MEN WHO MIGRATE, WOMEN WHO WAIT

Caroline B. Brettell

# MEN WHO MIGRATE, WOMEN WHO WAIT

*Population and History in a*
*Portuguese Parish*

PRINCETON UNIVERSITY PRESS
PRINCETON, NEW JERSEY

ISBN 0-691-09424-1

Publication of this book has been aided by a grant from
the Whitney Darrow Fund of Princeton University Press

This book has been composed in Linotron Sabon

Clothbound editions of Princeton University Press books
are printed on acid-free paper, and binding materials are
chosen for strength and durability. Paperbacks,
although satisfactory for personal collections, are not
usually suitable for library rebinding

Printed in the United States of America
by Princeton University Press
Princeton, New Jersey

Dedicated to João José da Silva, a teacher, a friend,
and an adopted *avô;*
and to the memory of Joyce Riegelhaupt.

# CONTENTS

# LIST OF TABLES

# LIST OF FIGURES

## ACKNOWLEDGMENTS

THE RESEARCH upon which this book is based began with a post-doctoral fellowship awarded to me by the National Institute for Child Health and Human Development. The person to whom I feel the greatest gratitude for encouraging me to apply for the grant, and for introducing me with careful but not overly domineering guidance to the field of historical demography, is Myron Gutmann. He recognized the potential of a vague idea and challenged me to address it in new ways. I would also like to thank Omer Galle who, as the Director of the Population Research Center of the University of Texas, warmly welcomed me on board and, perhaps more importantly, provided me with space and computer time. He and his colleagues and staff at the Center made the initial years of the project both stimulating and fruitful.

My second monetary debt is to the Wenner Gren Foundation, which furnished me with support for further research in Portugal during the summer of 1982. Their contribution truly made this an interdisciplinary study. Joyce Riegelhaupt had the task of writing a letter to them on my behalf. Joyce's critical responses to some of my ideas have always been helpful and I will miss her as a colleague and friend. She was a pioneer in bringing American anthropologists to the study of Portuguese society. Equally useful were the careful comments on the manuscript made by David Kertzer.

I would also like to thank the Newberry Library for providing a community of scholars to which I could attach myself upon my move to Chicago, and for facilitating my access to the Greenlee Collection, a resource that I used extensively in the preparation of Chapter Two. In Chicago, I have also benefited from the warm friendship and collegiality of Susan Tax Freeman. Her support and encouragement have been invaluable.

My debts in Portugal are extensive and I fear that in trying to set them down on paper I will forget someone or something. I hope not. In Lisbon, I would like to thank Robert Rowland and Brian O'Neill of the Núcleo de Sociología Histórica of the Gulbenkian Institute in Oeiras and Manuel Nazareth of the Universidade Nova. Although none of them has seen the final manuscript, the opportunity to exchange ideas about Portuguese demography with each of them was essential. Rui Feijó drew my attention to the electoral rolls for the District of Viana do Castelo. We share a mutual interest in this region that will, I hope, continue. Maria Beatriz Rocha Trindade secured funding for me from the Secretariado de Estado da Emigração during the summer when I initially explored the possibility of an historical demographic study. Her dedication to the problems of Portuguese emigrants and to research on Portuguese emigration shows no bounds.

In Viana do Castelo, Aristides de Arroteia facilitated my access to several important archives, and in the process became a very "simpático" friend and tireless voluntary co-worker. I owe him, Aurelio Barbosa, the editor of *Aurora de Lima,* Jorge Ramos of the Secretária do Governo Civil of Viana do Castelo, and Dr. António Matos Reis of the Municipal Museum Archives many thanks. In addition, the staffs at the Municipal Library, the Department of Justice, and the Department of Finances were extremely forthcoming and helpful. Prior to my arrival, no one had ever before asked for access to their collections and records for such lengthy periods of time, and somehow they found a quiet space for me to work. In Braga, I would like to thank the staff of the Arquivo do Distrito de Viana do Castelo of the Archiepiscopal Library. They too tolerated my presence day after day.

In Lanheses itself, this project could never have been realized without the assistance and encouragement of Padre Manuel Araujo de Castro. He permitted me to spend endless hours in the parish archives in his home, and trusted me enough to let me take irreplaceable volumes to the nearby town for xeroxing. During one summer, I stayed in the home of Joaquim Fernandes dos Santos. He, his wife, his son, and his daughter were all gracious hosts who somehow adapted to my strange habits. In fact, I owe an enormous debt of gratitude to the entire dos Santos family, and particularly to Virginia, who was my first contact with the parish. On another visit, I was for three weeks a guest of Lucia de Barros. She too took care of me, eliminating the worry of daily meals for the scholar hard at work.

There are innumerable other Lanhesans, young and old, who shared their thoughts and ideas with me, sometimes formally, but often in passing. To each of them, *muito obrigada*; but a special *orbigada* must go to João José da Silva, who shares the dedication of this book. I would say that João José is wise beyond his years, but he is already over ninety and has lived a long and hard life. He shared many of his experiences and insights with me, and during the hours which I spent sitting by his bedside I came indeed to love him as the grandfather I have never had.

I would like to thank the editorial staff at Princeton University Press for helping me to see this manuscript through to publication, and Mario Carelli, who cheerfully gave up precious hours as a fellow at the Newberry Library to verify that all accents were in place.

A final debt of gratitude goes to my husband Rick, who endured my absences in Portugal and all those weekends and evenings when I sat at my word processor to the neglect of him and everything else around me. I know he shares my admiration for the Portuguese people and their heroic history of emigration.

*Chicago, December 1985*

MEN WHO MIGRATE, WOMEN WHO WAIT

Map of Portugal Showing Administrative Districts and District Capitals

From *Portugal: A Country Study*, Eugene K. Keefe et. al. Washington, D.C.: United States Government as represented by the Secretary of the Army, 1985 (Second printing).

> By analyzing parish registers, listings of inhabi-
> tants, and the like, we can look into the lives of
> ordinary people in the past. . . . Where the nec-
> essary records are preserved, there is a chance to
> get down to the roots of society almost as a so-
> cial anthropologist tries to gain insight into a
> contemporary community by listening to its
> members tell of the great events of their lives
> and the clusters of social attitudes, customs,
> sanctions which relate to them. (Anthony Wrig-
> ley 1969:12)

> To sift through archives, documents or censuses
> is to give oneself the means to think about the
> reality of the past and the meaning of a tradi-
> tion. (Marc Augé 1982:103)

DURING the past decade or two, there have been significant attempts
within the scholarly community to cross the frontiers between disciplines, to share methodologies and theoretical insights and, in the
process, to raise new questions and create entirely new avenues of
exploration. One of the most fruitful interchanges is that which has
occurred between the disciplines of history and anthropology (Kertzer
1984a). On one level, the exchange has been both substantive and
specific. As Stone (1982) notes, anthropologists have been asking
questions about kinship structures, residence rules, marriage, and inheritance customs since the founding of their discipline, questions
that are of vital concern to a new generation of family and social
historians. The formulation of certain general principles about the
"nature of man" or the "nature of social life" on the basis of an
intensive study of the dynamics of life in a local community has an
equally long tradition within anthropology. In historical circles, it is
of more recent vintage. What Stone calls "total history" is nothing
other than what anthropologists have long referred to as "holism."
From an alternative perspective, history has helped to move anthropological analysis away from the structural-functional, static, and
synchronic approach that dominated the discipline in the mid-twentieth century. To some extent, the impetus has been greatest among
anthropologists working in Western cultures, where written records
are accessible, for it was the absence of such records that led the

great ethnographer of Melanesia, Malinowski, to conclude that it was only in the recurrent functions of cultural practices or social institutions that an explanation of cultural origins could be found. Of greater importance, perhaps, particularly if one accepts a more dynamic approach to one's subject matter, is the alternative that history provides to what is essentially an extremely "presentist" view of the forces of social change.[2] For example, phenomena that have traditionally been ascribed to urbanization, modernization, or industrial development may turn out to have greater historical depth. History allows the anthropologist to pose the questions of whether, when, and why change occurred in a more sophisticated and less assumption-bound manner. It permits him, as Marc Augé (1982:103) has put it, "to think about the reality of the past and the meaning of a tradition." If anthropology encourages comparisons across space, history encourages comparisons over time (Thomas 1963).

On another level, the cross-fertilization between these two disciplines of history and anthropology has been of a more general or abstract nature. To the extent that the historian tries to understand the documentary evidence of the past through the eyes of whoever left that evidence, his task differs little from that of the anthropologist who attempts to understand a society or culture on its own terms, through the eyes of a participant in that culture. To the extent that the goal of the anthropologist is to distinguish what people say they ought to do from what they actually do, his task is much the same as that of the historian who attempts to differentiate ideology, or the ideal of the historical past, from behavior in past times.[3] Both disciplines are concerned with the potential contrast between an insider's interpretation of events and that of an outsider or observer. Both are, or should be, equally attentive to the important difference between rules, whether of law or custom, and the bending of rules. Perhaps the advantage that the anthropologist has over his historical colleagues is that he can often elicit or observe both types of information, whereas the historian is frequently forced to speculate about one on the basis of the other as it appears or is reported in the written record. Yet this is not always the case, and it is certainly true that, when subjected to historical evidence, or even, for that matter, more rigorous quantifiable evidence, what have been interpreted by some anthropologists as longstanding rules for behavior or for sorting out individuals within a society have turned out to be expressions of an ideal that is not manifested in actual practice.

In the broadest sense, these are some of the principles that lie at the foundation of this study of demographic change and family history in a parish in northwestern Portugal during the eighteenth, nineteenth, and first half of the twentieth centuries, a study that combines an analysis of quantitative data drawn from parish registers and other historical documents with more qualitative data I have gathered as a field ethnographer, recording the recollections of individual participants in a society as well as my own observations of that society. Unlike the new community historian, who often chooses his locale on the basis of the quality of the historical documents at his disposal, it was my curiosity about the historical past of a village where I had previously worked as an anthropologist, and about the meaning of certain demographic and cultural traditions that were very much a part of contemporary life, which motivated my foray into the historical records.

My assumption was that not only could historical data provide a past to the ethnographic present, but also that observations made in the field could be used to examine more closely some of the conclusions drawn from strictly historical demographic studies, or at least provide a context within which to piece together and understand the written sources more fully.[4] On the one hand, I was fortunate enough to find that this parish had a very complete set of vital records dating from the late sixteenth century.[5] On the other hand, the insights about their past among villagers themselves have contributed enormously to a better understanding of the patterns that have emerged in the analysis of historical records. The connection between these two bodies of data, ethnographic and documentary, is apparent in the similarities between the core method of the historical demographer—family reconstitution—and that of at least some ethnographers—the collection of genealogies and oral histories.[6]

If the complementarity and compatibility of methods of research provide one explanation for the study on which this book is based, another is an interest in certain questions that I felt might best be addressed through intensive investigation of the population history of a local community. These questions fall roughly into three areas, one related to the so-called demographic transition (the shift from high to low fertility), which will be taken up in Chapter Four, the second to emigration, and the third to women's roles. These are not mutually exclusive areas. Indeed, the underlying aim of the book is to explore the relationship between emigration and a range of other demographic phenomena (including fertility) in a local context and, in doing so, to examine the connection between population patterns and sex roles. Recently, Ross and Rapp have drawn our attention to the ways in which anthropology and history can work together to describe the social embeddedness of individual sexuality. "Social relations," they suggest, "which appear peripheral to individual sexual practices may in fact influence them profoundly through intervening social forms" (1981:54). Although the idea is not necessarily new,[7] it merits further examination, and certain regions of northern Portugal, where emigration has been part of the way of life for several centuries, provide us with an excellent opportunity to do so. It is certainly safe to say that emigration is part of Portugal's cultural ethos. Its importance in Portuguese literature (Brettell 1979, Cesar 1969) is a reflection of its importance in Portuguese life.

As sociologists and anthropologists of modern life, we are accustomed to viewing emigration, particularly that from the rural countryside, as a solution to the problems of unemployment and underemployment, population density, and large families. We are also accustomed to viewing it as a recent phenomenon, the result of urbanization and industrialization; that is, of the pull factors associated with contemporary socioeconomic change. Until the appearance of Olwen Hufton's significant study of the poor of eighteenth-century France (1974), historians were perhaps equally guilty of projecting an image of an immobile rural society prior to the great age of industrialization and urban growth. However, what Hufton describes for the eighteenth century is a rural "economy of makeshifts" wherein "the emigrant's proceeds, like the remittances crucial to the Irish and southern Italian peasantry today, could buttress a frail regional economy" (1974:69).[8] She goes on to discuss different patterns of migration (seasonal, temporary, permanent), arguing that local cultural and socioeconomic factors will influence the predominant form that a migration stream assumes. In turn, it is possible to suggest that these varying patterns of migration, each of them differently motivated, may have quite distinct effects on the social, economic, and demographic life of the local rural community. Indeed, there is a tendency to look at migration as a dependent variable, the result of different forms of land tenure and inheritance practices or different kinship systems and household arrangements. Yet it is also an independent variable—cause as well as result.

Both the continuity and variety of particular patterns of emigration and their significance to a local or regional economy are important to consider in any study of the demographic history of northwestern Portugal; so too is its dual character as both cause and result of various forms of social and demographic behavior. Within such a framework, a range of questions can be posed. Is high emigration from northern Portugal a manifestation of the search for alternative sources of income, a substitute option for the children of large families? Was population pressure solved though migration rather than through the limitation of family size? On the other hand, is it not possible that a resistance to fertility control for some other reason (religion, for example) made emigration necessary, or that the more "modern-oriented" or ambitious simply migrated out, thereby effecting the preservation of norms or preferences for high fertility in their place of origin? Whether emigration is a force of conservatism or a stimulus for social change, and under what circumstances it is one,  or the other, or both, or changes its character, has yet to be decided definitively within sociological and anthropological circles, and therefore within historical circles.[9]

The issue of whether to view migration as the outcome of an adaptive response to population pressure, or as a phenomenon caused by other factors (but which has the useful consequence of being a successful means of population control) leads directly to the concept of homeostasis, a concept central to current theoretical debate in the fields of demography and historical demography.[10] Applied to demographic behavior, the thesis is that societies strive to maintain population equilibrium and that a range of phenomena (fertility, migration, age at marriage, permanent celibacy) are used by these societies as regulatory mechanisms to maintain the population at a given level. Clearly, the roots of this concept are to be found in Malthus, and, in contemporary thinking, are at the very core of the demographic transition model.

One of the classic formulations of homeostasis is contained in Kingsley Davis' 1963 address to the Population Association of America, published in the *Population Index* in the same year. Davis presents a "Theory of Change and Response in Demographic Behavior," arguing that when population pressures are great, societies respond in a "multiphasic" way to alleviate these pressures. Thus, following a period of declining mortality and sustained natural increase, the Japanese not only responded by increasing their abortion rate, but also through marriage postponement, sterilization and contraception programs, and outmigration. The same can be said for much of western Europe. Friedlander (1969:359–360) has taken the argument further, especially in relation to migration as a regulatory response. He hypothesizes that "an adjustment in reproductive behavior of a community in response to the rising of a 'strain' . . . may differ depending upon the ease with which the community can relieve the 'strain' through outmigration." In his concluding remarks, Friedlander calls for a thorough examination of the precise circumstances that lead people to use various demographic responses or combinations of demographic responses.[11] Daniel Scott Smith has reiterated the point, arguing that although the homeostatic model seems to work theoretically, our emphasis should be on homeostasis as "a pervasive empirical pattern whose causes need explication" (1977:38). He goes on to note the difference between societal norms and individual actions, suggesting that more attention should be paid to the latter.

This simultaneous polarity and interdependence between the individual (or family) and the group (or society) is one that has preoccupied both historians and social scientists. It is a particularly appropriate concern in any discussion of social change, for ultimately it is the individuals who, making their private decisions to alter some age-old custom, collectively cause a transition in the structure of the society or culture as a whole. In a classic study of social change, Daniel Lerner has made precisely this point: "The great drama of societal transition occurs through individuals involved in solving their personal problems and living their personal lives" (1958:74).[12]

That the relationship between the individual and the group is equally important to present-day social/demographic history is apparent in Wrigley's seminal article on group and individual strategies of family formation. He phrases the problem in terms of a difference between conscious and unconscious rationality: "Men's actions at all times are influenced by their appreciation of their personal interests and by their response to social norms, (and) it is interesting to examine strategies of family formation as if couples behaved in conformity with these stereotypes of thought and action" (1978:152). The essence of the problem is to discern which features lead individuals or families, making decisions about their personal lives, to choose the separate courses of action that combine to form collective behavior and produce a pattern of behavior, a homeostatic response. Conversely, what, if anything, do the patterns that are revealed at an aggregate level tell us about individual motivations? To what extent are historical demographers guilty of the so-called "ecological fallacy" when they ascribe rational and premeditated decisions to individuals on the basis of significant relationships among variables that they see for a community or society as a whole? The quantum leap from one level of analysis to the next is problematic, and mirrors broader sociological and anthropological concerns about the locus of norms or of "culture." In fact, it does a disservice to scholarship to view culture as the source of binding rules and regulations. Rather culture defines a continuum along which lie a range of acceptable actions or choices that can be taken by individuals in order to achieve their separate ends. In short, to equate the appearance of some fact of behavior with a particular motivation must be done quite cautiously and with an awareness of all the alternatives that may be possible within a particular cultural context. This brings us directly back to the relationship between the disciplines of history and anthropology, and particularly to the way in which Silverman (1976) has defined their intersection. Historical analysis, she suggests, reveals the structural constraints that influence decisions, whereas anthropological interviews reveal the actual choices that have been made.

Before turning to a specific discussion of the substantive focus of this book, a word more should be said about the problem of sex roles. Here again we are faced with a curious contradiction between ideology or norms for behavior and actual behavior. Certainly male dominance is as much a part of Portuguese culture as it is of other Mediterranean cultures, and yet in northwestern Portugal one also finds an element of, for want of a better word, "matri-centrality." To remain a virgin until marriage is an expressed value, and yet in northwestern Portugal illegitimacy has by no means been a rare phenomenon. In some ways, these contradictions reflect the differences between appearances and reality that have been described for other Mediterranean societies (Friedl 1967). As Gilmore (1982:180) has put it, "the view of woman [throughout the Mediterranean] is itself dualistic: she is both madonna and whore." While this contradiction is indeed complex, the phenomena of high illegitimacy and matri-centrality in some respects set Portugal, or at least northwestern Portugal, apart from its Mediterranean neighbors, although they are shared by the neighboring and therefore culturally and geographically similar region of Spanish Galicia. In both these areas, I would argue, emigration, as an integral part of their populations' histories, has had an instrumental impact. To understand the demography of women in these regions, and the pattern of sex roles in general, it is therefore crucial to consider migration patterns. Although this observation is by no means novel, it merits further examination, and this is what I will undertake as I move through the discussion of marriage, fertility, and illegitimacy in a parish in northwestern Portugal between 1700 and the present.

As with almost all research endeavors, the scope of this project has been altered and expanded as it has proceeded. Given my interest in combining qualitative data drawn from ethnographic fieldwork and oral histories with quantitative data based on an analysis of parish registers and census material, the study began with a focus on the late nineteenth century and the twentieth century. A starting date of

1860 was selected, first because enormous improvements in the recording of births, deaths, and marriages by parish priests occurred at that time, and second because the first national census in Portugal was taken in 1864. In addition, oral memory to flesh out the quantifiable data could perhaps be pushed back to the 1870s or 1880s. However, once certain patterns or trends became apparent, my curiosity to discover the origins of those patterns, or at least to see how much further back in time they could be found, was stimulated. Consequently, I incorporated another century and a half into my analysis of the parish registers and was, therefore, also able to include material drawn from other documentary sources that predated 1860. Clearly, this process of parish register "archaeology" could continue *ad infinitum* for as far back as the documents themselves go. However, I have adhered to the two-and-a-half century time frame from the beginning of the eighteenth century to the middle of the twentieth, for historical reasons.

The eighteenth century was the last great age of Portuguese prosperity and of primacy in international affairs. In 1687, gold had been discovered in the great Brazilian colony, a treasure trove that secured for the smaller parent country a steady source of income to pay for imports, including the grain imports necessary for a stagnating domestic economy. In 1703, a treaty between Portugal and England gave the latter country a preferential position with regard to wine exports, and at the same time removed limitations on the import of English trade goods. The close association, almost dependence, on both Brazil and England was to remain significant, if not ultimately detrimental, to the subsequent economic history of Portugal.

King John V (1706–1750) ruled the highly centralized government assertively until almost the end of his life. Upon his death in 1750, the reins of the Portuguese government were put into the hands of Sebastião José de Carvalho e Melo, later Marquis of Pombal, by the new king, José I (1750–1777). When King José ascended the throne, Portugal had little industry, and its agricultural sector was in disarray. Pombal, ruling virtually as an absolute dictator, reanimated commerce, regulated the markets for the port wine trade, expelled the Jesuits, reformulated taxes, limited the ambitions of the nobility and the clergy, and introduced a period of economic well-being under state control. With the death of José I and the demise of Pombal, the country fell under the leadership of the devout but eventually demented queen Maria I. Nevertheless, numerous restrictions imposed by Pombal were lifted, and a growing mercantile class led the country into the nineteenth century with continued prosperity and with much of its Old Regime intact.

Increasingly, however, the English assumed control of important commercial enterprises, and the trade balance became more unfavorable. The economic domination of Britain impelled Napoleon to send French troops to "liberate" the country, and by 1816 the royal court had fled to Brazil, where it ruled in exile under British protection. The Old Regime had collapsed and a century of political instability and economic fragility was ushered in. In 1822, King John VI accepted his position as constitutional monarch of Portugal and returned from Brazil. The latter country, meanwhile, ruled by King John's heir, Dom Pedro, declared independence, an event that dealt an enormous blow to the parent country and from which she took a long time to recover.

The weakened position of the Portuguese monarchy and the loss of Brazil split the country into two factions—the liberal and anticlerical radicals who supported continued political revolution, and the traditional monarchists who supported a return to absolutism. The decades of the mid-nineteenth century were characterized by heated struggles between these two factions, each with its own royal candidates. The liberals eventually gained control and ruled the country for much of the rest of the century. The economy continued to rely heavily upon the reexport of colonial goods, and internal agricultural production remained stagnant. The national debt grew, and at the dawn of the twentieth century Portugal was poor and backward, with little remaining from her epochs of political and economic splendor.

Although population grew dramatically during the latter half of the nineteenth century, the growth was virtually offset by the most massive emigration in the country's history, a movement unmatched until the post-1960 emigration to France. The causes and character of this late nineteenth century outmigration to Brazil are explored more fully in a later chapter, but it is important to emphasize that the rural peasant population of northern Portugal had already begun to emigrate to Brazil during the eighteenth century.

By 1914, emigration to Brazil had been curtailed and Portugal was experiencing, for the first time in her history, a republican government. However, after fifteen years, seven presidents, and eighteen military coups, the parliamentary regime collapsed, and leadership of the country was turned over to a military government and finally, in 1933, to an authoritarian New State headed by Dr. António de Oliveira Salazar. The Catholic Church, which had suffered enormous setbacks under the anticlerical First Republic, was gradually restored to its central position in the social life of Portugal. The national debt was alleviated under the guidance of Salazar's austerity programs; the burden of economic austerity fell most heavily upon the shoulders of the urban working class and the rural peasantry. Living standards improved in some areas, but in other areas, particularly in the northern and interior countrysides, the traditional way of life changed little. Only after World War II, and especially after 1960, with improvements in education and with prosperity from French francs flowing back to Portugal in the form of emigrant remittances, did life begin to change and only then did parts of rural Portugal truly enter the twentieth century. In short, despite the changes in forms of government over two hundred years—from Old Regime, to Constitutional Monarchy, to Republic, and finally to right-wing dictatorship—much of the population of Portugal in 1950 was coping with life in ways similar to those of their ancestors in 1750. This fact helps to explain the social and demographic system that is the subject of this book.

The parish of Lanheses, which provides the focus for this study, is located in the heart of the region of northern Portugal that has experienced the heaviest rural outmigration since the end of the eighteenth century. Today, it is what one might call a modernizing village, but that modernization has come only in recent decades, and at the moment the village is a curious amalgamation of the past and the present. Situated only fourteen kilometers inland, it is not particularly isolated, but it was only at the end of the nineteenth century, with improvements in national roads, that movement in and out of the parish, and to the sea coast in particular, was facilitated. Today it is a rather large village with a population approaching two thousand. A century ago, the population was only half that. In the early nineteenth century, Lanheses had the administrative status of *vila*, seat of the municipality (*concelho*) of Lanheses, which included several of the surrounding parishes. It has held, therefore, a pivotal position within its region and it is perhaps for this reason that the parish records have survived so completely to this day.

Although I would hesitate, as any anthropologist probably would, to call Lanheses a "typical Portuguese community," its demographic history is not, I would argue, uncharacteristic of the region in general, and it is certainly an appropriate locus for a study of the relationship between sex roles, emigration, and other population phenomena. Indeed, it was emigrants from Lanheses involved in the recent exodus to France who first introduced me to their native village, and in many ways they are simply carrying on a tradition that began with their ancestors of several centuries ago. Where possible, I have tried to indicate what might make Lanheses different from its near or distant neighboring communities, and to put its demographic history into a broader regional context. Although ideally a regional study of the questions addressed in this book might allay the fears of those who are distrustful of yet another community study (although certainly not "yet another" in the Portuguese context), such a study would sacrifice in depth what it gained in scope, and depth is the forte of the anthropologist. Recently, Peter Laslett (1983) referred to Portugal as "a puzzle." If this study puts a few more pieces of the puzzle in place, then it will have made its contribution.

There is one more point to be made about the localized focus of this book. MacFarlane (1977) has clearly spelled out the pros and cons of the community study method, addressing himself particularly to the problem of boundary delineation. How precisely do we delimit the community we are studying? Are its borders defined by the geographical arena within which marriages occur or within which economic goods are exchanged? Do we proceed according to some political or administrative division? Or do we focus on the group of people who worship together? Rarely do these overlap, and certainly they may change over time. Lanheses is no exception. Marriages have been and continue to be contracted with non-Lanhesans. Individuals from other villages have been bringing their goods to the bimonthly market (*feira*) since it was first established in the late eighteenth century. For several decades during the early nineteenth century, its status as vila implied administrative jurisdiction over several of the nearby parishes. Yet I think it is safe to argue that for as far back as can be documented, Lanhesans have worshiped in their own church, which has served at the center of their community as a symbol of their identity.[13] Although some have left the parish to marry or emigrate, and have consequently died and been buried elsewhere, the church where they were baptized remains as an anchor in their lives. Thus, we can begin with this parish community and its records, and move out from there, subjecting the other kinds of community with which Lanhesans have become involved to empirical investigation.

# CHAPTER ONE

# The Parish of Lanheses: Demography, Economy, Social Structure, and Religion

### HISTORY AND GENERAL CHARACTERISTICS OF POPULATION

The village of Lanheses is situated along the Lima River in the concelho of Viana do Castelo in the northwestern province of Minho. It is approximately fourteen kilometers from the coast, and midway between the provincial towns of Viana do Castelo and Ponte de Lima. Although the Lima River is one of several rivers that cut through the north of Portugal, flowing from the mountains in the interior toward the sea, it has inspired many Portuguese poets, and is thought by some to be the mythological River Lethe referred to by the Greek geographer and historian Strabo. According to Augusto Pinho Leal, the Romans believed that the Lima River produced forgetfulness, and they feared to cross it because, in doing so, they thought that they would forget Rome and remain in the area forever.[1] Perhaps a similar sentiment is what keeps contemporary natives of the region so attached to their homeland—to many of them, it is indeed the most beautiful part of the world, and a place to which emigrants hope and expect to return one day.

The early history of Lanheses itself is fragmented and must be viewed in the context of the history of northwestern Portugal as a whole. The entire region of Entre-Douro-e-Minho (the present provinces of Douro Litoral and Minho) was settled by primitive Lusitanians around 2000 B.C. Some writers have claimed that Lanheses was the seat of an old Lusitanian city called Lais, or city of the *laisenses*—hence one explanation for the origin of the name. After 900 B.C., Celtic herders and metalworkers entered the region, settled, and intermarried with the Lusitanians. The Romans appeared on the Iberian peninsula around 212 B.C., but it took them almost two hundred years to conquer the entire area, and their battles against the very independent Lusitanians were long and hard. After their conquest, the Romans set about to establish settled agricultural villages throughout the Iberian peninsula. Although remote from the rest of the Empire, Lusitania (Portugal) came to share the language, the legal structure, and later the religion of Rome.[2]

In A.D. 409, the Swabians crossed over the Pyrenees into Spain and eventually settled in Galicia and Lusitania. Whereas the south of Portugal remained Romanized and characterized by large estates and nucleated villages, the Swabians introduced the practice of more dispersed settlements and land holdings that were divided among heirs from one generation to the next. The system of minifundia that characterizes northern Portugal, and especially the province of Minho, was born.

Moors invaded Iberia in A.D. 711, and conquered much of the territory. However, the northwestern corner never came truly under their aegis, and within fifty years of the Moorish conquest, the kings of Asturias and Leon reconquered the major cities of Entre-Douro-e-Minho: Porto, Braga, Guimarães, and Viseu. In the late ninth century, these Christian kings reorganized the region under autonomous counts and called it the Província Portugalense (province of Portugal). By the eleventh century, these counts pushed their dominion southward to the city of Coimbra.

Raymond, the fourth son of Guillaume the Great of Burgandy, came to northern Spain and Portugal in 1086 or 1087. In 1090, he married Urraca, the legitimate daughter and heiress of Alfonso VI, king of Leon, Castille, Galicia, and Portugal. Raymond was granted the government of Entre-Douro-e-Minho (Portugal) and Coimbra in 1094, but in 1096 or early 1097, Alfonso gave Portugal and Coimbra to his son-in-law Henry of Burgandy as a dowry upon his marriage to Alfonso's illegitimate but favored daughter Teresa.[3] When Henry died, Teresa was left as a regent for her son Afonso Henriques. Local Portuguese barons, fearing Teresa's alliance with her Spanish kinsmen, turned to Afonso Henriques and encouraged him to claim the Portuguese territory as his own. Afonso expelled his mother in 1128, refused to pay homage to his Spanish cousin Alfonso VII (the son of Urraca), went on to oust the Moors from large portions of the country, and finally assumed the title of King of Portugal in 1143.

After the separation of the Kingdoms of Leon and Portugal, and under the successive leaderships of Afonso III (1248–1279) and D. Diniz (1279–1325), the conditions of the rural population in the province of Entre-Douro-e-Minho improved. The lands were distributed to colonists who paid a fixed tribute or *foro* in money or in kind.

> Each couple was given a sufficient portion of uncultivated land to
> plant, common land for pasturage, and furze-field for vegetable
> manure. All the land which was cultivated at the death of the cou-
> ple (*caseiros*) or principle emphyteuta was divided among the heirs.
> All the uncultivated land was returned to the crown, the country,
> or the seigneury, but as self interest animated agriculture, only bar-
> ren land remained undistributed. (Silva 1868:109)[4]

Allodial holdings became increasingly smaller, to the point, in some
cases, of being economically absurd. In this context, as the historian
Marques (1972) has noted, local migrations from one area to the
next, from countryside into towns, began. Numerous new towns (*vilas novas*) and villages (*aldeias novas*) were founded.[5] Much in line
with current theories about the relationship between partible inheritance, land fragmentation, and population growth, Marques draws a
connection between the breaking up of the old Roman villas, the
access of later-born sons to property revenue, and an increase in population in Portugal in the eleventh, twelfth, and thirteenth centuries.
However, like the rest of Europe, Portugal suffered a population set-
back with the arrival of the Black Death in the mid-fourteenth century.[6]

From the late Middle Ages (approximately 1130) until the middle
of the sixteenth century, the village of Lanheses, together with the
neighboring villages of Vila Mou, Meixedo, and Nogueira belonged
to the *couto* conceded by D. Afonso to the monastery of San Salvador da Torre, a Benedictine monastery supposedly founded in A.D.
570 by St. Martin of Dume and, according to some sources, restored
around 1066 by Frei Ordonho, a relative of D. Payo Vermudez (whom
some called the Count of Tuy).[7] This monastery, like the rest of the
area north of the Lima River, was part of the Gallegan diocese of
Tuy until 1440. It was then transferred to the bishopric of Ceuta in
Africa and, finally, in 1512, to the archbishopric of Braga.[8]

The population of Portugal began a steady increase after 1450 and
throughout the sixteenth century, despite periodic plagues. In 1527,
King João III ordered a census of the nation (Freire 1905). At this
time, 2,104 dwellings were counted in the town and vicinity of Viana
do Castelo, and 101 dwellings in the village of Lanheses itself. The
entire population of Entre-Douro-e-Minho was counted at 275,330,
making it, as it had been since the birth of the nation, the most
densely inhabited region of Portugal—approximately 20 percent of
the total population living on 13 percent of the area. The population

for the country as a whole was estimated at between one and one-and-a-half million at the time.[9]

Lanheses existed at the easternmost extent of what was defined as the *termo*, or limits, of the town of Viana do Castelo. Viana had remained a small fishing town until the great age of discovery changed it into a major port for overseas trade. It flourished throughout the fifteenth and early sixteenth centuries. Attracted by its commercial prosperity, José Martins de Ricalde (or Rigua), a native of the Spanish province of Biscaya, came to Viana in the fifteenth century. The family prospered, and in 1548 a descendent, João Martins de Ricalde, acquired half of the patronage of Lanheses from the convent of San Salvador da Torre,[10] and built a manor house in the village. One of his great-grandsons became the priest of Lanheses and erected a family tomb in the main parish church. In the early years of the nineteenth century, a descendent, D. Maria Francisca Abreu Pereira Cyrne, only child of the tenth *senhor* of the manor of Lanheses, married the second count of Almada, and the property thus passed into the hands of one of the important noble families of Portugal, a family about which more will be said later in this chapter. When Portugal came under Spanish rule (1580–1640), commerce in Viana do Castelo was paralyzed, and the town stagnated. Only when gold and diamonds were discovered in Brazil did the town and its region thrive again.

In Padre António Carvalho da Costa's chorography of Portugal, originally published between 1706 and 1712 and reissued in 1868, Lanheses is listed as having 170 dwellings.[11] By the middle of the eighteenth century, the number of dwellings had only grown to 173 (Cardoso 1767), and in 1793, despite the fact that it was neither urban nor politically important, the queen of Portugal, Maria I, elevated Lanheses to the status of vila, the administrative seat of a *concelho. Together with other villages in the concelho that came under* the jurisdiction of the new vila in 1795, Lanheses constituted a seigneury (*senhorio*), which was given *de jure et herdade* to Sebastião de Abreu Pereira Cyrne "in remuneration for the many and valiant services" of his uncle, Sr. José Ricardo Pereira de Castro, chancellor major of the kingdom, and in exchange for the seigneury of Lindoso, which Sebastião's father, Francisco de Abreu Pereira Cyrne Peixoto (brother of José) had had since 1750. A pillory was erected to symbolize this new status of vila, as were a town hall and a prison. In 1796, a bimonthly market (*feira*) was established, and by 1799 this market had usurped the cattle trading business from the smaller feira in the village of Meixedo. Except for scattered election portfolios that give us some indication of the more respected citizens of the new vila, a few tribunal records listing petty offenses, and a book of local laws, little else survives from this period of Lanheses' history.[12]

There are, however, two sources that provide some indication of the population of the new vila at the dawn of the nineteenth century. Pina Manique's 1798 census (1970) listed 188 households, and 476 for the new concelho as a whole.[13] The cadastre of the province of Minho prepared by the engineer José Gomes Villas Boas at roughly the same time (Cruz 1970) still listed Lanheses as a couto—one of thirteen in the territory of Viana do Castelo at that time—and counted 801 souls living in 186 households.[14] The population was further subdivided as follows: 265 men over age 14, 304 women over age 14, 125 boys under age 14, and 107 girls under age 14. According to Villas Boas, Lanheses had, at this time, three clerics, and 960 *reis* were collected for the annual tithe paid to the church.[15] The population for the entire territory of Viana do Castelo was 124,197 individuals living in 32,144 households.[16]

With the independence of Brazil in the 1820s, the silting up of the port, and the collapse of the shipbuilding industry in the region, Viana do Castelo's period of economic prosperity waned.[17] In 1834, in accordance with nationwide administrative changes and with the dissolution of both seigneuries and ecclesiastical patronages (*padroadas*), Lanheses lost its status as a vila and was, instead, incorporated into the concelho of Viana do Castelo. Although the pillory and oral historical pride are the only signs remaining to indicate the village's former political glory, the bimonthly market survives to this day and has helped to sustain Lanheses' economic centrality within its region.

Although the population of Portugal had grown steadily during most of the sixteenth century, a plague in 1581, sixty years of Spanish rule, and the war of restoration in 1640 initiated a period of lethargic population growth through most of the seventeenth century. By the middle of the seventeenth century, the population of the country as a whole was estimated at two million. According to Balbi (1822), in one of the first "statistical essays" on Portugal, certain regulations supported by João IV (1640–1656) and his successors, as well as religious intolerance that discouraged foreigners from settling, impeded Portugal from regaining its former growth pattern as quickly as it might have.

Population grew slowly during the first half of the eighteenth century under the reigns of Pedro II (1668–1706) and João V (1706–1750) despite a plague in Lisbon in 1723, certain political intrigues with which these sovereigns involved themselves, and sometimes contradictory legislation with regard to agriculture, commerce, and industry. By 1758, the population was estimated to be at two-and-a-half million. By 1800 it had reached approximately three million, and by 1820, 3.1 million. Yet, according to Marques (1972), Lisbon was not growing as fast as other major capital cities in western Europe, and the growth of the city of Porto, by contrast, was symptomatic of the economic development and prosperity of northern Portugal in the eighteenth and early nineteenth centuries. If we accept early population counts for Lanheses itself, growth was indeed slow. Between 1527 and 1712, an average of one new household was formed every two-and-a-half years; only three new households were established in the fifty-five years between 1712 and 1767, whereas one new household was established every other year in the thirty-three years between 1767 and the dawn of the nineteenth century.

The real takeoff in Portugal's population growth occurred after the middle of the nineteenth century, and especially between 1860 and 1911. As in other parts of western Europe, this takeoff was largely coincident with an abrupt fall in mortality. Morgado has pointedly observed, "if three hundred and thirty years had been needed for the population (of Portugal) to reach a figure of three and a half million, only a further century was needed before it passed eight million" (1979:319).

The first national census of Portugal was taken in 1864, and from that time on we have a more or less accurate monitoring of population trends, nationally, regionally, and, to a lesser extent, locally. The census figures for the concelho of Viana do Castelo and for the village of Lanheses appear to indicate that population growth in this area did not really take off until the 1920s and 1930s. However, a closer examination of the rates of actual and natural increase (based, of course, on aggregate calculations from parish registers in combination with census figures) demonstrate that indeed there was population growth, but that it was offset to a great extent by emigration (Table 1.1). In the fourteen years between 1864 and 1878, fifty new households were established, while the population itself declined by almost two hundred individuals—hence a dramatic drop in mean household size, as well. A more thorough discussion of the nature of household formation during the late nineteenth century is included in Chapter Three.

Figure 1.1 shows trends in the gross numbers of baptisms, deaths, and marriages in the parish for the little more than two-and-a-half centuries between 1700 and 1960. Baptisms show a general decline

TABLE 1.1 DEMOGRAPHIC RATES FOR LANHESES, 1864–1970

| Period | Birth Rate | Death Rate | Migration Rate | | | Rate of Increase | |
|---|---|---|---|---|---|---|---|
| | | | Male | Female | Overall | Natural | Actual |
| 1864–1878 | 27.9 | 27.5 | −31.9 | − 7.7 | −15.9 | 0.4 | −15.5 |
| 1878–1890 | 24.5 | 18.2 | −18.0 | − 3.1 | − 9.0 | 6.3 | − 2.7 |
| 1890–1900 | 26.7 | 19.6 | − 3.0 | − 5.3 | − 4.3 | 7.1 | 2.8 |
| 1900–1911 | 29.5 | 19.4 | −13.0 | 0.0 | − 5.1 | 10.1 | 5.4 |
| 1911–1920 | 23.4 | 20.2 | − 6.2 | − 2.0 | − 3.7 | 3.2 | − 0.5 |
| 1920–1930 | 29.5 | 14.9 | − 6.2 | 5.7 | 0.9 | 14.6 | 15.5 |
| 1930–1940 | 31.3 | 11.4 | − 3.0 | − 7.7 | − 5.7 | 19.9 | 14.2 |
| 1940–1950 | 28.6 | 12.8 | − 1.7 | 6.2 | 2.7 | 15.8 | 18.5 |
| 1950–1960 | 25.9 | 9.4 | −14.0 | −12.7 | −13.3 | 16.5 | 3.2 |
| 1960–1970 | 17.7 | 8.1 | −11.6 | −16.1 | −14.0 | 9.6 | − 4.4 |

NOTE: Birth and death rates are calculated as the number of baptisms / deaths divided by the population at mid-period and multiplied by 1,000. Migration rates (overall and by sex) are calculated as net migration (the population at the end of the time period minus what the estimated population at the end would be as the sum of the population at the beginning and the natural increase—births minus deaths) divided by the mid-period population and multiplied by 1,000. The rate of natural increase is the birth rate minus the death rate, and the rate of actual increase is the rate of natural increase minus the migration rate.

SOURCE: Portuguese National Censuses: taken on January 1 in 1864 and 1878; on December 1 in 1890, 1900, 1911, 1920, and 1930; on December 12 in 1940; on December 15 in 1960 and 1970. The figures for 1970 are from the preliminary results and exclude children born in France but baptized in Lanheses. Figures for births and deaths are taken from the parish registers.

throughout the later eighteenth century, followed by an increase during the first thirty years of the nineteenth century.

Between 1830 and 1890 there were short-term fluctuations in natality and, subsequently, a second period of rapid increase at the dawn of the twentieth century and especially after 1920. The momentary drop between 1910 and 1919 seems to be directly associated with a momentary drop in marriages, as well—both most likely a result of the impact of World War I. Although not shown on the graph, the number of baptisms in the parish declined quite dramatically during the 1960s, a direct result of emigration to France, which coincides with a negative rate of actual population increase after forty years of population growth. Couples in the 1960s were often marrying in Lanheses and subsequently departing together for France, although many have had children born in France baptized in the village.

Marriages show more short-term fluctuations after 1810, but generally, the average number of marriages per year remained fairly con-

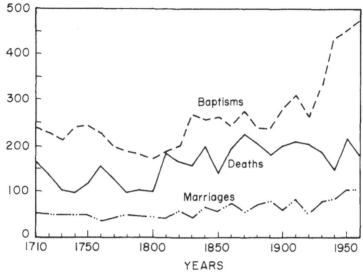

FIGURE 1.1 Demographic Trends, Lanheses, 1700–1960

stant until the late nineteenth and early twentieth centuries. Deaths appear to have varied as much as births over the short term. In general, the low figures probably reflect an underreporting of childhood mortality before first-communion prior to the mid-nineteenth century. The dramatic rise in deaths between 1800 and 1810 is most likely the result of the Napoleonic invasions in the later years of that decade. The rise between 1830 and 1840 reflects the impact of the worldwide cholera epidemic (Morris 1970)—thirty-two individuals died in August and September of 1832 alone.[18] A similar epidemic, the Spanish flu, hit the parish in 1918, killing twenty-seven people during the month of October. This latter epidemic is not forgotten by Lanhesans, especially those who lost a relative, and an annual pilgrimage in early June is made by inhabitants of all the villages in the region to commemorate this tragic and mortal event.

## GEOGRAPHY AND ECONOMY

> In no other region is the cultivator so routine, and in no other region, perhaps, is the routine of cultivation more empirical and more ruinous. (Ortigão 1885:53)

> If Egypt is a present of the Nile as Herodotus suggested, Minho is without doubt the result of the labors of her inhabitants. (Sampaio 1923:455)

The province of Minho (the districts of Viana do Castelo, Braga, and Porto) has often been described as the garden of Portugal. Its rolling, verdant landscape and favorable precipitation and climate have made the land fertile and productive despite the pressures of a dense population.[19] During the nineteenth century, much of the region was covered with chestnut trees, which provided one of the staples in the peasant diet. Today, the major trees are maritime pines, which furnish the peasants with fuel or with emergency cash. In the early part of the present century, wood was very important in the economy of the village of Lanheses and in the Lima Valley in general. Men and women were employed as wood choppers, as *carteiros* (those who transported wood from the mountains to the river's edge), or as boatsmen (*barqueiros*) who ferried the wood in shallow vessels down the Lima River to the port at Viana do Castelo.

The pine trees are located in mountain properties (*bouças*); the rest of the land in the province of Minho, particularly that in the flatter river valleys, is planted under a crop rotation system. Some of this land is irrigated in summer when spring rainfall has been insufficient. In the past, before the introduction of piped water, water was carefully regulated. Each peasant farmer had a set time and turn to irrigate his fields with this so-called *água da rega*, and if his turn came in the middle of the night, he had to be ready to take it. As in other parts of peasant Europe, the sharing of water was often a source of dispute.[20]

As mentioned earlier, property in Minho is divided into small plots and any single family is likely to own or rent numerous fields, campos and bouças, dispersed throughout their native village and perhaps in neighboring villages.[21] Ramalho Ortigão once remarked in jest that the ownership of land in several villages has given the Minhotan peasant the "right to be buried in all of them, though the right to vote in only one" (1885:159). Pery (1875) estimated the average size of plots in the districts of Viana do Castelo, Braga, and Porto at the end of the nineteenth century as 0.58, 0.65, and 0.89 hectares, respectively. He went on to note that even larger properties were divided into smaller parcels and rented out to peasant farmers. Today, the concelho of Viana do Castelo is the region of Portugal with the greatest percentage of owner-proprietors in the agricultural population. This was not the case either a century or half century ago however. In Portugal as a whole, 95 percent of agricultural exploitations occupy 32 percent of the land surface, whereas in Greece 95 percent of the agricultural exploitations are on 80 percent of the land surface (Barros 1972). This difference reflects the contrast in Portugal between the latifundia south and the minifundia north. More will be said about property in the next section of this chapter.

The major cereal crop throughout Minho is corn, which was introduced at the end of the sixteenth century, and which subsequently altered the entire rural economy of northwestern Portugal. Cabral (1974:29–30) has labeled the "corn revolution" the most significant change in Portugal's economic history after the Roman conquest. It caused the suppression of fallow land, an increase in irrigated land and in intensive small-scale agriculture, a decline in pasture land and in communal labor, the building of walls between land parcels, and the fostering of individualism (Ribeiro 1945). Corn is sown in May and irrigated (if necessary) three or four times a month until its maturation and harvest in late August and throughout September. Between the rows of corn, the peasants plant beans and other vegetables, thus making use of every piece of terrain they can. After the corn is harvested, the land is planted with grass, and the fields thus serve throughout the winter months as pasture for the farm animals. Plots that have been planted with corn may subsequently be planted with potatoes or winter cabbages and turnips.

After corn was introduced, as the population of the region grew, its cultivation was extended into fields that had traditionally been reserved for other uses. This particularly caused a change in vine cultivation. Instead of planting vines in low rows on sunny hillsides (as is done in the Douro valley or in the south of France, for example), the peasants of the province of Minho began to train their vines up granite posts and tree trunks, and along arbors between their plots of corn-sown land. The grapes, raised up and partially sheltered by their own foliage, do not mature as quickly, and for this reason the wine in the region has come to be known as *vinho verde* (green or immature wine).

Although the cultivation of corn spread up into the mountainsides and caused the terracing of lands and the takeover of pasture land in some parts of upper Minho, some high lands remained reserved for pasturage and, more importantly, as furze-field—that is, for the production of underbush (*mato*) used to create beds for the farm animals and, ultimately, much-needed manure.[22] In the past, cattle and sheep were extremely important for the production of milk, cheese, butter, and wool. However, the expansion of corn and the simultaneous decline in the number of fields devoted to pasturage led to a decline in dairy production, and olive oil eventually began to replace butter.

Although this system has its critics, the French geographer Pierre Birot (n.d.:73–74) once described it as "the most perfect type of vertical agricultural integration imaginable," a system that has furnished the peasants of the region simultaneously with fruit, cooking oil, beverages, vegetables, bread, and food for cattle and pigs. This agricultural system, and the methods of farming, have been handed down from one generation to the next. That what we see today is little different from the way of life two centuries ago is confirmed by observations made by eighteenth- and nineteenth-century northern European travelers who passed through the region.

> I travelled on a very bad road, through a pleasant country in general, which appeared populous, cultivated as high as the hills would permit with indian corn and vines; met many people, they had a neat appearance, but the women were without shoes and stockings. (Dalrymple 1777:121)

> Here small fields of maize, and even rye and barley and more rarely of wheat are surrounded by high German oaks, chestnuts, and poplars, artificially watered by brooks. Every tree supporting a vine which spreads over its crown, and not infrequently reaching the summit of the high oak. (Link 1801:331)

A second important feature of the rural agricultural system in northwestern Portugal and in Lanheses, and a feature clearly linked to population density, is dispersed settlement. The countryside is made up of small village after village, and one hardly notices where one ends and the next begins. Although Lanheses is one of the larger villages within its region, occupying an area of approximately eleven square kilometers of cultivated, uncultivated, and residential territory, it is, itself, composed of twenty-five smaller hamlets or localities (*lugares*), each with its own name.[23] There is some degree of "hamlet-pride," but whatever chauvinism one can find is normally at the village level. The most important lugar is the Lugar da Feira, the area in the center of the village surrounding the village square. Here the bimonthly market is held, and here are located the majority of small stores and cafés. The first *Casa do Povo* was built on the village square in the 1930s, and the only remaining functioning wood-burning bakery is located nearby.[24]

According to Candido Furtado Coelho's 1861 statistical analysis of the district of Viana do Castelo, 59 percent of the active population during the latter half of the nineteenth century were salaried laborers. However, it is unclear whether this figure referred strictly to salaried industrial laborers, or included salaried agricultural laborers, as well. More recently Jaime Reis (1981) has analyzed a "forgotten" industrial inquiry made in the district of Viana in 1839, an inquiry that was to cover agricultural, manufacturing, and commercial industry. In response to a question about the number of factories in the concelho of Viana, the respondent recorded three: a crockery factory in Darque (across the river from the town of Viana do Castelo) and two for tanning in Viana itself. The report continues:

> All these factories are in decadence since the appearance of other crockery establishments in Porto which sell their products for less, and of tanning houses in Galicia. In the crockery factory, the metals and dyes used are foreign and the leathers used in tanning are from Brazil. The crockery factory employs eight workers and the tanning factories six to eight in each. (Reis: 1981:194)

In short, what industry there was in the concelho of Viana, and in Lanheses, prior to the twentieth century was primarily cottage industry, engaged in during seasons of the year when agricultural labors were less burdensome, and primarily, although clearly not exclusively, for home consumption.

In the district of Viana do Castelo, it was the women who often contributed most to domestic industry. During the winter months, they spun and wove linen and made heavy covers of rags. The manufacture of linen was, in fact, a very important and time-consuming activity until the early 1950s (Felgueiras 1932). The following observation was made by an Englishman who passed through northern Portugal in the 1790s:

> It is much to the credit of the women of Portugal that they manufacture all the linen used in the kingdom through its various branches; they sow the grain, reap the produce, and hatchet the flax; afterwards, they weave the yarn and make up the linen . . . even the tables of the poorest peasant has a clean cloth and napkin. (Murphy 1795:20)

This linen industry supported a range of occupations: spinners, weavers, cloth merchants, lacemakers, seamstresses, ropemakers, and ribbonmakers (Bezerra 1785:50). The regional importance of linen manufacture is also reflected in numerous old and popular maxims that make reference to the distaff and spindle.

> Não há casa farta onde a roca não anda.
> There is not a prosperous house where the distaff is not at work.
>
> Tome casa com lar e mulher que saiba fiar.
> Take a house with a hearth and a woman who knows how to spin.

The primary nonagricultural profession (*arte*) of Minhotan men was and is that of mason (*pedreiro*). Granite is the major stone base, and the men of the region have become adept at cutting and working with it. Their expertise has been valued throughout Portugal and abroad, a factor which explains, at least to some extent, the paths of emigration that Minhotan stone masons have followed, particularly into Spain. In recent decades, they have taken these skills to France, adapting themselves to working with cement blocks and steel frames.

In addition to professions as masons, there were Lanhesans who called themselves carpenters and painters, and occasionally, after the dawn of the twentieth century, stuccoers. Several men were also occupied as boatsmen until better roads and ground transportation became more prevalent after 1930. Indeed, in the "inquérito industrial" studied by Reis (1981), the following answer was given by the concelho of Viana to a question about transportation: "The commodities produced in this municipality are brought in carts from the houses of proprietors to the shores of the Lima River, and from there in boats to the ships." Among other masculine professions mentioned in various historical sources are tailors, shoemakers, clog makers, potters (about which more will be said shortly), basketweavers, and small merchants. However, despite this rather motley assortment of professions for a small rural place, it is safe to say that most families were equally involved in some form of cultivation. These nonagricultural, artisanal activities were a necessary complement to a minifundia type of agricultural economy.

There are three other aspects of the historical local economy of Lanheses which are worthy of mention. Costa (1868) makes reference to mines in the vicinity of Lanheses that have been exploited at various times, but particularly during the second World War, when Portugal was providing raw minerals to both the Allies and the Axis. Almost everyone in Lanheses worked in the wolfram and tin mines nearby and at the height of demand collected anywhere from sixty to one hundred escudos per kilogram of tin or wolfram (the escudo in 1940 was worth approximately $0.037). Some "made it rich," particularly if mines were found on their property. The family of the present priest of Lanheses prospered in precisely this way. Those who remember this period in Lanheses' history recall that so many people left the fields that there was soon a food shortage, and the price of bread escalated to such an extent that even the village baker became rich, providing bread made from things that were inedible and selling it for exorbitant prices. The "mania" of money that spread through Lanheses and the region is mentioned repeatedly by many of the old-timers, and is realistically recorded by Aquilino Ribeiro in his fictional account of this period, *Volfrâmio*.

Another important aspect of the local economy of Lanheses has been the fabrication of ceramic roof tiles and housewares. Tiles made in Lanheses are said to have been sent to the monastery of Mafra when it was built in the eighteenth century. Leal (1873) mentions that "plentiful and excellent tiles, in addition to other forms of pottery—jugs, large bowls, cooking pots—are made in Lanheses." Candido Furtado Coelho, in 1861, counted seven pottery workshops in the district of Viana, all of them in Lanheses. In fact, certain extended families of potters (*oleiros*) worked almost exclusively in the production of domestic items, and the skill was passed on from one generation to the next. One such family came to Lanheses from a village near Prado in the district of Braga, an area famous for its domestic pottery. Other families were involved strictly in the seasonal production of tiles that were baked in private ovens and only at certain times of the year because of the excessive smoke which this process produced. When Padre Cardoso counted in the 1760s, there were eight ovens; Coelho (1861) counted twenty-two in the concelho of Viana a century later, although he mentions no figure for Lanheses itself; at the time of the First World War, according to one villager, there were forty ovens in Lanheses, half of them concentrated in one lugar. Today, this activity has disappeared, but when Lanhesans participate in the procession of the annual Feira da Agonia, the important fair in the town of Viana do Castelo, they frequently remind people of the importance of the pottery industry in their past. Tastes have changed and factory-manufactured products are more readily available to the people of the rural north. Although peasant households still own and use the ruddy-colored pottery, their preference is for the type of ironstone china seen on dinner tables throughout the Western world. Roof tiles are still used for construction, but they are mass-produced today and transported throughout the country.

One final element of the local economy that is important to mention is the cattle trade, the *comércio de boi* or *comércio de gado*. Every peasant family, if it were successfully to farm its land, required a team of oxen. Some families, to make extra cash, raised these oxen from young bullocks, using their labor while they owned them, and then selling them at the local markets for a profit. Others, if they could not afford to own a team of oxen outright, took a *gado a ganho* from a local dealer or contractor (there were several in the region). They fed the beasts, used their labor, and then, when the team was sold, half the profit went to the farmer and the other half to the cattle contractor. This practice of gado a ganho was so common that often families did not know who owned oxen teams and who rented them, and it was the cattle trade that made the bimonthly market of Lanheses so important in the past. One old-timer mentioned that as a boy his parents sent him to the feira to collect the manure for the fields. It was free to anyone who came to gather it. He and others alluded to one of the larger cattle dealers in Lanheses who was an important individual in village politics during the first several decades of the twentieth century. Today, there is very little cattle trading left, although some peasant households still continue to buy and sell. What trade there is takes place largely at the monthly feira in the town of Ponte de Lima, eight kilometers to the west.

Before concluding this brief discussion of the geography and economy of Lanheses and its region, it is important to make some reference to the process of modernization. Changes in the village economy have been fairly recent, and, even so, there are still families who are farming their land much as their ancestors did two centuries ago. Electricity was brought into the parish in the 1930s. Piped water is more recent. An elementary school was also built in the 1930s, but only in the 1960s were four years of primary education made obligatory by the government. There were teachers who instructed children in Lanheses during the nineteenth century, but in their own homes and whenever children appeared. In 1859, Coelho (1861) counted twenty-six students in school in Lanheses, and literacy figures in the national census demonstrate the backwardness of basic education until quite recently. Today, numerous women over age sixty can neither read nor write, and rarely have adults over thirty-five received much more than a few years of primary schooling.

According to Lanhesans themselves, the real thrust of modernization has come with the post-1960 emigration to France. No family is "poor" any more; new houses are being built by the so-called *franceses* throughout the village; the village square has been revived as new stores, cafés, and other businesses have been opened. In 1978, a new Casa do Povo, complete with clinic and recreation center, was opened to serve Lanheses and neighboring villages, and since the mid 1970s the priest has been running a local high school program that also serves the region. The road along the northern shore of the Lima River between Viana do Castelo and Ponte de Lima was improved in the latter nineteenth century, and the first motor car passed through in the early part of the twentieth century. Bus service has existed since the 1930s, and in 1980 a new bridge was built across the Lima River at Lanheses, facilitating access to Porto and points south. In short, the pace of change has been much more rapid in the past two or three decades than in the previous two centuries. It is important to remember this if one believes that the changes in values and ideas that accompany technological modernization are significant to subsequent changes in demographic behavior. This is a question to which we will return later in the book.

## LAND TENURE AND SOCIAL STRUCTURE

In most discussions of the nature of land tenure and social structure in Portugal, the north is characterized as a region of minifundia, partible inheritance, and small-scale, self-subsistent, independent peasant family farms, whereas the south is characterized as a region of latifundia, absentee landlords, and a rural proletarian agricultural population. Although this characterization is not inaccurate, it obscures somewhat the complexity of property ownership and social stratification, particularly in northwestern Portugal. Clearly, given the extensiveness of emigration in certain regions of the north, the "independence" of the peasant family was, as Cabral (1974) has observed, a "pseudo-independence" at best. Furthermore, not every so-called peasant family owned all the land they farmed, nor were all peasant families living in the rural north landowners. In this and the following section, I would like to explore the complexity of this social system further through a discussion of social stratification, land tenure, and inheritance in the parish of Lanheses.

Although one cannot necessarily argue that a rural village like Lanheses is divided into distinct social classes, it is safe to suggest that the population was and is by no means homogenous, and that there is a system of stratification that, until recently, was essentially based upon the ownership of land. Except at the uppermost level, there has been a great deal of fluidity, which has depended to some extent on emigration. Within the history of the village, there are identifiable cases of families who have become rich through the success of one or more of its members in Brazil, and of others who have descended a few notches because of a large number of offspring or some other "misfortune." The exploration of the relationship between social position and other demographic phenomena is reserved for later chapters, but it is important to outline the major characteristics of local social structure at this point.

In general, a small-scale peasantry farms the land, but the peasantry is itself subdivided into small and medium-sized property owners, tenant farmers, sharecroppers, and agricultural laborers. In addition, and this is particularly true of the Lima River valley, there are ennobled and high-ranking military/government families who have owned property throughout the upper Minho, property which was, in many cases, granted to them several centuries ago by one or another of Portugal's monarchs. Indeed, the Conde de Aurora (1929) once referred to the Lima Valley as the "forcing bed for Portuguese fidalgos."[25] Although the amount of land owned by any one of these families was in no way as extensive as that owned by some of the large landowners in the south of Portugal, their presence in the region has nevertheless been felt, and their very existence is crucial to the way in which land was owned and farmed throughout most of the history of Minho in general, Lanheses in particular. One cannot speak of the sharecropper (*caseiro*) or tenant farmer (*lavrador-rendeiro*) without speaking of these wealthier landowners with their manor houses (*solares*) and large farms (*quintas*).

## Fidalgos: The Rural Aristocracy

During the Middle Ages, most of the land in northern Portugal was owned by the Church and, to a somewhat lesser extent, by the nobility. By the thirteenth century, much of the property that had been granted to the nobility by the kings of Portugal (*honras*) was entailed (*vinculado*) and transferred in one piece, generally according to a practice of male primogeniture (*morgado*). The number of morgados multiplied, especially during the reign of Manuel I. However, despite the fact that the Church and the aristocracy owned the bulk of the land, most of it was farmed under leases or *foros*, a system that had its origins in the post-Roman *villa-colon* system. This system contributed greatly to land fragmentation, since the more small plots that could be leased out, the greater the amount of rental income on the land an owner could collect. Peasants, as tenant farmers, were required to pay a fixed amount of rent, usually in agricultural goods, each year, the amount of which was unrelated to the quantity of goods produced in any one year. These contracts for rent were generally long term, and were passed on from one generation of tenant farmers to the next.[26]

Two families best represent the importance of the *honra-vinculo-morgado-foro* system in the history of property ownership and land cultivation in Lanheses. By far the more important, and the only aristocratic family that still retains a house and property in the parish, is that of the counts of Almada. The Almadas established themselves in Lanheses in 1818, when a daughter of the Ricalde family married D. Antão, the second count of Almada. The Ricaldes, as mentioned earlier in this chapter, were descended from João Martins de Ricalde (or Rigua), an Asturian who had fled from Spain in the early sixteenth century and settled in the town of Viana do Castelo. The *quinta* of Lanheses was given to him as part of the dowry of Ana da Rocha (of the Rocha family in the neighboring village of Meixedo) when they married. In 1548, their son purchased half of the patronage of Lanheses from the convent of San Salvador da Torre, and another descendent, abbot of the village between 1594 and 1621, purchased the remaining half in 1618.

The Ricaldes allied themselves and intermarried with other ennobled families in the region (the Abreus, the Pereiras, the Castros, and the Lobatos) as the generations suceeded one another. Many of them assumed distinguished government posts, among them Frei Sebastião Pereira de Castro, a minister of King João V (1706–1750). He was a son by the second marriage of Francisco de Abreu Pereira, who, in the middle of the eighteenth century, built a new manor house in Lanheses to replace the original house, which had fallen into ruin by the seventeenth century. Frei Sebastião's brother, José Pereira de Brito Abreu, assumed the role of senhor of the manor in Lanheses on his father's death and married his cousin Dona Isabel Maria Peixoto Cyrne. His son Francisco Abreu Pereira Cyrne married Dona Maria Victoria Menezes Bacelar of the house of Covas, further in the interior of the Lima Valley, and his grandson Sebastião married Maria José de Lencestre, daughter of Gonçalo Pereira da Silva, first heir to the solar of Bertiandos, a closely neighboring village. Sebastião's and Maria José's daughter and sole offspring, Maria Francisca, who was born in 1801, married her cousin D. Antão, the second count of Almada and the fourteenth count of Abranches, in 1818. The Almadas had been given the title Count of Abranches by King Charles VII of France because of their heroism. The achievements of this family continued in Portugal through D. Antão Vaz de Almada, who was one of the forty fidalgos who plotted the restoration of Portugal in 1640. The descendents of D. Antão Vaz all held governmental positions and intermarried with other noble families.

D. Antão's son, D. Lourenço, succeeded his father as third count of Almada in 1835, and he in turn was succeeded by his fourth child and second son (the eldest was demented), D. Miguel, in 1874. D. Miguel is remembered by old-timers in Lanheses for some of the advances he made in local agriculture, whereas the fourth countess, Dona Leocadia, is remembered for her "kindness." Many of the young girls from village families worked for the count and countess, whether in the village solar or in the house in Lisbon, where the family resided for eight or nine months of the year. When D. Miguel died heirless in 1916, D. Lourenço Vaz Almada, his nephew, became the fifth count, and it is his eldest son who is currently the sixth count of Almada, though the title has now legally disappeared.

In the past, much of the land owned by the Almadas in Lanheses was overseen by a steward who had families living on the property and working for him (*caseiros*). Some of the land was also rented out to local peasant farmers. Today, the present count, who lives in the city of Porto, has formed an association with one caseiro family. This family works the land and the fruits of their labors are divided with the Almada family. Although there are no extant data to indicate precisely how much land in Lanheses was owned by the Almada-Ricalde family in the past, the property records of 1940 list ninety-three separate plots within the boundaries of the parish in their name for a total of 343,361 square meters (approximately 34 hectares) of territory.[27] Five of these properties, those which appear to have been inherited directly through the family line, are over 10,000 square meters (63,381, 75,724, 27,953, 26,420, and 11,560 square meters, respectively), and if these are omitted from the total amount of land, the average size of plots is 1571.85 square meters, or less than a quarter of a hectare. The majority of these plots seem to have been acquired from other villagers, although the time of their acquisition is not clear. They vary in nature—some planted with corn, others covered with underbush (*mato*). Clearly, although the Almadas are the biggest property owners in Lanheses, and, church-owned lands aside, probably were in the past, the total amount of land in their name in no way compares to the large-scale properties in the south of Portugal. Furthermore—and this is the important point to reiterate—about one-third of the total amount of land owned by this family is divided up into minute parcels rented and farmed by other villagers. Finally, the bulk of land has been passed on over the generations to a single male heir. Indeed, many of the daughters never married, whereas later-born sons seem to have taken up religious or military careers.

The other distinguished "house" in Lanheses is the Casa da Barrosa, with its chapel constructed on the site of a hermitage of unknown date that had been erected in honor of Our Lady of Hope. By the early eighteenth century, this hermitage had fallen into ruin, and one of the priests in the archbishopric who came to Lanheses on a regular annual visitation in 1723 ordered that the chapel either be destroyed or restored. In 1732, a priest and village native, Francisco Alves Franco, who had acquired a fortune in Brazil, took it upon himself to restore the chapel, and subsequently built a house adjacent to it on property purchased from the rector of Correlhã (a village further inland), who had himself purchased the land from the founder of the original hermitage. The chapel was restored in 1737, and the house erected.

When Padre Francisco died in 1749, he left the administration of the chapel to his niece Maria Micaella, a daughter of his sister Isabel, and her husband Domingos da Rocha. In his will, he entailed the property, a restriction that most likely survived until the 1860s when entailments (*vinculos*) were finally abolished throughout Portugal. This will exists in an extant book of testaments for the parish of Lanheses, and is worth quoting in part, since it provides an excellent example of how large properties were dealt with in order to secure the social position of a family that had risen to wealth on the basis of resources of a priest returned from Brazil.

> I declare that from my fixed property will be separated property worth four thousand cruzados, among which I include what I own in Casal Maior, in the field in Agra, and the debts associated with these properties. Excluded from this is the property of Barrosa, and the farmland in Agra de Baixo and Campo de Rio—property which my nephew João, son of my sister Isabel and her husband Domingos, will have when he is ordained a priest; and if he does not assume this position, the property will go to his brother António when he becomes a priest, with the obligation, to whomever of these, to say every Sunday and on holy days and Saturdays, a mass for my soul in the Chapel of Our Lady of Hope . . . and these goods they will have by entailment, so that at no time can they sell it, but must keep it together and undivided.

The testator, Padre Francisco Alves Franco, goes on to indicate that the chaplain should, if possible, always be a relative of the administrator of the vinculo, and that he can ordain himself at the expense of the vinculo associated with the chapel. If the administrator neglects to send the eldest son to study for the priesthood, then the closest relative to the administrator who is a priest can be designated as the chaplain. He then specifies his niece Maria Micaella as the administrator "with the condition that she does not marry a person from a loathsome nation, a Negro, mulatto, or Moor, nor any from any other nation of those rejected by law." He obliges his niece and future administrators to live in the house of Barrosa for at least half the year. Finally, he stipulates that the form of succession for the Casa da Barrosa should give preference to the eldest female of his niece Maria Micaella, and so on down. Although this is a curious indication of the emphasis on female heirs, in a codicil to the will dated 1748 this preference is revoked in favor of the eldest male.

My best guess is that the codicil was written at the request of Maria Micaella's husband. In 1745, prior to Padre Francisco's death in 1749, Maria Micaella had married Dr. Miguel Tinoco de Sá Pereira Velho of Viana do Castelo. It was as a result of this marriage, and with the codicil to Padre Francisco's will, that the Casa da Barrosa was passed into the hands of the Tinoco family, a family with substantial property in the neighboring village of Fontão. Miguel Tinoco and Maria Micaella had one son, who married a woman from the village of Darque in 1779 and inherited the Casa da Barrosa upon his mother's death. They in turn had two sons, José Joaquim, who died while still a youth, and Miguel. Miguel inherited the property in Lanheses and later married Dona Maria José Pimenta Furtado de Mendonça of the village of Miranda in the concelho of Arcos de Val de Vez.[28] Four children were born of this union: António, who died single; José, the heir; Catarina, who married the "lord" of the manor in the village of Vitorino das Donas (across the river from Lanheses); and Maria José, who married a gentleman from Santo Tirso near Porto and died without offspring. In addition, there was an illegitimate son, Joaquim José, who became a priest and who was mentioned in his father's will.

The heir, José, who was born around 1816 in the neighboring village of Fontão, married a widow, Dona Ana José Malheiro de Meneses of Monção in Lanheses in 1843. Dona Ana died in 1882 without producing an heir. However, two illegitimate children, Miguel and Rosa Maria, were born to José Tinoco and a servant, Francisca Rosa da Silva, in the 1870s. Prior to his death in 1893, José Tinoco was persuaded by the priest of Lanheses to marry Francisca Rosa and thereby to legitimize his two children. According to old-timers in Lanheses, this woman became an "egoist" once she had assumed the role as "patroness." "She used to go out into the fields with a sunshade to make sure that the poor laborers were working and none of the laborers complained because they needed the work."

Upon José Tinoco's death, Miguel became the heir. His sister, who had married a young man from Arcos de Val de Vez, died while still a young woman with no children. José Tinoco also had another illegitimate son, José dos Passos, born in Fontão to Dona Maria da Agonia of Viana. This son inherited the Casa de Retiro, the Tinoco family estate in Fontão, married, and had eleven children. Miguel

Tinoco never married, and when he died in the 1950s, his property was divided between his paternal half brother José and the daughter of his maternal half sister (an illegitimate daughter of Francisca Rosa by another man). This half sister had also inherited property upon her mother's death, but she had married a man who, to pay for frequent trips he made back and forth to Brazil, sold much of what his wife had inherited back to Miguel Tinoco. Today, the Tinoco family no longer exists in Lanheses, and the Quinta and Casa da Barrosa have recently been purchased by a local entrepreneur who made his money in Angola but returned to Portugal soon after the revolution of 1974. The chapel was sold to the brother of the current priest of Lanheses, an emigrant in the United States, who subsequently turned it over to the village ecclesiastical corporation.

Of the other important wealthy landed families who at one time or another lived in Lanheses, or at least owned property in the parish, we know much less. Their presence is indicated by oral history, by a few marriages that took place in the parish, by occasional obituaries recorded in the parish register, and by periodic references in notarial records, wills, and other documents in which specific plots of land are mentioned. The Pimenta da Gama was one such family. They owned land and employed caseiros until just after the Second World War. In the electoral list of 1870, a certain António Pimenta da Gama Barretto is listed with property in the village assessed at 9,320$500, the highest on the document. Presumably Tinoco and Almada voted elsewhere. The name of this late nineteenth-century Pimenta da Gama indicates that at some point in local history, the Pimenta da Gama family was connected (clearly by marriage) with the Regos Barretos, viscounts in the village of Geraz de Lima on the southern shores of the Lima River. Indeed, Rego Barretos were also residents and property owners in Lanheses in the later eighteenth and early nineteenth centuries.

Although these aristocratic families are not the focus of attention in this book, it is important to acknowledge the influence they may have had on village life. Their sheer presence underscores the fact that Lanheses was neither isolated nor without social hierarchical differences. They stood as a vivid reminder of the differences between rich and poor and of the fact that these differences were measured primarily by ownership of land. Presumably, they followed certain practices—primogeniture, consanguineous marriages—in order to maintain their wealth and social position. Finally, they provided employment opportunities for poorer Lanhesans, whether as domestic servants, day laborers, or tenant farmers.

## Lavradores: The Land-Owning Peasants

Below the fidalgo class are the landowning peasant farmers. In the province of Minho, the term *lavrador* is applied to all those who work their own land, whether as small or large property owners. However, in Lanheses, it is important to distinguish between well-to-do peasants, the so-called *lavradores abastados,* and the average lavradores who worked on land that they rented in addition to land they owned. Whereas the lavradores abastados cultivated their land themselves, using the hired labor of landless peasants during harvest seasons, the average small-scale peasant farmer either combined the farming of land with some sort of artisanal skill (mason, carpenter, and so on), or hired himself or his offspring out to work on the land owned by wealthier peasants or the aristocracy.

In an 1871 arrolamento dos bens (property roll), 253 households were listed in Lanheses, 164 of which were headed by lavradores (Table 1.2). For each household, a value was given to its property in

TABLE 1.2 HOUSEHOLDS BY PROFESSION
OF HEAD OF HOUSEHOLD,
LANHESES, 1871

| | | |
|---|---|---|
| Total Number of Households | | 253 |
| Lavrador households | | 164 |
|    male headed | 118 | |
|    female headed | 46 | |
| Jornaleiro households | | 36 |
|    male headed | 19 | |
|    female headed | 17 | |
| Pedreiro households | | 13 |
| Potter households | | 6 |
| Tailor / seamstress households | | 10 |
|    male headed | 6 | |
|    female headed | 4 | |
| Shoemaker households | | 6 |
| Other artisans | | 10 |
|    male headed | 9 | |
|    female headed | 1 | |
| Others (boatsmen, surgeon, druggist, miller, baker, etc.) | | 8 |
|    male headed | 6 | |
|    female headed | 2 | |

SOURCE: Arrolamento dos Bens, 1871; Arquivo Municipal de Viana do Castelo.

reis. Although it is not clear quite how this figure was arrived at (one presumes that it was some kind of tax), these values give us a good idea of the constituents of the lavrador class during the latter third of the nineteenth century. Approximately 64 percent of these households were assigned a value under a thousand reis; another 32 percent were valued between a thousand and two thousand reis; and the remaining 5 percent were valued at over two thousand reis. Of the six households at the top of the scale, three are headed by siblings— two sisters and a brother—the three eldest children of a family that has been in the village at least since 1700. All of these families still had adult sons—in their late twenties and early thirties—living with them, although this is equally characteristic of medium and small-scale lavradores, as well. Several of these wealthier peasants are associated with important quintas in Lanheses, some of which still remain, but others of which have been broken up in the recent past. Indeed, oral history corroborates the fact that these well-to-do peasant farmers often came into wealth through inheritance or through money earned abroad, and used it to purchase land.

The wealthier lavrador families identified by old-timers do not correspond to the six identified from the 1871 arrolamento. Of these orally identified lavradores abastados, one, the proprietress of the Quinta da Boa Vista in the lugar of Corredoura had been married to a man who was an apothecary and who emigrated to Brazil and made a fortune; a second owns the Quinta da Granja, a piece of property acquired through the good fortune of a son who had been a priest and made his money in Brazil during the early years of the twentieth century; a third was established when a young man, a native of Refoios further in the interior and the steward of a quinta in Lanheses in the 1840s, was left wealthy by two of his brothers who were priests, and subsequently acquired land for himself in Lanheses.

There are several extant, though sporadic, electoral rolls for Lanheses dating to the mid-nineteenth century that also give some indication of the variations in wealth among the lavrador class of Lanheses. These rolls are not, as the arrolamento of 1871, a complete list of households, but only of male heads of household who are eligible to vote (largely on the basis of a minimum fee they were able to pay). Table 1.3 provides a summary of the electoral rolls for 1855 and 1864. As in the 1871 arrolamento, the majority of lavradores are in the lower category of small property owners. In addition, and more clearly in 1855 than in 1864, it appears that the upper category is composed of older lavradores who have accumulated their wealth over time.

TABLE 1.3 SUMMARY OF ELECTORAL LISTS FOR LANHESES FOR 1855 AND 1864

| Number with a Decima Quota and other Contribution between: | | Profession | | | Marital Status | | |
|---|---|---|---|---|---|---|---|
| | | Lavrador | Other* | Mean Age | Sing. | Marr. | Widow |
| *1855* | | | | | | | |
| 1$000–1$999 | 47 (51%) | 40 | 7 | 49.5 | 2 | 45 | 1 |
| 2$000–2$999 | 23 (25%) | 22 | 1 | 55.9 | 1 | 21 | 1 |
| 3$000–3$999 | 11 (12%) | 10 | 1 | 57.0 | 0 | 11 | 0 |
| 4$000–4$999 | 5 (5%) | 5 | 0 | | 0 | 5 | 0 |
| 5$000–5$999 | 4 ⎫ (7%) | 4 | 1 | | 0 | 4 | 0 |
| 6$000+ | 2 ⎭ | 1 | 1 | 61.3 | 0 | 1 | 1 |
| *1864* | | | | | | | |
| 1$000–1$999 | 40 (46%) | 37 | 3 | 52.0 | 4 | 31 | 5 |
| 2$000–2$999 | 21 (24%) | 19 | 2 | 49.9 | 1 | 18 | 2 |
| 3$000–3$999 | 13 (15%) | 10 | 3 | 51.8 | 2 | 10 | 1 |
| 4$000–4$999 | 5 (6%) | 4 | 1 | | 1 | 4 | 0 |
| 5$000–5$999 | 4 ⎫ (9%) | 3 | 1 | | 0 | 4 | 0 |
| 6$000+ | 4 ⎭ | 4 | 0 | 58.6 | 0 | 4 | 0 |

* Among other professions in the 1$000–1$999 category are tavern keepers (*vendeiros*), shoemakers, a boatsman, a blacksmith, a surgeon, and a miller. The other professions in the 2$000–2$999 category are a druggist, a mason, and a baker; in the 3$000–3$999 category, a tavern keeper, a cleric, a merchant, and a druggist; in the 4$000–4$999 category, a cleric; in the 5$000–5$999 category, a surgeon; and in the 6$000+ category, a proprietor—Miguel Tinoco.

SOURCE: Rois Eleitorais, 1855, 1864; Arquivo Municipal de Viana do Castelo.

## Day Laborers, Sharecroppers, and Tenant Farmers

In 1864, according to Sampaio (1979), only 24.5 percent of the population in the upper Minho owned land, a factor that explains, he claims, the number of *arrendeiros* (or *lavradores-rendeiros*), *jornaleiros*, and *caseiros* among the total population. These three groups comprise the three lowest levels of the socioeconomic hierarchy in the region in general, and in Lanheses in particular.

At the bottom are the jornaleiros, those families with essentially no land who made (and make) their living working for others in agriculture for daily wages. A popular saying about the jornaleiro is that he had "neither a threshing floor, a river bank, nor the shade of a fig tree" (não tem eira, nem beira, nem sombra da figueira). In fact, many, if not most, of these jornaleiro families may have had a small plot (*quintalejo*) of land abutting their home where they could grow cabbage, turnips, and perhaps a few potatoes, but nothing big enough to accommodate a crop of corn. Basilio Teles (1903) observed that the jornaleiros were truly the people in northern Portugal who lived in the most misery: "Their salaries are irregular and scanty . . . two hundred, two hundred and forty, three hundred reis from time to time . . . hardly enough to meet the expenses of a family, above all a family so numerous and composed largely of minors." (Teles 1903:18).

In Lanheses, at the dawn of the twentieth century, the going salary for a jornaleiro was three hundred reis *seco* (dry) or one hundred reis plus food; for women the salary was two hundred reis seco. Among these families, there were many in which the husband had some other kind of low-paying occupation, such as shoemaker, clog-maker, or boatman, while his wife worked as a jornaleira. Indeed, women made up a large proportion of the jornaleiros because they could be paid less and because agricultural work, especially for wages, was traditionally a female domain. Girls began to earn income for their families at a young age, and, if they never married, they may have worked all their lives as day laborers. In some cases, particularly when a young girl came from a large family, she was sent to live with a wealthier lavrador family as a *criada* (maid servant), a term that implies, in the rural Portuguese context, work not only in domestic service but also in the fields. In the 1871 arrolamento, there are almost as many female-headed as male-headed jornaleiro households (all given a valuation of 180 reis). Indeed, many women who had had illegitimate children lived alone as heads of households and worked as jornaleiras; it was the major means by which they could support themselves.

Whereas female jornaleiras were frequently the daughters of caseiros, poor lavradores, or jornaleiros already established in the parish, it seems that many of the male jornaleiros whom we can identify as such throughout Lanheses' history came to the parish from elsewhere, married, and settled down. This is not only an indication of the geographic mobility characteristic of the region, but also of the availability of work for members of this low social group in the parish of Lanheses. The fact that the parish had a bimonthly feira may have made it a stopping-off place for young men in search of work.

Slightly above the jornaleiros (mostly because of greater economic stability) were the so-called caseiros, sharecroppers of sorts who made

their living working the lands of the ennobled families in the region.
Many of these caseiros were originally recruited from among the jornaleiro class—the more enterprising, perhaps. About the caseiro class, Teles (1903) had the following comment:

> Their needs are little, the most important being the need to eat, and the fruits of the property they rent satisfied that need. As long as the land gives them bread, vegetables, wine to feed themselves and their families and to pay the rent, what does it matter to them if the price of vegetables, wine, or bread rises. . . . They can almost always maintain an economic equilibrium. . . . Their only problem is when the rent goes up . . . in that case the man has no doubts about returning to day labor, looking for work in the cities, or trying his luck in Brazil. (Teles 1903:15–16)

There is evidence that caseiros have always been a part of the social make-up of the parish, though probably a small part. For example, in 1706 Domingos Alves Seixas married Maximina Franca Rocha. When Maximina had a child the following year, the couple were listed as residents on the Quinta de San João, and Francisco Abreu Pereira Cirne was named as the godfather of their daughter— a good patron-client relationship contracted between a poor caseiro and his wealthy employer. In October of 1722, a certain Bento Alves married Andresa da Costa. At his death in 1769 he was described as a "caseiro of the Tenente Coronel (a military officer) António Luis Bandeira." Presumably the Tenente Coronel lived elsewhere, as did many other individuals who had tenure to property in Lanheses that was cultivated by caseiros.

In the nineteenth century, it seems that most of the caseiro families came from neighboring villages to work on the lands of the Almadas, the Pimentas da Gama and, in the latter part of the century on the property of the military family of Pereira de Castro, which owned a large quinta in Lanheses. According to one informant, many of these caseiros came from Santa Marta and Perre, villages nearer the provincial town of Viana do Castelo, where impartible inheritance was supposedly more common. Caseiros were, in his assessment, the disinherited offspring who looked elsewhere in the region for some sort of stability in agriculture. The descendents of some of these families still remain in the village; others have disappeared. Some of the male heads of caseiro households did follow the late nineteenth-century and early twentieth-century emigration streams to Brazil and Spain together with their lavrador compatriots.

The third group to consider in this category of families who worked land they did not own were the lavradores-rendeiros, who may have owned a small amount of land but probably rented the bulk of what they cultivated. Indeed, in the electoral rolls or the arrolamento dos bens it is possible that many of the lavradores taxed at the smaller amounts were in fact lavradores-rendeiros. Lavradores-rendeiros were small-scale agriculturalists who managed to scrape by, probably experiencing hard times during bad harvest years. In some instances, the distinction between them and caseiros is not very apparent—indeed, in the absence of property records we are not able to compile a total ownership/rental profile for any single family. Full-fledged caseiros did not own any land, and indeed those identified as such during the latter nineteenth century do not appear on the 1871 arrolamento dos bens.

Rents on land were normally a fixed amount of the crop, determined according to the size of the plot rather than the size of the annual yield. Extant wills and notarial records give us some indication of the nature of these rental contracts, many of which were long-term agreements in the form of foros made with various religious institutions or individuals outside the village who owned land within it. For example, in a joint testament of 1795, João Araujo and his wife Maria Alves stated that they were "masters and owners" of a contract with the Convent of S. Domingos for a plot of land in the lowlands (*veiga*) of Lanheses and for which they paid, annually, twelve *razas* (probably about sixty liters) of corn. They bequeathed this contract to their son and daughter-in-law, asking them to pay the annual sum. In a will written two years earlier, José da Rocha left his daughter Luisa his *prazos* in Casal Maior and Bajouca, both of which belonged to the Convent of Santa Cruz in Viana, and to which he paid an annual pension of two-and-a-half *alqueires* of corn.[29] In other wills, these inherited foros and prazos were divided equally between heirs. Notarial records dating from the early nineteenth century contain numerous examples of the actual establishment of such contracts. They specify the location and amount of land, the amount of the pension, the length of the contract, the day on which the pension is to be paid, and the penalty for forfeit.

One of the largest property owners in the parish, from whom villagers could lease land to cultivate, was the Church. In 1789, for example, a young man of fifteen named José Martins, with the authority of his father Bento Martins, recognized the obligations he had as tenant (*emphiteuta*) to the "Reverend Priest" for the prazo of Casal Maior. The annual rent was 0$540, three hens, and two chickens.[30] Another couple, Carlos António and Esperança da Costa, farmed seven small plots under the proprietorship of the village church, for which they paid seven alqueires of corn each year. Further, such "recognitions" (*reconhecimentos*) of obligation are among the papers preserved in the parish archives, most of them dating to the later eighteenth century. In March of 1790, the widower Paulo Gonçalves, together with three married men—Domingos Alves, José Gonçalves, and Bento Alves—each recognized land that was owned by the parish church and that they cultivated in return for annual pensions of one, one-and-a-half, two-and-a-half, and five alqueires of corn, respectively. All of these plots were in the veiga down by the river's edge, and were apparently long and narrow strips, one as narrow as three-and-a-half *varas*, or approximately 3.85 meters. In another reconhecimento of the same year, one couple paid an alqueire for a third of a plot which they shared with a widow who also paid an alqueire. All three are described in the document as *simples colonos*, a phrase that clearly harks back to the colonos of the thirteenth century, and therefore suggests the persistence of a certain form of land tenure across several centuries. Although we do not know specifically what happened to the church properties in Lanheses in the 1830s, there were thirty-eight different individuals recorded on a list of foros paid by Lanhesans in 1875, and some individuals were listed more than once. The sums paid ranged from 0$015 to over 1$000.

Clearly, these poorer agriculturalists, whether as caseiros, lavradores-rendeiros, or jornaleiros, depended on the well-to-do lavradores, the northern rural aristocracy, and the Church for their livelihood in a system that was characterized by both inequality and fluidity. Jornaleiras occasionally married "aristocrats"; enterprising tenant farmers or day laborers could, particularly if they were lucky in emigration, return and buy some land. Owning land was a mark of socioeconomic status; having at least some land to farm (even if it was farmed for wages) was necessary for survival. We thus need to turn to the issue of how this land, once procured, was passed on from one generation to the next. Although keeping one's social and economic position was clearly important among the aristocracy, was it important among the landowning peasant classes? Was it even feasible? Although the inheritance of land will figure again in the discussion of marriage patterns in Lanheses, it is useful here to set out some of the broad parameters within which property was transmitted.

## The Inheritance of Property

In the village of Lanheses, there are three extant books of testaments that cover a period between 1742 and 1859. It is apparent that not everyone who died in the village during this hundred-year period made a will, or, if they did, they were not recorded in one of the Livros dos Testamentos that still survive. However, those wills which are available for study provide us with important, though not necessarily quantifiable and systematic, historical insights about what was valued, what was transferred at death, and about family relationships in general. Furthermore, they indicate that even within this regime of supposedly partible inheritance, one offspring was generally favored over all the others to receive the têrço or third portion. It seems useful to explore the content of these wills after the discussion of land tenure and social structure, thereby providing a basis for later examination of the relationship between inheritance patterns and other demographic phenomena. I will begin by making a few generalizations about these wills as a group, and then explore several of them in greater detail—that is, to look at the ways in which they are similar and then to examine their variety.

The majority of testaments were written at the bedside of the testator soon before his or her actual death; some of them revoked an earlier document. They are generally recorded by what was apparently a village scribe (such an individual still exists today to write for those who cannot) and in the presence of one or two witnesses. As Descamps (1935:72) once observed, many of these wills were essentially religious documents, specifying at the outset and in rather formulaic language the robes in which the testator wished to be buried (for Lanhesans, the most popular habit seems to have been that of St. Francis) and the number of masses that the dying individual wanted to have said for his or her own soul and sometimes for the souls of relatives who had already passed away. If anything, the making of a will was, in Descamps' view (1959), an obligation morally imposed upon the individual by the Church. The following testament of Domingos Rodrigues das Possas, widower, written in 1759, will serve as an example of the religious aspects of these documents:

Say I, Domingos Rodrigues, widower of Antonia Gonçalves, of the lugar of Possas in this village of Lanheses, in the vicinity of the town of Vianna, that sensing that I am going into the hands of God, our Lord Jesus Christ, and therefore that I am in the last days of my life, and being in a perfect state of mind, this is my last wish—I ask for ten masses for my soul and another ten for the soul of my companion, each one with an offering of four vinténs (0$80); also I ask that ten masses be spoken for the soul of my father and my mother, each for 0$80 reis; also ten masses for the

souls of my father-in-law and my mother-in-law, each with an offering of four vinténs.

After these sometimes lengthy preambles, the testaments move on
to a discussion of more mundane matters, chiefly indicating the executor of the will and the recipient of the *têrço dos bens moveis e de
raiz* (the third share of movable and fixed real property). If a couple
was making a will together *(de mão comum)*, something that happened not infrequently and that probably indicates a marriage between socioeconomic equals, the têrço was left to the one who survived and then, upon the survivor's death, to a specified heir. Generally,
the testator acknowledged whether or not he had obligatory heirs
*(herdeiros forçosos)*, direct offspring recognized by name, and, if not,
he was then free to choose whomever he wished as an heir. For example, António Rodrigues and Maria Gomes da Rocha, in a common will of 1826, stated that "they had no legitimate children, nor
natural children, nor adulterous children, nor incestuous children,
and for this reason were free to dispose of their property." Clearly,
this excerpt indicates that the rights of illegitimate children were recognized. To this point I will return in Chapter Five.

Although there are numerous examples, a few of which will be
explored shortly, of seemingly equal inheritance (each child receiving
some part of his parents' property), a single heir was normally favored to receive the third share, the têrço. As Descamps (1935) has
emphasized, this favored heir was never chosen without motive, and
in general was a person (a child, relative, or even unrelated individual) who had cared for the testator in his old age and illness and
whom he hoped would continue to do so until he finally passed away.
For example, a portion of the will of António Alves Franco, widower
of Maria Rodrigues, who died in 1857 at the age of eighty-two, reads:

> Considering the good services and many benefits that he (António,
> the testator) has received from his daughter Maria who is in his
> company, caring for him in all his illnesses and leaving him want-
> ing for nothing, in remuneration for all these services, leaves the
> third share of all his movable and fixed real property.

In this case, Maria's husband, José da Costa, was asked to serve as
the executor of the will. António Alves Franco had had four daughters, two of whom (Maria and Domingas) survived to adulthood and
marriage (they married two brothers). In another will, that of the
widow Francisca Luisa who died in 1819, the testator acknowledged
that she had two surviving children (of six born to her), a son João

who emigrated and married in Spain, and a daughter Maria who remained celibate and in her mother's company. For the assistance that Maria had given her in sickness and in health, her mother left as compensation "this house where I live, with all its furnishings, courtyard, threshing floor, and privy near the house of Manuel Correia." The heir, Maria, died celibate in 1875 at the age of seventy-six. She had had illegitimate offspring.

In some cases, certain restrictions were tied to the legacy. João Franco de Castro and his wife Isabel Gonçalves made a will in 1845 in which they left all of their property to a relative, Isabel, daughter of José Correia and Luisa da Costa, "as long as she (Isabel the heir) continues always with the same love and care that she has shown to this point, living honestly, and if she wants to marry during the lives or life of one of the testators, that she chooses a boy to her liking and to that of the testators . . . if she does not fulfill these wishes, whosoever of the testators who survives the other may name another heir."[31] A similar condition was set by Manuel Morais and Luisa Gonçalves in a will of 1792 written four years before Manuel's death. Since this couple had no surviving legitimate offspring (they had two children, both of whom died in infancy), they left the têrço to one another and the final inheritance to the discretion of the survivor. They added, however, "we raised a niece in our household by the name of Francisca, daughter of Simão Luiz and our sister-in-law and cousin Domingas Gonçalves, and this niece, because we love her and have received many services from her which we hope she will continue to provide, we leave her our house in the lugar of Rocha and the lands, stables, vines, threshing floor, and outbuildings . . . on the condition that she behaves well and that she does not marry without our consent, and that she remains with us until we die, because if she shows ingratitude, this legacy will not have effect."[32] Indeed, there are a few indications of changes of mind. In a notarial entry dated 1813, the spinster Maria Pires revoked an earlier document wherein she had left all her property to José Gonçalves Pereira and his wife. The couple had not cared for her to her liking, and she had therefore been forced to depend upon the "Christianity" of the community. In the new document, she leaves her property to the Church. This is the only case among the surviving testaments in which such an action was taken.

A final example of the process and motives behind heir designation is contained in the will of Manuel Barbosa de Castro, who passed away six years before his wife in 1849, leaving six offspring. He left the share of the house and the property on which it was located to the son or daughter who stayed with his wife until the end of her life. If more than one stayed, he instructed that his wife was to choose from among them the recipient of the têrço (which presumably included the house). In 1855, when his wife died, there was no new will. By this time, a daughter Rosa Luisa had married, but son Francisco (age eighteen), and daughters Luisa (thirty-two) and Rosa (sixteen) were still apparently in the household. A year later, Luisa died, unmarried, and wrote her own testament, specifying her sister Rosa Luisa and her brother-in-law Francisco Antunes as the "universal heirs" of her property. To her goddaughter, Rosa, Rosa Luisa's and Francisco's child of fourteen months, she left "a field in Trogal de Veiga, a field which her mother could use (usufruct) while she was alive." To her brother Francisco she left 40$000, and to her executor, Gonçalo da Monte, she left her "field of underbrush and pine trees in the vicinity of the chapel of Senhor do Cruzeiro." I will return to a discussion of the testaments of unmarried individuals shortly, but clearly the above examples demonstrate that inheritance, or more exactly, the designation of a favored heir, was used by elderly people to ensure that someone would care for them in their old age. They had the right, it appears, to discriminate, and they exercised this right astutely. This motive of "social insurance" seems to have been more powerful than any motive related to keeping property intact. The fact that women, often daughters who had remained celibate, were frequently heirs of the têrço, is further proof of this "security/reward" motivation.

Testators were apparently aware that favoring one individual, especially one child, over the others might cause some friction. This fear of disharmony led some of them to ask their offspring, in the context of their wills, to "behave themselves." For example, Isabel Francisca de Castro, widow of Felipe Gonçalves da Fonte, made a will in November of 1831 which revoked one made earlier with her husband. In this new will, she named her son Manuel as executor, left him her têrço, and asked him to pay for the expenses of her funeral out of it. She then requested that, after the têrço had been extracted, the rest of the property be divided equally among all her children—she had had five, four of whom, two sons and two daughters, were still alive and all of whom were married by 1831. She called upon "all her sons and daughters not to make demands and to create disorder in the apportionment, but to conserve peace and friendship so that they would be blessed by God." Manuel, her favored heir, was the eldest son, and the earlier will, made just prior to his father's death in 1821, indicated that he was living with his parents (most likely with his wife, whom he had married in 1810, and his own children). In this earlier will, the older couple had specified that one hundred reis be given to Manuel, fifty at the death of the first and fifty at the death of the second.

A fear similar to that expressed by Isabel Francisca de Castro is contained in the will of Vitoria Araujo, widow of João Araujo, who died in March of 1837. Although not favoring one of her three children (Maria, married, age 56; Vitoria, married, age 53; and Manuel, married, age 49) over the others, she hoped that they would "behave as brothers and that there would be no discord, and that they would conduct the apportionment amicably according to God's law." As executor she designated her son, and for this service left him an offering of 30$000. Vitoria mentioned in her will that she was living "in the house of the Quinta de Pillar," perhaps an indication that this was a well-to-do lavrador family.

A slightly different choice was made by Isabel da Rocha, the widow of Joaquim Soares (who had died in 1842) in her will of 1849. Isabel disinherited her only son, a son by her first marriage to Bento Alves in 1797, in favor of a man whose house she had been living in and who, together with his family, "had treated her with love." About her son she said: "I state that my son went to Spain as a boy and married there many years ago without giving me anything, nor serving as a support in my advanced age and major illnesses. . . . I declare further that my son ought not to take badly my deposition because when he came here I gave him money, clothing, and gold, and in this fashion he left and never wrote to me again." Clearly, she felt that she had done enough for him and that he had done nothing for her in return. She felt gratitude instead to the favored heir she specified, a man whose relation to her is not clear, but "in whose house she finds herself paralyzed." She also asked in the body of her will that all those people who owed her money pay it to her heir, Manuel Gonçalves Marinho, and his wife Maria Alves Franco after her death.

References like that which Isabel da Rocha made to her son's departure to Spain appear over and over again in the wills of this period. In some cases, the children of testators died abroad or disappeared (that is, their fate was unknown to their parents). In other cases, their children used money earned in Spain to renovate their parents' property or to buy additional land or a team of oxen. Maria da Costa Pereira died at age seventy-two in 1828, the widow of Felipe António Gonçalves. In her will she stated that she had six children, "some of whom have already died in Spain."[33] To those surviving, she bequeathed two shares of her inheritance, the other share having already been promised to her daughter Maria on the occasion of her marriage to Manuel Machado da Rocha. Similarly, Maria Franco da Rua, widow of João Esteves, acknowledged six children in her will of 1841. Her son António died in Spain, her son Francisco in the Overseas Territories. She left her têrço to her daughter Maria, who had "treated her well, and to ease her conscience because Maria was over eighteen when her husband died, and could have asked her mother for wages as part of the agreement to stay with her."

José Barbosa de Castro, in a will written five days before his death in November of 1851, left his têrço to his three children: Maria (born in 1830), Domingos (born in 1834), and António (born in 1838). His eldest son Manuel (born in 1825) "has been in Brazil for more than six years and he has heard nothing from him." Isabel Francisca de Castro, in her testament of 1843, asked that masses be said for the souls of her daughter Maria (born in 1785), and for her sons José (born in 1786 and married into another village), and Frutuoso (born in 1790), the latter "if he is dead, since he has been absent in America for some time." She left her têrço to her illegitimate daughter Luisa (who was born in 1799, three years after her husband's death) "for the kindness with which she has always treated me" on the condition that half will be for Luisa's daughter Maria. Her son José, she claimed, received his portion when he married. That part which belongs to Frutuoso "will remain in abeyance until his death is verified and will then pass to Luisa with the obligation that she have two masses said each year for the soul of Frutuoso." Isabel asked her son-in-law, José Alexandre, Luisa's husband, to be the executor of her will, and left him 48$000 for his service. She also requested that her daughter give an alqueire of corn to her *compadre* (the godfather of her child) Manuel da Cunha on the first day of St. Michael (September 30) which comes after her death.[34]

When sons returned from Brazil or Spain, a major concern expressed by parents in their testaments was that whatever these sons had contributed to the family patrimony not be included in the assessment and division of property. José Martins da Costa, widower of Maria Francisca, made a will in 1830 leaving his têrço to his daughter Maria Franca, wife of José de Sousa Vieira. He stated that his son-in-law had purchased some additional land with money earned in Spain, and that none of this land should therefore be counted in the division of property between Maria and his two other offspring. António Correia made a similar statement in 1820 with reference to his third (of four surviving) son João (born in 1786 and married in 1814), who was living with his father.

> For the satisfaction of the money that he spent for the good of the soul of my wife and in gratitude for the work he gave me and the expenses he incurred, I leave him his portion of the oxen team which we have to work our land, and I declare that some of the land we farm was bought by him with money he earned in the Kingdom of Castille and should not, therefore, be brought into question in the apportionment after my death.

José da Costa, who died a widower in 1844, offers a rather lengthy explanation of his affairs. He states that he has four children, two sons and two daughters, and three of them were "dowered" with 100$000 at the time of their marriages. In addition, his son José received an arbor of vines in Campello valued at 24$000. His youngest son António (born in 1802 and married in 1826) was not dowered, but rather gave his father 60$000 to complete the portion of his daughter Ana on the occasion of her marriage in 1825 and, in addition, gave him another 40$000. For this reason, he leaves his son António his têrço, "from which 20$000 should be extracted and given to his grandson António, son of João Abrigueiro, for being in my company." He goes on to declare that his son António purchased some land of his own and a wine press, and that neither of these should be considered as part of the property to be divided. All of these purchases, he states, were made with money his son António earned in Spain.

A final and much earlier example that makes reference to emigration, and that also emphasizes the notion of equality and fairness to its fullest is contained in the will of the widow Vitoria Pereira written in 1779. Vitoria declares that she had four children (António, Francisca, José, and João), and that all are her legitimate heirs. She further states that her son José spent 28$800 for a voyage to Brazil and that she wishes this amount to be deducted from his legitimate portion "because I never wanted, nor was it my intention to abuse with this expense the legitimate inheritance of my other children." She continues:

> I leave to my daughter-in-law, wife of my son João Pereira, my loom, for the assistance she has given me in my illness, and which I hope she will continue to give me until the end of my life. I leave my new mantilla to my granddaughter Maria, daughter of Antó-

nio, also for helping me in my illness. Also, I leave my cask for
wine to my granddaughter Maria, daughter of António da Costa.
I declare that my son João Pereira paid interest of 8$950 to Bar-
rosa which I had left when I moved to this lugar. I declare that
António has 25$000 and António da Costa 30$000 of my portion,
sums which I wish to have extracted from their legitimate inheritances so that everyone will remain equal. I declare that my son
José, for the voyage to Brazil, sold the field of Borralha, which
belonged to us. I leave my barrel for wine to my son João for the
help he has given me and which I hope he will continue to give me
until the end of my life. I also leave to my granddaughter Maria,
daughter of António, a plot of land where she can make a threshing floor and where her husband, José Gonçalves, can make tiles—
this too for her helpful aid.

The will of Vitoria Pereira demonstrates a number of other aspects
worth pursuing further: the attempt, despite the têrço, to arrive at
some sort of equality, the settling of final debts (that is, indicating
where money was owed), and some indication of what kinds of items,
in addition to land, were valued enough to be mentioned in the context of a last will and testament.

João Martins da Costa died a widower one month after his wife
had passed away in March of 1850 at the age of sixty-four. At the
time of his death, he had five daughters (Ana, born in 1819 and
married in 1848; Maria, born in 1823 and married in 1861; Josefa,
born in 1825 and unmarried at her death; Luisa, born in 1827 and
unmarried at her death; and Rosa, born in 1829 and unmarried at
her death) and one son, Manuel, born in 1831 and married in 1871.
He left his têrço to his four unmarried daughters with the condition
that his sister-in-law Ana would have usufruct rights. Out of this
têrço, he obliged his daughters to give 5$000 to his son Manuel and
2$000 to his married and eldest daughter Ana. He also acknowl-
edged that his daughter Ana had fifteen alqueires of corn and a loom
in her possession, both of which were to be assessed in the division.
He designated his son Manuel or his sister-in-law Ana as executor
and also declared that his daughter, when she married, took some
linen and other things from the household and that his other daughters should each receive the equivalent in value.

Finally, Asumpção Alves da Costa emphasizes equality in a rather
unusual way in her will of 1849. Although she left the third share of
her half of the property to her husband and her sister for them to
use while they still lived, she asked that it be divided among her

daughters and son Manuel after her husband's and sister's deaths, but expressed the wish that her daughter Ana not have a share because she had already inherited from the testator's sister. Furthermore, she requested that her têrço be fulfilled equally in "upper property" (mato) and "lower property" (veiga) so that there would be no injustice among her heirs.[35]

The notion of equality toward offspring was also raised in several wills when testators had sons whom they had sent into the priesthood. José Gonçalves Pereira died a widower in 1842 at the age of forty-two. He named his four children Gualter, João, Maria, and Luisa as heirs, "not mentioning his son Padre António because he has already received his patrimony and should expect nothing more." In addition to these shares of inheritance that are apparently given by parents prior to their deaths to send sons through seminaries in preparation for the priesthood, some parents also bestowed a dowry (dote) of sorts upon their children prior to their death, and if this had occurred, they felt obliged to mention it in the context of their will. One example was referred to earlier (see note 34), but there are numerous others. Simão Luis de Castro and Catarina Rodrigues Pereira mentioned in their joint testament of 1759 that they had given their daughter a dowry of 100$000 in addition to her trousseau. To their son António they had given the sum of 30$000. João Lourenço da Rua, who had married Domingas Castro in 1706, had seven children, one who died as an infant, five who married, and one (the second son) who died a bachelor at the age of eighty-five. When João died in 1754, he left his youngest son Domingos (who had married six years earlier) a value of 20$000 in the houses of his residence above that which he and his siblings would receive at their mother's death. In addition, he mentions giving 15$000 to his eldest son to marry in 1743; 70$000 to his eldest daughter Maria for her marriage in 1733; and 60$000 to his daughter Sebronia on her marriage in 1738. At the time, these were substantial sums and indicate a prosperous family. When Domingas his wife died two years later, she confirmed all these monetary dotes and designated her son Domingos as the recipient of her half of the house "in reward for all the personal expenses he has had." When the bachelor son Manuel died in 1802, he named his nephew and godson Manuel as his universal heir.

A final example is contained in the will of António José Pereira Palma and his wife Ana da Rocha Lima made just prior to António's death in 1831. They state that their youngest daughter Maria had been promised a half of their têrço upon the death of the last, so that she could marry José Machado da Rocha, a sergeant in the twenty-second regiment. The other half was to go to their daughter Ana on the condition that she stayed with them until the end, treating and respecting them "as good children should."[36] In fact, in some instances dote refers not to a sum of money or bequest actually conferred at the time of marriage, but simply to a promise of inheritance at the time of death of the parents.

One of the most elaborate cases of detailed and explicit division of property is contained in the will of Lourenço Pereira, widower of Mariana Josefa, who died in 1822 at the age of eighty-six. This couple had had no children of their own (Mariana was forty when they married), but apparently had a young orphan (*exposta*), Rosa Maria, living with them. Lourenço designated his nephew, João Pereira, Rosa Maria's husband, as his heir. Rosa Maria herself had died in 1818, and Lourenço Pereira stipulated that if João Pereira were to remarry, his sole heirs would be the offspring (Lourenço, António, Maria, and Manuel) of the marriage between João Pereira and Rosa Maria Exposta. He then went on to leave specific items (land and other property) to these four offspring, and to other relatives. To Lourenço, he bequeathed the house and "place" (*sitio*) that belonged to Ana Franca in Roupeiras, and also a field in the same spot that belonged to manuel Pereira; to António, he left a field in Agra de Baixo; to Maria, a field in Bajouca; to Manuel, a field in the lowlands of Ponte de Linhares; to his sister Ana Pereira, two gardens in Roupeiras where she lived and one olive grove near the fountain of Roupeiras ("when she dies this should pass to her godson Lourenço"); to his sister Maria, a pine tree near the fountain of Roupeiras and a piece of land in Salgueiras; to his sister Ana, a stand of rushes at the foot of the olive tree; to his nephew and godson Lourenço Gonçalves Pereira, son of Francisco Gonçalves and Ana Pereira, a piece of land with an olive tree, two peach trees, oak trees, and some underbrush in the vicinity of the fountain of Roupeiras; to his sister Domingas, half of a field in Fujacos de Cima, and a field of underbrush and oak trees in the field in Tres Lamas; to his goddaughter Maria, daughter of Ana Pereira, a field that belonged to Manuel Seixinha; and finally to his godson José, some oak trees near the fountain of Roupeiras.

Whereas several testaments, like that of Lourenço Pereira, indicate specific plots of land and designate to whom they are to go, there are other items that were seemingly highly valued and that were therefore also mentioned specifically in wills: houses of residence; objects such as wine barrels, carts, and iron cooking vessels; gold coins and gold chains; pieces of linen, whether clothing (distinctions were made between everyday wear and special items), tablecloths, or bedding;

looms and other furniture, specifically chests for the storage of linens; and finally, as has been demonstrated, specific sums of money. A good example of the variety of items included in a legacy is contained in the 1828 will of widow Francisca Gonçalves. To her daughter Antónia, she left everything that had belonged to her dead daughter Ana—"the fields in the place of residence with fruit trees, two additional fields in Fontainhas, a field in Armeiros, a pine box which she herself had had made, and gold, as well as clothing, including a skirt, a mantilla, and underwear, and also some linen sheets; in addition, a field in Largo which is under a foro of one alqueire of corn, a field of vines with olive trees, and a field of chestnuts, all in the same lugar." In addition, she left half of the house, "all in payment for her labors."

The will of Lourenço Pereira mentioned above is also interesting as an example of who inherited the property of couples who had no direct offspring of their own, a not infrequent occurrence in Lanheses' history. Generally, nephews or nieces, some of whom were also godchildren or living with their aunt or uncle, were the major beneficiaries. Another good example is contained in the legacy of Maria Correia Pereira, widow of Domingos Alves, who died in 1837. She and her husband had had two children, but both died in their childhood. When Maria passed away, she designated as her universal heir her nephew Albino Pereira de Castro, the illegitimate son of her brother António, or his wife Ana Rodrigues Franco. However, she also specified other recipients. To her brother-in-law Manuel Alves Franco, she left two fields; to her sister-in-law Domingas, a field in the Campo da Veiga (with the provision that if her husband did not pay the security of five coins he owed to José António Monteiro of Viana, then this field should be used to pay the debt); to her husband's nephew, two fields (one *bouça*—mountain plot—and one *campo*—cultivated field); 48$000 to another nephew of her husband's; 18$000 and 30$000 to her nephew José, sums she had loaned to him to buy a cart; to her nephew Lourenço, half of the field in Fujacos (the other half having been given to Albino); and to a niece and goddaughter, 0$800.

In addition to childless couples, single people, particularly single women who had never married but who clearly had property to dispense, were also free to choose their own heirs. Luisa Gonçalves Marinho, "feeling infirm," made a will in September of 1833. She was a spinster of forty-six years, one of the five surviving children born to Manuel José Marinho and Antónia Gonçalves. She designated her immediately elder sister Ana Quiteria, wife of António do

Rego, as her universal heir. To her eldest sister Maria, the wife of António da Rocha, she left five coins that she owed her and one half of an onion field. To Maria's daughter Rosa she left another field. To her youngest brother Manuel, she left five coins that he owed her, and another 39$000 that he owed her and that was recorded in a notarial note together with interest. To Margarida Exposta, an orphan who was living with her, she left 60$000 in metal money, a sum which her brother Manuel would be obliged to bestow on her on the day of her marriage or, if this did not occur before she reached twenty-five, then she was to be given 60$000 with interest counted from the day of the testator's death when she reached that age. In addition, she left her sister and heir 40$000, and asked her to take charge of Margarida as if she were her own daughter and that Margarida, until she married or reached age twenty-five, was to give her sister the interest on the 60$000 to cover expenses. She went on to name several other recipients, some of them godchildren, of various items, and concluded with a list of all the people who owed her small sums of money, noting that these debts should be settled with her sister and heir after her death.

The desire to spell out debts, whether what the testator owed or what was owed to him, is quite explicit in the testaments that survive from Lanheses' past. In numerous cases, the testators gave the debt to their debtor as an offering, exonerating him, so to speak. For example, Maria Fernandes da Rocha, spinster, in a will of 1828, claimed that her brother owed her five Spanish coins (*puros duros castilharios*) which she gave his son to pay a debt, and she absolved him of this obligation. In other cases, as with Luisa Gonçalves Marinho's will mentioned above, the debt was simply transferred to the new heir. Luiz Pinto, who died single in 1816, specified that the heir of his house and the land on which it was located pay the 30$000 that he owed with interest to the Confraria (brotherhood) of St. Anthony. Finally, still other testators chose to make it known that a debt had been cleared. António de Castro Palma, widower, declared in a testament of December 1830 that his daughter Domingas and her husband had already "satisfied" the sum of 16$660 that they owed him.

One final observation is worth making about these wills. There are several cases of individuals, with or without obligatory heirs, who recognized the service of a servant (*criado/criada*) who had worked for them. In 1813, Maria Gomes da Rocha, widow of António Rodrigues, left her servant Domingas a field in Estonturas, "in satisfaction of unpaid wages and those which may fall due until the day of my death." Others left small amounts to the village priest, and on rarer occasions actually named the priest as executor of their will.

Clearly, the extant testaments in Lanheses demonstrate that plots of land, houses, and other property were transferred at death (post-mortem inheritance) according to quite explicit instructions. However, there are also indications in the testaments and in notarial records that some property was transferred at marriage in the form of an "endowment," perhaps to ensure a favorable match.[37] There is also evidence that a good deal of land was bought and sold during the lifetime of any particular individual. In a writ of January 1820, Francisco Alves Pereira and his wife Francisca Teresa de Sousa sold a plot of land with a "regressive agreement of three years" to João da Silva. The plot included vines, a vegetable garden, and an olive tree, and was leased (under a foro) for the annual sum of 0$025 from the parish church. The sellers also acknowledged that the same plot had been mortgaged to the Brotherhood of Almas for the amount of 24$000, which they wished to remit at the time of the writ because of judicial pressure to do so, and which had increased to 35$832 with interest. The plot was therefore sold with the same foro for 37$500 with the three-year regressive agreement that obligated the sellers to pay an annual pension of six alqueires and one quarto of corn to the buyer. If the sellers failed to pay this annual pension, the buyer was given the right to possess the land. This particular couple appears to have sold several plots of land at this period of time. The husband was in his sixties and had eight children, the youngest under ten years of age. We can only speculate that they were facing personal hard times and were therefore forced to sell. The buyer was roughly the same age, a widower with two grown and married daughters.

Other sales of land, with or without foros, and with or without "regressive agreements of specified length" were transacted during the period between 1770 and 1850. In 1777, for example, a couple living in the village of Vitorino das Donas across the Lima River sold a plot in Lanheses that they had inherited, together with its foro and property tax (*dízimo*), for 8$000. In another writ of April 1820, Isabel Alves Rocha, widow of José da Costa, sold various plots of land to Captain Miguel Tinoco, a member, as has been shown, of the village aristocracy. The sale included a field in Sobral for 21$000, a field in the site of Alvite for 15$500, a field in the site of Colada for 2$500; another in the same site for 20$000, an arbor of vines for 3$000, and an uncultivated plot for 10$000.

These particular cases also reinforce the fact that much of the land in Lanheses was farmed by sharecroppers and tenant farmers under rental contracts of varying lengths. Yet another example is contained in a notarial agreement dated August 1819. In this contract, António Rodrigues and his wife Maria Gomes of the lugar da Feira agreed to pay Francisco Alves Franco and his wife Francisca Teresa de Sousa 9$000 in metal money on St. Michael's day each year for the rental of a portion of arable land with fruit trees, an olive tree, and vines, measuring 48.5 varas (53.5 meters) in length and 15.5 varas (17.1 meters) in width at the northern end and six varas (6.6 meters) in width at the southern end. Included in the agreement was half the water from a well on the property. The contract was to be null and void at the first year that the lessors or their heirs faulted in their payments. The lessors were also required to "conserve the portion of land in the state in which they found it, treating it as if it were their own and, if they did not, they would be thrown off and would answer to all the charges."

Some of the other notarial records deal with debts that were owed, with interest (5 percent), to individuals or to the various religious brotherhoods in the village—about which more will be said shortly. Plots of land or a house were put forth as collateral. The loans themselves were largely taken to improve a home or to augment the amount of land under cultivation. For example, João de Araujo and his wife Vitoria Francisca de Castro borrowed 67$200 from António Franco, a bachelor from S. Salvador, in 1819 so that they could "ensure the security of their home." As collateral, they put up a cultivated field in the veiga of Vila Mou that had an annual pension of six alqueires of corn paid to the monastery of S. Salvador.

This rather lengthy analysis of the extant books of testaments and notarial records for Lanheses demonstrate several factors that are worth reemphasizing. First, assuming a foundation of equality toward all offspring, the testators were free to choose—and often did choose— a single offspring or individual as the preferred heir of the third portion or têrço.[38] The major criterion that determined their choice appears to have been nurturance—that is, who had taken care of them and would continue to do so in their illnesses and old age. Given this criterion, it is not at all surprising that celibate daughters were frequent heirs. What this suggests is that we should perhaps consider reversing our understanding of the causal relationship between inheritance and permanent spinsterhood, or at least admit a more complex and culturally varied relationship. To this point I will return in Chapter Three.

Second, the freedom to designate, as well as the evidence that property was frequently bought, sold, or mortgaged, suggests a flexible regime wherein it would have been unrealistic for offspring to guide their lives by the expectation of inheritance. Clearly, this has enormous ramifications for hypotheses that relate either the fact of marriage or age at marriage to the inheritance of land and to parental age at death. The connections may not be straightforward, and it is in a complex context that one has to consider the role of emigration. This point too will be further examined later in the book.

Third, although historical demographers have contributed enormously to our quantifiable knowledge of peasant family life in the European historical past, we may never have a complete picture of the more qualitative aspects of family relationships among these rural populations. However, attitudes gleaned from an analysis of documents like the *livros dos testamentos* do open a small window on the quality of such relationships in the Portuguese village of the past. The possibilities of discord arising over property divisions would not have been mentioned so often by parents in their wills had such discords not been frequent. Even today, land division remains a potentially volatile situation. Furthermore, in several other less forthright aspects, these wills tend to indicate not quite "happy families." There is a businesslike element to paying children wages (even in the form of a promise of the *têrço*) as compensation for their continued attentiveness. To refer to them as being "like servants" is the most extreme expression of this attitude, which in the long run underscores the emphasis placed upon the independence of the individual rather than upon the unity of a piece of property or a household, as one finds in other parts of western and southern Europe. In this region of Portugal, property was most important as a means by which the social relationships between generations could be reinforced.

Finally, these wills offer little support to some of Goody's theories (1983) about the omnipotent control of the Church, at least in the Portuguese case. It appears that childless couples, spinsters, and bachelors found heirs. Nieces and nephews, illegitimate children, foster children brought back from foundling homes, even servants were among the designated recipients in such cases. Although the Church was present at the making of these "last wills and testaments" and benefited in the form of contributions made for the masses in honor of the dying person's soul or the souls of loved ones, in only one instance was there any mention of the Church receiving the bulk of an individuals's estate, and in only a few instances were special sums bequeathed to parish priests. Yet, the very religious preambles to these wills persist into the late nineteenth century, a fact that Daniel Scott Smith might argue to be a measure of a sustained high level of religiosity in this population, particularly in contrast to the population of Hingham, Massachusetts, where the religious preambles to wills began to wane during the mid-eighteenth century and had virtually disappeared by 1820. Furthermore, earlier discussion has already alluded to the fact that the Church was a significant landholder in the region, at least until the confiscation of its properties in the 1830s and again during the First Republic. There is no doubt that the role of the Church in the history of Lanheses is a complicated one, and I would like to explore this role in the final section of this chapter.

## The Church and Religion

Livi Bacci, in his study of Portuguese fertility, concludes by suggesting that religiosity may be the most significant variable explaining regional variations in demographic behavior in Portugal. Although there are enormous difficulties associated with trying to assess the impact of religion on behavior, it is nevertheless clear that the Church has been the most important national institution at the local level throughout Portuguese history, and the focal point of village life in northern Portugal until the present day. Indeed, it is the Church which interceded at important life cycle events—a birth, a confirmation, a marriage, a death—and which recorded these events for the historical demographer of the future. Although I will return in later chapters to a more complete assessment of religion in relation to fertility and illegitimacy, it is important in the final section of this chapter to discuss, however briefly, the position of Church and priest in the history of Lanheses.

One necessarily begins by stating that it is impossible to understand the role of the Church in a local community apart from its role within a nation as a whole. For the two-and-a-half centuries that provide the time frame for this study, the position of the Catholic Church in Portugal has risen and fallen with the changes in government and as the tides of anticlericalism have ebbed and flowed. Throughout much of its early history, the Portuguese Church had enjoyed a privileged status. Extensive property in the rural countryside was owned by various religious institutions, granted to them by successive monarchs.[39] As was noted earlier, Lanheses was itself part of such a land grant (*couto*) until the sixteenth century. Once Portuguese overseas expansion was underway, the partnership between Church and State was further enhanced. In their joint mission of conquest and settlement they developed a relationship that was mutually beneficial and that contributed to the financial prosperity and political power of both.

While the "mission Church" maintained its position of strength and importance into the present century, the "mother Church" in the homeland began to witness the erosion of both economic and political power with the ascendency of the Marquis de Pombal in the 1750s. Pombal severed relations with Rome, expelled the Jesuits, and placed education under State control, setting in motion a process of secularization that was to continue throughout much of the nineteenth century. Many of Pombal's specific reforms were rescinded under the reign of the devout Queen Maria. Her successors followed a course which, while recognizing the Catholic religion as the official State religion, sought more widespread monarchic control both of the clergy and of numerous church regulations.

In 1831, a second wave of anticlericalism swept through the country as monasteries, convents, and colleges belonging to various religious orders were abolished. The Inquisition was dissolved, and much of the property controlled by the Church was auctioned off. Although many of the religious orders were restored later in the century, the Church had been virtually divested of its wealth. Anticlerical sentiments persisted, but in the financial and political chaos of the late nineteenth century, they were not vociferously expressed. Only with the advent of the First Portuguese Republic in 1910 did a new and stronger movement emerge. The theological faculties within Portuguese universities were closed, religious education in schools was abolished, divorce laws were changed, and church festivals were discouraged. Under a new Law of Separation, all church property was seized, and priests and nuns were forbidden to wear clerical garb. The Church was the supreme symbol of a traditional order that the New Republic wished to dissolve completely. A Congress of Free Thought held in 1911 prophesied that in two generations Catholicism would disappear from Portugal. However, in 1917 three shepherd children reported that they had seen the Virgin Mary on a hillside near the town of Fatima. A new cult was born which laid the basis for the strengthening of the position of the Portuguese Catholic Church under the New State formed by Dr. António Salazar.

Although Salazar finalized the separation of Church and State with the 1940 Concordat, one of his closest friends was the Cardinal Patriarch of Lisbon, Manuel Cerejeira. Together these two men fashioned a new order fundamentally rooted in Catholic principles. Although the role of the Church in the politics of the State was severely limited, its role in the social, educational, and moral life of the Portuguese people was revived, if not expanded.

The result of almost two centuries of secularization, riddled with sometimes heated anticlerical movements, was the creation of an important segment of society which, though nominally Catholic, was generally uninterested in or opposed to any form of religious expression and unwilling to allow the clergy to influence their lives in any way. However, it is important to recognize that nominally Catholic anticlericals were only a segment of Portuguese society, and a regionally concentrated segment, at that. Although low church attendance or the seeking of alternative religions, especially Protestantism, have characterized the way of life in southern and urban Portugal, the rural north has remained committed to the Catholic Church.[40] During the civil war of the 1830s, it was the rural clergy which mobilized the northern peasantry against the liberal cause, and a decade later, in 1846 and 1847, clerical influence was again at work in the mass uprising commonly known as the "Maria da Fonte" movement.[41] More than a century later, in the aftermath of the 1974 revolution that toppled almost fifty years of Salazarism, the northern peasantry again rallied in support of a Catholic Church, which came increasingly under attack for the role it had played in the "New State," and against the "threat" of Communism that they envisioned as a real possibility in the fledgling years of the new democracy.[42]

It is not easy to find explanations for the enormous regional differences in the status of the Portuguese Catholic Church. Nor is it easy to assess historically (with the exception of movements like Maria da Fonte) the impact of shifts in the position of the Church over time upon the population living a day-to-day existence in the small, often isolated, villages of the northern countryside, where priests were frequently the only literate individuals and the only major link with the world beyond the local region. Clearly, the fact that the seat of the Portuguese Church, as well as seven (eight as of 1980) of its bishoprics are located in the north has something to do with its greater influence in that region. However, this is, in turn, probably explained by the fact that the north is more densely populated. Until quite recently, every parish, no matter how small, had its own priest, and often one or two curates in addition.[43] It is also possible that in a densely populated area of small-scale agriculture, where priests were frequently though not always of the same peasant background as their parishioners, there was more tolerance for these men of the cloth than in the south, where clerics were often the second sons of wealthy landowners, and where differences in wealth were clearly more apparent.

This does not mean that anticlericalism did not exist in the north, for indeed it did and still does—but anticlericalism of a special nature, directed more toward the priest as an individual than toward the church as an institution or toward religion as a set of beliefs (Cabral 1981, Riegelhaupt 1973). The great Portuguese ethnographer Joaquim Leite de Vasconcellos, in his "Notes on the Religiosity of the Portuguese" (1985), went so far as to suggest that this anticlericalism was an indication that the Portuguese were not *fundamentally* religious.

> There is no doubt that the Catholic religion has had a great influence for a long time. . . . But among (the Portuguese) there has never developed the type of mysticism which exists in Spain, and there has always existed here a strong spirit . . . which scoffs at the clergy similar to what one encounters in medieval French literature, where at every step clerics are castigated. (Vasconcellos 1958:508)

Yet, to be anticlerical does not mean that one is either antireligious or areligious (Riegelhaupt 1973).

One of the major facets of rural anticlericalism is embodied in criticisms of the morality of priests, and it is indeed in the character and therefore influence of individual priests at the local level that one probably has to look for the strength of religious observances or religious beliefs at any particular time. Did they earn respect? Did they instill fear or inspire piety? In contrast to Ireland, or at least postfamine Ireland, where priests are known to have practiced what they preached and are commended for their purity (Connell 1968, Larkin 1972, 1976), references to the lack of chasteness among the Portuguese clergy have deep historical roots. Dias (1960) has noted that as early as the fourteenth century there were public protests about the scandalous behavior of Catholic priests, who were called *homens estravagueiros e barregueiros*—rather potent words referring to men who kept mistresses. In the seventeenth century *Memórias* of the Cortes of Santarém, clerics are accused of setting bad examples for the laymen to whom they should be teaching doctrine and good upbringing through their own good conduct. Several English travelers (who, granted, may have had an anti-clerical bias themselves) wrote forthrightly about the lack of upright moral behavior on the part of the Portuguese clergy.

The men are laborious and brave, and the women are chaste. For these good qualities they are solely indebted to Providence, and not in the least to their clergy, most of whom employ their leisure in devising means of debauching their female parishioners. Such are the advantages of the vow of celibacy. (A.P.D.G. 1826:340)

This observer goes on to refer to the "tyrannical influence which priests exercise over the private concerns and interior economy of every family".[44]

Apparently, the Portuguese Catholic hierarchy was itself aware of the problem. For example, among the documents kept with the parish archives in Lanheses is a circular sent to all local priests from the Archbishop of Braga in 1856. The archbishop advises his clerics that one of their most important duties is to provide the populace with evidence of their honesty and to avoid any behavior that might elicit criticism. For this reason he informs his clerics that it is prohibited to have in their house or company individuals of the female sex who are under fifty who are not their mothers, sisters, or nieces within the second degree of consanguinity. They are further prohibited from hearing the confessions of women of whatever age in hermitages, in private homes, in the sacristy, or at night. Confession is only permitted "in wooden confessionals with partitions which completely separate the penitent from the confessor and which are located in places in the church which are in full view of anyone entering the church".[45]

A circular sent out four years later indicates that word had reached the archbishop telling of priests who were participating in *esfolhados* (the traditional celebrations surrounding the activity of husking corn in late August and September) "in indecent dress, dancing, and having contact with people of different sex after dark." The archbishop condemns all such activities and calls for their cessation. Although it is clearly impossible to claim that any of these circulars had particular reference to the clerics of Lanheses, it is nevertheless within this framework that one has to consider the role of church and priest in a single northern Portuguese rural parish.

Lanheses has been a separate parish with its own priest to administer to the needs of the people since at least the mid-sixteenth century. Some of these priests have been natives of the village, whereas others have been outsiders; some have been of relatively humble origins; a few have been members of the wealthier families discussed earlier in this chapter. Older villagers living in Lanheses today are quite able to talk about and compare the priests and resident clerics they can remember in their lifetime: the one who officiated between

1890 and 1911, who was a *lavrador* like everyone else and who only wanted his *beatas* (the word refers to devout women) on Sundays; the son of a local family, priest in Nogueira, who was forced to flee to Brazil after the advent of the First Republic because of his outspoken support of monarchist causes, and who returned more than a decade later with a fortune; the "saintly and pious cleric" who led the community between 1911 and 1927 and who is rumored to have "slept on a bed of nails"; and the severe disciplinarian who dominated village life for almost as long as Salazarism prevailed in Portugal (1927–1967).[46]

Lanhesans also speak of the children of priests, but only one example falls within recent memory.[47] In the eighteenth century a few cases appear in the registers which indicate that the illegitimate children of priests did exist, although none of these appear to be the children of Lanhesan priests or curates (that is, they are the illegitimate children of women originating from other parishes). In addition to criticizing present-day priests for their excessive interest in money, occasional references are made to their "sensuality," although ultimately many Lanhesans, like northern Portuguese peasants in general, (Cabral 1981) admit that priests are "men like other men."

The comparisons between past priests and those today are manifestations of the type of anticlericalism currently expressed in Portugal. That they are the focus of gossip is itself an indication of the important role they play in parish life. Certainly one can argue in favor of the present priest in Lanheses, as many parishioners recognize, that he has been instrumental in bringing increasing educational opportunities to his parish. Much of his time is occupied today in running the secondary school program, a program that did not exist locally prior to his assumption of responsibilities as parish priest. Although his manner may not be much to the liking of individual Lanhesans, he appears, at least to an outsider, to be a true village chauvinist who wants to see his community evolve.

If the priest is the human center of religious life in Lanheses, the parish church itself is the geographical center. Situated on a rise at the heart of the village, and therefore seen from quite a distance, the present church structure dates from the latter half of the eighteenth century, though it has been restored and altered frequently since then, the most recent work having been carried out in the early 1970s with the help of contributions made largely by emigrants in France, Australia, Canada, and the United States. Indeed, over the years several of the changes and additions have been the result of the generosity of Lanhesans abroad (in 1928, a group of emigrants in Brazil purchased the clock). The property surrounding the church building, the *passal*, constituted the land that the priest was entitled to cultivate. The church was divested of this land during the First Republic, and it is now owned by an emigrant in Canada, having passed through the hands of several proprietors prior to his purchase of it. Although the rectory adjacent to the church was also confiscated at that time, it was purchased by the parish soon after and maintained as a residence for the priest. Today, since the current priest is a native of the village and lives in his paternal home, the rectory has been converted into a classroom building to house the local secondary school.

The village cemetery, located to the northwest of the church, was inaugurated in the 1890s. Prior to that time, people were buried in the church plaza (*adro*) and, before the early nineteenth-century reforms, in sepulchers in the church itself. In addition to the main church, there are several smaller chapels scattered throughout the village, some of them associated with specific rituals that fill the annual agricultural and/or religious calendar, and others originally built as private chapels by some of the local landed "aristocracy".

The association between various argicultural events and the cult of saints is an excellent example of the character of folk religion in northern Portugal. In Lanheses, every May, there is an annual procession to the chapel of St. Anthony in order to bless the oxen and milk cattle. New wine is traditionally first tasted on St. Martin's Day in November, and agricultural rents are due on St. Michael's Day in late September. Every year on December 8, there is a solemn mass and procession to the chapel of St. Frutuoso in the lugar of Outeiro in celebration of the patroness of Lanheses, Santa Eulalia.[48]

The most important, and most architecturally significant, of Lanheses' chapels is that of Senhor do Cruzeiro, built in the middle of the eighteenth century on land immediately adjacent to the parish church. Records in the district archives in Braga reveal that in 1756 Padre Manuel da Silva and other officials of Lanheses, in a petition to the archbishop of Braga, claimed that "they had a large cross with the image of the crucified Christ in the parish, that the image had made and makes miracles, and with donations they hoped to cover the image with a sculptured arch and closed niche." With that petition, a chapel was built and, a decade later, the confraternity of Senhor do Cruzeiro was founded with the following statutes:

1. there will be in this *confraria* a juiz (chairman), secretary, treasurer, and two majordomos elected by the officials of the previous year (this was the mesa or table of the confraternity);

2. the officials will be obliged, through their revenues, to celebrate a solemn festa each year in the said chapel on the day of the invention of the cross (May 3).[49]

Although not the festa of the patron saint, the festa of Senhor do Cruzeiro has become the most important annual celebration on the religious calendar.

As the national Catholic Church went in and out of favor, both the confraria and the festa of Senhor do Cruzeiro experienced periods of prosperity and popularity and periods of decline. In recent years, the festa in particular has been revived, in part through the energies of the current parish priest, who sees it as a way to raise money in the village, and in part through the dedication of emigrants in France who time their summer vacations to coincide with the festa weekend, and for whom it provides an opportunity to manifest their continued attachment to the village and their homeland. However, by mentioning both the festa and the confraria of Senhor do Cruzeiro, it is possible to address in a more general way the significance of both brotherhoods and festivals in the religious, social, and economic life of Lanheses and the province of Minho more generally.

Although they are now frequently a point of contention between the so-called "modern priests" '(Cabral 1981) and the lay public, festas and pilgrimages (romarias) have been an important part of the religious life throughout northern Portugal and especially in the province of Minho. The festa of Senhor do Cruzeiro in Lanheses is today one of a cycle of festas celebrated throughout the Lima Valley during the summer, which culminates in the perhaps more secular Feira da Agonia held in the town of Viana do Castelo at the end of August. Indeed, most of these festivals combine the sacred with the secular, the social and commercial with the religious, a characteristic that Sanchis (1976) points to as an excellent example of the practical nature of religion in northern Portugal. Although this has been and continues to be a problem for the church hierarchy, for the people it presents no such conflict. Devotion to the saint, the making and fulfilling of a religious vow (promessa), and a family picnic are all fundamental and acceptable parts of these religious events. In addition to participating in their own festa, Lanhesans frequently take part in many of the other regional festas and romarias, some of which have as old a history as the Festa of Senhor do Cruzeiro. One of the most important pilgrimages in the region is that to the hermitage of S. João de Arga in the Serra de Arga in the mountains north of the parish. Promessas symbolize the close intersection between religion and health: S. João de Arga is supposed to cure cysts and other skin diseases; Santa Justa (who also has a mountain hermitage) protects people from gout; S. Braz intercedes in illnesses of the throat; and Santa Marta in female illnesses (Araujo 1957). Indeed, the close connection between popular religion and folk medicine is manifested in these saintly devotions.

If the festas have both their sacred and secular aspects, so too do the local confrarias. Lanheses has seven confrarias, and virtually every parishioner is a member of at least one, if not all seven. Each member is required to make a small annual contribution and, in return, is guaranteed a funeral as well as a certain number of masses each year after his or her death. In addition, each member is entitled to have the banner of the confraria or confrarias he or she belongs to carried at the funeral. According to one villager, to have no banners is shameful, a declaration of not being very Catholic, and something people will criticize and talk about, "and no one wants to be criticized after he is dead!"

The historical documentation on these local brotherhoods is scanty, and it is impossible to determine precisely how old some of them are, but they most certainly date back to the early eighteenth century, and therefore existed throughout the period covered by this study. Although their role in the religious life of the community, particularly that associated with death, is important to emphasize, their role as lending institutions within the local village economy is equally, if not more, significant. Extant confraria records demonstrate that numerous villagers borrowed various sums of money, generally at 5 percent interest, from these confrarias, designating plots of land as security, and sometimes specific individuals as guarantors or bailsmen (*fiador*). For example, in an entry dated February 1876 in the record book of the Confraria das Almas, it is stated that José Machado da Rocha of Lanheses owed said confraria the sum of 20$000 at 5 percent interest in accordance with a contract registered with the notary Barreto of Viana do Castelo; as security he offered an arable field, vines, and olive trees adjacent to his house and as a guarantor he stipulated his son José. As late as 1975, one Lanhesan bought a house and land in the Lugar da Feira (which she has made over into a café and boarding house) from a widow. Both domicile and property were mortgaged to the Confraria do Rosario in February of 1889 for 60$900 at 6 percent interest. When the purchaser paid the debt almost a century later in order to acquire the land, the amount owed had risen to over seven thousand escudos.

These debts were frequently passed on from one generation to the next, and generally recorded in notarized agreements. The notarial records for the vila of Lanheses between 1826 and 1835, as well as records in the towns of Ponte de Lima and Viana do Castelo, contain numerous examples of these written contracts for loans. In short, in the days before any form of state supported rural credit, the Church, through its various brotherhoods, performed this vital role, and in this way entered into—indeed, partially controlled—the economic life of its parishioners.

In addition to the contributions made to confrarias and the accumulation of debts, parishioners also paid an annual tithe. Even today, this particular contribution survives, obligating parishioners more by sanction than by law to make yearly gifts to their priests. It is part of the annual Easter celebrations. Traditionally priest and *mordomos* (more recently the sacristan) visited each household, were given food and a glass of wine, eggs, and chickens. Today, the priest sends out envelopes for money, a practice that some villagers dislike. The nature of this and other contributions was formally spelled out in a document of November 10, 1779, in which the inhabitants of the parish acknowledged their "habits and customs" (*usos e costumes*) with regard to their "religious" duties. Much as the State today takes a certain percentage of production through taxation, so too did the village priest in eighteenth- and presumably nineteenth-century rural Portugal. This document is reproduced in full in the Appendix, and stands as a strong indication in and of itself of the central position of the Church in the life of the local village community.

Supplementing the Church's, and therefore the priest's, intervention at important points in the individual life cycle and its potential role in the economic life of the Lanhesan peasant family, was its role in the political life of the village. The priest has served and continues to serve as an intermediary between village and nation, reading important circulars during Sunday mass or interpreting important government legislation, today through the vehicle of the parish newspaper. Prior to the First Republic, priests were actively involved in the local political body, the Junta da Freguesia. Indeed, the priest who officiated at the turn of the century was at one point the president of the Junta. Clearly, this political position was undermined between 1910 and 1926, and villagers insist that their "saintly" leader during this period, Padre Couto, did not enter into politics at all. Under Salazar, local church councils (Comissões Fabriqueiras) were set up, consisting of the parish priest and two laymen. Although not the same as the civil body—the Junta—these Comissões, depending on the personality of the priest, could have been as powerful as local governing bodies. Furthermore, even as only an ex officio member of the village Junta, the priest continued to wield an enormous amount of power in village decision making, particularly as one of the few fully literate individuals at hand. As more laymen have become both literate and political, conflicts with the priest over the control of the political life of the village have increased. Indeed, such conflicts have become more significant since the revolution of 1974. If Lanheses is any example, and despite a separation of Church and State which even Salazar supported, the Church through its vehicle, the parish priest, continues to involve itself in the secular/civil life of the northern Portuguese parish. For example, when a new state-built Casa do Povo was opened in Lanheses in 1978, the celebrations were held on August 15, one of the major holy days in the Catholic church calendar.

In a recent study of family and marriage in Europe, Goody (1983:45) argues that the Church "insinuated itself into the very fabric of domestic life, of heirship, and of marriage. . . . Religion entered into the basic units of production and reproduction. The whole world was sinning and paying for it." The Church, in his view, had to accumulate property in order to provide for the devout and for those who had committed themselves to carrying out its work. Accumulating property meant controlling the transmission of property, and controlling the transmission of property meant influencing patterns of marriage, fertility, legitimacy, and illegitimacy.[50] Clearly, the power that the Church had in these areas of life waxed and waned as its relationship with the State waxed and waned. And, as Goody himself notes, the "practices of the people" frequently diverged from the "ideology of the Church" (p. 185). They sinned, but paid for their sins.

To the extent that it is possible, the convergence and divergence between ideology and practice in relation to marriage, fertility, and illegitimacy in Lanheses will be explored in subsequent chapters in order to make some assessment about the role of the Church in the lives of Lanhesans over two or more centuries, and therefore of the impact of "religiosity" on demographic behavior. Yet, throughout these discussions it will be necessary to keep in mind that the Church itself, or more appropriately its servants, may not have practiced what they preached, either. They may have been sinning too, but unlike the general populace, *not* paying for it except to the extent that their influence over their parishioners, especially their male parishioners, may have been undermined. Whether individual priests who have served the parish of Lanheses since 1700 instilled fear, piety, and obedience, or skepticism and independence is probably impossible to answer, but we can at least entertain the question in relation to domestic issues which, if Goody is right, may have mattered enormously to the Church. In fact, if one is to take Goody to a logical conclusion with reference to Portugal, the contrast between a population composed primarily of poor and landless day laborers in the south, and a population of landowning, if only small-scale landowning peasants in the north, may go a long way in explaining some of the differences in the extent of "religiosity" in these two regions.

# CHAPTER TWO

# Emigration and Return Migration in Portuguese History

> Emigration is a complex phenomenon in its causes, conditions, and results. (Alexandre Herculano 1873:107)

## INTRODUCTION

In the summer of 1889, Maria Josefa de Castro married Francisco José Rodrigues. He was twenty-seven and she was twenty-six, and they both worked as jornaleiros. After their marriage, they established an independent household adjacent to Maria Josefa's paternal home. During their married life, they produced seven children, all but one of whom grew up and married in the parish. Francisco José had emigrated to Spain as a young boy, the first time when he was only eleven years old to accompany his father. After his marriage, he continued to emigrate because the family was large and they had little land.

When his eldest son António José was ten years old, he began to accompany his father on these temporary migrations to Spain. He worked as a mason's apprentice and earned virtually nothing. In 1912, however, when he reached his eighteenth birthday, he resolved to emigrate to Brazil, and his father, fearing that if he went to Brazil alone he would never return, decided to accompany his son. They left with five other men from Lanheses—two cousins, an uncle, and two other young men. Four of them were single and three were married. They took a boat out of Porto, a nineteen-day journey, and the trip cost thirty-seven escudos each. António José and his father had to borrow the money to pay for the passage. They left during the height of emigration to Brazil, when there was plenty of well-paid work, especially in construction. In 1912, an artisan earned three *tostões* (300 reis) a day in the Lanheses region, five in Lisbon; in Brazil, the going wage was the equivalent of two thousand reis in Portuguese money.

Once World War I began, work in Brazil became harder to find. By 1915, there was virtually nothing, and many of the Portuguese in

Brazil, including Francisco and his son António José, decided to return to Portugal. António José took a job as a chauffeur, although he had no driver's license, and his father found work in a factory, where he earned only enough to buy their food. António José later found employment as a gardener and then as a delivery boy. But none of these jobs paid enough to make it possible to save for the return passage. Finally, father and son found work on a small construction project and were able to put aside the money for the voyage home. Others were less fortunate and had to remain in Brazil.

In 1917, after he had returned to Portugal, António José was inducted into the army. He was twenty-two. However, when Portugal began to send men to France to fight in the war, he decided to flee from the barracks in Viana do Castelo with nine others. He went to Spain, to Galicia, and eventually found work. Only when the war was over did he return to Portugal. In the interim, his father had died, succumbing to the outbreak of Spanish flu that hit the region and the village in October of 1918. His father was only fifty-six, and the burden of responsibility for the wife and children he left behind fell on António José's shoulders. Thus, soon after his return from Spain, António José was forced to go to Lisbon in search of work. He was determined to help his mother pay off all the debts his father had left at his death, including the loan for which the paternal home had been offered as security. When work in Lisbon proved difficult to find, he returned to Spain. During these years, António José thought little about marriage. All the money he earned went to his family.

One day, however, during the summer of 1921 when he was working in Lanheses, he was joking with a friend who suggested that he marry Rosa Araujo. He responded that she was perhaps "too high for him; that she was the niece of priests and the sister of a doctor of laws; that she was from a family of certain social distinction, and he from a family of poor jornaleiros." Yet, the idea was placed in his mind. He was already twenty-seven. Later during the same summer, he found himself working with a cousin of Rosa Araujo on a stone wall near her house. Rosa's father passed by. In jest, he commented to the other young fellow, "look, it is my father-in-law." Rosa's cousin repeated to his sister what António José had said and she in turn passed it on to Rosa. In this fashion, his suit was announced. But Rosa's father, brothers, and uncles were opposed to the marriage, though Rosa herself accepted the idea. Discouraged, António José returned to Spain.

The following summer he returned to Portugal to complete his military service in Viana do Castelo. A year later, on the day of his dismissal from the army, there was a festa in the neighboring village of Vila Mou. At the festa he met Rosa's father, who told him that his opinion had changed, that he saw that António José was a "good and hard-working lad," and that he would give his consent to the marriage. António José told his future bride that he wanted to wait until October to marry so that he could save some money. She replied that she had no money either and that they would marry and earn together. António José borrowed 450$000, sold a small calf for another 400$000 in order to buy his bride a gold chain, and earned the rest of the money for the wedding by making roof tiles for sale.

Once married, they moved in with Rosa's father. Six days later, Rosa's father died. In his will, he left the house to his two sons, both of whom were no longer living in the parish. António José was annoyed, moved his family into a small rented house, and resolved to emigrate once more in order to amass the money to buy the house from his brothers-in-law. He left three months after his marriage. In April of 1924, he returned to see his first child, a daughter. He spent the summer in the village and then returned to Spain again in September. His life of seasonal migration continued for four years, until he had set aside enough money. Even after the purchase of the house, he continued to emigrate to Spain as his family grew. Only in 1931, when political turmoil in Spain disrupted all the possibilities for work, did his emigrating days end for good.

António José and Rosa had nine children. Most of his sons and sons-in-law, like their fathers and grandfathers before them, have been abroad, but in France rather than in Spain or Brazil. This new migration, according to the veteran migrant António José, has been much more lucrative. All his offspring have earned enough abroad to build big new homes. Some have returned to live in them; others have remained in France. His large extended family, which includes over forty grandchildren and at least a dozen great grandchildren, is composed of a number of intersecting households within the village and abroad. António José, who has been widowed for more than twenty-five years, still lives in his wife's paternal household in the company of his youngest daughter.

António José's saga of emigration is one among many that could be told by Lanhesans, and probably by Portuguese throughout the province of Minho. Since emigration is a central theme in this book, this chapter explores the character of Portuguese emigration from the beginning of the great age of discovery into the present century, demonstrating its continuity despite changes in scope and destination.

Historical emigration, and even much of more recent emigration, is difficult to document at both national and local levels. But to have some knowledge of its extent within a larger context sets the stage for an appreciation of its impact at the local level. Indeed, as will be demonstrated in later chapters, in the absence of census manuscripts or population registers like those which exist, for example, for Belgium, Italy, and parts of Scandinavia, an estimation of emigration requires creativity and a fundamental understanding of Portuguese culture.

## PORTUGUESE EMIGRATION: MAJOR THEMES

Emigration in Portugal is as old as her Golden Age, the great age of discovery when Portuguese ships explored the coasts of India, Asia, and America. Portugal's leadership in pulling Europe out of her so-called "crisis of feudalism" was, as Wallerstein (1974) has noted, quite logical, given the country's geographical location and her relative internal stability compared with other European nations at the time. The age of Portuguese exploration lasted for over three centuries, enough time to instill a spirit of adventure and of looking elsewhere in Portuguese national consciousness, a national consciousness that touched nobleman and peasant alike. Indeed, the geographer Orlando Ribeiro once referred to emigration as a "demographic vocation" in Portugal, particularly among the people of the northwestern province of Entre-Douro-e-Minho (1970:345).

For the first few centuries, gold and spices were the driving forces behind this overseas expansion. To the demand for these luxury items was added the need for increased food supply, a factor that quickly changed Portuguese explorations from missions of trade to missions of colonization and "civilization" (Godinho 1955). The Portuguese world and the Christian world were to be enlarged by the massive settlement of natives of the continent in the overseas territories. Between 1500 and 1800, these lands absorbed a major portion of Portugal's population growth. In the first quarter of the nineteenth century, a little more than three million people were counted in continental Portugal and the Atlantic Islands, while almost seven million were counted in Brazil, America, Asia, and Africa. Of course, the annual rates of emigration varied. Godinho (1971) provides us with the following estimates of departures: 280,000 between 1500 and 1580; 300,000 between 1580 and 1640; 120,000 between 1640 and 1700; and 600,000 between 1700 and 1760.

The eighteenth century was, according to the Portuguese demographic historian Joel Serrão, the turning point in Portuguese emigration, the point at which the Portuguese emigrant *sensu strictu* came into being. The *colonizador* of the Portuguese Old Regime was an individual who had abandoned his native soil "under state initiative or as part of a national enterprise." The *emigrante* was an individual who abandoned his country "for exclusively personal reasons, independent of official solicitations and sometimes in opposition to them" (1974:88). It was this dramatic surge of emigration in the first half of the eighteenth century, a surge stimulated by the discovery of gold in Brazil at the end of the seventeenth century, which led officials and native observers to express concern that overseas expansion and the "colonization mission" had gone too far, that too many were leaving the homeland and depleting the country of its valuable agricultural population. This preoccupation, directed largely toward the emigration of the poorer classes of northern Portugal, was to remain throughout the nineteenth century, and indeed resurfaced in the decade of the 1960s, when Portugal demonstrated a 2 percent loss in population per year, largely as a result of emigration to France. It provides the basis for one of the major themes of Portuguese emigration: was it a population problem or a population solution? Clearly, it should not be an either-or question, and the answer depends, to a large extent, on the perspective one adopts—that of the nation state or that of the individual emigrant. Furthermore, the question itself reveals a great deal about widespread attitudes toward the rural population of Portugal over the last four centuries and, to a lesser extent, about the perceptions that those of the countryside themselves had of their own society.

If one buries oneself in the major commentaries from the mid-seventeenth century on, emigration was a national problem requiring a solution in economic and social change within continental Portugal. This problem orientation is clearly reflected in the title of Manuel Severim de Faria's 1655 essay "Remédios para a falta de gente" (Remedies for the shortage of people) (Faria 1974). Faria attributed what had come to be perceived as a grave issue of underpopulation to three factors: the conquest, the lack of industry, and the shortage of land to cultivate.[1] Much as contemporary historians of proto-industrialization argue today, Faria noted that men who did not have the wherewithal to sustain themselves, let alone a family, did not want to marry. Some became beggars, while others emigrated, hoping to find that wherewithal in other nations. Writing shortly prior to the beginnings of significant rural outmigration to Brazil, Faria directed his comments to the massive exodus to Spain, an emigration about which we know very little, but which figures significantly in the demographic history of Lanheses and the province of Minho in general.[2]

> They go to foreign kingdoms, especially to Castille, because of its proximity. . . . Many people have said that a quarter of the inhabitants of Seville were born in Portugal and that in many streets of that city our language rather than Castillian is spoken. The same can be said of Madrid; and throughout Old Castille and Estremadura it is well known that the majority of mechanics were born in Portugal, men who go there to make their living because they do not have work here. (Faria 1974:190)

Faria's solutions to the problem of the *falta de gente* were solutions that have been raised repeatedly, and to little avail, right into contemporary times. He called for industrial development, for the building of factories, and for the limitation of primary goods export. He also called for the internal colonization of the less populated south and for agrarian reform that would not only result in population increase, but also in the expansion of the wheat crop. Wheat was in short supply in his view not "because of some natural defect, but because of the cupidity of those who wish simply to enlarge their properties, those who, the more land they have, the less they cultivate. There is no farmer so rich as to have enough money for such large estates and therefore, the bigger the estate, the more it is divided into small parcels" (Faria 1974:208).[3]

Duarte Ribeiro de Macedo, in his *Discursos Sobre a Introdução das Artes no Reino* (1675) also emphasized the importance of industry that would lead peasants to move from a subsistence economy to one of surplus. As people become more prosperous, he argued, they will be encouraged to marry and to have families and, consequently, the country will become richer and more populated. In his view, the colonies and overseas expansion were not the major causes of population loss because those who had an ability to make a living did not leave for foreign lands. Indirectly, of course, both Macedo and Faria were referring to emigration as an economic solution for the poorer classes of rural Portugal. The interesting aspect of both their arguments, however, is the fundamental belief that economic well-being would not only stem emigration, but would also increase fertility and, hence, solve the perceived "problem" of underpopulation.

A similar argument was put forth more then a century later by Antonio de Araujo Travessos in his *Discurso Político Sobre a Agricultura, Particularmente a de Portugal* (1792):

> The facility of living and abundance are the principle causes of marriages and the raising of children; as a result, where work is well paid the human species multiplies and the population even increases as a result of immigrants who come from poorer countries; and the increase in population moderates naturally the price of work. (quoted in Amzalak 1923:98)

These early analysts of Portugal's demographic situation clearly perceived a connection between economic conditions, emigration, nuptiality, and fertility.

Travessos' concern over the price of work, essentially the augmentation of salaries supposedly resulting from the shortage of manual labor in the countryside, eventually became the primary preoccupation of those who viewed emigration as a national problem. The low salaries and poor living conditions that were fundamental causes of massive exodus were shoved aside. The result of this preoccupation was the creation of restrictive emigration laws in the early part of the eighteenth century. According to a decree of March 20, 1720, only those who could justify with documents that they were going abroad on important or official business were granted passports. This legislation, with the aim of solving the supposed crisis of agricultural labor, lasted well into the nineteenth century, and is one of the major explanations for consistently high levels of clandestine emigration, whether to Spain or across the Atlantic (Costa 1911). In short, the laws did little to stem the tide, and even in the mid-nineteenth century similar complaints were heard about the "pernicious effects of the feverish mania of emigration which has taken possession of the laboring classes. . . . Proprietors who, a few years ago, found with facility and for a reasonable price, as many day laborers as they needed, today look in vain despite offering a hefty salary" (*O Vianense* January 18, 1858).

The great nineteenth-century Portuguese historian Alexandre Herculano, in his essay on emigration in *Opúsculos* (1873–1875), condemned the attempts to halt emigration with the sole motive of maintaining low salaries in agriculture. "To my way of seeing," he said, "the problem does not stem from the scarcity of labor; it stems from the erroneous path which agriculture has followed, from the deplorable ignorance of certain economic laws and certain indisputable principles of agricultural science" (Herculano 1873:107). He pointed to price inflation (between 1862 and 1871, the price of corn rose in numerous concelhos in the northern coastal districts of Aveiro, Porto, and Viana do Castelo), and cited as one possible cause, though by no means the major one, the return of *brasileiros*, of those who had made it rich in Brazil.[4] Salaries were simply insufficient, and any increase was barely enough to meet rising prices. Improving the material conditions of the laboring classes was the major problem to be solved. A similar viewpoint linking one crisis to another appeared in an 1888 editorial in the northern regional newspaper *Aurora de Lima*.

> The scarcity in our fields, the high prices of agricultural products without compensation to those who cultivate, and all the economic ills resulting from the agricultural crisis can be attributed to emigration . . . Why do farm workers leave? Certainly because agriculture does not remunerate them for their work; they leave in the greatest misery. . . . How much do they earn? The salaries of day laborers are between 280 and 360 reis per day. It is therefore natural that the worker procures in other areas of the kingdom or in foreign countries a remuneration which will rid him of the misery of slavery . . . It is necessary to address, with respect to emigration, the development of the population and the division of rural property. . . . Emigration under these conditions cannot justifiably be repressed. (*Aurora de Lima* October 1, 1888)

The renewed and voluminous writing about emigration toward the end of the nineteenth century was a response to the outflow of population which occurred after 1870 and which reached its peak in the years just prior to World War I. Between 1888, when slavery was finally abolished in Brazil, and 1929, the annual rate of emigration from Portugal was approximately 15,000, with 59,000 leaving in 1911, 87,000 in 1912, and 77,000 in 1913. The population of emigrants represented roughly 77 percent of Portuguese population growth in the late nineteenth century.[5] Miriam Halpern Pereira (1981) argues that Portuguese emigration took on a different character in the nineteenth century, and that the status of the Portuguese immigrant in Brazil declined dramatically. From being a person of privilege, he became the object of hostility.[6] Nevertheless, emigration still remained a channel for social mobility because of the significant difference in salaries between Portugal and Brazil and the fluidity of the labor-short Brazilian market.

The causes of this emigration explosion are complex and, as Basilio Teles (1903) has noted, varied from one region to another.[7] In

general, however, the latter half of the nineteenth century was a period in Portugal when demographic pressures upon the land were
increasing as a result of population growth (Pereira 1971, 1981).
Compounding these demographic pressures were growing economic
crises. In the 1860s and 1870s, export prices fell. The phylloxera
disease all but demolished the viticultural industry in the north, particularly in the Douro region. In 1862, throughout the upper Minho
in northern Portugal, there were revolts against the second ministry
of the Marquis of Loulé and the taxes which the bourgeoisie wanted
to impose upon rural work. In the 1880s, taxes, including those imposed upon the transfer of property, were increased dramatically.
Land throughout the upper Minho was subject to severe price speculation and increasing fragmentation, especially after the legal changes
of the 1860s. In 1867, the new Civil Code called for strict partibility
in the inheritance of property, for the abolition of all forms of privileged inheritance among the rural aristocracy (*vinculos* and *morgados*), for the registration of all *foros*, and for the division of common
pasture lands.[8]

According to the Parliamentary Inquiry on Emigration of 1873,
the number of property owners in the district of Viana do Castelo
increased from 47,354 in 1862 to 50,584 in 1872 (by 6.8 percent).
Although this was by no means the greatest increase (in Braga the
proportional increase was 17.9 percent and in Viseu 13.2 percent), it
was significant enough to further impoverish the landowning population of this region. This trend continued until the turn of the century. During the final years of the nineteenth century, the number of
small rural properties throughout the northwest increased by close to
10 percent (Cabral 1979). Simultaneously, there was a great deal of
price speculation and expropriation, both of which were to the advantage of the richer peasants and the bourgeoisie. Many poor peasants were forced to sell in order to eat or simply because what they
had was not enough to support them.[9] Small rural industries were
also on the decline, a phenomenon Cabral (1979) presents as an explanation for the rising number of artisans among the population of
emigrants to Brazil.

In the opinion of Basilio Teles (1903), who is responsible for one
of the best accounts of Portuguese rural life at the dawn of the twentieth century, the young son who went off to Brazil was his parents'
economic security, their reserve capital in a situation where both taxes
and interest rates were rising. To these economic motives, he added
to desire to avoid military service, a motive which again played an
important role in the post-1961 massive emigration to France (Bret-

tell 1978, 1984).[10] For the Portuguese woman, according to the ethnographers Joaquim and Fernando Pires de Lima (1938), the departure of fiancés, sons, or husbands for military service or for war was almost the same as death. Indeed, popular songs and poetry abound with examples of this abhorrence for army life.

> Antes quería morrer
> O meu corpo dar a terra
> Do que ver o meu amor
> Ir combater para a guerra
>
> First I would like to die
> To give my body to the earth
> Than to see my love
> Go to fight in war.
> (Lima 1942:14)

Although the economic and demographic pressures were quite real, there were skeptics among those who commented upon the emigration phenomenon, skeptics who placed their emphasis less upon the wish to escape rural poverty and misery than on ambition and the desire to make a fortune.

> Portugal is a poor country say those who advocate emigration to Brazil, it has too many people. . . . But this is sophism. . . . The principal cause of Portuguese emigration to Brazil and one that we can never tire of repeating, is the unconscious ambition of emigrants. (Percheiro 1878:32)

Although the response to the question "What are the causes of foreign emigration?" in the First Parliamentary Inquiry on Portuguese Emigration (Anonymous 1873) acknowledged all of the above-mentioned socioeconomic causes, the first reason cited was "the ambition to acquire riches fomented and developed by the example of those who return with good fortunes, and for which the idea that most of the emigrants who remain abroad, victims of misery and ill health, does not serve as an obstacle." Indeed, in suggesting solutions to stem the flow, the inquiry called upon local priests to inform their parishioners of the negative aspects of emigration. Embedded in this notion of ambition, therefore, lies what is perhaps the second major theme of Portuguese emigration: was it prompted by necessity or by a desire to get ahead?

The image of the Portuguese emigrant as a fortune seeker who left his country with the hope of striking it rich and the expectation to return one day to show off his wealth is one that has permeated Portuguese society since the days of the so-called *mineiros* (miners) of the seventeenth and early eighteenth centuries. In the nineteenth century, the mineiro became the brasileiro. Brasileiro is a term which, since the nineteenth century, has been used to refer not only to a native-born Brazilian, but also, and often more frequently, to a native-born Portuguese who emigrates to Brazil, makes it rich, and then returns to Portugal to display his wealth. Substantial evidence for the vitality of this national archetype can be found in writings on Portugal—historical, philosophical, and literary. Every peasant family was thought to produce at least one brasileiro.

> The race of the peasant is prolific. In youth, he has ordinarily more brothers on the fig tree than sparrows above him chirping away. As a result, since the figs cannot feed them all, it is necessary to send each one out according to the vocation and talents which God has bestowed upon him. The stupidest becomes a teacher; the most disorganized a chief magistrate; the laziest a priest; and the cleverest goes to Brazil. The teacher dies of hunger; the priest turns fat and procreates; the magistrate mistreats everyone; and the Brazilian either establishes himself there and no one talks of him anymore or he comes back to establish himself in his own village and becomes a viscount. (Ortigão 1885:24)

Examples of verses that exalt the status of the brasileiro can be found even in popular poetry.

> Voce diz que me não quer
> Eu que não tenho dinheiro?
> Tenho meu pai no Brasil
> Sou filha dum brasileiro
>
> You say you do not love me
> I who have no money?
> My father is in Brazil
> I am the daughter of a brasileiro.
> (Lima and Lima 1938:104)

Some essayists referred to these returned emigrants as "deceived compatriots who see in Brazil a new promised land (Percheiro 1878:dedication). The emphasis on "deceived" is important, because it suggests that the disadvantageous expenditures (monetary, emotional, and physical) which are necessary in order to get to Brazil outweigh all the advantages. But "the Portuguese who emigrates does not see it this way. He only thinks that at the end of several years he must return from Brazil" (*ibid.*:18). It is this desire to return which gives the term brasileiro its true meaning.

> The first idea, perhaps, that this word suggests is of an individual whose principal and almost exclusive characteristics are to live with more or less largesse and not to have been born in Brazil; he is a man who left Portugal in his boyhood or youth, more or less poor, and who, many years later, returns more or less rich. (Herculano 1873:111–112)

Not only does the brasileiro return rich, he returns to display his wealth. The most common way to do so was to build a house, a tiled extravaganza with "columns painted in green and walls with yellow bases and scarlet vertexes" (Branco 1966:24). Julio Dinis has perhaps best captured this *brasileiro de torna viagem* (returned brasileiro) in his depiction of the character Eusebio Seabra in his novel *A Morgadinha dos Canaviais*. Seabra is a man who

> left the village as a child and went to try his fortune in Brazil. . . . He was there forty years and returned as the serious man we see, and rich. How he made it rich no one knows—He came to build a large house on the spot where he was born, a large house with tiles and sculpture, with three floors, verandahs, and a garden with pottery statues. . . . The ambitions of Eusebio Seabra are to be the chief personage of influence in the village, and to this end he began with some repairs in the parochial church, some new vestments for the altar saints, and a new bell. At his own expense he paid for the festa of the patron saint. (Dinis 1964:137)[11]

The First Parliamentary Inquiry on Emigration (1873:117) makes reference to the fact that some of these successful brasileiros became local moneylenders in their native villages because they were the ones with disposable capital. The report goes on to affirm that "the best properties one finds, or the newest buildings almost all belong to those individuals who are called Portuguese in Brazil and Brazilian in Portugal" (*ibid.*:177). Percheiro (1878:47) points out that the Portuguese emigrant who prior to his departure worked in "our fertile fields" goes to Brazil to work as a "water-carrier, cartman, boatman, or in the immense diversity of services which (in Portugal) are performed by the sons of Galicia." Indeed, in James Taylor's Portuguese-English dictionary (1958), the word *galego* is defined as a deprecatory epithet applied to the Portuguese in Brazil. An eighteenth-century English traveler estimated that some 30,000 Galicians entered Portugal each year to participate in the cereal and wine harvests. He went on to add, "I am told that almost all of the livery servants throughout this kingdom come from Galicia, it being scarcely possible to persuade the Portuguese to wear the badge of dependence" (Dalrymple 1777:126).[12] What this discussion of the Galicians in Portugal underscores, however, is a view of emigration as somewhat hypocritical, of people working at jobs abroad that they would never undertake at home.

Although most nineteenth-century descriptions of the brasileiros are similar to that of Julio Dinis, and essentially poke fun at their excessiveness,[13] Ramalho Ortigão made an exception for the brasileiro of the Lima Valley. In this region, he claimed, the brasileiro is a little brasileiro, "so little that he hardly passes as a boy who went to Brazil."

> The beauty of the land, the modest grace of the customs, the simplicity of life, exerts here, more than elsewhere, this nostalgic magnetism which leads the emigrant to repatriate as soon as he can. As soon as he has earned enough to buy a plot he has had his eyes on, enough to build a story on the paternal home, enough to buy two more cows, and enough to defray the luxury of a nag to go to the *Feira da Agonia* . . . the emigrant from between the Minho and the Lima returns modestly in the second class of the Royal Mail. (Ortigão 1885:8)[14]

Some placed the blame for the folly of the brasileiro almost entirely on the ignorance of the rural population. The following passage is indicative of this point of view and is worth quoting in full.

> An ordinary man destines his son from childhood to be a brasileiro, and, with this in mind, sends his son to school to learn how to read, and write, and count. It does not enter into the mind of that father that of a hundred who go to America, ninety-five are lost to this country, some swallowed by the waves, others taken sick or assassinated, others consumed by the insupportable work they have in the mines or in the fields. . . . And what of those laborers who go every year to the Alentejo, to Lisbon, to Spain. . . . They leave (if they are married) their wives as widows, or single, unable to procreate, and if in ten years of absence they had remained and had had four children, these children would be the greatest richness for them and for the country . . . because a good farmer or a good artisan is worth a lot of money. (Bezerra 1785:190)

The final observation made by this writer about the impact of emigration on fertility is important to our later discussion, but for our purposes here his emphasis is clearly upon the foolishness of emigration—that it brings more trouble than it is worth. Percheiro (1878) concurs with this point of view, providing a series of calculations to support the argument that emigration is unprofitable both monetarily and in terms of health. Indeed, the regional newspapers during the late nineteenth century published lists of Portuguese nationals who had died in Brazil, many suffering from tuberculosis or yellow fever. In November of 1860, for example, the following was reported from Brazil:

> A ship with 250 colonos arrived here recently. These colonos were taken to an island at three leagues distance from this city. The majority died and the others are being punished here for their sins. After they arrive is when they repent having abandoned their country.

Yet, the Minhotan emigrant appears to have ignored all of these variously motivated admonitions, seeing instead the emigrants who returned to "build palaces beside his hut" (Costa 1874).

Others blamed ambition-motivated emigration less upon the ignorance of the emigrant than upon the men who acted as intermediaries, the so-called *engajadores* who made money rounding up men willing to go to work in foreign countries. Indeed, like the term brasileiro, the term engajador has special meaning—it derives from the verb *engajar*, which literally means "to hook," but which more conventionally means "to entice men for labor migration." These engajadores frequently offered a pound (*libra*) to anyone who was able to convince another person to emigrate. By the late nineteenth century, regional newspapers in the north were full of editorials calling for a halt to such practices. The engajadores were accused of issuing deceptive contracts that did not make the potential emigrant aware of the differences in currency values between Portugal and Brazil. Nevertheless, these same newspapers simultaneously permitted engajadores to advertise in their pages. On December 12, 1890, for example, an announcement appeared in the *Aurora de Lima* offering free passage to Brazil on bimonthly ships to all married farm laborers or artisans, as well as to single men, and to single women who wanted to work in domestic service. The offer was supposedly supported by the government of Brazil, and all matters could be handled in Viana do Castelo, the provincial town where the newspaper itself was published. The consul of Maranhão, in a communication of December 7, 1874, characterized these engajadores as "perverse men, true parasites who amuse themselves in deluding, with the most ingratiating smiles, their unwary brothers about a happiness which is completely ephemeral" (quoted in Percheiro 1878:170).[15] Pereira (1981) describes various individuals from parish priests to the captains of ships who became involved in and profited from the business of *engajamento*. Clearly, these engajadores, like their twentieth-century counterparts the *passadores* who helped clandestine emigrants travel from Portugal to France in the 1960s, were middlemen, serving the politics of migration in both sending and receiving areas. The historian Herculano, sympathetic to the cause of the Portuguese peasant-emigrant, called for the improvement of primary education as a way to help the rural classes to avoid being enticed by the deceiving engajadores. Yet he simultaneously recognized that knowing how to read would not, ultimately, help them to see the truth; rather, they needed work (Herculano 1873:175).

It is not known exactly how many Portuguese actually did return from Brazil during the late nineteenth and early twentieth centuries. Martins (1885) estimates that roughly 50 percent of those who departed during the latter half of the nineteenth century eventually came back. Pereira (1981) refers to a rate of return between 1864 and 1872 which fluctuated between 30 and 40 percent. Passport registers and oral histories indicate that even with emigration to Brazil there were cases of individuals who left for a period of time, returned, and then departed again. Others departed as single men and returned, perhaps as much as twenty years later, to marry. Still others came back ill and destitute or to live our their final years before death in their native villages. Carqueja (1916:416–417) notes that of 73,831 who entered the port of Lisbon in 1890–1891, 4,062 were sick and 672 tubercular. Certainly, a significant homeward flow occurred after the outbreak of World War I, as employment became increasingly difficult in Brazil, and again with the contraction of the labor market after 1929 (Simões 1934). It is impossible, however, to calculate with any degree of accuracy the extent of return migration because prior to the mid-twentieth century such figures are unavailable. Even today, most figures for the number of return migrants from France and other northern European countries can be little more than educated guesses. It is important to emphasize, however, that the goal of return must be treated differently from the fact of return, since it is often a fundamental part of the original migration project.

Furthermore, this "ideology of return" (divorced from the number of those who actually return) was supported by national emigration policy because the economy of the country was bolstered by the remittances that emigrants sent back to their homeland. Pereira (1981:43) points out that during the sixty years between 1870 and 1930, Brazilian money not only led to the monetarization of rural life in Portugal but also stimulated investment in property and construction. There was an enormous influx of money from Brazil in the period between 1860 and 1875 (Pery 1875). Estimates for the volume of remittances between 1881 and 1890 vary between eight and twelve thousand *contos* (Pereira 1981).[16] Carqueja (1916) has estimated that an annual average of approximately one hundred seventeen thousand contos entered Portugal between 1911 and 1914. These funds were directed primarily, and in order of highest to lowest amount, to the following districts: Porto, Lisbon, Viseu, Viana do Castelo, and Aveiro. Only with emigration to France in the 1960s and 1970s did remittances from emigrants again reach and surpass such proportions.[17] Although the data on nineteenth-century remittances from Brazil have yet to be fully explored, Pereira (1981) points to some very important differences. The majority of the funds were apparently sent to male recipients, a factor that Pereira argues to be an indication that the remitters were primarily sons sending money back to their fathers. However, in the district of Braga, a different pattern existed. There, the majority of funds were remitted to women, suggesting that in this region the majority of emigrants were married men. Clearly, it is necessary to direct one's attention more closely to the sociodemographic and regional character of emigration.

## PORTUGUESE EMIGRATION: REGIONAL AND LOCAL CHARACTERISTICS

Pre-nineteenth-century figures on emigration are difficult to obtain, and the estimates of Godinho cited above are perhaps the best available figures for the total volume of outflow to Brazil prior to 1800. In addition, references have been made to migration to Spain, although merely to the existence of this movement rather than to any precise numbers. To this should be added the seasonal internal movement of peasants from the north of Portugal to the south, the so-called *ratinhos* about whom several scholars have written (Carqueja 1916, Pereira 1981, Picão 1947).[18] Serrão (1974) observes that even throughout the nineteenth century, until 1868, little of a very exact quantitative nature is known about Portuguese emigration. He cites some random counts of the number of Portuguese entering Brazil— 24,000 between 1808 and 1817; 11,557 in 1855; and an average of 4,000 per year between 1860 and 1868 (the lowest rate in the entire

TABLE 2.1 AVERAGE ANNUAL EMIGRATION (1866–1913) BY DISTRICT

| District | A. | Pop. 1864 | B. | Pop. 1878 | C. | Pop. 1890 | D. | Pop. 1911 |
|---|---|---|---|---|---|---|---|---|
| Aveiro | 1027 | 238,700 | 959 | 257,059 | 2509 | 287,437 | 5992 | 336,243 |
| Beja | 47 | 135,508 | 8 | 142,119 | 86 | 157,571 | 708 | 192,499 |
| Braga | 973 | 309,508 | 1128 | 319,464 | 1497 | 338,308 | 4123 | 382,276 |
| Bragança | 23 | 156,909 | 17 | 168,651 | 939 | 179,678 | 8675 | 192,024 |
| C. Branco | 7 | 159,505 | 19 | 173,983 | 74 | 205,211 | 614 | 241,184 |
| Coimbra | 189 | 268,894 | 1162 | 292,037 | 2172 | 316,624 | 6213 | 359,387 |
| Évora | 0 | 98,104 | 1 | 106,858 | 270 | 118,408 | 27 | 148,295 |
| Faro | 2 | 172,660 | 48 | 199,142 | 156 | 228,635 | 1087 | 272,861 |
| Guarda | 29 | 210,414 | 82 | 228,494 | 1194 | 250,154 | 6190 | 271,616 |
| Leiria | 19 | 173,916 | 145 | 192,982 | 799 | 217,278 | 4229 | 262,632 |
| Lisbon | 45 | 438,464 | 1187 | 498,059 | 1249 | 611,168 | 620 | 852,354 |
| Portalegre | 3 | 95,665 | 1 | 101,126 | 18 | 112,834 | 36 | 141,481 |
| Porto | 2741 | 410,665 | 2867 | 461,881 | 3845 | 546,262 | 6198 | 679,540 |
| Santarém | 8 | 196,617 | 4 | 220,881 | 142 | 254,844 | 250 | 325,775 |
| V. Castelo | 390 | 195,257 | 693 | 201,390 | 947 | 207,366 | 2560 | 227,250 |
| Vila Real | 344 | 213,289 | 791 | 224,628 | 1936 | 237,302 | 6658 | 245,547 |
| Viseu | 390 | 353,543 | 1474 | 371,571 | 2699 | 391,015 | 10156 | 416,744 |

NOTE: A. Emigration, 1866–1871; B. Emigration, 1880–1882; C. Emigration, 1896–1898; D. Emigration, 1911–1913. Population is de facto.
SOURCE: Carqueja (1916:388); Portuguese National Censuses.

nineteenth century). After 1868, the figures become more readily available, and they rise, as pointed out earlier, to reach their peak in the years just prior to World War I.

Table 2.1 presents the average annual emigration by district between 1866 and 1913, when emigration to Brazil was at its height. Table 2.2 describes emigration by district for the twentieth century and includes the impact of the most recent emigration of Portuguese people to France in the post-World War II era. Both of these tables demonstrate the regional concentration of emigration in the northern half of the century. Tables 2.3 and 2.4 present the sex ratios (males per hundred females) of the population by district in various census years between 1864 and 1970, and distinguish the single population from the married population. There are two factors that these latter tables demonstrate which are worth pursuing in the context of this study: the male-biased pattern of emigration and the especially disproportionate ratios for the district of Viana do Castelo—especially among the married population—in comparison with other districts at similar points in time.

TABLE 2.2 OFFICIAL EMIGRANTS BY DISTRICT, 1901–1970

| District | 1901–1930 | 1931–1940 | 1941–1950 | 1951–1960 | 1961–1970 |
|---|---|---|---|---|---|
| Aveiro | 106,574 | 14,402 | 11,190 | 36,190 | 44,621 |
| Beja | 3,949 | 159 | 159 | 670 | 9,009 |
| Braga | 64,506 | 6,689 | 4,095 | 21,400 | 64,125 |
| Bragança | 62,923 | 5,536 | 4,106 | 21,972 | 24,491 |
| C. Branco | 10,221 | 986 | 970 | 4,899 | 34,667 |
| Coimbra | 88,479 | 7,165 | 5,471 | 15,420 | 19,961 |
| Évora | 999 | 124 | 56 | 315 | 2,855 |
| Faro | 20,761 | 4,184 | 3,271 | 8,195 | 25,933 |
| Guarda | 72,626 | 7,519 | 6,410 | 21,478 | 37,813 |
| Leiria | 45,335 | 3,531 | 2,361 | 14,614 | 52,636 |
| Lisbon | 25,759 | 1,692 | 1,687 | 7,980 | 58,598 |
| Portalegre | 1,911 | 232 | 91 | 576 | 2,470 |
| Porto | 118,501 | 12,950 | 8,684 | 35,615 | 59,140 |
| Santarém | 12,352 | 1,195 | 907 | 7,299 | 25,735 |
| Setúbal | | 97 | 183 | 1,237 | 12,529 |
| V. Castelo | 36,360 | 4,590 | 3,372 | 16,254 | 37,236 |
| Vila Real | 74,134 | 6,043 | 3,761 | 19,499 | 26,272 |
| Viseu | 131,551 | 16,480 | 11,007 | 35,981 | 33,611 |

SOURCE: Boletims, Junta de Emigração

Historians of Portugal have repeatedly observed that the province of Minho (the districts of Porto, Braga, and Viana do Castelo) has been the center of emigration for several centuries. This corresponds with the fact that Minho has been the most densely populated region of Portugal since the founding of the country as a nation in the twelfth century. It also corresponds with a custom of land division that substantially predates the legislation supporting strict partibility enacted during the latter nineteenth century, and that has essentially made it necessary for people from this region to emigrate in search of supplemental income.

Within the province of Minho, the district of Viana do Castelo has consistently played an important role in emigration, although it has not always been the region with the highest outmigration. Rather, it has had a steady outflow over time, a factor that further enhances the argument that it was constant population density and constant population pressure upon the land that made emigration necessary, rather than short-term economic crises such as the phylloxera disaster, for example, which stimulated the massive outflow from the Douro valley in the 1870s and 1880s. Within the district of Viana do Castelo, there has been some variation in the rates of emigration among

TABLE 2.3 SEX RATIO OF THE SINGLE POPULATION BY DISTRICT, 1864–1970 (males/100 females, de facto population)

| District | 1864 | 1878 | 1890 | 1900 | 1911 | 1920 | 1930 | 1940 | 1950 | 1960 | 1970[a] |
|---|---|---|---|---|---|---|---|---|---|---|---|
| Aveiro | 82.3 | 81.3 | 86.4 | 86.3 | 86.5 | 85.3 | 89.5 | 93.9 | 97.1 | 96.2 | 95.5 |
| Beja | 112.2 | 141.5 | 115.5 | 111.6 | 112.3 | 110.1 | 111.5 | 109.7 | 110.5 | 110.0 | 109.2 |
| Braga | 76.6 | 76.8 | 81.8 | 82.3 | 85.2 | 84.8 | 89.9 | 93.2 | 96.1 | 96.1 | 95.2 |
| Bragança | 108.5 | 104.8 | 105.6 | 103.5 | 103.3 | 100.8 | 103.4 | 107.6 | 108.5 | 99.3 | 102.6 |
| C. Branco | 100.7 | 100.3 | 104.6 | 100.8 | 100.0 | 98.5 | 100.3 | 103.1 | 104.5 | 99.3 | 100.0 |
| Coimbra | 91.8 | 88.9 | 91.3 | 88.6 | 88.4 | 87.1 | 90.5 | 91.5 | 92.6 | 91.5 | 93.0 |
| Évora | 115.1 | 118.9 | 117.9 | 114.8 | 112.5 | 111.4 | 109.7 | 109.2 | 108.9 | 105.3 | 102.2 |
| Faro | 107.4 | 106.8 | 109.2 | 107.9 | 103.2 | 103.9 | 103.4 | 106.7 | 110.3 | 109.1 | 112.1 |
| Guarda | 98.1 | 97.2 | 96.8 | 96.6 | 94.9 | 92.9 | 96.2 | 100.4 | 103.5 | 99.6 | 95.5 |
| Leiria | 103.0 | 100.8 | 102.8 | 101.6 | 99.8 | 98.5 | 102.5 | 102.5 | 104.4 | 105.6 | 102.9 |
| Lisbon | 117.5 | 117.7 | 117.5 | 112.1 | 108.2 | 106.3 | 109.8 | 99.8 | 98.2 | 94.9 | 94.1 |
| | | | | | | | | 92.9[b] | 89.5[b] | 84.3[b] | |
| Portalegre | 116.2 | 113.9 | 116.3 | 112.7 | 107.6 | 107.1 | 109.8 | 110.1 | 108.4 | 104.9 | 102.1 |
| Porto | 81.5 | 85.6 | 90.4 | 89.9 | 90.3 | 91.2 | 92.6 | 95.2 | 94.7 | 94.6 | 96.3 |
| | | | | | | | | 83.9[b] | 79.8[b] | 77.6[b] | |
| Santarém | 108.8 | 106.6 | 104.7 | 104.1 | 101.8 | 101.7 | 104.8 | 105.8 | 105.4 | 101.4 | 100.1 |
| Setúbal | | | | | | | 113.4 | 113.4 | 115.4 | 110.3 | 108.2 |
| V. Castelo | 77.6 | 76.6 | 76.1 | 76.6 | 77.4 | 77.0 | 76.8 | 82.8 | 84.5 | 83.0 | 80.5 |
| Vila Real | 98.1 | 95.2 | 94.0 | 94.8 | 91.8 | 95.0 | 97.7 | 103.8 | 106.6 | 105.5 | 102.6 |
| Viseu | 91.6 | 88.9 | 88.1 | 87.8 | 86.7 | 86.5 | 89.2 | 96.5 | 98.4 | 97.3 | 95.8 |

[a] Figures for 1970 are based on the 20 percent estimate.
[b] Figures for the cities of Lisbon and Porto considered apart from the district.
SOURCE: Portuguese National Censuses, 1864–1970.

TABLE 2.4 SEX RATIO OF THE MARRIED POPULATION BY DISTRICT, 1864–1970 (males/100 females, de facto population)

| District | 1864 | 1878 | 1890 | 1900 | 1911 | 1920 | 1930 | 1940 | 1950 | 1960 | 1970[a] |
|---|---|---|---|---|---|---|---|---|---|---|---|
| Aveiro | 94.3 | 92.3 | 91.4 | 91.6 | 87.5 | 88.5 | 88.6 | 92.3 | 92.3 | 93.5 | 95.4 |
| Beja | 101.4 | 100.9 | 102.3 | 100.8 | 101.2 | 99.3 | 102.6 | 102.0 | 100.0 | 99.5 | 98.0 |
| Braga | 97.4 | 97.1 | 96.6 | 96.2 | 94.0 | 91.6 | 96.1 | 95.7 | 95.6 | 94.3 | 93.4 |
| Bragança | 102.4 | 101.8 | 100.9 | 98.9 | 96.6 | 95.6 | 100.9 | 98.8 | 98.1 | 98.4 | 95.7 |
| C. Branco | 99.9 | 100.7 | 102.5 | 99.3 | 98.5 | 96.9 | 98.4 | 100.3 | 98.9 | 98.5 | 96.4 |
| Coimbra | 97.7 | 95.6 | 93.9 | 91.0 | 87.0 | 89.4 | 91.1 | 92.5 | 93.3 | 95.0 | 96.1 |
| Évora | 100.7 | 100.8 | 100.5 | 101.8 | 99.5 | 98.8 | 99.9 | 100.0 | 98.8 | 99.5 | 99.2 |
| Faro | 96.5 | 98.2 | 100.8 | 99.3 | 95.5 | 96.5 | 93.4 | 96.9 | 96.4 | 96.8 | 96.5 |
| Guarda | 99.7 | 99.8 | 98.2 | 96.6 | 91.7 | 91.1 | 90.0 | 94.7 | 95.5 | 95.8 | 94.3 |
| Leiria | 98.5 | 97.0 | 97.5 | 96.2 | 92.5 | 94.6 | 95.4 | 95.6 | 95.9 | 97.3 | 96.1 |
| Lisbon | 107.9 | 106.8 | 107.2 | 105.2 | 105.8 | 102.8 | 104.6 | 103.4 103.5[b] | 101.2 101.5[b] | 99.5 99.3[b] | 98.0 |
| Portalegre | 103.9 | 101.1 | 102.5 | 99.4 | 98.8 | 97.8 | 106.6 | 102.0 | 99.2 | 99.9 | 98.7 |
| Porto | 96.8 | 96.1 | 96.7 | 96.4 | 92.6 | 93.9 | 95.2 | 95.5 99.1[b] | 95.9 98.2[b] | 96.4 97.9[b] | 96.3 |
| Santarém | 99.9 | 100.2 | 101.5 | 98.4 | 100.2 | 97.7 | 99.8 | 97.4 | 97.5 | 98.1 | 98.3 |
| Setúbal | | | | | | | 105.2 | 102.7 | 100.7 | 99.4 | 98.2 |
| V. Castelo | 95.3 | 94.5 | 91.1 | 92.3 | 89.2 | 88.1 | 87.5 | 88.0 | 89.9 | 87.5 | 86.5 |
| Vila Real | 101.4 | 100.7 | 98.7 | 99.2 | 92.9 | 94.4 | 96.9 | 96.4 | 98.1 | 97.1 | 94.2 |
| Viseu | 99.2 | 96.8 | 95.0 | 93.6 | 87.6 | 88.2 | 90.3 | 90.8 | 93.6 | 94.0 | 93.8 |

[a] Figures for 1970 are based on the 20 percent estimate.
[b] Figures for the cities of Lisbon and Porto considered apart from the district.
SOURCE: Portuguese National Censuses, 1864–1970.

concelhos during the last one hundred years, but the concelho of Viana do Castelo itself (where the parish of Lanheses is situated) has consistently been a source for both single and married male emigrants since the last quarter of the nineteenth century.

In addition to census data, regional newspapers also provide valuable commentary about emigration from the district of Viana do Castelo during the second half of the nineteenth century. Two were published in the town of Viana do Castelo itself—the short-lived *O Vianense* (1856–1868) and the *Aurora de Lima*, first issued in 1855 and still published today. In addition to printing long editorial articles on emigration, which have been referred to in the first section of this chapter, these papers documented the number of boats that set out from various Portuguese ports with Brazil as their destination, and included numerous shipping notices advertising ticket prices and promising comfortable passage.[19] In the 1850s and 1860s, the cost of first-, second-, and third-class passage was 144$000, 117$000, and 38$000 reis, respectively, for a trip from Lisbon to Rio on the Hamburg-Brazilian or the Europa-America lines (both English companies). On Portuguese ships, the prices were appreciably less—72$000, 60$000, and 33$000 reis, respectively. A day laborer in the early 1870s earned about 0$200 reis per day, masons and carpenters about 0$300 reis per day, tailors and shoemakers about 0$280 reis. Given these wages, a day laborer would have to have worked approximately 165 days in order to save up enough money to buy a third-class ticket on a Portuguese line, and this calculation excludes (absurdly, of course) the daily cost of living. Many emigrants, needless to say, went into debt to pay for their passage.

On occasion, the regional newspapers also published figures for the number of annual departures from the district. For example, the November 29, 1858, issue of the *Vianense* reported that 218 passports from the district had been issued for Brazil during that year.[20] Of these, 165 were to single men, 47 to married men, 3 to widowers, and 3 to women. By profession, these individuals were classified as follows: 7 businessmen, 1 shop assistant, 9 masons, 11 carpenters, 6 tailors, 5 blacksmiths, 1 painter, 1 firework maker, 54 farmers (*lavradores*), and 122 with no profession. The passport registers from which these figures are taken provide information not only on the occupations of emigrants, but also on their age distribution and marital status. Whereas 43.3 percent of the individuals who applied for passports in the District of Viana do Castelo in 1865 were under age nineteen, only 11.3 percent fell into this age group in 1890. Conversely, only 23 percent in 1865 were between thirty and forty-nine, compared with 39.3 percent in 1890. The change in the composition of the emigrant population is equally reflected in the marital status of applicants for passports. In 1865, 85.8 percent were single, compared with only 57.9 percent in 1890.

During the third quarter of the nineteenth century, the most common profession cited was that of shop clerk (*caixeiro*). By the end of the century, the peasant farmer (*lavrador*) had become more frequent. Martins (1885:231) provides the following breakdown for the year 1887:

| | |
|---|---|
| Rural workers (lavrador, jornaleiro) | 32% |
| Proprietors | 4% |
| Shop clerks | 8% |
| Office workers | 6% |
| Sailors | 2% |
| Servants (criadas de servir) | 7% |
| Unclassified | 41% |

In discussing these figures, he notes that the monopoly that Portuguese immigrants had over the butcher's trade in Brazil was challenged by the end of the century by immigrants from Italy, and that this challenge was instrumental in the shift from "classic" shop-clerk emigration to "agriculturalist" emigration. A later breakdown by profession is provided by Bento Carqueja for the period between 1911 and 1913. He separates two classes of "rural workers"—*agricultores* and *operários agrícolas*—the former perhaps roughly equivalent to lavradores and the latter to jornaleiros.

| | |
|---|---|
| Agricultores | 15% |
| Carpenters | 3% |
| Masons | 3% |
| Agricultural Workers | 24% |
| Domestic Industries | 4% |
| Unclassified | 51% |

These figures raise the essential question of whether the majority of those who emigrated from farming backgrounds were landless laborers or small property owners. This is an important point of controversy that has been raised more generally and perhaps most recently by the historian Charles Tilly (1978). As suggested in the previous chapter, the social structure of northern Portugal, and especially of the province of Minho, is complex enough to make it difficult to argue one side or the other with any degree of assuredness. Indeed, it is not always clear precisely where a family belongs within any model of social stratification which requires classification into a single cell or level.

The national censuses also provide us with information on the impact of emigration on the sex ratio of the local population of Lanheses (Table 2.5). These local data roughly parallel (in terms of time period) the effects of migration on the sex ratios for the district of Viana do Castelo as a whole, and demonstrate that the two major periods of outmigration were between 1878 and 1890 and again between 1900 and 1911, the latter period having an impact on the married population of the parish in particular.

In addition to the national censuses, there are a few alternative sources that can be drawn upon to provide both a qualitative and quantitative impression of emigration from the parish of Lanheses in particular. Furthermore, and unlike the census data, these sources are nominative, providing us with migration data on specific individuals. The passport registers are one such source, since they do identify emigrants by name and place of birth. Although it was very common by the middle of the century for individuals to depart for Brazil without a passport and therefore for these registers to grossly underrepresent the extent of movement, we can at least derive some idea of the makeup of the Lanhesan emigrant population from these documents. In general, it seems that the pattern of movement out of this parish closely paralleled the pattern for the region as a whole.

In the 1830s and 1840s the names of only seven men from Lanheses appear, all of them single, three of them in their early twenties and three under twenty. Five of these men were related, and in one instance two young cousins emigrated together. During the 1870s, twenty-five Lanhesans are listed, including twenty-one single men, three married men, and one single woman. Fifteen of the single men were in their twenties. The occupations of the men were varied, including six lavradores, six stonemasons, a carpenter, a few potters, a boatsman, an ironsmith, and a few shopkeepers. During this decade, one man who called himself a merchant (*negociante*) went back and forth to Brazil three times. In fact, all were going to Brazil, with the exception of one shop clerk traveling to Luanda.

During the next decade, twenty-five Lanhesans again applied for passports, three of them (two married men and one single man) more than once. The number of married men increased to seven, most of them in their mid-thirties or early forties. The occupations were similar to that of the previous decade except for the fact that four young tailors were included. In the 1890s, the number of married Lanhesan men who applied for passports expanded dramatically. Of the thirty-

TABLE 2.5 SEX RATIOS OF THE LANHESAN
POPULATION BY MARITAL STATUS, 1864–1960
(males/100 females)

| Year | Single | Married | Widowed |
|------|--------|---------|---------|
| 1864 | 85.9 | 102.4 | 42.2 |
| 1878 | 67.4 | 90.2 | 44.4 |
| 1890 | 53.4 | 78.1 | 44.2 |
| 1900 | 64.2 | 87.4 | 37.9 |
| 1911 | 63.9 | 72.5 | 31.8 |
| 1920 | 66.5 | 80.3 | 37.1 |
| 1930 | 82.1 | 86.9 | 23.2 |
| 1940 | 81.3 | 87.8 | 14.7 |
| 1950 | 77.2 | 91.0 | 19.7 |
| 1960 | 84.6 | 91.1 | 25.8 |

SOURCE: Portuguese National Censuses, 1864–1960.

three who were apparently leaving for the first time, twenty-three were married. During this decade the pattern of going back and forth two or three times became more widespread, and three men, in fact, returned to reemigrate with their families.

A second source that can be used to provide nominative data on emigration from Lanheses in the absence of census manuscripts are the Rois da Desobriga, lists kept by the parish priest to record communicants and confessants and annual household donations to the parish church. Those not present in the parish at the time the roll was taken were marked as absent (*ausente*). Although we cannot be sure that the priest was entirely accurate in his record keeping, counting these ausentes does demonstrate that emigration was a factor in the life of Lanhesans during the latter half of the nineteenth century and the early twentieth century, and that it was much more extensive than is suggested by the passport registers.

The data from these rois are contained in Table 2.6, and they merit a few observations. First, it is clear that emigration was already important by 1850, although it expanded in the 1880s and 1890s.[21] Second, whereas single men constituted the bulk of emigrants during the nineteenth century, in the early part of the twentieth century there were as many, if not more, married men absent from the parish. Third, whereas single women account for roughly 25 percent of the absences after 1887 (a third in 1899), my reading of this proportion is that many of these women were absent as local migrants rather than as international emigrants. In numerous cases, they were young

TABLE 2.6 "AUSENTES" FROM LANHESES IN THE ROIS DA
DESOBRIGA, 1850–1927 (absolute numbers)

| | Males | | | Females | | |
|---|---|---|---|---|---|---|
| Year | Single | Married | Widowed | Single | Married | Widowed |
| 1850 (T = 101) | 66 | 29 | 0 | 6 | 0 | 0 |
| 1870 (T = 125) | 85 | 17 | 1 | 22 | 0 | 0 |
| 1881 (T = 131) | 95 | 16 | 2 | 17 | 1[a] | 0 |
| 1887 (T = 135) | 62 | 42 | 2 | 29 | 0 | 0 |
| 1892 (T = 122) | 50 | 34 | 4 | 30 | 3[b] | 0 |
| 1899 (T = 81) | 32 | 21 | 0 | 27 | 1[a] | 0 |
| 1907 (T = 100) | 37 | 37 | 2 | 24 | 0 | 0 |
| 1913 (T = 103) | 42 | 46 | 0 | 14 | 1[a] | 0 |
| 1920 (T = 79) | 34 | 27 | 0 | 18 | 0 | 0 |
| 1927 (T = 105) | 46 | 35 | 1 | 22 | 0 | 1 |

[a] In each case an entire nuclear family was marked absent.
[b] One was absent with her husband, the other two were absent with an entire nuclear family.
SOURCE: Rois da Desobriga, Lanheses.

women from the poorer day laboring families, and quite frequently two or three daughters from single households were absent at the same time. These young women (sometimes girls between the ages of eight and thirteen) were sent to serve in the households of local aristocrats throughout the Lima Valley region. In a few cases, they were marked as servants (*criadas*) in Lanhesan lavrador households, and then marked absent. About this servant population more will be said later. Thus, although the rois demonstrate the geographic mobility of women as well as that of men, we are dealing with a different type of mobility.[22] It is safe to argue, and I am by no means the first to do so, that not only was emigration abroad from continental Portugal concentrated in the northern half of the nation, but it was also predominantly an emigration of men, whether single or married.

The figures themselves, whether local, regional, or national, demonstrate this sex bias, whereas historical evidence, particularly traveler's accounts, point to the effects of this sex bias on the rural countryside. One of the observations made most frequently by these travelers was the prevalence of women who worked in the fields. Though the connection between this observation and male emigration was not always stressed, clearly the phenomenon was considered unusual enough to comment upon. The following excerpts are characteristic of a wealth of similar remarks made about the economic roles of women in northern Portugal throughout the two-and-a-half centuries that are covered by the present study.

> Two things are notable among the people of the countryside; first that the women dig, plow, and do all the agricultural work as the men; the second is that, given their ordinary sustenance, a frugal and rustic meal, they endure the greatest toils without succumbing to the work or damaging their health. (Costa 1789:xix)

> Such are the normal duties of women here, for the men of the district, possessed with an unconquerable aversion for this form of labor, are well content to leave the soil to their wives and daughters while they, for their part, go out into the world and adopt the less strenuous callings of carpenters, masons, and waiters. (Koebel 1909:230)

The second quotation points to the division of labor that has evolved in northern Portugal, whereby women work in the fields and men work as artisans or emigrate or both. These roles complement one another and, in this context, emigration must be viewed as a temporary departure, as a means by which to supplement household income. While their husbands were gone, the women of northern Portugal, especially those from the province of Minho, customarily dressed themselves in black and eventually earned the epithet of *viuvas dos vivos*, widows of the living. They farmed the land, raised the children, and waited for the day when their husbands would return from Spain, Brazil, or some other far-off place. The important economic roles of these northern peasant women will figure at several points in this study and should be kept in mind. In some ways, they are the result of a long tradition of male emigration; in other ways, they have contributed to its perpetuation.[23] It is certainly possible to suggest that whether as stimulus or consequence, there are important connections to be made between male emigration, women's economic roles, and a broad range of alternative demographic phenomena.

The Rois da Desobriga, when linked with other historical documents, can also lend some insight into the socioeconomic status of the Lanhesan emigrant population during the late nineteenth century. The majority of those who were absent in 1870, whether married heads of households or unmarried sons, were from lavrador households, but from the poorest to the wealthiest of these. Villagers today, in discussions of more recent emigration to France, talk about the bulk of emigrants who departed because it was necessary to do so—because the population was too great, the land too little, and because agricultural life simply yielded little (*não dá para nada*). However, they also talk about men who emigrated although they did not need to, men who had property and were living reasonably well. They say of them "they did not want to be left behind" (*não querem ficar atrás*). If others made fortunes abroad, they wished to make theirs too.[24] Surely it is possible that this assessment holds for the eighteenth and nineteenth centuries as well as for the present, especially given the fact that even the more well-to-do lavradores were not enormously rich in land, and that several offspring could easily erode a family's status. Clearly, the conclusion one is forced to draw is that emigration can be differently motivated depending on one's socioeconomic position, and that some, indeed, can be guided more by ambition, if that is even the right word, than by necessity. The status of even the more well-to-do Portuguese lavradores was threatened during the later nineteenth century, and emigration was one means by which to preserve that status.

The occupational status of Lanhesan emigrants after the turn of the century was somewhat different. Of those marked absent on the 1907 rol who were either heads of households or sons of heads of households, fifteen were masons and three sons of masons, one was a tailor and two were tailor's sons, thirteen were jornaleiros and one a jornaleiro's son, twelve were lavradores and seven the sons of lavradores, and ten more were associated with other activities (blacksmiths, shoemakers, basketmakers, stuccoers, carpenters). This probably reflects both a change in the socioeconomic composition of the parish and, as suggested earlier, a change in the socioeconomic composition of the migrant population per se. These issues will be further treated in the next chapter.

## Conclusion

The causes of Portuguese emigration, particularly that which has occurred since 1850, are complex. As Martins (1885:165) has suggested, a combination of factors probably stimulated this massive overflow: Portugal's coastal position, her colonial history, the example set by the "rich returnees" who somehow survived the "meatmarket" in Brazil, and the "laws of subsistence" in the province of Minho and the Azores in particular. Interestingly enough, Martins observed at the same time the paradoxical impact that this emigration had upon population growth: "That in no country, under such conditions, can a population grow or diminish, if not by virtue of the increase or decrease in the amount of food. If there is emigration, more people are born; if there is no emigration, fewer are born." (Martins 1885:164). Habakkuk's (1955) thesis about the relationship between marriage and inheritance patterns, population growth, and emigration is almost embodied in this last phrase, as is the general premise of emigration as a safety valve which, by siphoning off excess population, made it unnecessary for other measures of population control such as reduced fertility to be employed. However, it is not completely clear that the demographic system in northern Portugal worked in precisely the way specified by Martins or theorized by Habakkuk. And there is the element of return in emigration to consider. What is certain is that the parallel phenomena of emigration and return migration have had a significant impact on other aspects of the population history of northern Portugal, and it is to this impact that we now turn.

# CHAPTER THREE

# Family and Household: Nuptiality in Lanheses

## INTRODUCTION

In June of 1882, with a dispensation, Maria Alves da Costa married a second cousin, Manuel Martins. She was thirty-two, the older of two children born to José Correia and Ana Maria da Costa. Her groom was forty-four, the second of eight children (six of whom lived) born to Manuel Martins and Maria Franca. Maria and Manuel were both marrying for the first time, and after their marriage they lived with Maria's widowed mother. During the next decade, they had three children of their own, two of whom (a son and a daughter) survived childhood. Their son, born in 1887, married in 1907 and brought his own bride to live with his parents, Manuel having become head of the household upon his mother-in-law's death in 1906.

Both Manuel and Maria came from lavrador families with long histories in Lanheses. Although we do not know precisely how much land their respective families owned and cultivated, Manuel's mother was among the top seven lavrador families listed in the 1871 arrolamento dos bens, whereas Maria's widowed mother could be classified as a small lavrador. Historical records are silent about the precise reasons why Manuel waited until his forties to marry or why he chose to marry a relative, a woman twelve years his junior.

However, we do know one crucial piece of information about Manuel. Ten years prior to his marriage, in June of 1872, Manuel emigrated to Brazil with his younger brother (by six years), João. In the 1881 rol da desobriga, João and Manuel were still listed as "absent," as were two more of Maria Franca's unwed sons, António and Joaquim. Indeed, the only son who returned to Lanheses to marry was Manuel; the others were lost to parish history forever. Whereas Manuel moved in with his wife's family after his marriage, his only sister and youngest sibling Maria remained with his mother, marrying in 1881 (at age thirty-two) and bringing her husband (who was four years her junior) to live with his mother-in-law. This couple had three daughters, the oldest and youngest of whom died as spinsters in 1975 (at age ninety-two) and 1972 (at age eighty-five), respectively. The middle daughter married in 1915 at age thirty.

A little more than a century before the marriage of Manuel Martins and Maria Alves da Costa, their great-grandparents, António Correia and Isabel da Rocha, were wed. He was twenty-four, the sixth of nine children (though second oldest of those who survived past childhood) born to António Correia and Quitéria Rodrigues, a couple who had moved to Lanheses from Santa Marinha Geraz de Lima across the river. Isabel was twenty-eight, the oldest child of Francisco da Rocha of Meixedo and Maria Alves Lima of Lanheses. Her mother was sixteen at her wedding thirty years earlier, though her maternal grandmother was closer to her own age (twenty-nine) when she married more than a half century earlier, in 1719. António and Isabel had five sons, four of whom grew up and married in Lanheses. All of them were in their twenties and had started their own families well before their parents passed away. The third son, João, Maria Alves da Costa's paternal grandfather, was the last to marry and was the heir to the paternal home and his father's têrço.

These marriages across the generations of a single family illustrate a number of characteristics of nuptiality in Lanheses. They indicate some variations in age at marriage over time as well as among individuals. They suggest a relationship between property, age at marriage, and emigration that is perhaps not as straightforward as has so far been presumed. They allude to permanent female spinsterhood as a phenomenon not to be ignored. And, finally, they hint at the presence of multiple family household arrangements. All of these aspects of marriage are the subject of the present chapter.

## WHEN LANHESANS MARRIED: GENERAL TRENDS IN THE AGE AT MARRIAGE

Perhaps the most significant difference between Manuel Martins and Maria Alves da Costa and their great-grandparents António Correia and Isabel da Rocha was the ages at which they first married, a difference which, at least in this example, is most dramatic for the men. Although there are several short-term fluctuations in the mean age at marriage in the parish of Lanheses between 1700 and the present, in general, ages at marriage for men were on the increase between 1720 and 1780, dropped abruptly during the 1780s, rose again during the two succeeding decades, declined to meet their mid-eighteenth-century levels between 1810 and 1840, and then experienced a dramatic and steady increase to unprecedented levels by the end of the nineteenth century (Figure 3.1). Female mean ages generally followed the same course as those for men, with the exception of the period between 1800 and 1820, when they moved in the opposite direction. It is likely that what caused the variations during this period (essentially effecting a short-term increase in the male mean age at marriage) was the Napoleonic invasion. The final downward trend for both sexes occurred in the present century; yet, a mean age of twenty-six at marriage for women as late as the 1940s is late indeed.

The highest levels for both men and women were reached during the last several decades of the nineteenth century (Table 3.1).[1] Between 1870 and 1879, for example, women were marrying on average 4.4 years later than they had been fifty years earlier; for men, the difference was 4.8 years. Male mean age at marriage reached its peak of almost thirty-two during the final decade of the past century, when female mean age at marriage was beginning its gradual decline. During the first decade of the present century, the average age at which Lanhesan men married declined dramatically (by 4.0 years), a factor that makes the late-nineteenth-century apogee even more intriguing. Another important factor to note is that the mean and median ages for men and women diverge by a greater amount during the final decades of the nineteenth century than in any of the preceding six or

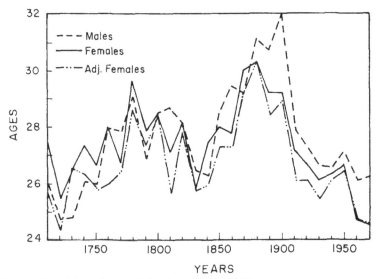

FIGURE 3.1 Mean Ages at Marriage, 1700–1970

TABLE 3.1 MEAN AGE AT MARRIAGE BY SEX FOR TEN-YEAR MARRIAGE
COHORTS, 1700–1970 (those marrying single only)

| | Males | | | | | Females | | | |
|---|---|---|---|---|---|---|---|---|---|
| Period | No. | Mean | Median | Min. | Max. | No. | Mean | Median | Min. | Max. |
| 1700–09 | 28 | 26.1 | 25.0 | 19 | 36 | 39 | 27.6 | 27.0 | 15 | 44 |
| 1710–19 | 23 | 24.8 | 24.0 | 19 | 38 | 31 | 25.5 | 24.0 | 15 | 43 |
| 1720–29 | 27 | 24.9 | 24.0 | 18 | 43 | 41 | 26.5 | 26.0 | 14 | 40 |
| 1730–39 | 28 | 26.1 | 25.0 | 17 | 34 | 41 | 27.4 | 27.0 | 18 | 47 |
| 1740–49 | 22 | 26.0 | 26.5 | 17 | 33 | 39 | 26.7 | 27.0 | 14 | 42 |
| 1750–59 | 19 | 28.0 | 28.0 | 19 | 36 | 31 | 28.1 | 27.0 | 17 | 47 |
| 1760–69 | 32 | 27.9 | 27.0 | 20 | 40 | 37 | 26.8 | 27.0 | 18 | 42 |
| 1770–79 | 37 | 29.1 | 28.0 | 18 | 46 | 43 | 29.7 | 30.0 | 19 | 45 |
| 1780–89 | 33 | 26.9 | 26.0 | 19 | 37 | 36 | 27.9 | 27.0 | 19 | 42 |
| 1790–99 | 30 | 28.5 | 26.0 | 21 | 48 | 35 | 28.5 | 27.0 | 20 | 43 |
| 1800–09 | 27 | 28.7 | 26.0 | 22 | 58 | 32 | 27.1 | 24.5 | 19 | 69 |
| 1810–19 | 36 | 28.2 | 28.0 | 17 | 50 | 46 | 28.1 | 26.0 | 19 | 49 |
| 1820–29 | 30 | 26.5 | 25.0 | 19 | 38 | 37 | 25.8 | 25.0 | 16 | 41 |
| 1830–39 | 45 | 26.3 | 26.0 | 19 | 39 | 57 | 27.4 | 26.0 | 16 | 46 |
| 1840–49 | 43 | 28.5 | 27.0 | 20 | 46 | 50 | 28.0 | 26.0 | 19 | 53 |
| 1850–59 | 49 | 29.5 | 29.0 | 19 | 45 | 62 | 27.8 | 27.0 | 17 | 45 |
| 1860–69 | 47 | 29.2 | 28.0 | 19 | 45 | 50 | 30.0 | 28.5 | 20 | 44 |
| 1870–79 | 62 | 31.1 | 30.0 | 19 | 60 | 64 | 30.3 | 30.5 | 18 | 44 |
| 1880–89 | 70 | 30.7 | 28.5 | 21 | 53 | 76 | 29.2 | 27.0 | 18 | 52 |
| 1890–99 | 55 | 31.9 | 29.0 | 19 | 81 | 57 | 29.2 | 27.0 | 19 | 61 |
| 1900–09 | 71 | 27.9 | 26.0 | 18 | 52 | 75 | 27.2 | 26.0 | 17 | 45 |
| 1910–19 | 47 | 27.3 | 28.0 | 20 | 37 | 49 | 26.7 | 26.0 | 17 | 43 |
| 1920–29 | 68 | 26.6 | 25.5 | 20 | 47 | 72 | 26.1 | 24.0 | 18 | 46 |
| 1930–39 | 79 | 26.5 | 25.0 | 19 | 59 | 81 | 26.3 | 25.0 | 18 | 42 |
| 1940–49 | 96 | 27.1 | 25.0 | 19 | 44 | 100 | 26.6 | 24.0 | 15 | 62 |
| 1950–59 | 100 | 26.1 | 25.0 | 20 | 47 | 100 | 24.8 | 24.0 | 16 | 42 |
| 1960–70 | 134 | 26.2 | 25.0 | 19 | 52 | 138 | 24.5 | 24.0 | 17 | 43 |

NOTE: Cases are omitted from total where no age was available—largely for men born in
other parishes.
SOURCE: Family Reconstitution Data, Lanheses.

seven decades. A similar divergence occurs for men between 1790
and 1809 and for women between 1800 and 1819.

One needs to be cautious with reference to these singulate mean
ages at marriage. If the age at marriage for single individuals marrying widows or widowers is omitted from the calculation (in the standard procedure these ages are included), the mean age, particularly

for women, is appreciably different during certain decades (Figure 3.1—Adjusted Females), frequently by more than a year, in one decade by as much as two years. Throughout much of the first part of the eighteenth century, the mean age for women marrying for the first time hovered around twenty-six, and the means—which approach twenty-seven and twenty-eight prior to 1770—are biased upward by the number of older women who married widowers. Had they not married these widowers, they might not have married at all. Conversely, the high mean ages at marriage at the end of the nineteenth century, especially in the 1870s and the 1890s, as well as the slow decline until 1950, are hardly affected by the remarriage of widowers despite the fact that virtually the same number of widowers remarried single women between 1760 and 1800 as between 1860 and 1900. It should be noted, however, that the decline in the adjusted mean age at marriage for women during the first decade of the twentieth century is somewhat more dramatic.

Frequency distributions for the singulate age at marriage illustrate in a slightly different way the late-nineteenth-century peak that has been referred to (Table 3.2). During the final three decades of the nineteenth century, approximately one-quarter of all the men marrying for the first time in Lanheses were over thirty-five, a proportion unprecedented during any decade before or after. For women, slightly more than a quarter were over age thirty-five during the 1770s, the 1860s, and the 1870s, whereas in the 1780s and 1880s and the first decade of the twentieth century, approximately 20 percent were over age thirty-five. In the 1870s, more than half of both men and women who married were over thirty, and in the 1890s, close to half of the men and a third of the women were over age thirty. Even when the percentages for women marying over thirty and over thirty-five are corrected to exclude those marrying widowers, the level remains high, in some decades higher. In the 1860s and 1870s, virtually all of the late marriages for women are accounted for by factors other than the remarriage of widowers. One further point to note about these frequency distributions is the percentage of women who married under age nineteen. Whereas 10.5 percent of all the women who married in Lanheses between 1700 and 1749 were under nineteen, during the next hundred and fifty years only 4.1 percent married so young, and as late as the 1950s and 1960s the proportions were only 7.9 percent and 8.4 percent, respectively. In short, the level of the 1700–1749 period has not been reached again (Table 3.3).

A final aspect of age at marriage merits brief mention at this point. Until 1850, approximately 7.5 percent of all single men marrying

TABLE 3.2 PROPORTION OF SINGLE MEN AND WOMEN MARRYING
OVER THIRTY AND OVER THIRTY-FIVE BY PERIOD, 1700–1970
(percent)

| | Males | | Females | | | |
|---|---|---|---|---|---|---|
| | | | Over 30 | | Over 35 | |
| Period | Over 30 | Over 35 | A | B | A | B |
| 1700–09 | 25.0 | 7.1 | 35.9 | 22.2 | 10.2 | 3.7 |
| 1710–19 | 8.7 | 8.7 | 22.6 | 16.0 | 9.7 | 4.0 |
| 1720–29 | 11.1 | 3.7 | 24.4 | 27.8 | 12.2 | 13.9 |
| 1730–39 | 17.8 | 0.0 | 24.4 | 15.1 | 12.2 | 6.1 |
| 1740–49 | 27.3 | 0.0 | 30.8 | 22.8 | 10.2 | 8.6 |
| 1750–59 | 31.6 | 10.0 | 32.2 | 20.0 | 12.9 | 0.0 |
| 1760–69 | 37.5 | 9.3 | 29.7 | 31.2 | 8.1 | 6.2 |
| 1770–79 | 37.8 | 13.5 | 48.8 | 40.5 | 27.9 | 21.6 |
| 1780–89 | 33.3 | 6.1 | 41.7 | 35.3 | 19.4 | 14.7 |
| 1790–99 | 30.0 | 16.7 | 40.0 | 38.7 | 14.3 | 16.1 |
| 1800–09 | 25.9 | 14.8 | 25.0 | 22.6 | 6.2 | 3.2 |
| 1810–19 | 25.0 | 13.9 | 30.4 | 28.6 | 17.4 | 14.3 |
| 1820–29 | 33.3 | 10.0 | 18.9 | 16.2 | 18.1 | 5.4 |
| 1830–39 | 15.5 | 2.2 | 29.8 | 14.3 | 12.3 | 6.1 |
| 1840–49 | 34.9 | 9.3 | 36.0 | 31.8 | 14.0 | 11.4 |
| 1850–59 | 46.9 | 12.2 | 33.9 | 30.5 | 16.1 | 11.9 |
| 1860–69 | 44.7 | 19.1 | 46.0 | 40.0 | 28.0 | 31.4 |
| 1870–79 | 52.4 | 25.4 | 56.2 | 56.7 | 28.1 | 28.3 |
| 1880–89 | 44.3 | 24.3 | 40.8 | 34.9 | 19.7 | 15.9 |
| 1890–99 | 49.1 | 25.4 | 33.3 | 36.4 | 14.0 | 16.4 |
| 1900–09 | 30.9 | 14.1 | 28.9 | 24.6 | 19.7 | 15.9 |
| 1910–19 | 31.9 | 10.6 | 34.7 | 25.5 | 10.2 | 2.1 |
| 1920–29 | 22.0 | 5.9 | 25.0 | 21.2 | 11.1 | 10.6 |
| 1930–39 | 24.0 | 3.8 | 20.9 | 20.0 | 1.9 | 8.7 |
| 1940–49 | 23.9 | 13.5 | 27.0 | 27.4 | 13.0 | 12.6 |
| 1950–59 | 17.0 | 3.0 | 14.0 | 17.2 | 3.0 | 12.6 |
| 1960–70 | 16.4 | 2.9 | 11.6 | 10.2 | 2.2 | 1.4 |

NOTE: A. those marrying widowers included; B. those marrying widowers excluded.
SOURCE: Family Reconstitution Data, Lanheses.

single women were ten or more years older than their brides (Table
3.4). Between 1850 and the end of the nineteenth century, this proportion rose to almost 13.5 percent. The percentage of women who
were ten or more years older than their husbands hovered around 4
percent from 1700 to 1949 and then dropped to almost nothing after
1950. In addition, whereas 20 percent of brides were six or more

TABLE 3.3 FREQUENCY DISTRIBUTION OF SINGULATE MEAN AGE AT
MARRIAGE BY SEX AND PERIOD, 1700–1970

| Period | Ages | | | | | | | |
|---|---|---|---|---|---|---|---|---|
| | 14–19 | 20–24 | 25–29 | 30–34 | 35–39 | 40–44 | 45–49 | 50+ |
| | Males | | | | | | | |
| 1700–49 | 10.9 | 36.7 | 34.4 | 14.1 | 3.1 | 0.8 | 0.0 | 0.0 |
| 1750–99 | 2.0 | 29.1 | 34.4 | 23.1 | 6.0 | 3.3 | 0.7 | 0.0 |
| 1800–49 | 2.8 | 27.6 | 43.1 | 17.7 | 5.0 | 1.6 | 1.6 | 0.5 |
| 1850–99 | 1.8 | 19.4 | 31.4 | 25.8 | 9.2 | 6.7 | 2.8 | 2.8 |
| 1900–49 | 2.2 | 37.7 | 34.1 | 16.3 | 4.1 | 4.1 | 0.6 | 0.8 |
| 1950–70 | 1.3 | 39.7 | 42.3 | 13.7 | 1.7 | 0.4 | 0.4 | 0.4 |
| | Females | | | | | | | |
| 1700–49 | 10.5 | 27.7 | 34.0 | 16.7 | 6.3 | 4.2 | 0.5 | 0.0 |
| 1750–99 | 3.8 | 28.0 | 29.1 | 22.1 | 9.9 | 6.0 | 1.0 | 0.0 |
| 1800–49 | 4.5 | 33.3 | 33.3 | 16.7 | 7.2 | 2.7 | 1.3 | 0.9 |
| 1850–99 | 3.9 | 21.0 | 32.4 | 21.0 | 12.0 | 8.1 | 0.6 | 1.0 |
| 1900–49 | 7.9 | 38.7 | 26.8 | 13.5 | 8.5 | 2.6 | 1.1 | 0.8 |
| 1950–70 | 8.4 | 49.1 | 29.8 | 10.1 | 0.8 | 1.3 | 0.4 | 0.0 |

SOURCE: Family Reconstitution Data, Lanheses.

TABLE 3.4 AGE DIFFERENCES BETWEEN HUSBANDS AND WIVES BY
PROPORTION OF MARRIAGES IN EACH CATEGORY, 1700–1969
(those marrying as singles only, in percents of N)

| Period | H > W by | | | | | W > H by | | | | | H = W |
|---|---|---|---|---|---|---|---|---|---|---|---|
| | 1 | 2–3 | 4–5 | 6–9 | 10+ | 1 | 2–3 | 4–5 | 6–9 | 10+ | |
| | | | Years | | | | | Years | | | |
| 1700–1749 | | | | | | | | | | | |
| N = 114 | 2.6 | 19.3 | 10.5 | 8.8 | 8.8 | 3.5 | 7.1 | 13.1 | 12.3 | 4.4 | 9.6 |
| 1750–1799 | | | | | | | | | | | |
| N = 136 | 4.4 | 16.9 | 8.8 | 16.2 | 7.3 | 2.2 | 11.8 | 5.1 | 16.2 | 4.4 | 6.6 |
| 1800–1849 | | | | | | | | | | | |
| N = 166 | 11.4 | 18.7 | 12.0 | 9.0 | 7.2 | 7.2 | 9.6 | 6.6 | 7.8 | 3.8 | 6.6 |
| 1850–1899 | | | | | | | | | | | |
| N = 283 | 7.8 | 13.1 | 8.5 | 11.3 | 13.4 | 5.3 | 11.7 | 8.8 | 7.8 | 4.6 | 7.8 |
| 1900–1949 | | | | | | | | | | | |
| N = 361 | 9.9 | 14.1 | 8.6 | 12.7 | 6.9 | 8.3 | 13.6 | 5.5 | 5.8 | 4.1 | 10.2 |
| 1950–1969 | | | | | | | | | | | |
| N = 223 | 13.4 | 21.1 | 14.3 | 8.9 | 4.0 | 10.8 | 8.5 | 4.5 | 3.1 | 0.4 | 10.8 |

NOTE: The age of one or both spouses was unknown in 71 marriages between 1700 and
1749; in 40 marriages between 1750 and 1799; and in 66 marriages between 1800 and
1849.
SOURCE: Family Reconstitution Data, Lanheses.

years older than their husbands during the latter half of the eighteenth century, only 12 percent had this seniority during the latter half of the nineteenth century. What factors induced young men to select women older than themselves as brides during the first hundred years, and what factors seemingly encouraged a shift in attitude during the next hundred fifty years? In fact, the change in age differences between spouses might not be very important by itself, but taken together with the other changes in the age at which Lanhesans married during the latter half of the nineteenth century, it virtually demands further consideration.

The trends in age at marriage in the parish of Lanheses are characteristic of the region as a whole during the late nineteenth century and the first half of the twentieth century. Livi Bacci (1971:47) demonstrates that in the district of Viana do Castelo the proportion of married women among all women between the ages of twenty and twenty-four is *consistently* the lowest for all continental districts between 1864 and 1940. Furthermore, whereas the greatest incidence of married women between twenty and twenty-four occurred south of the Tagus River in the nineteenth century, the lowest incidence occurred in the north. After 1930, however, the southern districts of Evora and Portalegre begin to appear among the districts with the lowest incidence of women married between twenty and twenty-four.

High ages at marriage are clearly not unique to northern Portuguese rural society. Indeed, they are part of a so-called "western European marriage pattern" first outlined by the historian Hajnal (1965) and documented numerous times since then by family and demographic historians. This pattern, in a good Malthusian tradition, combined a tendency to postponed marriage with high levels of permanent celibacy. Wrigley (1982) has recently suggested a modification in order to point to intermediate forms between west and east. Specifically, he introduces a "Mediterranean" pattern found in southern Europe and characterized by late ages at marriage for men combined with early ages at marriage for women. Thus, whereas in the classic western pattern "there is a small mean age gap between spouses with many first marriages in which the wife is the older partner," in the Mediterranean pattern the mean age gap is large. Despite the fact that Portugal can be considered part of southern Europe, the marriage patterns in Lanheses, and probably throughout northwestern Portugal, are much more compatible with the classic western European pattern than with the Mediterranean pattern. Not only are the mean ages for both men and women high well into the present century, but until the 1940s, 10 percent or more of wives were older than their husbands by six years or more. Indeed, if the anthropologist of European culture areas were to use such demographic phenomena as an indication for the placement of Portugal, or at least northern Portugal, within a broader regional cultural tradition, they would call for inclusion within the northwestern European "Atlantic fringe" together with countries like Ireland and regions of France such as Brittany.[2] What one needs to consider in this light are the social and economic characteristics shared by these countries or regions which have tended to produce similar demographic responses.

Not only have the recent spate of family reconstitution studies demonstrated variations in the mean age at marriage from country to country and region to region, but they have also demonstrated variations in the timing of rises and declines (Gaskin 1978). Unfortunately, many of these studies stop before the middle of the nineteenth century, and the comparative date from 1850 onward derive essentially from aggregate census data. Although late marriage became a disappearing custom in several western European countries by the turn of the twentieth century, it remained prevalent in others (Dixon 1971, 1978, Sklar 1974), most notably Ireland, where as late as 1950 grooms were an average age of thirty-three and brides an average age of twenty-eight.[3] Although northern Portugal was among those regions of western Europe to have retained relatively high mean ages at marriage well into the present century, it has clearly not been as extreme a case as Ireland.

In attempting to understand the trends in nuptiality in Lanheses, particularly in the age at marriage, there are two areas to focus on: first, the reasons for the late-nineteenth-century peak and for the sudden drop after the turn of the twentieth century; and second, the conditions that sustained a relatively high mean age at marriage and certain other characteristics of nuptiality (such as remarriage and age differences) from at least the middle of the eighteenth century until after the Second World War. In the first case, we are clearly dealing with a crisis situation that had an impact on other demographic trends as well; in the second case, we are dealing with one element in a sociodemographic system of long standing.

## CONTINUITY AND CRISIS: MARRIAGE, LAND TENURE, AND EMIGRATION

In the rural areas of "traditional" Europe, it has been suggested that the most crucial variable affecting the timing and extent of nuptiality was the ownership or inheritance of land. Three decades ago, H. J.

Habakkuk (1955) distinguished marriage patterns under different systems of inheritance—partible and impartible. Under an impartible system, one child is favored to inherit the family patrimony while his siblings are forced to emigrate or to work as laborers and to marry late, if at all. This system has been shown to be associated with a stem family form of household structure (Berkner 1976, Goldschmidt and Kunkel 1971). In a partible system, all children receive a share of the patrimony and therefore have some source of economic support. This system is supposedly accompanied by nuclear family households, a greater number of marriages, and earlier marriage. Recently, Berkner and Mendels (1978) have reviewed these arguments, noting that strict impartibility or partibility are ideal types which, in reality, are subject to enormous flexibility. Indeed, where joint family households have been documented, the ideal of partibility is compromised by the practicalities of impartibility. Berkner and Shaffer (1978), in a discussion of the joint family in the Nivernais, demonstrate how the tenuousness of relations between individuals, family groups, and land tenure have ultimately threatened the survival of joint households.[4] One further criticism of this hypothesis can and has been made. The intricacy of rural social structure, both the fact that not all land is locally owned and that not everyone in a local community owned land, complicates a pure relationship between the inheritance of land and the ability and decision to marry. There is clearly some connection between the way in which property was owned and transmitted from one generation to the next and specific demographic phenomena, but to understand that connection it is necessary to understand both the inheritance system in practice and the local economy and social structure associated with it (Berkner and Mendels 1978). Whether property was transmitted at marriage or at death, whether it was divided equally among all offspring or bequeathed in full to a single heir, and whether an heir was defined by birth order or chosen at the discretion of parents are among the important variables to consider.[5]

In the absence of any property records prior to 1940 or of any consistent individual level data on social class prior to 1860, the evidence on land tenure in Lanheses is scanty. However, the discussion of wills contained in Chapter One clearly indicates that the mechanisms for the transference of property in this parish, and probably in other parishes throughout the region, were by no means systematic and uniform.[6] In principle, the underlying ideal was one of partibility, but one child, frequently a daughter and often a daughter who never married, was generally the recipient of the têrço or third share, which usually included the parental home and was bequeathed purely as a matter of parental choice. Although testaments and notarial records indicate that in some instances children were "dowered" at the time of their marriage, this does not appear to have been the norm. Rather, the custom was for post-mortem inheritance with usufruct rights left to the surviving spouse, if there was one, for the duration of his or her life.

The testaments also suggest that in the eighteenth and nineteenth centuries, as in earlier centuries, much of the land in Lanheses was probably farmed under rental or sub-rental contracts of short or long term (*prazos, foros*), that the plots were small, and that many of these contracts were passed on from one generation to the next, thereby creating further subdivisions. Families such as the Pereira-Cyrne/Almadas, the Rego-Barretos, and the Tinocos used the services of jornaleiros or caseiros, or leased their lands to lavradores-rendeiros in the eighteenth century just as they did in the nineteenth and early twentieth centuries. Religious organizations and the local parish church did likewise. Although we do not know precisely what happened to this church property during the 1830s, when national regulations called for the sale of vast quantities of land owned by religious orders, it is apparent that in the early 1870s, when the registration of all foros was required by law, a number of plots in Lanheses were still farmed in this manner.

Where Lanheses *foreiros* who appeared on an 1875 list found in the Municipal Archives in Viana do Castelo could be linked to heads of households appearing on the 1871 arrolamento dos bens, the majority were small-scale lavradores with property assessed at 0$540 or 0$960 reis. Indeed, the fact that in this 1871 arrolamento more than 60 percent of the heads of household who were called lavradores were assessed at under 1$000 is a clear indication of the small amounts of land which they owned outright. Although this excessive fragmentation was no doubt aggravated during the latter part of the nineteenth century, it is probably safe to conclude that the bulk of Lanhesan families, during the eighteenth as well as the nineteenth centuries, were supporting themselves on small amounts of land, and that many of them were farming land they did not own and were therefore faced with annual rents which, in bad harvest years, may have been hard to meet.

These facts, as well as the fact that the bequeathing of property in Lanheses was discretionary, generally post-mortem, and semi-egalitarian are reflected in the absence of the clear-cut patterns in certain aspects of demographic behavior that have been found in other areas, particularly in areas where impartibility and perhaps primogeniture were practiced. In these latter areas, to the extent that individuals relied upon land for their livelihood, each new generation had to await the passing on (or retirement) of an earlier generation before it could assume control of the family patrimony. Philip Greven (1970), for example, has demonstrated the way in which delays in the transmission of land from parents to children effectively influenced the postponement of marriage for younger sons in seventeenth- and eighteenth-century Andover, Massachusetts. Although Vinovskis (1974) has criticized some aspects of Greven's analysis,[7] a number of scholars have essentially accepted this so-called marriage-inheritance hypothesis, demonstrating, for example, correlations between a father's age at death and the age at which his children married (Smith 1978). The implication of Smith's argument, as mentioned earlier, is that only with the death of a father will title to land be passed on to his son, thereby facilitating marriage. The focus on the father's age at death assumes a patriarchal order of things which is not totally appropriate in the northwestern Portuguese context, where women inherited equally and frequently remained as heads of households in widowhood. Yet, for comparative purposes it is useful to begin by examining the relationship between these two variables (father's age at death and mean age at marriage for offspring) for the Lanheses data.

Table 3.5 shows the mean age at marriage by father's age at death (below or above sixty) for birth cohorts of both sons and daughters

TABLE 3.5 MEAN AGE AT MARRIAGE BY FATHER'S AGE AT DEATH, 1700–1949 (by birth cohorts of children born to complete marriages)

| Birth Cohort | Father Died under 60 Years | | | | Father Died over 60 Years | | | | | |
| | Sons | | Daughters | | Sons | | | Daughters | | |
| | No. | $\overline{X}$ | No. | $\overline{X}$ | No. | $\overline{X}$ | % Waiting | No. | $\overline{X}$ | % Waiting |
|---|---|---|---|---|---|---|---|---|---|---|
| 1700–1749 | 17 | 27.5 | 32 | 29.1 | 59 | 28.9 | 20.3% | 68 | 26.9 | 14.5% |
| 1750–1799 | 32 | 27.7 | 46 | 27.1 | 48 | 28.2 | 24.5% | 60 | 27.8 | 16.4% |
| 1800–1849 | 41 | 29.4 | 55 | 27.2 | 70 | 31.7 | 32.8% | 86 | 30.2 | 24.2% |
| 1850–1899 | 26 | 26.2 | 36 | 27.2 | 92 | 28.7 | 26.1% | 120 | 28.7 | 22.5% |
| 1900–1949 | 47 | 26.4 | 43 | 25.0 | 163 | 27.5 | 17.8% | 154 | 27.7 | 22.1% |

NOTE: $\overline{X}$ indicates mean age at marriage.
SOURCE: Family Reconstitution Data, Lanheses.

between 1700 and 1949. The differences (over sixty mean minus under sixty mean) for each cohort are as follows:

| Cohorts | Sons | Daughters |
|---------|------|-----------|
| 1700–49 | + 1.4 | + 2.2 |
| 1750–99 | + 0.5 | + 0.7 |
| 1800–49 | + 2.3 | + 3.0 |
| 1850–99 | + 2.5 | + 1.5 |
| 1900–49 | + 1.1 | + 2.7 |

With the exception of the birth cohort born during the latter half of the eighteenth century which, for the last decade or two, would correspond roughly to marriages occurring in the post-Napoleonic period when overall mean ages at marriage were declining, there appears to have been some relationship between father's age at death and the mean age at marriage of both sons and daughters in Lanheses. Yet, if we examine the same data according to whether the marriages of sons or daughters occurred before or after the death of a father who was more than sixty when he died, the relationship is not as clear-cut. Only about one-quarter of those sons and daughters whose fathers died over age sixty waited until after the death of their fathers to marry.

Although the birth cohort of the early nineteenth century clearly stands out, it is important to realize that many of the young men and women included in this cohort were marrying after 1850 as age at marriage itself rose in response, in part, to the changing economic conditions that characterized this half century of crisis. In essence, although a father's age at death, and the inheritance of property that may have been associated with it, might have had some influence upon the timing of marriage for some segment of the Lanhesan population, it was a less determinative relationship in this northwestern Portuguese parish than it was, for example, in the New England towns of Andover and Hingham. We have to consider the fact that for many Lanhesan families who owned very little land (the lavradores-rendeiros) or none at all (the caseiros and jornaleiros), inheritance of property from a father or mother would clearly have mattered little. Indeed, it is probably wiser to argue that the postponement of a marriage while a father was still alive was motivated more by the desire of parents to maintain the labor or potential income of unmarried children, both sons and daughters, for as long as possible.[8] If the present is any example for the past, young men and young women, working as day laborers, domestic servants, or in any other income-producing activity, surrendered the bulk of what they earned to their parents.

A village byway, lugar de corredoura

Looking onto the lugar da feira

Jornaleiro houses

Lavrador houses

Solar of the Almada family

A "Casa Francesa" built by a recent emigrant to France

The primary school built in the 1930s

Old pottery and tile factory

The parish church

Parish priest (1927-1967) with communicants

Village chapel

Chapel of Senhor do Cruzeiro

Mordomas in procession at the festa

Woman at work husking corn

The testaments demonstrate that money made by unmarried sons working in Spain was often given to parents, and that this donation to the household was remembered at the death of the senior generation. Alternatively, parents may have put a certain portion of what their children earned aside to form part of a marriage gift or trousseau. Certainly this is a practice that has continued into the post-World War II period.

Ideally, to support the arguments which suggest that the age at marriage may only have been linked to the inheritance of property for a certain segment of the population who had enough property to matter, we need data on the socioeconomic status of individuals. Unfortunately, these data are lacking prior to 1860. However, the post-1860 data reveal a few intriguing associations. Table 3.6 categorizes the mean ages at marriage for men and women according to the husband's profession (as listed on the marriage register) between 1860 and 1949. Unfortunately, though characteristically, all lavradores were classified together, and clearly as a group were marrying later than either jornaleiros or artisans. The number of jornaleiros prior to 1890 is too small to warrant discussion, but it is curious that although both the lavrador group and the artisan and craftsmen groups experienced very dramatic decreases in the mean age of men at marriage during the first decade of the twentieth century, the jornaleiro group experienced an increase of almost two years in their mean age at marriage. At the same time, almost double the total number of male jornaleiros married in the parish. Half of these men were the sons of lavradores, and almost as many were jornaleiros from other parishes.

Both these factors are symptomatic of the endemic and progressive proletarianization of the northern Portuguese countryside during the late nineteenth century, which not only swelled the ranks of the landless but also stimulated massive emigration. In short, several of these turn-of-the-century jornaleiros were recent members of the small lavrador class, and in the short run probably still held the world view of their small-scale peasant parents. They too may have been delaying marriage in the hope of acquiring money to buy land of their own, thereby reestablishing themselves in the propertied class. The other curious factor to note about these jornaleiros is that, except in the first decade of the twentieth century, they were generally marrying women who were older than themselves. A perusal of individual cases indicates that most commonly the women themselves were also jornaleiras, that none of the marriages was precipitated by a premarital pregnancy, and that in several cases the couples were described as poor (the epithet *mendigos* [beggars] was ascribed to them at the

TABLE 3.6 MEAN AGES AT MARRIAGE FOR MEN AND WOMEN BY
HUSBAND'S PROFESSION, 1860–1949
(single grooms marrying single brides)

| Year | Lavradores | | Jornaleiros | | Artisans | | Craftsmen | |
|------|-----|-----|-----|-----|-----|-----|-----|-----|
| | M | F | M | F | M | F | M | F |
| 1860–1869 | 30.1 (28) | 29.6 (28) | 24.5 (2) | 25.5 (2) | 27.7 (7) | 25.3 (7) | 27.8 (8) | 31.4 (8) |
| 1870–1879 | 32.4 (35) | 31.3 (35) | 25.2 (5) | 34.2 (5) | 29.0 (12) | 27.4 (12) | 26.0 (8) | 26.4 (8) |
| 1880–1889 | 31.5 (36) | 28.9 (36) | 31.6 (5) | 31.8 (5) | 30.2 (17) | 28.0 (17) | 26.5 (10) | 25.7 (10) |
| 1890–1899 | 33.9 (29) | 29.4 (29) | 26.9 (11) | 28.9 (11) | 29.2 (4) | 25.2 (4) | 29.6 (10) | 24.0 (10) |
| 1900–1909 | 28.5 (29) | 27.4 (29) | 28.8 (20) | 25.3 (20) | 23.0 (7) | 24.1 (7) | 26.3 (12) | 26.2 (12) |
| 1910–1919 | 32.0 (17) | 27.5 (17) | 22.7 (6) | 24.8 (6) | 25.7 (11) | 25.4 (11) | 26.5 (8) | 25.7 (8) |
| 1920–1929 | 26.9 (29) | 26.2 (29) | 23.0 (11) | 30.2 (11) | 26.7 (16) | 24.4 (16) | 24.6 (15) | 23.3 (15) |
| 1930–1939 | 26.6 (40) | 26.5 (40) | 25.5 (11) | 25.9 (11) | 27.7 (13) | 26.1 (13) | 25.8 (13) | 27.4 (13) |
| 1940–1949 | 28.4 (33) | 27.7 (33) | 29.0 (17) | 31.0 (17) | 26.2 (24) | 24.9 (24) | 25.4 (10) | 23.5 (10) |

NOTE: Included in the artisans' category are masons, carpenters, stuccoers, and painters;
    included in the craftsmen's category are potters, tailors, shoemakers, basketmakers,
    blacksmiths, boatsmen, and barbers; excluded from consideration are merchants, phar-
    macists, soldiers, bus drivers, and clerks.
SOURCE: Family Reconstitution Data, Lanheses.

death of one or the other of the spouses). Can we interpret these as
opportunistic marriages on the part of the young jornaleiro male?
Certainly, no land was involved. To the issues of age differences and
of "opportunistic" marriages I will return later in this section.

While Table 3.6 tends to indicate that until 1920 those men and
women whose livelihood depended most directly on the access to
property that they could farm themselves married later, but that the
relationship between land and marriage is not as clear-cut in this
region of northwestern Portugal as it is in other areas of Europe. The
same can be said about the relationship between land and emigration. As noted above, Habakkuk (1955) and those who have based
their explorations of impartible inheritance on his thesis have sug-

gested that such a system results in a limitation of the total number of marriages (low nuptiality), a high level of outmigration and/or permanent celibacy, and slow population growth, whereas partibility results in increasing land fragmentation, rapid population growth, high rates of marriage, and low rates of permanent celibacy.

What seems to have been overlooked in most of the discussions that spring from Habakkuk's original formulations is that both systems of inheritance can be and are associated with geographic mobility. The important point is that the character of this mobility differs and that this difference has a significant effect on the character of nuptiality. As Habakkuk himself observed,

> Long distance migration for seasonal or short periods was common throughout Europe, whatever the prevailing rules of inheritance. There is something to be said for the view that equal division prompted such migration (as a) method by which the sons of a peasant household who enjoyed a certain expectation of a share in the patrimonial property could acquire money to enlarge their holdings and supplement their family income. . . . Seasonal migration was not an escape from the peasant family, but a condition of its survival. The peasant went, not to acquire a new occupation in a different society, but to improve his position in the old. (Habakkuk 1955:7)

The anthropologist Eric Wolf, in a study of two villages in the Italian Tyrol, points to precisely this difference. In the village of St. Felix, where land is impartibly inherited, younger siblings who migrate become "socially irrelevant to the family remaining in the village," whereas in the village of Tret, where land is divided equally among all heirs, "the ties with migrant children and kin are maintained" (Wolf 1962:19).

The distinction that Habakkuk and Wolf make between permanent and temporary migration is crucial to an understanding of nuptiality in northwestern Portugal and in Lanheses, given the "ideology of return" described in the previous chapter. Migrant children were certainly remembered by their parents as they wrote their wills. Reconsider Isabel Francisca de Castro, who asked in her will of 1843 that the portion to which her son Frutuoso, "absent in America for some time," was entitled should "remain in abeyance until his death was verified." These were not disinherited offspring who were sent off and forgotten by their family remaining in the village.

Given the nature of emigration from northwestern Portugal, it is possible to argue first, that the high ages of marriage in Lanheses, as well as certain characteristics of age differences that were mentioned earlier, are related at least in part to a system of land fragmentation and small-scale ownership, combined very frequently with tenant farming, that has always made it necessary for potential heirs to migrate to establish themselves in independent households and to supplement the income they could expect (if they had any such expectation) to receive from land to which they would eventually have title; second, that an increase toward the end of the eighteenth century in the number of young men who went to Spain to make some money before settling down may have contributed to the short-term rise in the age at marriage at that time, and that both may have been responses to short-lived economic and political difficulties in the nation as a whole; third, that the dramatic increase in the age at marriage at the end of the nineteenth century is explained not only by an aggravation of the land fragmentation process and a general worsening of economic conditions, but also by a change in the character of emigration from predominantly seasonal migration to Spain to more long-distance migration to Brazil; and fourth, that both these migration streams (to Spain and to Brazil) occurred within the context of an expectation of return, despite the fact that many who left never came back. If marriage was to be postponed for economic reasons, emigration was the means to an end, but as a means it may have operated to further postpone marriage if not, as we will see, eliminate it entirely.

Essentially, I am arguing that in the context of extensive land fragmentation and the delayed transfer of what little property was owned or cultivated by any one family, what the majority of young men expected they might inherit or what their future wife might inherit was insufficient to sustain a family, and therefore that many of them, prior to their marriage, went abroad to Spain or Brazil to earn money to buy land or to build a house or both. Even the acquisition of a rented prazo required capital to purchase a team of oxen and a plow. Thus, the determining factor in when and who married among the offspring of any particular couple was not necessarily who was to inherit the patrimony, but the fact that what was to be inherited was rarely sufficient to support an independent household. Young men were very often forced to seek alternative sources of income that would permit them to marry, and in a region where opportunities for lucrative, salaried nonagricultural labor were limited, emigration offered the best chance. If young men postponed their marriages, then so too did young women. Courtships of five or more years were perfectly acceptable. The following popular song expresses allegorically a young man's request that his *namorada* wait for him:

> Rosa que está na roseira
> Deixa-te estar até ver
> Que eu vou ao Brasil e venho
> Inda te hei de vir colher

> Rose on the rosebush
> Stay there until you see
> That I go to Brazil and return
> Still to come and gather you

The data that I will draw upon to support the above propositions about the intervening effect of emigration on age at marriage are neither systematic nor rigorous, because of the difficulties of documenting emigration at the local level. However, I think they are sufficient to suggest that more attention should be paid to different patterns of and motives for migration as they affect nuptiality. The first piece of evidence comes from the marriage registers themselves. Throughout most of the two-and-a-half centuries between 1700 and 1950, it seems that grooms were required to "justify their free state" or "justify their absences" (account for their time as bachelors, and presumably prove that they had no other wife) at the time of their marriage. Although we do not know how faithfully the priests in Lanheses recorded this fact on the marriage record (indeed, it seems that the priest who officiated during the final decade of the nineteenth century and the first decade of the twentieth century, as well as Padre Couto who succeeded him [1911–1926] did not make notes of these justifications), the number of times that they do appear provides some indication of the extensiveness of emigration prior to marriage.

During the first half of the eighteenth century, 12 percent of the grooms who married in Lanheses "justified their absences," most of them for the period of time that they had spent in Spain, a few for migration to other parts of Portugal. The mean age of marriage for this group of grooms was 24.9, below the overall mean for all grooms marrying within the parish at this time. However, many of the grooms of these decades were from other parishes, and we do not have their ages at marriage. Furthermore, in the 1720s almost half the men who married had been absent, and their mean age at marriage (27.4) was well above that for the marriage cohort of this decade as a whole.

Indeed, it is during the 1720s and 1730s that these justifications of absence for the first part of the eighteenth century are concentrated.

Between 1750 and 1790, either there was little emigration, or the priests were negligent in their record of justifications of absences, or no young men who emigrated returned to marry in the parish. The death records tend to suggest one of the latter two conclusions. During those forty years, twenty-four obituary notices of young Lanhesan men who died in Spain were recorded. Most of them were in their twenties. Eleven more notices recorded the deaths of single men in Brazil and Lisbon, although three of those who died in Brazil may have departed as early as the 1730s or 1740s—they were each over fifty at their deaths. In addition, there were ten obituaries for married men who died abroad, mostly in Spain, during the same time period. Although these may not seem like very many deaths, one has to remember that not all deaths abroad were reported back to the parish, and that many of those who emigrated did not return (though they may have intended to), or returned to marry elsewhere.[9]

These death records lend further support to the conclusion that throughout the eighteenth century emigration was a fact of life in the parish of Lanheses. Indeed, during the last two decades of that century, it seems to have become more extensive. Between 1790 and 1799, there were eleven notices of young Lanhesan men who had died in Spain and, in addition, twenty-six of the forty-three men who married in the parish during that decade had been in Spain, one had been in Brazil, and six more in other parts of Portugal. The mean age at marriage for these men was 29.5, a year older than the mean age for the marital cohort as a whole. This trend of emigration to Spain continued into the first decades of the nineteenth century: twenty-four men who married between 1800 and 1809 had been "absent," as had seventeen of those marrying in the succeeding decade. Their mean ages at marriage were 28.3 and 31.7, respectively. During the next several decades, between 1830 and 1870, the notations of absences dwindled off once more, although again we cannot be certain as to whether this was due to an oversight on the priest's part or an actual decline in the number of young men who went to Spain. No deaths of young Lanhesan men abroad were reported during the 1820s, 1830s, and 1840s, and during these and the subsequent two decades only twenty-two grooms justified their absences, an average of approximately four per decade. The average age at which these men married once they had returned to the parish remained, however, higher than that of the male population as a whole (30.6).

In the 1870s and 1880s, eighteen young men acknowledged a period of emigration, eight of them in Spain, seven in Brazil, and three in other parts of Portugal (Coimbra and Lisbon). The mean age at marriage of these men was 35.4 years, and for those who went to Brazil, 38.0 years. Curiously, all but one of these Brazilian returned emigrants married women who were related to them, three of them, like Manuel Martins, whose marriage to Maria Alves da Costa opened this chapter, within the third degree of consanguinity (second cousins) and three within the second degree of consanguinity (first cousins). The average age at marriage for these seven brides was 32.7. This behavior cannot be explained with any assurance, but it may have been an attempt in the face of increasing economic straits to combine wealth, that perhaps brought back by the emigrant with the land which he and a close cousin could reunite through their marriage. Such consanguineous marriages are discussed further later in the section.

Although these justifications of absence in no way represent the extent of emigration from Lanheses during the late nineteenth century (clearly many left and never returned), it is interesting to look at the two peaks in emigration—during the last two or three decades of the eighteenth century and during the last decades of the nineteenth century— in broader economic terms. Based on on tabulations for the regional market of Ponte de Lima kept by the Miseracordia (Reis 1980), Figure 3.2 plots the fluctuations in the prices of both wheat and corn from the mid-eighteenth to the early twentieth centuries. These fluctuations provide a general indication of the economic well-being of a region. The prices of these two major cereals began to rise dramatically in 1790, and had skyrocketed by 1815. Between 1815 and 1850 they turned downward. In 1866, there was a worldwide depression that had an impact on the Portuguese economy, causing a sudden drop in export prices and a rise in unemployment. The port of Viana do Castelo was importing almost everything except corn and potatoes and, even so, the price of corn rose between 1850 and 1885, although not as dramatically as it had during the early nineteenth century. After a momentary drop, it continued its slow rise, remaining high during the first two decades of the twentieth century. Prices of other major commodities also experienced sharp increases between the 1840s and the 1860s: meat rose by approximately 60 percent; coffee by 140 percent; oil by 48 percent; wine by 200 percent; and rents by 40 percent (Sampaio 1978).

The trends in the prices of grain in the Lima Valley do tend to correlate roughly with fluctuations in the age of marriage in Lanheses, and broadly coincide with identifiable periods of significant emigra-

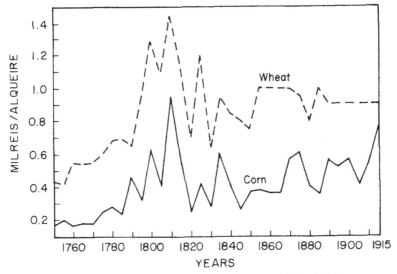

FIGURE 3.2 Prices in the Market of Ponte de Lima, 1750–1915

tion, as well. All three were on the rise by the last decades of the eighteenth century. The first two decades of the nineteenth century were undoubtedly decades of chaos. Napoleon's troops assaulted the northern countryside, arriving in 1809 during the month of April and disrupting the sowing season. The crisis into which these invasions led the country may very well have disrupted marriage plans for the peasants of northern Portugal, including Lanheses. Indeed, although there are no documents to confirm it, it is possible that young Lanhesan men were called up to serve in the army, or that they emigrated to Spain in order to avoid military service. Certainly in the latter case there are subsequent parallels during World War I, and more recently in the massive and clandestine emigration flow to France to avoid service in the African colonial wars. As was noted in Chapter Two, popular folklore abounds with indications of the distaste for military service among the northern Portuguese peasantry, and there are extant military lists (of males between the ages of seventeen and thirty-nine who are subject to recruitment) which date to the early nineteenth century for the District of Viana do Castelo, although none for Lanheses itself has as yet been found.[10]

Although the years succeeding the Napoleonic invasion were by no means peaceful politically, there is a close correspondance during the 1820s and 1830s between the declining mean ages at marriage for both men and women in Lanheses and the falling off of grain prices in the region. Compared to the decades preceding and succeeding them, the 1820s and 1830s were probably relatively stable economically, at least within the rural context. There is virtually no solid evidence on local emigration trends during this period. However, during the last decades of the nineteenth century all three began to rise again, although prices rose less dramatically than previously, indicating a new phase of economic difficulties for the country and the region.[11]

As mentioned above, during the first decades of the twentieth century the records of justifications of absence are negligible and most certainly inaccurate, given the knowledge of the extent of emigration to Brazil that comes to us through other documentary sources and through oral history. However, it is also true that many of these early-twentieth-century departures occurred after marriage rather than before, and therefore had an impact on fertility different from the impact mediated through advanced ages at marriage. This problem is discussed in the next chapter. Only in the last several years of the 1920s and during the 1930s do justifications of absences appear again, most of them for periods of time spent in Spain. For the entire period between 1900 and 1949, the marriage registers record thirty-three young men who justified their time away from the parish, seventeen of these in Spain, two in Brazil, and fourteen with no precise location given. The mean age at marriage for these men was 28.8 years.

Ethnographic evidence suggests that the seasonal migrations to Spain occurred primarily during the late fall and winter months, when agricultural work in Portugal was less demanding. If this was true, then it might have had a visible effect on the seasonality of marriages, as well as on the seasonality of conceptions in the case of married migrants. Although the latter phenomenon will be discussed in the next chapter, variations over time in the proportions of marriages by season may further elucidate periods of extensive or less extensive migration among the young unmarried male population. Table 3.7 presents these proportions by month of marriage beginning in 1700 and ending in 1970. The latter half of the eighteenth century certainly stands out, with almost half the marriages occurring during the summer harvest months of July, August, and September. If this period is examined more closely, it appears that in the 1760s, 1770s, and 1780s in particular, more than 65 percent (and in two of those decades as high as 76 percent) of marriages were celebrated between April and September. This is also true for the first decade of the nineteenth century. Conversely, the disproportionate concentration of marriages in these summer months falls off during the 1820s and 1830s. It is

TABLE 3.7 SEASONALITY OF MARRIAGES BY MONTH AND
HALF-CENTURY, 1700–1949 (as percent of total)

|  | 1700–49 | 1750–99 | 1800–49 | 1850–99 | 1900–49 | 1950–70 |
|---|---|---|---|---|---|---|
| January | 10.6 | 2.4 | 6.7 | 5.5 | 9.1 | 23.3 |
| February | 7.7 | 6.2 | 4.3 | 10.0 | 9.1 | 10.0 |
| March | 3.6 | 3.8 | 1.6 | 4.2 | 4.7 | 3.3 |
| April | 4.1 | 4.3 | 7.4 | 5.5 | 7.2 | 7.1 |
| May | 6.5 | 5.7 | 8.2 | 6.7 | 9.8 | 5.8 |
| June | 13.0 | 8.1 | 10.9 | 10.3 | 6.2 | 4.5 |
| July | 7.7 | 17.6 | 13.7 | 9.4 | 7.5 | 3.7 |
| August | 11.4 | 21.9 | 11.8 | 14.0 | 8.0 | 12.1 |
| September | 8.9 | 10.5 | 12.9 | 14.0 | 10.9 | 7.9 |
| October | 13.8 | 8.1 | 10.6 | 9.7 | 9.6 | 6.2 |
| November | 10.2 | 9.0 | 5.9 | 6.1 | 10.4 | 5.4 |
| December | 2.4 | 2.4 | 5.9 | 4.5 | 7.5 | 10.4 |

SOURCE: Parish registers, Lanheses.

possible that during these years seasonal migrations did decline. Certainly, the mean age at marriage dropped. That the later nineteenth century does not experience as dramatic an increase as the later eighteenth century could be explained by the fact that by this time the predominant form of migration was to Brazil, and that the optimum time for travel overseas was during the spring, summer, and fall, and not in the winter. Furthermore, we are clearly no longer talking about a seasonal migration, despite the fact that several Lanhesans apparently traveled back and forth to Brazil more than once. Even so, more than a quarter of the marriages contracted during the latter half of the nineteenth century occurred during the two months of August and September.

Although the argument here may be somewhat stretched, it is interesting to note that during periods when we know that there was little emigration from the parish—between 1914 and 1918 and again between 1940 and 1945—more marriages took place between the months of October and March than between April and September. This is a pattern characteristic of a strictly agrarian community, where spring and summer are taken up with too many cultivating activities to leave time for the "frivolity" of weddings.[12] The latter pattern, curiously, emerges most strongly during the two decades between 1950 and 1970, when a full third of the marriages celebrated in the parish occurred in December and January. To my mind this is explained not by the disappearance of seasonal migration but by a new schedule of seasonality. By the late 1950s, men from Lanheses were emigrating to France to work in construction. Clearly, the off-season in this business occurred during the winter months, and at that time many came home. In fact, during the decade of the 1960s the disproportion in favor of January marriages emerges most strongly, with 45 of the 138 marriages for the entire decade occuring in that month.

The rois da desobriga provide us with complementary data on emigration and age at marriage. As mentioned in the previous chapter, on each of these lists the parish priest recorded absences from the village. When these lists are compared with family reconstitution data, it is possible to discern from among the young men marked absent at one point or another which ones returned to marry in the parish. Although the numbers in no way represent the total number of those who returned as opposed to those who remained abroad (some may have returned and married in another parish), it is possible to take the subsample of those who married in Lanheses and compare the average age at which they married to the mean age at marriage for the population as a whole. A further limitation is that these lists do not tell us where the young men returned from. We can only surmise, given the extensiveness of emigration to Brazil throughout northwestern Portugal by the last decades of the nineteenth century, that this was a probable destination for many of them.

In general, throughout the late nineteenth century the mean ages at marriage for these returned emigrants are above the mean for the marrying male population as a whole, averaging approximately 32.8 years for those linked to the rois of 1850, 1870, 1881, 1887, and 1892. Furthermore, during the 1880s and 1890s the proportion of marriages in the parish that involved a returned emigrant were 26 and 33 percent, respectively. These represented a significant increase from 16 percent of the marriages contracted during the 1870s. The proportion of marriages involving a returned emigrant during the first decade of the twentieth century declined to 20 percent, but rose again to 26 percent of the marriages between 1910 and 1919.

Since these rois are by no means a totally accurate accounting of the emigration of single men from Lanheses, the above proportions for all decades are probably low estimates, and the conclusion one is led to is that the delayed marriages of returned migrants may indeed have contributed to the particularly high mean ages at marriage for the village population as a whole during the late nineteenth century.

In this light, it is intriguing to return to the changes in age differences between spouses outlined in Table 3.4. Although one can only speculate about these figures, I see three possible explanations that can be associated with emigration. One is that among the marriages between a man and a woman ten or more years his junior were several contracted by returned male emigrants who, when they arrived back in the village, found few women within their close age cohort who were not already married. However, given the high rates of female spinsterhood in Lanheses throughout the late nineteenth century, a phenomenon to which we will return in the next section of this chapter, this does not seem likely unless we reason that only the most "undesirable" women (in domestic and agricultural skills and social position, as well as in physical appearance) were left among the women who were in their thirties and still spinsters.

A second possibility is that returning emigrants may have been viewed by younger women as attractive prospects for husbands. They may indeed have come home with enough money to establish a new household or buy some land. However, among those young men who were recorded as absent on one or more rois who married in the parish in the 1870s, 1880s, or 1890s, only one-fifth (10/50) married women ten years or more younger than themselves. Two married women substantially older than themselves, one by as much as seventeen years. Almost half (22/50) married women close to themselves in age (0–3 years older or younger), suggesting that these couples were namorados (fiancés) who had simply postponed their marriage, the young women faithfully waiting for their beaus to return from abroad. Indeed, the growing spinster population of the late nineteenth century probably included several young women whose fiancés never returned.

A third explanation rests in the demography of age-sex ratios. As young men reached their twenties, they emigrated. Some young women who preferred to marry rather than wait or face the prospect of spinsterhood had to look to older men, whether emigrants or not, as potential husbands, since many of the men who were closer to their own age were absent. The mean age at marriage of women who married men ten or more years older than themselves in the 1870s, 1880s, and 1890s was 27.4, as compared to an average mean for the entire population marrying during these three decades of 29.6. Furthermore, among those women who married between twenty and twenty-four during the last three decades of the nineteenth century, 25 percent (10/40) married men ten or more years older than themselves. Although the numbers are too small to offer conclusive support to one explanation over another (indeed both arguments may be needed to explain individual cases), they do suggest a possible relationship between male emigration and an increase in the proportion of brides taking substantially older grooms during the late nineteenth century.

Of course, there are other potential explanations for the age differences between spouses that are more directly associated with land tenure and inheritance. Bell (1979), for example, views it as evidence of parental control in the contracting of marriages. Curiously, however, in Nissoria, the southern Italian village that he describes as "populated by pure peasants," and where 80 percent of family heads were medium or small-scale landowners who occasionally supplemented their income from the land with additional work (that is, where the economy appears to have been most like that of Lanheses), 60 percent of females were under twenty-one at marriage. Unfortunately, Bell provides no comparable figures for males, although by all indications they were older, and therefore demonstrate the so-called Mediterranean demographic pattern. Certainly, these very young Italian brides may have been more susceptible to parental choices for actual partners than were the brides of Lanheses, only a third of whom, until 1900, were under twenty-five at the time of their marriage. Even as late as 1970, the proportion of brides who were under twenty-five at marriage was less than 60 percent. Furthermore, throughout the eighteenth and nineteenth centuries, between 40 and 50 percent of the marriages in Lanheses were contracted between young people who were only a few years apart in age, if not of the same age. This could suggest a substantial amount of individual choice in mate selection, which apparently has increased with the unfolding of the twentieth century, such that approximately 65 percent of the marriages between 1950 and 1969 were contracted between young people who differed from zero to three years in age.

None of this negates the fact, however, that marriages where parents had an influential role in the selection of a spouse—that is, marriages of *interesse* (of economic interest)—did occur. Indeed, Lanhesans today talk of these in references to the past, but describe them as having been most common among the well-to-do lavradores. And as indications of this element of interesse, they are more likely to point to marriages contracted between relatives, to a marriage between a young man and an older woman, or to the marriage of a single man to a widow.

Clearly, a marriage with a close relative could serve as a mechanism for averting land fragmentation and maintaining certain properties within the family, especially in a region where women were as likely to inherit as men. As one informant put it, "two related families see properties next to one another which they farm independently. They think that if there was a marriage between them these two properties could be reunited in the next generation and divided among the children of one couple rather than among the children of two couples." Generally, however, when asked about such consanguineal marriages, Lanhesans tended to compare their own village with the neighboring village of Fontão, and to claim that among the richer lavradores of the latter, marriages between cousins were more common. Yet, an analysis of the parish records reveals that such marriages were certainly not uncommon in Lanheses. Table 3.8 indicates that the number of consanguineous marriages increased during the nineteenth century, although it was by no means negligible during the eighteenth century. Even in the twentieth century, and despite the fact that the proportions are low, the bulk of such marriages were those requiring dispensations for a second-degree (first cousin) or third-degree (second cousin) relationship. In fact, if we recalculate these proportions to take account of endogamous marriages only—where both bride and groom were natives of the parish—the percentages are more dramatic.

| | |
|---|---|
| 1700–1749 | 19.9% |
| 1750–1799 | 17.3% |
| 1800–1849 | 32.9% |
| 1850–1899 | 30.5% |
| 1900–1949 | 11.4% |

Lanhesans are not, however, totally misguided in their perception of the state of affairs with respect to cousin marriage in their parish, for it is true more often than not that when we have some evidence of the socioeconomic status of the bride and groom involved in a consanguineal marriage, particularly one of the second or third degree, they are young people from the more well-to-do lavrador families in the parish. The case opening this chapter provides one example. So too do the marriages over successive generations of the well-to-do Artilheiro family.

In July of 1762, Manuel Alves Artilheiro married a fourth cousin, Maria Luisa de Castro. They had six children, but only the three youngest sons survived to adulthood. The eldest of these, Manuel, never married. He was the recipient of his mother's têrço, and in all the electoral rolls of the mid-nineteenth century he was assessed at the upper end of the socioeconomic scale. Although he remained a bachelor, in 1820 a certain Rita Exposta, a woman whose name indicates that she was abandoned at birth and most likely worked as a

TABLE 3.8 MARRIAGES WITH DISPENSATIONS OF CONSANGUINITY
AND AFFINITY, 1700–1949

| Period | Consanguinity | | | | Affinity | | | |
|---|---|---|---|---|---|---|---|---|
| | 2° | 3° | 4° | % Consang. within 4° | 1° | 2° | 3° | 4° |
| 1700–1749 | 0 | 14 | 17 | 12.6 | 0 | 1 | 1 | 1 |
| 1750–1799 | 2 | 8 | 17 | 12.8 | 0 | 0 | 1 | 0 |
| 1800–1849 | 3 | 24 | 23 | 19.5 | 0 | 1 | 5 | 1 |
| 1850–1899 | 9 | 22 | 26 | 17.3 | 2 | 1 | 0 | 2 |
| 1900–1949 | 8 | 19 | 3 | 7.7 | 0 | 0 | 0 | 0 |
| 1950–1959 | 3 | 5 | 0 | 7.8 | 0 | 0 | 0 | 0 |

NOTE: Several of these marriages had consanguineal and/or affinal ties along more than
one genealogical line. They have been classified according to the highest level of consanguinity (2>4). One marriage was classified as consanguineal because of an "illicit
copulation" with a cousin of the bride. Another was classified as first-degree affinity
because of "carnal copulation" with a sister of the bride.

The 1900–1949 period may be underrepresented. The priest of Lanheses between
1911 and 1926 was negligent in making a note of dispensations and justifications of
absence on the marriage register. This underrepresentation may also be due to the fact
that in 1917 the official ban on marriages within the fourth degree (third cousins)
established by the Catholic Church in the sixteenth century was lifted.

SOURCE: Parish registers, Lanheses.

domestic servant in Lanheses (perhaps for Manuel Artilheiro junior),
gave birth to Manuel junior's illegitimate daughter Camilla Rosa. In
1843, Camilla Rosa married her first cousin and Manuel's twenty-
one-year-old nephew José Luiz, the youngest son of Manuel's brother
Domingos. This young couple moved in with Manuel and inherited
his property upon his death in 1859.

José Luiz and Camilla Rosa had ten children. A daughter Maria
das Dores, who was born in 1857, married her first cousin António
José Alves Pinto in 1882. He was fifteen years her senior, a son of
the parish apothecary, and had spent many years in Brazil prior to
his marriage. Maria das Dores, who outlived her husband, was a
wealthy landowner of the early twentieth century, labeled a *lavradeira abastada* by villagers who remember her. The youngest son of
José Luiz and Camilla Rosa, João Luiz, married Maria Rosa Castro
in 1891, when he was twenty-seven and she was thirty. Maria Rosa
and João Luiz were first and second cousins along one genealogical
line and second and third cousins along the other. One of their
daughters, known colloquially as Maria Barbosa, was also labeled as
"woman of property."

Among the descendents of Manuel Alves Artilheiro junior's other brothers, there were also several close consanguineal marriages. One great-nephew, Manuel José Marinho, married a second cousin, Rosa Franco, in 1861, when she was forty and he only twenty-six. Another, António Monteiro, married a first cousin of his father in 1890, when he was twenty-nine. His bride was forty-nine. A third, Maria José Monteiro, married a first cousin, Manuel António de Castro, in 1905, when she was forty-two and he twenty-six. Clearly the age gaps in these three marriages, with the wives appreciably older than their husbands, is not to be ignored. It is probably a very precise indication of a marriage of interest in which the larger kinship group was involved and in cases where the brides were substantial heirs. Furthermore, it was a fairly safe guarantee that few offspring would be born, thereby permitting the realignment of properties in future generations. Certainly in António Monteiro's case we can wonder about the affection he felt towards a wife so much older. At the turn of the century, he emigrated to Brazil, although there was no financial need to do so. When his wife died in 1919, António took up with one of the domestic servants in the household, a thirty-five-year-old illegitimately born jornaleira from Moreira de Lima. Seven months after the death of his first wife, he married her. She was pregnant with his child.

Indeed, if the fact that women were as likely to inherit as men made marriages between cousins good matches, it also made widows and older women in general attractive prospects for younger men. Although widower remarriage was motivated more by the need to find a woman to replace a dead wife than by economic considerations, particularly if one was left with children to raise, the same cannot necessarily be claimed for widow remarriage. When one discusses remarriage with female villagers today, they speak disapprovingly, fearing that a stepfather for their children might not be the best solution, since he would "never love them as their natural father," and certainly throughout Lanheses' history widow remarriage has been less frequent than widower remarriage. When it occurred, it was often to younger and as yet unmarried men, and in several instances the widow was pregnant at the time of her marriage. From the widow's perspective, this may have been a means of entrapment. Furthermore, a younger man over whom, simply by virtue of seniority in age of more than ten years, she would have had greater control and influence, would have been a good choice in light of the fears of abusive stepfathers.[13] From the young man's perspective, such a marriage may have been particularly advantageous. His wife was already established in a household, and she probably had land under cultivation to which she held actual or usufruct rights. The same could be said for young men who married older but as yet unmarried women. Very often, these older women were the ones who had remained with their parents until their death and were therefore the recipients of their têrços. In short, the fact that women were frequent heirs adds another dimension to certain characteristics of age differences between spouses.

The proportions of marriages of men to women ten years older than themselves remained steady at roughly 4 percent of all marriages celebrated in the parish between 1700 and 1949. During the two decades between 1950 and 1970, this proportion was negligible, and the proportion of women who were from one to nine years older than their husbands fell to below 30 percent for the first time in Lanheses' history. This may be an indication of the diminishing importance of land as a factor crucial to a marriage decision, and therefore reflect a move toward a choice of marriage partners made purely on the basis of romantic interest rather than economic interest. Yet, I am by no means convinced that "love marriages" and individual choices were not present in the historical past, as well. Popular songs and poetry abound with references to romantic interests and romantic attachments (Cortesão 1942). Furthermore, we have to consider the independence, both financial and emotional, vis-à-vis a family of orientation developed by those young men who had emigrated to Spain and to Brazil and who returned with cash to help their parents buy more land, pay off debts, or aid in the marriage of another sibling. That parents recognized this independence and respected their sons for it is evident in their wills when they tried to isolate the contributions of these emigrant sons to the family patrimony.

Nevertheless, even for those who chose a marriage partner on their own, economic considerations were of vital importance to the timing of marriage, indeed, even to the fact of marriage. The gold chains worn by peasant brides of Minho as part of the traditional wedding costume were viewed as a statement of wealth in hand, and poor was the bride who went to church without any gold around her neck, even if some of it was borrowed. Land, however, as a source of steady income, or the promise of some sort of supplementary income through emigration and/or the development of a craft was the real prerequisite to the establishment of a new household. One informant who waited until he was thirty before marrying a woman of similar age said it was because he had no money, "certainly not enough to start a family." He added that one of his sisters had married earlier, had many children, and lived in misery. This was a strong deterrent to his own early marriage. Although the shorter childbearing period of his thirty-year-old wife was not necessarily a conscious motive for waiting, what this man was expressing was an awareness that many children meant economic hardship.

The preceding discussion has delineated a complex relationship between land tenure, emigration, and age at marriage. Although no claim is being made that emigration is the direct and only cause of delays in the age at which young people contracted marriages in the parish, it clearly had this consequence, since it was rarely conceived of as a permanent departure. The sounder conclusion, perhaps, is that short-term increases in the emigration flow were themselves symptomatic of worsening economic, if not political, conditions, and that both emigration and delayed marriages were responses to those conditions. The sudden drop in the mean age at marriage at the dawn of the twentieth century simply reflected a return to more customary levels. Yet emigration did not decline at the same time. What did occur, however, was a change in the composition of the emigrant population and in the socioeconomic character of the parish population in general. More of the men who emigrated were already married. Although there have always been married male emigrants, their numbers increased because the ranks of the rural proletariat and the small-scale lavrador increased.

Whereas lavradores comprised almost two-thirds of the male heads of household listed on the 1871 arrolamento dos bens, they made up only a third on a 1945 list of resident proprietors prepared to serve as the basis for a municipal tax. Another third in 1945 was composed of propertyless jornaleiros and so-called *trabalhadores rurais* (rural workers). Almost 11 percent of the population in 1945 comprised individuals classified as *proprietários*, and among them were Miguel Tinoco and the Conde Almada. These were clearly the largest landowners and, in addition to the "rural aristocrats," included a number of families who were independently identified as *lavradores abastados* by village informants, or who had made their money in nonagricultural activities and used it to purchase property in the parish.[14] In 1871, 8.8 percent (six) of the lavrador households were taxed at an amount over 2$000.

The fact that almost a third of the residents of the parish were landless by the mid-twentieth century may contribute significantly to an explanation of the steady decline in the mean age at marriage. Acquiring land, whether through purchase or bequest, prior to marriage was becoming increasingly unimportant or hopeless for a greater segment of the population. In the parish today, there is virtually no emphasis placed upon owning property or having access to farmland as a prerequisite to marriage. "Today," said one old-timer, "the swallows marry and then make their nest."

New opportunities have emerged in the post-World War II era, including the development of several local and regional industries. In Lanheses itself, enterprising men have introduced olive oil processing, lumber processing, and sand dredging for cement. To the east, in the parish of Santa Comba, a cheese factory was opened in the early 1950s. To the west, in the parish of Santa Marta, Germans have built a textile factory. Across the river at Darque, a pulp processing factory was built in the early 1970s. Lanhesans work in each of these. Finally, there is work to be had in a booming local construction industry, itself the result of the most recent emigration flow—that to northern Europe. Indeed, much of the valuable farmland is being converted into lots for the new houses—the so-called *casas franceses*—which the emigrants to France have built. This in itself is a clear indication that it is no longer viewed as a primary source of livelihood. As a consequence, some elderly parents are dividing their land early. The favoring of unmarried daughters as recipients of the paternal home and the têrço still exists, however, although the motive of social insurance is less pressing since the introduction of rural pensions in the post-Salazar era.

Villagers view France as the most lucrative destination to date, if not as a savior for their poor country. With good jobs abroad, there is no reason to postpone marriage. Indeed, for the first time in Portuguese history, and beginning in the mid-1960s, women have emigrated on a par with men, some of them single, some of them married. Furthermore, until the mid-1970s remittances flowing back from France created a new prosperity throughout northwestern Portugal. Indeed, it may be that the increase in the volume of remittances from Brazil during the years just prior to World War I created a similar, though short-lived, prosperity throughout the province of Minho, which initiated the decline in the mean age at marriage in Lanheses from its late-nineteenth-century peak. Yet, for all of these most recent changes, and despite the two periods of crisis in the late eighteenth and the late nineteenth centuries, the trends in age at marriage in Lanheses reflect a certain continuity. In 1950, men and women were marrying on average at approximately the same stage of life as they were in 1700. Only time will tell if the drop to a mean age of twenty-four for women in the 1960s and 1970s will be followed by a drop in the male mean age, and if in time the decline will proceed even further.

## NON-MARRIAGE: THE CELIBATE POPULATION

Manuel Martins' younger sister had three daughters, only one of whom—the middle one—married. The other two died as spinsters, one in her eighties, the other in her nineties. Indeed, equally important as the age at marriage to an understanding of the character of nuptiality in Lanheses is the extent of permanent celibacy.[15] Although the timing and degree of nuptiality are generally discussed together, recently a few scholars (Brandes 1976, Dixon 1971) have suggested that they may not, in fact, be as closely related as we would expect. In order to explain the lack of patterned congruence between these two phenomena, Dixon outlines three important factors that appear to intervene between social structure and nuptiality: the feasibility of marriage, the availability of mates, and the desirability of marriage. The first encompasses economic conditions; the second, the demographic structure; and the third, cultural features.

With regard to economic feasibility, clearly some of the same factors that supposedly influence the age at marriage probably influence the degree of marriage; again, the most significant of these, as well as the most commonly explored, is the pattern of inheritance. To return once again to Habakkuk's original formulation: where land is passed on intact to a single heir, there are high levels of outmigration and/or permanent celibacy; conversely, where it is divided equally among all offspring, nuptiality rates are high and lifelong bachelorhood or spinsterhood is at a minimum. The predictable connection between impartible inheritance, nonmarriage, and emigration has been demonstrated repeatedly by anthropologists and historians alike (Abelson 1978, Bauer 1983, Berkner 1972, Bourdieu 1962, Douglass 1974, Goody 1973, Iszaevich 1974), the archetypal example being post-famine Ireland (Arensberg and Kimball 1940, Connell 1968). That between partible inheritance and a supposedly low incidence of permanent celibacy has received less attention, perhaps because the relationship is less clear-cut, and partible inheritance is itself an ideal type that is often not rigorously adhered to in practice or custom.

Northwestern Portugal presents us with a situation in which a tendency toward an equal division of property after the designation of the têrço (resulting over the centuries in a high degree of minifundia) is nevertheless associated with extensive permanent celibacy, primarily among the female population. Indeed, it is important to consider quite seriously variations in the composition of the celibate population by sex. As Knodel and Maynes (1976) conclude in their study of differences in urban and rural marriage patterns in Imperial Germany,

> the sex ratio is most strongly related with the male-female differences in nuptiality rather than with either male or female nuptiality separately since it is the marriage probability of one sex *relative* to the other that is most directly influenced by sex ratios. (Knodel and Maynes 1976:154; emphasis added)

Within northwestern Portugal, it is the district of Viana do Castelo which has, at least since the later nineteenth century, had the highest levels of spinsterhood (Livi Bacci 1971:49). To explore, therefore, to the extent that we are able, the causes and character of spinsterhood in Lanheses (a parish at the heart of this district) should prove fruitful to a fuller understanding of nonmarriage in general. Table 3.9 illustrates the patterns of permanent celibacy in Lanheses between 1860 and the present, based on the number of men and women dying over age fifty who are still single. Since the quality of the death records improved after 1860, and age at death was itself included on the obituary notice, it is only from this point on that we can be certain of the accuracy of this particular measure. This still provides an indication of the likelihood of marriage for birth cohorts from approximately 1810 on. Table 3.10 gives the distribution according to marital status and sex for Lanhesans who died between 1750 and 1859. This distribution is based on whether an individual was registered as *solteiro/a* (single), *casado/a* (married), or *viuvo/a* (widowed) on the obituary. All those who could be positively identified as infants or children (under age twenty) at their death were eliminated from the "singles" category. Similarly, young adults in their twenties, including young men who died in Spain, were also eliminated. However, due to certain limitations imposed by the problems of record linkage, no age could be established for many among those included in the "singles" category on Table 3.10.[16] Thus, the proportions dying single should be taken only as an indication of the parameters for permanent spinsterhood or bachelorhood prior to 1860. They are probably all somewhat high.

Focusing for the moment on the post-1860 data, it is clear that in Lanheses, as throughout northwestern Portugal, nonmarriage was consistently and distinctively higher for women than for men. It also demonstrates that the likelihood of a woman marrying became less

TABLE 3.9 PROPORTION CELIBATE IN LANHESES, 1860–1970
(based on proportion of those dying over 50 who are single)

| Period | Females | | Males | |
|---|---|---|---|---|
| | No. Deaths | % Celibate[a] | No. Deaths | % Celibate[a] |
| 1860–69[b] | 62 | 33.9 | 40 | 10.0 |
| 1870–79[c] | 63 | 33.3 | 42 | 11.9 |
| 1880–89 | 55 | 18.2 | 43 | 11.6 |
| 1890–99 | 70 | 24.3 | 49 | 8.2 |
| 1900–09 | 74 | 33.8 | 43 | 9.3 |
| 1910–19[d] | 71 | 28.2 | 49 | 6.5 |
| 1920–29 | 64 | 37.5 | 44 | 4.5 |
| 1930–39 | 61 | 32.8 | 32 | 6.3 |
| 1940–49[e] | 68 | 29.4 | 47 | 6.4 |
| 1950–59 | 69 | 24.6 | 46 | 15.2 |
| 1960–70[f] | 64 | 31.2 | 49 | 10.2 |

[a] Included among celibate men are four priests; among celibate women, one nun.
[b] One male of unknown age excluded.
[c] Three females of unknown age excluded.
[d] One divorced male excluded.
[e] One male and one female of unknown ages excluded.
[f] Three females and one male of unknown ages excluded.
SOURCE: Parish registers, Lanheses.


TABLE 3.10 DISTRIBUTION OF DEATHS BY MARITAL STATUS AND SEX, 1750–1859

| Period | Females | | | | | | Males | | | | | |
|---|---|---|---|---|---|---|---|---|---|---|---|---|
| | Single* | | Married | | Widowed | | Single* | | Married | | Widowed | |
| | No. | % | No. | % | No. | % | No. | % | No. | % | No. | % |
| 1750–1759 | 22 | 33.3 | 23 | 34.8 | 21 | 31.8 | 15 | 28.3 | 26 | 49.0 | 12 | 22.6 |
| 1760–1769 | 12 | 19.7 | 29 | 47.5 | 20 | 32.8 | 13 | 30.2 | 22 | 51.2 | 8 | 18.6 |
| 1770–1779 | 14 | 35.9 | 9 | 23.1 | 16 | 41.0 | 6 | 18.2 | 14 | 42.4 | 13 | 39.4 |
| 1780–1789 | 25 | 40.3 | 22 | 35.5 | 15 | 24.2 | 11 | 27.5 | 19 | 47.5 | 10 | 25.0 |
| 1790–1799 | 20 | 36.4 | 27 | 49.1 | 8 | 14.5 | 8 | 14.3 | 24 | 42.8 | 24 | 42.8 |
| 1800–1809 | 13 | 21.7 | 24 | 40.0 | 23 | 38.3 | 11 | 22.9 | 22 | 45.8 | 15 | 31.2 |
| 1810–1819 | 17 | 28.8 | 20 | 33.9 | 22 | 37.3 | 16 | 39.0 | 15 | 36.6 | 10 | 24.4 |
| 1820–1829 | 21 | 35.6 | 15 | 25.4 | 23 | 38.9 | 1 | 2.4 | 21 | 50.0 | 20 | 47.6 |
| 1830–1839 | 20 | 29.8 | 23 | 34.3 | 24 | 35.8 | 8 | 16.6 | 20 | 41.7 | 20 | 41.7 |
| 1840–1849 | 19 | 40.4 | 16 | 34.0 | 12 | 25.5 | 6 | 16.2 | 16 | 43.2 | 15 | 40.5 |
| 1850–1859 | 24 | 32.9 | 24 | 32.9 | 25 | 34.2 | 18 | 32.1 | 26 | 46.4 | 12 | 21.4 |

* Excludes all those who died as infants or children (under 20), and many of those identified to have been in their twenties at the time of their death.
SOURCE: Parish registers, Lanheses.

and less toward the end of the nineteenth century and during the first decade of the twentieth century. This is reflected in the high percentages of women over fifty who died single in the 1920s and 1930s and who would have reached marriage age in the 1870s, 1880s, and early 1890s. This is at precisely the same period that the age at marriage reached unprecedented levels, suggesting that in Lanheses and probably throughout the region, there was indeed a close connection between these two phenomena, both probably affected by the dire economic conditions of the late nineteenth century. The highest level of permanent male celibacy occurs several decades later (in the 1950s), corresponding roughly to cohorts born between 1870 and 1900 who would have reached marriage age during the latter 1890s and the first two decades of the twentieth century. Whatever was influencing female nonmarriage, especially during the final decade of the nineteenth century, also seems to have affected male nonmarriage, although to a lesser extent. Conversely, and perhaps of greater interest, is the fact that the male cohort corresponding to the cohort of women who experienced the highest levels of permanent celibacy (those who died between 1920 and 1939) had the lowest levels of permanent celibacy. Although the economic conditions of the late nineteenth century may have had their impact in raising the levels of permanent celibacy for both men and women, the variations in the extent of nonmarriage for these corresponding male and female death cohorts suggests that the demographic imbalance in the population resulting from the male-biased pattern of emigration must have been significant in increasing the likelihood of permanent spinsterhood among the female population of Lanheses and rural Minho in general. At the height of emigration in the late nineteenth century, there were simply not enough young men available for marriage.

Although probably enhanced during the late nineteenth century, the relationship between male emigration and spinsterhood is, I think, a longstanding one in Lanheses. The data are less rigorous prior to 1860, and yet there are some indications that justify such a claim. We have already noticed that prior to the mid-nineteenth century, one of the major destinations for Lanhesan emigrants was Spain, and that many young men had to justify their absences prior to their marriage. A more or less constant phenomenon within the demographic history of the parish, the migratory movement to the neighboring Iberian kingdom seems to have increased significantly during the last decades of the eighteenth century. If the marriage registers provide us with indications of this movement, so too do the death registers.

Although some of those who died abroad were married men, the majority were young (in their twenties) and single, adventurous youths who had gone to Spain to make some money to enable them to buy land, a team of oxen, or a house, and therefore to marry. Such goals were clearly achieved by some, as was pointed out in Chapter One in the discussion of the wills of Lanhesans from the mid-eighteenth century on, in which migratory sons were frequently mentioned. Others were not so successful, meeting their end on foreign soil. Indeed, during certain decades such deaths of young Lanhesan men who were in Spain was disproportionate both to the number of young men who died in their twenties who had remained in the parish, and to the number of young Lanhesan women in this age group who died. Clearly, one result was a depletion of the population of marriageable spouses for the young women of the village. Furthermore, it is important to emphasize again that we do not know how many more died abroad whose deaths were not reported to the priest in Lanheses, and we can therefore probably assume that these figures are a low estimate of this phenomenon.

If these notices represent only partially the extent of the migratory movement to Spain, then the increase in the number of women who died single during certain decades of the late eighteenth century or in the early to mid-nineteenth century begins to make sense, although we do not know for many of these women the ages at which they died and therefore whether we can indeed consider them spinsters. For example, the death cohorts of the 1780s and 1790s would correspond to young women who reached marriage age somewhere during the middle third of the eighteenth century, a time when, it seems, the emigration of young Lanhesan males to Spain was already a regularly established movement. In the 1790s, of the twenty women included in the *solteira* category on Table 3.10, eleven are known to have been over fifty and therefore permanent celibates. Five of the thirteen dying in the succeeding decade have been established as being over fifty. The 1840 to 1849 death cohort corresponds at the upper age levels to women who would have reached marriage age during the 1790s, clearly a period when migration to Spain was quite extensive. Seven of the women who died "solteira" have been positively identified as being over fifty at their death.

Although this is not "hard" evidence, as it includes only those few women who were described as "solteira" by the priest in the obituary notice and could be matched without question to a birth record, it does at least suggest the possibility of a relationship between male emigration and female spinsterhood in Lanheses during the eighteenth and nineteenth centuries. Certainly one further factor to consider, although there is no documented evidence to support it, is the number of these spinsters who may have been betrothed to young men who went abroad to try to make a fortune. They waited for year after year, never receiving any word as to whether their namorado was alive or dead, until they reached an age when there was no longer much hope for marriage.

That the relationship between the demographic structure and non-marriage should not be dispensed with as easily as, for example, Brandes (1976) does in his micro-level study of a parish in Spain is corroborated by a comparison with other situations in which the sexual composition of the celibate population differs from that characteristic of northwestern Portugal. Patrice Bourdelais (1981) documents especially high rates of female celibacy in specific regions of France (Brittany, the eastern and central mountains) during the latter half of the nineteenth century, and raises the possibility that at least some of this (especially in the mountainous regions) can be linked with male emigration. Conversely, Jegouzo and Brangeon (1974) have linked recent high rates of male celibacy in rural France with the departure of women who are disenchanted with life in the countryside and with the prospects it has to offer them. The same can be said for rural Ireland throughout much of the late nineteenth century and most of the twentieth century. Indeed, the comparison between northern Portugal and rural Ireland is quite revealing.

In Ireland, women have predominated among the population of emigrants, a fact little appreciated despite Ravenstein's reference to it almost a century ago in his discussion of the "laws of migration" (1885). This has been true, as Kennedy (1973) has pointed out in his study of Irish demographic history, for all periods except those in which there were major wars involving Britain that took men out of the countryside—the Boer War and the two World Wars of the present century. Scheper-Hughes further substantiates this pattern in her study of the rural Country Kerry parish of Ballybran.

Although fleeting courtships and flirtations occur between adolescent secondary school pupils during the year, a trail of broken romances follows each summer at graduation time, when the vivacious and mobile young women migrate. They leave behind a large proportion of their beaus who are committed, as the girls are not, to carrying on the family farm and name—a task rendered

> more absurd each year as these men come to recognize that they
> are not likely to produce any heir of their own. (Scheper-Hughes
> 1979a:53)

Clearly these Irish "colleens" are as put off by their future in the countryside as the young French girls referred to by Jegouzo and Brangeon. The result has been that in rural Ireland, as in parts of rural France today, male celibacy has exceeded female celibacy.

It is important to consider further the impetus for these differently sex-biased migration streams. In Ireland, young women were free, if not encouraged, to emigrate, despite the extremely patriarchal and male-dominant character of Irish rural society. Indeed, given the system of impartible male-heir inheritance that was reestablished in the country after the Great Famine, it is understandable that a young woman would choose to emigrate rather than to spend her life as a celibate spinster working for her parents or for her brother and sister-in-law. Kennedy (1973:7) has described the choice quite precisely, not as one "between rural unemployment or urban work as a domestic servant, but rather a choice between the subordinate role of an unpaid helper in her own family and the freedom and independence which a paying job in a distant city promised." Furthermore, as Kennedy himself points out, there were enormous opportunities for Irish women in Britain and in America, in countries where their maternal tongue was spoken and where the status of women, as a result of various emancipation movements, was much greater than in Ireland.

Portugal clearly differs from Ireland in a number of ways. First, married women were not free by law to emigrate without the permission of a husband, and single women under twenty-one had to have their father's permission (and when they did, it was generally for short distance and short-term movement to work in domestic or agricultural service). In fact, custom required securing a father's permission long after the legal age of majority was reached. The restrictive laws on female emigration remained in effect into the 1960s and, consequently, affected the movement of women who wished to take part in the most recent phase of Portuguese emigration, that to France. Coincident with these legal restrictions was a negative attitude toward female migration that has also persisted well into the mid-twentieth century. It was believed that young women who left their father's household would be led astray and hence become "used goods." As we will see in Chapter Five, such an assessment was frequently borne out. Young men in the village did not want to marry these girls and thus any girl who hoped for marriage thought twice about migration, even on a short-term basis. Furthermore, to be forced to send a daughter out into service was an indication of poverty, a factor that made these young women that much more undesirable as potential spouses.

A second difference between rural Ireland and northwestern rural Portugal, one that has already been noted repeatedly, is the fact that in Portugal there is no discrimination against daughters as potential heirs, as there is in Ireland. Indeed, the wills demonstrate that in many instances they were favored. As heirs, and frequent recipients of the têrço, women had a certain independence and, therefore, a certain status denied to women in rural Ireland.

Third, the division of labor in Portugal has been such that women perform a large share of the major agricultural tasks. These agricultural responsibilities have been an important deterrent to female emigration, although initially they may have been assumed by women who were replacing migrating males. They have given women in rural Portugal a certain freedom of movement outside the household and, in the case of married women, enhanced their power and influence within the family. Migration on any more than a regional and temporary basis was unnecessary and, especially in the case of more well-to-do lavrador families who needed all the labor they could get, undesirable. It is interesting to note in this vein that as rural Ireland has become increasingly mechanized, especially after 1950, the emigration of Irish males has increased significantly (Kennedy 1973).

In northwestern Portugal and in Lanheses, daughters were a definite economic asset and their labor contributions to the household were at least as important as those of sons. Fathers may have preferred to keep them unmarried for as long as possible, or unmarried altogether in order to retain them as an economic resource; the fact that many of them waited until their father's death to marry is an indication of this. And many of those who waited found themselves beyond a "marriageable age," *dura* (literally, hard; a reference to undesirable; *pão duro* is stale bread), as the Portuguese would say. Differences in the expectations or expected roles for sons and daughters, men and women, can account to a large extent for variations by sex in both patterns of emigration and permanent celibacy.

Yet, as mentioned above, there has been some recent questioning of the emphasis placed upon the sex ratio as the major determinant of the extent and character of nonmarriage. Brandes (1976:208), for example, has warned that it is frequently "impossible to determine the group within which the sex ratio should be considered." Lanhes-

Table 3.11 Marital Endogamy and Exogamy in Lanheses, 1700–1969

| Period | Endogamous Marriages | | Exogamous Marriages | | | Both Bride and Groom Nonnative |
| | No. | % | Total No. | % Groom Nonnative | % Bride Nonnative | No. |
|---|---|---|---|---|---|---|
| 1700–1749 | 156 | 68.4 | 72 | 90.3 | 9.7 | 18 |
| 1750–1799 | 156 | 76.5 | 48 | 81.2 | 19.8 | 7 |
| 1800–1849 | 152 | 66.1 | 78 | 87.2 | 12.8 | 22 |
| 1850–1899 | 187 | 59.7 | 126 | 77.0 | 23.0 | 16 |
| 1900–1949 | 264 | 69.3 | 117 | 88.0 | 12.0 | 1 |
| 1950–1969 | 145 | 60.4 | 95 | 74.7 | 25.3 | 9 |

Note: Native and nonnative are defined by birth in or outside the parish. Thus, among those classified as nonnatives there may be individuals who, although born elsewhere, may have been residing in Lanheses in the years preceding their marriage.

Source: Parish registers, Lanheses.

ans have always married with outsiders—with people from the surrounding villages and sometimes from more distant regions, including Spain. Since at least 1700, between one-quarter and one-third of all the marriages celebrated in the parish have been between a native bride and non-native groom or vice versa, the former clearly being more prevalent given the greater tendency to marry in the bride's village (Table 3.11). Yet, in the Portuguese case this reaching out beyond the frontiers of the parish does not, I think, diminish the importance of the so-called "availability of mates" and its impact on nonmarriage, for within the district of Viana do Castelo as a whole the sex ratio imbalance of the unmarried population has been great since at least the late nineteenth century, and probably even earlier. Indeed, between 80 and 90 percent of all the exogamous marriages in Lanheses were contracted with other natives of the district, a third of these throughout the nineteenth century with individuals from the immediately neighboring villages of Meixedo, Vila Mou, Fontão, and S. Pedro de Arcos (Table 3.12). In fact, the figures on exogamous marriages add another dimension to the crisis situation of the late nineteenth century. Not only did the proportion of endogamous marriages drop to below 60 percent for the first time, but the number of exogamous marriages with spouses originating from a concelho other than Viana do Castelo rose to close to 20 percent. Both phenomena are indications of the greater mobility of the rural population—even the female population—at this time.

TABLE 3.12 PLACE OF BIRTH OF NONNATIVE SPOUSES, 1700–1969

| | Non-Native Spouse From | | | | | | | |
|---|---|---|---|---|---|---|---|---|
| | Neigh-boring Village | | Same Concelho (Viana) | | Neigh-boring Concelho (Ponte de Lima) | | Different Concelho | | Foreign Country |
| Period | No. | % | No. | % | No. | % | No. | % | No. |
| 1700–1749 | 30 | 41.7 | 20 | 27.8 | 15 | 20.8 | 6 | 8.3 | 1 |
| 1750–1799 | 22 | 45.8 | 12 | 25.0 | 6 | 12.5 | 8 | 16.7 | 0 |
| 1800–1849 | 26 | 33.3 | 24 | 30.8 | 10 | 12.8 | 13 | 16.7 | 5 |
| 1850–1899 | 42 | 33.3 | 39 | 30.9 | 20 | 15.9 | 23 | 18.2 | 2 |
| 1900–1949 | 59 | 50.4 | 27 | 23.1 | 14 | 11.9 | 17 | 14.5 | 0 |
| 1950–1969 | 32 | 33.7 | 23 | 24.2 | 20 | 21.0 | 17 | 17.9 | 3 |

NOTE: Neighboring villages include Vila Mou, Meixedo, Fontão, and S. Pedro de Arcos; only those marriages in which one of the spouses is a nonnative are included on this table; throughout the eighteenth and nineteenth centuries, the foreigners who married Lanhesans were all natives of Spain.

SOURCE: Parish registers, Lanheses.

There is, however, significant merit to Brandes' question of why, if men are in such a favorable position to marry, there are celibate men at all. In short, this brings us to the desirability of marriage and to a range of other social and cultural factors that may have been important in determining the extent of spinsterhood or bachelorhood. Dixon (1971:222), adopting the female perspective, has argued that the desirability of marriage is determined by "the availability of social and institutional alternatives to marriage and childbearing and by the extent to which these alternatives are considered rewarding." Clearly, where women could support themselves without the aid of a husband, through agricultural work and with the expectation of title to some land and possibly a house, the pressures and the necessity to marry may not have been great; nonmarriage was thus economically viable. Furthermore, the stigma attached to the single status would have been minimal where such a status was as common as it was in rural Portugal from at least the mid-eighteenth century on; nonmarriage was thus socially viable. Third, whereas the Civil Code gave a certain degree of autonomy to single girls who were over twenty-one, married women were under the complete authority of their husbands; nonmarriage was thus legally attractive. Finally, although we cannot be sure whether approval was bestowed before or after the fact, there are numerous proverbs and popular songs within the folkloric culture of northern Portugal that glorify spinsterhood and denigrate marriage, and which embody, therefore, a definite and prevalent cultural attitude.[17]

Antes que cases, vê o que fazes
Before you marry, watch what you are doing

Solteirinha não te cases. Goza-te de boa vontade
Single one do not marry. Enjoy yourself at will

Mãe o que é casar? Filha é penar, parir, chorar!
Mother, what is marriage?
Daughter it is trouble, giving birth, and tears!

Quando eu era solteirinha, usava fitas aos milhos.
Agora sou casada, traga lágrimas nos olhos.

When I was single, I used ribbons and ties
Now that I am married, I have tears in my eyes.

Eu casei-me, cativei-me
Troquei a prata ao cobre
Troquei minha liberdade
Por dinheiro que não corre

I married and entrapped myself
I exchanged silver for copper
I bartered my freedom
For money which does not flow

Solteirinha solta solta
Casada, prisão, prisão
Mais vale uma só solteira
Que quantas casadas hão

Single one, flee, flee
Marriage is a prison, a prison
One unmarried woman is of more
Value than all the married women
    there are

Although Brandes suggests that few in the village of Becedas in Spain would choose to remain single, the popular adages and songs cited above suggest that among Portuguese women, celibate "bliss" may have been viewed as preferable to wedded "misery." This attitude has been corroborated by several Lanhesans in discussions of their own spinsterhood or that of a relative or fellow villager. They spoke of the "fear" of marriage, of the fear of hunger and poverty that might accompany the task of establishing a new household and of having to nurture the endless stream of children that might be born. Such fears, some said, were greater in the past when there was more economic hardship than there is today. Some simply decided that they would be better off remaining in their father's household. Others, claimed that it was their father who discouraged a marriage because he did not want to see them worse off than they were in his household. Such, for example, was the reasoning of José dos Santos, a shrewd businessman who made and traded in leather goods used in farm work and whose household was *uma casa farta* (a household of abundance), according to several local residents.

José and his wife Virginia had ten children between 1896 and 1914. The eldest and only surviving son was born in December of 1896. He was followed by four daughters. The first, Teresa, was born in 1899 and in 1922 married João da Costa, a stone mason who worked here and there (he was absent from the parish in the 1924 and 1927 rois), "cared little for his wife, and never amounted to much." Teresa bore four children (of whom three lived) before dying of a pulmonary infection in 1930. The next two daughters of José and Virginia, Dores and Gracinda, never married. Spinsterhood was also the fate of a younger daughter, Josefa. All three had suitors, but José, faced perhaps with the misfortune of his eldest daughter, felt that none of them was prosperous enough to care for his daughters as he could. Even when Gracinda became pregnant and produced an illegitimate daughter, born in 1931, he vetoed her marriage to the father of her child. Indeed, this young man's "price" to save Gracinda's honor was a team of oxen and the revenue from the sale of Gracinda's gold chain. José dos Santos adamantly refused. Josefa, in a conversation about some of the namorados in her life who had come and gone, once put it this way:

> My father would rather have seen his daughters dead than married and in misery. And pretty soon you have passed the age for marrying anyway.

Four more children of José and Virginia died, two in early childhood and two as victims of the flu epidemic of 1918. The youngest daughter, Amelia, was born in 1914. She had a namorado in Fontão for twelve years before her father finally agreed to let her marry him at the age of thirty-one. After the marriage, the couple moved to Fontão. Five months later and already pregnant, Amelia fainted while working with her husband in the fields. She had a miscarriage and died shortly afterwards. Her sisters blame her death on the lack of hygiene and the fact that she caught an infection that no one did anything about. Her death dismayed José, since she was his youngest and favorite daughter. It set him further against any thought of marriage for his other daughters. When José died in 1951, he left his estate in the hands of his son José (who had married) and his eldest surviving daughter, Dores. They were in turn to take care of the spinster sisters and allow them to live in the family household until their deaths.

Clearly, discouraging daughters from marrying worked to the favor of the parental generation, who could be guaranteed someone to care for them in old age, a concern that testaments demonstrate was foremost in their minds, and whom they could "reward" for such service by bestowing on them their têrços. Furthermore, bestowing the têrço on a spinster daughter was a mechanism whereby properties could be reunited rather than further divided. Spinster aunts favored a nephew or niece, especially one who may have lived with them since childhood and cared for them.

One final attitude is epitomized by the case of an elderly spinster named Luisa. Born in 1900 in Sá (concelho of Ponte de Lima), Luisa came to Lanheses in 1913 after her mother had married her stepfather, a marriage to which she had been opposed but which her mother had told her "must be my destiny." Her stepfather was a violent man who frequently beat his new wife and stepdaughter. They never complained, she said, "because in those days people were more ignorant and illiterate." She emphasized that her stepfather already had two other wives who had died young, and that her own mother passed away when she was only fifty-five. All these premature deaths she blamed on the abuse of her stepfather. Although Luisa had several suitors and several opportunities to marry, the negative memories of her stepfather had convinced her "never to make the mistake her mother had made."

If cultural attitudes toward spinsterhood and marriage seem to have been important, we might also examine socioeconomic factors, the status of individual families, and the roles of particular children within those families. One line of inquiry to pursue is whether a daughter's birth order had anything to do with whether or not she married. Is there, for example, a tendency for the oldest daughter to remain a spinster because the onus of helping her mother care for younger siblings falls upon her at an early age? Or, conversely, is there a tendency for the youngest daughter to remain unmarried, because on her shoulders falls the task of caring for her aged parents, her older brothers and sisters having already married and formed new households of their own? Certainly there are examples of both types of situations in the ethnographic record. There are equally examples in the historical record, but in the context of the entire population of celibate daughters examined according to birth order, being the oldest or the youngest was not a statistically significant determining factor.

For sons, the number of cases during any decade about which we can be certain of permanent bachelorhood is so few that it is difficult to arrive at any conclusion except that it was in the long run not in itself an important part of the demographic picture. In a few cases, permanent bachelors were only sons or eldest sons in families with all sons, but there have also been cases of middle sons, with both older and younger married brothers and sisters, who themselves remained single.

What does seem apparent is that there has been some tendency for permanent spinsterhood or bachelorhood to run in families. However, upon closer examination of these families based on the sometimes scanty socioeconomic data that is available, it is not possible to argue that the practice was more common among one socioeconomic group than another. Throughout much of the nineteenth century, the offspring of both middle and well-to-do lavrador families seem to have shown a roughly equal tendency to celibacy. For example, the lavrador Artilheiro family that was discussed earlier produced celibate sons across several generations, including one who officiated as the priest of the parish between 1849 and 1863. Indeed, all five native-son priests whose deaths are recorded in the Lanheses registers during the nineteenth century were from the more substantial lavrador families. The cost of a seminary education was such that only families with some means could afford it. Unlike the aristocratic classes, however, this was not necessarily a means of disenfranchising them from any further claim to property, for in some cases priest-sons were the recipients of their parents' têrços.

Another example is provided by the case of the offspring of João Martins da Costa, a lavrador taxed on the 1845 electoral roll at the upper end of the range for that year. João was married in 1812 to Ascenção da Costa. Both bride and groom died within a month of one another in 1850. The couple had nine children, six of whom lived to adulthood. The eldest two of the five daughters married, one before her parents' death at age twenty-nine, and the other afterwards, in 1861, at the age of thirty-eight. The youngest child and only son also married in 1870 at the age of thirty-nine. The remaining three daughters all remained celibate, dying in 1900, 1897, and 1911 at the ages of seventy-five, seventy, and eighty-two, respectively. In 1850 the three spinster daughters and their younger brother were living together with a maiden aunt, one of their mother's sisters, in a house in Lamas, where they continued to live for the rest of the century. They had all inherited equally from their parents, and when the aunt died in 1859 she too left what she owned to her nieces and nephew in equal portions.

At the other end of the socioeconomic scale, among the less prosperous lavradores, there are also numerous examples of families with several offspring who never married. One is provided by the children of Manuel José de Sousa and Luisa Pereira. Manuel does not appear on any of the extant electoral rolls prior to his death, suggesting perhaps that he did not have enough wealth to qualify. He had married Luisa in 1823, and during the next eighteen years Luisa bore him eight children, six of whom survived. The eldest son, António, never married; the second child, a daughter, married in 1871 at the age of thirty; the next two daughters never married, and the youngest daughter and son both married, the daughter in 1872 at age thirty-three and the son in 1869 at age twenty-eight. The parents had died prior to any of these marriages, Manuel in 1846 and his widow in 1869. António de Sousa, who was listed as a lavrador in the 1871 arrolamento dos bens with one team of oxen and property assessed at 0$960, and his two spinster sisters continued to live in their paternal home in the Lugar da Feira until their deaths in the first decade of the twentieth century. When the youngest brother Manuel married, he established a new household nearby.

There are also cases of poor jornaleiro families or of families in which the head of household was primarily an artisan who had a number of unwed offspring. For example, of the six sons who survived into adulthood of the shoemaker Leandro do Val, who was married in 1841 and assessed, in the 1871 arrolamento dos bens, at 0$900, only one, the second-born, married in the parish. The eldest son had disappeared from the rois da desobriga by 1870, and the third and sixth were both marked absent by 1881. The fourth, marked absent on several rois, died celibate in 1938 at the age of eighty-seven, and his immediately younger brother died a bachelor in 1906 at the age of fifty-three. Of the four daughters born to this couple, only one, the youngest, never married, and she died a spinster in 1944 at the age of seventy-eight. However, two of her older sisters waited to marry until after both parents had passed away, the mother as a widow in 1893. One was thirty-one and the other forty-two.

Although all the cases discussed so far derive from marriages contracted during the first half of the nineteenth century, similar cases could be cited for the latter half of the same century. Spinsterhood seems equally to have occurred in pairs and trios within particular families. There appears to have been a somewhat greater tendency than during the first half of the century in families with only one unwed daughter for that daughter to be an only daughter or the eldest daughter. Another trend that continued from the earlier part of the century and that has not yet been mentioned was that the daughters who never married were often among the population of women in the village who had had children out of wedlock. Indeed, this could be one explanation for their "celibate" status. Abandoned by a young man to whom she had yielded, a young woman's chances of finding a husband were jeopardized. However, there are other ways to look at the entire question of illegitimate births, a subject that will be explored more thoroughly in Chapter Five.

About the few bachelor sons of couples who married between 1860 and the turn of the century, little of any conclusive or general nature can be said. In one case, ethnographic data tells us that the man spent many years abroad as an emigrant, returned to the village rather late in life, and spent the rest of his life living in rather slovenly conditions with his spinster sister. In another case, the elder of two sons born to António Araujo was *demente* (demented) and therefore remained unmarried. Brandes (1976) has in fact suggested that mental and physiological defects within a family may have affected the marital status of members of that family in general. Although it is not apparent in Lanheses that an otherwise healthy individual would be marked by the ailment or physical deformity of a sibling to the extent that Brandes describes for the village of Becedas (indeed it did not come up in any explanation of why spinsterhood or bachelorhood ran in families), the physical deformities of any particular individual would have been reason enough for nonmarriage.

Clearly, economic, demographic, and cultural factors should be equally considered in any attempt to understand nonmarriage in northwestern Portugal or elsewhere. For women in northwestern Portugal, there were social alternatives to marriage and childbearing that were rewarding. Although unmarried women continue to be addressed as *menina* (girl) until well into their thirties (implying that the possibility of marriage still exists), at a certain point they become *tias* (aunts) (implying the transition to permanent spinsterhood). Yet, *tia* is a very respectable position and is, in fact, a form of address extended to nonrelatives as well. *Tias* inherit; *tias* serve as godmothers; *tias* help married sisters or widowed brothers who do not remarry to raise their children, and very often live in the same household. Indeed, it could be argued that there is an entire female culture of spinsterhood ("tia-dom") in northwestern Portugal, and it is clearly far from being conceived of as an unfortunate state of affairs. Spinsters work together on their own land or as jornaleiras or criadas. They support church activities, teaching cathechism classes and singing at Sunday masses. As one informant put it, "*ficam para vestir imagens*" (they remain to dress the altar images). In short, they make a major contribution to the religious life of the parish.

Although there are young women in present-day Lanheses who are not marrying, the attitudes toward spinsterhood are changing. As the region becomes more prosperous, the fear that marriage leads to penury has diminished. In fact, as emigration opportunities for women opened up in France, the number of single Portuguese women who went abroad increased. Some went in search of husbands—a reaction to the demographic imbalance created by the dramatic rise in clandestine male emigration to avoid military service in the early 1960s. Others, accepting their probably permanent spinsterhood, went in search of a better salary, planning to save their earnings abroad to build a new house, buy rental property, or establish a small business (Brettell 1978), and thereby attain both independence and economic security. In Lanheses, one such spinster used her nest egg to open the first hotel (*pensão*) in the parish. Another bought an apartment in Viana do Castelo.

The important point to be made, however, is that spinsters in Lanheses are not and probably were not pitied or considered unfortunate for never marrying. They did and can lead full lives. The result of a situation in which a spinster is robbed of some of the important roles associated with such a full life is most tragically epitomized by the case of Palmira Ferreira. One of many children of António Ferreira, Palmira never married. She spent much of her early adult life caring for her widowed father and, when he died, for her three bachelor brothers, Balthazar (who was retarded), Casimiro (who was studying to be a priest), and António (who spent many years in France during the 1960s).

António's goal in emigrating to France was to earn enough money to buy back the property and the house that his father had been forced to sell to the Conde in the 1930s as a result of economic difficulties. In 1970, when he had amassed the sum, António returned from France for good. A few months later he decided to marry. His decision greatly upset Palmira for two reasons. As his bride, António had chosen the sister of a young man with whom Palmira had once been "conversing." At that time, because Palmira was poor, his family had refused to let him marry her. To see this family change their tune and permit their daughter to marry her brother now that he owned a house and a large piece of property was a blow to her pride. Second, she feared that in this new household, where her new sister-in-law would be in charge, she would have no role. She would be replaced as the woman in charge. These are the explanations that the family and friends of Palmira have given to justify her suicide. On December 21, 1970, just one month before her brother was to be married, Palmira threw herself into a deep well. It was two days before they found her body.

## MARRIAGE AND THE FORMATION OF HOUSEHOLDS

When Manuel Martins and Maria Alves de Castro married in 1882, they moved in with Manuel's widowed mother. At her death, Manuel became the head of household, and when his son in turn married in 1907, he and his bride moved in with Manuel and Maria. For whatever reasons, neither of these couples seems to have had much concern for the prerequisite expressed in the popular and often quoted Portuguese dictum *quem casa, quer casa* (whoever marries wants a house).[18] Isabel da Rocha, on the other hand, did. Born during the last decade of the nineteenth century, Isabel was raised in a small two-room house by a maternal aunt. From an early age she worked as a jornaleira on the lands of the Tinoco and Pimenta da Gama. When she was in her mid-twenties, she had a proposal of marriage from a young man from Santa Comba, a parish further inland. He was an only son and "would have been a good match." But Isabel did not want to leave Lanheses and the house she would inherit when her aunt passed away. Several suitors from Lanheses were also discouraged, primarily at the request of her maiden aunt, who "did not want her niece to bring a strange man" into the house. Isabel respected her aunt's wishes. Besides, her aunt was "a little crazy" (*tolinha*), and Isabel "did not want any embarrassments with a new husband." Only after her aunt died, and when Isabel was already thirty-seven, did she marry Joaquim dos Reis, a man nine years younger.

Although originally from the parish of Sá in the concelho of Ponte de Lima, Joaquim had been working as a jornaleiro for the Tinoco family for several years. He was poor, but "a hard worker, a saver, and an honest man." And they had a place to live which, though modest, was fully their own. For Isabel, inheriting this little house was clearly an important consideration in her marriage plans, and until she owned it outright and was free of any responsibility toward her aunt, she preferred to postpone any thought of taking a husband. Isabel's case suggests that the possibility of establishing a new household is an important factor to consider when trying to understand the characteristics of nuptiality. This possibility is clearly limited by the availability of housing, by the economic potential of a couple to build or pay for a new shelter and to acquire the land on which it is located, or by the facility with which a newly married couple can move into a house already occupied by some other member or members of the bride's or groom's family.

It is around the issue of household structure and residence patterns that much of the recent research in family history has been concentrated. And it is this same issue that brings anthropologists and historians into intensive and sometimes contrary discussion. With the material available to him, the historian can provide measures of the statistical predominance of certain types of residential groups, but what precisely does statistical predominance mean? Verdon (1980) raises a number of insightful questions in this regard. If we have a community with 50 percent nuclear households, is this high or low, and does it reflect a norm or cultural rule? Does the residential group that an historian can describe have anything to do with the domestic groups that anthropologists observe? And are residence patterns per se of any interest apart from what they can tell us about marriage, economics, and kinship relations? Clearly, the historian is limited by his data in this regard. Census lists tell us nothing about the motives behind the formation of one kind of household as opposed to another. Yet with some appreciation of cultural context and of certain structural constraints, be they economic, demographic, political, social, or cultural, we can at least offer educated guesses about why certain domestic arrangements are more prevalent than others.

To determine more precisely the nature of household formation and family structure in Lanheses and the relationship between what appears to be an ideal of neolocality and nuclearity (at least Lanhesans today clearly express it as an ideal) and the actual distribution of different types of households is important, particularly given differences of opinion about the theoretical connections between certain household and family forms and the characteristics of nuptiality per se. On the one hand, there is a line of reasoning which suggests that because nuclear families place more pressures upon limited economic resources, age at marriage will be higher because it takes that much longer to assemble the necessary means for the establishment of a new household. On the other hand, nuclear family households have also been associated with high nuptiality, both being the direct result (in an ideal system) of partible inheritance practices. Indeed, nuclear family households have frequently been called the most adaptive form of household in an area of partibility, whereas extended family households are presumably correlated with impartibility, high emigration, and low nuptiality (Habakkuk 1955). Again, northwestern Portugal provides us with some challenging puzzles, since it is an area with a tendency for partibility (albeit not totally egalitarian), yet characterized by both high ages at marriage and low overall nuptiality.

Furthermore, there is some disagreement in both the historical and ethnographic literature as to whether and where families are more commonly extended, multiple, or nuclear, and what the prevalence of any one of these forms might mean for some evaluation of the nature of the Portuguese family.[19] In this literature, the north of Portugal is characterized as a region in which extended family households prevail, and the south as an area predominated by nuclear family households (see Rowland 1983). Boisvert (1968:96), on the other hand, views the difference in vertical rather than spatial terms, arguing that "nuclear families dominate among the popular sectors in the countryside and in the cities (whereas) families with patriarchal tendencies are more frequent among middle and large-scale property owners and the urban middle classes."

In the absence of either census manuscripts or anything equivalent to civil population registers, the most useful source for individual-level data on household structure in Lanheses are the rois da desobriga. The earliest extant roll for Lanheses dates to 1850; they are sporadic until 1900; and were then kept fairly systematically until 1927.[20] Due to the time limitations of this data on households, the discussion here is focused upon the late nineteenth and early twentieth centuries. However, since this is precisely the time during which other more strictly demographic phenomena appear to have reached unprecedented levels, an emphasis on this particular period is appropriate. When linked with data from the parish registers, these lists, despite their lack of periodicity, do demonstrate some intriguing relationships between nuptiality and household formation in Lanheses.

Table 3.13 provides the percentage distribution of different household types for different years between 1850 and 1927. Households

TABLE 3.13 DISTRIBUTION OF HOUSEHOLD TYPES IN LANHESES,
1850–1927 (percent)

| Type | 1850 | 1870 | 1881 | 1887 | 1892 | 1899 | 1907 | 1913 | 1920 | 1927 |
|------|------|------|------|------|------|------|------|------|------|------|
| | | | | *Solitaries* | | | | | | |
| 1a(M) | 0.0 | 1.4 | 1.0 | 1.1 | 1.9 | 1.1 | 1.5 | 1.5 | 1.5 | 1.1 |
| 1a(F) | 1.6 | 3.4 | 2.7 | 1.8 | 1.1 | 1.9 | 1.5 | 2.7 | 5.2 | 2.1 |
| 1a(T) | 1.6 | 4.8 | 3.7 | 2.9 | 3.0 | 3.0 | 3.0 | 4.2 | 6.7 | 3.2 |
| 1b(M) | 0.6 | 4.8 | 5.3* | 2.2 | 1.8 | 1.9 | 0.7 | 1.2 | 1.5 | 3.2 |
| 1b(F) | 4.8 | 7.2 | 6.3 | 6.2 | 6.7 | 7.1 | 5.2 | 5.8 | 3.7 | 3.6 |
| 1b(T) | 5.4 | 12.0 | 11.6 | 8.4 | 8.5 | 9.0 | 5.9 | 7.0 | 5.2 | 6.8 |
| | | | | *Coresident Singles* | | | | | | |
| 2a | 2.4 | 4.1 | 4.0 | 4.4 | 4.4 | 3.0 | 3.4 | 1.5 | 1.1 | 2.5 |
| 2b | 2.4 | 0.7 | 1.3 | 1.8 | 0.7 | 1.5 | 3.0 | 3.5 | 3.7 | 3.2 |
| 2c | 0.0 | 0.0 | 0.0 | 0.4 | 0.3 | 0.0 | 0.0 | 0.0 | 0.4 | 0.0 |
| | | | | *Simple Family Households* | | | | | | |
| 3a | 10.0† | 14.5‡ | 8.6 | 8.1 | 7.4 | 6.7 | 7.9 | 6.6 | 7.5 | 6.5 |
| 3b | 35.4† | 36.2‡ | 46.2 | 31.6 | 33.3 | 32.1 | 34.4 | 33.7 | 36.2 | 37.1 |
| 3c | 3.3 | 3.8 | 3.0 | 2.2 | 1.1 | 3.0 | 2.6 | 1.9 | 3.3 | 2.1 |
| 3d | 5.3 | 9.3 | 8.6 | 8.8 | 6.7 | 10.4 | 5.6 | 9.3 | 10.1 | 7.9 |
| 3a–3d | 54.0 | 63.8 | 66.4 | 50.7 | 48.5 | 52.2 | 50.5 | 51.5 | 57.1 | 53.9 |
| | | | | *Single Mothers with Offspring* | | | | | | |
| 3e | 4.8 | 3.8 | 2.3 | 3.3 | 3.3 | 4.8 | 4.1 | 3.1 | 4.9 | 5.0 |
| 3f | | | | | 0.4 | | | | | |
| | | | | *Extended Family Households* | | | | | | |
| 4a | 0.4 | 0.3 | 0.3 | 3.7 | 6.3 | 4.1 | 1.9 | 1.6 | 1.5 | 4.6 |
| 4b | 1.9 | 0.0 | 0.0 | 0.7 | 1.5 | 0.4 | 1.5 | 0.4 | 0.0 | 1.8 |
| 4c | 1.4 | 2.1 | 5.0 | 4.4 | 3.7 | 5.2 | 5.6 | 4.3 | 2.6 | 4.6 |
| 4d | 2.4 | 1.0 | 1.3 | 0.0 | 0.7 | 1.5 | 0.4 | 2.3 | 1.5 | 1.1 |
| 4e | 3.3 | 3.4 | 2.3 | 4.4 | 5.6 | 6.0 | 3.7 | 5.0 | 3.7 | 2.9 |
| 4f | 2.9 | 1.0 | 1.0 | 1.5 | 3.3 | 1.8 | 2.6 | 1.5 | 3.4 | 2.9 |
| 4a–4f | 12.3 | 7.8 | 9.9 | 14.7 | 21.1 | 19.0 | 15.7 | 15.1 | 12.7 | 17.9 |
| | | | | *Multiple Family Households* | | | | | | |
| 5b | 1.4 | 0.3 | 0.3 | 2.6 | 2.6 | 1.1 | 1.5 | 2.7 | 0.4 | 0.4 |
| 5c | 4.3 | 0.0 | 0.0 | 3.3 | 1.1 | 1.5 | 1.1 | 0.8 | 1.9 | 1.8 |
| 5d | 5.2 | 0.3 | 0.3 | 2.2 | 2.9 | 2.2 | 4.5 | 2.7 | 0.7 | 1.4 |
| 5e | 3.3 | 1.7 | 0.0 | 4.0 | 2.2 | 1.5 | 4.9 | 6.2 | 4.5 | 1.8 |
| 5b–5e | 14.2 | 2.3 | 0.6 | 12.1 | 8.8 | 6.3 | 12.0 | 12.4 | 7.5 | 5.4 |

TABLE 3.13 DISTRIBUTION OF HOUSEHOLD TYPES IN LANHESES, 1850–1927 (percent) (*continued*)

| Type | 1850 | 1870 | 1881 | 1887 | 1892 | 1899 | 1907 | 1913 | 1920 | 1927 |
|------|------|------|------|------|------|------|------|------|------|------|
| *Other Multiples/Unclassifiable* | | | | | | | | | | |
| 5g | 0.4 | | | 0.3 | | | | | | |
| 5h | | | 0.7 | | | 0.4 | 0.7 | 1.2 | 0.7 | 0.7 |
| 5ı | | | | | 0.7 | 0.4 | 0.4 | 0.3 | | 1.4 |
| 6a | 2.4 | 0.7 | 0.0 | 0.0 | | 0.4 | 1.1 | | | |
| Total (N) | 210 | 290 | 301 | 272 | 270 | 268 | 267 | 258 | 268 | 280 |

NOTES:

* Includes two priests in addition to the parish priest, who each year is among the single male households, generally living with servants and in one instance with a sister and therefore classified as 2a.

† Revised figures (see text) are 3a, 6.2%; 3b, 38.2%.

‡ Revised figures (see text) are 3a, 10.7%; 3b, 39.2%.

SOURCE: Rois da Desobriga, Lanheses.

have been classified according to the Laslett and Wall (1972) scheme with several important modifications.[21] Furthermore, as mentioned in the notes to this table, the 1850 and 1870 distributions for couples living alone (3a) and for simple nuclear families (3b) have been amended through record linkage with family reconstitution data because, for these two years, children under seven (before their first communion) were not included on the rolls. The amendment is fairly complete, but not entirely accurate, since the data do not permit correction for couples who were not married in the parish but who were living there at the time of both these rolls.[22]

There are a number of things to be learned from these distributions. The first is the dramatic decrease in the proportion of complex households (both multiple and extended) between 1850 and 1881. The corresponding increase is in simple households (especially nuclear family households—3b) and, to a lesser extent, in households made up of single men and single women (1b) living alone. Clearly, the creation of ninety-one new households in the thirty-one-year interval between 1850 and 1881 (approximately three per year) is a reflection of these shifts in household type. However, by 1887 the trend reversed itself; there was a resurgence of extended and multiple family households, while the percentage of nuclear family households declined and remained relatively constant (hovering around 50 percent) during the next three decades. Data drawn from the national

FIGURE 3.3  KEY TO HOUSEHOLD TYPE CLASSIFICATIONS FOR
LANHESES DATA

Solitaries
 1a  Widow / widower living alone
 1b  Unmarried men or women living alone

Coresident singles
 2a  Coresident siblings
 2b  Coresident relatives of other kinds
 2c  Coresident singles of unknown relationship

Simple family households
 3a  Married couple living alone
 3b  Married couple with children (nuclear family household)
 3c  Widower with children
 3d  Widow with children
 3e  Single mother with offspring
 3f  Single mother with offspring and one or more of her siblings

Extended family households
 4a  Extended upward through parent / parent-in-law of head
 4b  Extended upward through other relative of head
 4c  Extended downward through grandchild of head
 4d  Extended downward through other relative of head
 4e  Extended laterally through sibling / sibling-in-law of head
 4f  Any combination of above

Multiple family households
 5a  Secondary couple extended up
 5b  Secondary couple extended down through male line—both spouses in both generations alive
 5c  Secondary couple extended down through male line—widow or widower in senior generation
 5d  Secondary couple extended down through female line—both spouses in both generations alive
 5e  Secondary couple extended down through female line—widow or widower in senior generation
 5f  Frereches
 5g  Other multiple
 5h  Single mother, married illegitimate offspring with spouse and children
 5i  Widow / er, widowed child and widowed child's offspring

Others
 6a  Unclassifiable

population censuses confirm the trends in household formation that emerge from an analysis of the rois. According to the census, fifty new households were established in Lanheses between 1864 and 1878. This represents a rather dramatic increase, considering the fact that during the next decade the number of households declined by twenty and then remained roughly stationary until the 1920s (Table 3.14).

Corresponding to these changes in the proportion of households by type or structure were changes in the size of households. Whereas 18.7 percent of the households in 1850 had seven or more people, only 9.9 percent were this large in 1870.[23] In 1881, the proportion of larger households begins to increase again and continues to rise until 1913, when 27.1 percent of the households in the parish had seven or more people. Whether based on census data or rois data, and whether de jure or de facto, households did increase in size during the first several decades of the twentieth century and, with the exception of the decade of the 1940s, apparently continued to do so during the 1950s and 1960s (Table 3.14). This pattern is clearly contrary to trends that have been described for other parts of western Europe. Segalen (1980), for example, found a mean household size of 6.2 in the French village of St. Jean Tromilon in 1836, a mean of 5.8 in 1866, of 5.5 in 1896, of 4.4 in 1926, and of 2.8 in 1975. In the same period, the proportion of multiple households in St. Jean Tromilon declined from 16.3 percent to 3.6 percent, and extended households, after experiencing a significant increase during the late nineteenth and early twentieth centuries, returned to their 1836 level of 4.5 percent by 1975. It is interesting to note, however, that the mean household size in Lanheses was never as high as that for Segalen's French village, even in the early enumerations of 1712 and 1800. A decline in infant mortality or an increase in fertility (as a consequence of a lowered age at marriage) could account for the twentieth-century trends. But for the early twentieth century, so too could the high proportion of complex households.

It is useful, in fact, to distinguish, as Table 3.13 does, between different types of multiple and extended households within the complex household category. In the 1890s, extended households comprised one-fifth of the total number of households, an increase of roughly 10 percent from the early 1880s. This increase can be accounted for, to a large extent, by a sharp rise in the number of households extended upward by the addition of a parent or parent-in-law of the head of household (4a). One of the major causes of this trend (a function to some degree of the way the data have been classified) is a shift in the designation of household head, reflecting, per-

TABLE 3.14 Growth in the Number of Households in Lanheses, 1527–1960

| Year | No. Households | Population | | Population per Household | | Year | No. Households | Population | | Population per Household | |
|---|---|---|---|---|---|---|---|---|---|---|---|
| | | de jure | de facto | de jure | de facto | | | de jure | de facto | de jure | de facto |
| 1527 | 101 | | | | | 1850[a] | 210 | 984 | 883 | 4.7 | 4.2 |
| 1712 | 170 | | 680 | | 4.0 | 1870[a] | 290 | 1061 | 936 | 3.6 | 3.3[b] |
| 1767 | 173 | | | | | 1881 | 301 | 1176 | 1045 | 3.9 | 3.5[c] |
| 1800 | 186 | | 801 | | 4.3 | 1887 | 272 | 1161 | 1026 | 4.3 | 3.8 |
| 1864 | 243 | 1191 | 1207 | 4.9 | 4.9 | 1892 | 270 | 1151 | 1029 | 4.3 | 3.8[d] |
| 1878 | 293 | 1140 | 1034 | 3.9 | 3.5 | 1899 | 268 | 1128 | 1047 | 4.2 | 3.9 |
| 1890 | 271 | 1073 | 1000 | 3.9 | 3.6 | 1907 | 267 | 1212 | 1112 | 4.5 | 4.2 |
| 1900 | 270 | 1028 | 1029 | 3.8 | 3.8 | 1913 | 258 | 1217 | 1114 | 4.7 | 4.3 |
| 1911 | 267 | 1200 | 1087 | 4.5 | 4.1 | 1920 | 268 | 1191 | 1112 | 4.4 | 4.1 |
| 1920 | 269 | 1161 | 1083 | 4.3 | 4.0 | 1927 | 280 | 1277 | 1172 | 4.6 | 4.2 |
| 1930 | 287 | 1218 | 1265 | 4.2 | 4.4 | | | | | | |
| 1940 | 368 | 1515 | 1459 | 4.1 | 3.9 | | | | | | |
| 1950 | 355 | 1816 | 1754 | 5.1 | 4.5 | | | | | | |
| 1960 | 362 | | 1810 | | 5.0 | | | | | | |

[a]The total population figures for these years are underestimated since children under seven were not included on the rois.

[b]The total number of de facto households is 287.

[c]The total number of de facto households is 298.

[d]The total number of de facto households is 269.

SOURCES: Columns 2–6, National population censuses, 1864–1960; columns 8–12, Rois da Desobriga, Lanheses.

haps, a shift in the locus of power and authority. A son or son-in-law who was listed in a previous roll as a subordinate in the household has been elevated to the status of household head, probably when the senior parent became too old to manage the affairs of the household—thus, the corresponding decline in the percentage of multiple households, particularly those that were headed by a widowed parent or parent-in-law, more often a widow than a widower. Over time, the figures tend to suggest that this passing on of authority, as measured by who is designated as head of household, is cyclical and therefore by no means undermines the fact that widowed women were definitely recognized as the heads of simple, extended, or multiple family households for as long as they were able to fulfill the responsibilities that such a position entailed. Indeed, women composed between approximately 13 and 20 percent of all simple and complex household heads (solitaries and coresident singles excluded) between 1850 and 1907, and as much as 24 and 25 percent in 1913 and 1920. This is quite different from what Kertzer (1984b), for example, has found in central Italy in the late nineteenth and early twentieth centuries, and clearly underscores the importance of women in northwestern Portuguese rural society.

Equally important in the extended household category are the number of households extended downward by the addition of a grandchild (4c), in most cases the offspring of an unmarried daughter. Sieder and Mitterauer (1983) have found precisely the same type of three-generation household in Lower Austria, and have linked it to widespread acceptance of illegitimacy in that region. As Chapter Five will demonstrate, it was toward the last decade of the nineteenth century and the first decade of the twentieth that illegitimacy in Lanheses reached unprecedented levels. In 1899, almost 5 percent of the households were composed of single women with their illegitimate offspring (3e), and in another 5 percent these young women were living with their parents (4c). A few more illegitimate grandchildren are included in households that were extended in more than one direction (4f).

The number of households extended laterally by the presence of a sibling or sibling-in-law (4e) is also not to be ignored. In several cases, this was the result of the younger couple in a multiple household taking over the household at the death of the parental generation, with siblings already in the household continuing to live there. Generally these siblings or siblings-in-law were unmarried females. It is worth noting, therefore, that both of these extended family household types (4c and 4e), insofar as they reflect an increase in the number of young women who never married, may have been indirect results of male emigration. The increase in the number of single women living alone between 1850 and 1870 and the stability of that figure at between 6 and 7 percent of all the households until the end of the century are clearly associated with male emigration, as well. Finally, the decline in the proportion of households made up of single men living alone from 5 percent in 1881 to a proportion varying between roughly 1 and 2 percent thereafter is also not to be overlooked in this regard.

The most significant long-term change in household structure in Lanheses between 1850 and 1920 was the decline in multiple family households by 50 percent. Simple family households and extended family households remained in roughly equal proportions at the beginning of the period as at the end. Yet, if we combine both extended and multiple households and consider them together as representative of a complex household structure, then the ratio of simple to complex was also roughly the same in 1927 as it was in 1850. Clearly, what is of most interest is the short-term decline in the proportion of complex households sometime in the 1850s or 1860s, and the persistence of this trend into the mid 1880s.

One has to wonder whether the changes in land tenure resulting from the new Civil Code of 1867 facilitated the expansion of independent households, at least in the short term. This code, it will be recalled, specified strictly egalitarian inheritance, the abolition of all vinculos, the registration of all foros, and the distribution of common pasture lands. Yet, by the 1880s, and aggravated by increasing population, the process of division had proceeded to the point of inviability, such that land for both housing and subsistence farming was no longer readily available. Furthermore, new taxation laws introduced in the 1880s imposed a severe enough burden on the rural populations of northwestern Portugal, Lanheses included, to halt the tendency toward independent households. Foro lands in particular were taxed mightily, forcing owners to sell innumerable small plots and thereby threaten the livelihood of innumerable lavradores-rendeiros (Martins 1885).

In this context, emigration soared in the 1880s and continued until the First World War. Emigration operated not only to reduce the total number of households, but also to increase the proportion of complex households. Indeed, perhaps the most distinctive feature of residence patterns in Lanheses is the strong uxorilocal tendency. Some of these uxorilocal households were the result of a non-native groom moving to the parish after marriage, but even among couples both of whom were native Lanhesans, there was a greater tendency to live with the bride's parents than with the grooms. The emigration of a spouse can partially explain this residential bias. If a wife was to be left alone, she preferred to be with her own parents than with those of her husband, and perhaps with her parents rather than in her own separate household.[24] Furthermore, if a young couple were continuing to help farm the lands of the parental generation after marriage, given the fact that women worked in agriculture more than men (a division of labor that has itself emerged from a tradition of male-biased emigration), a uxorilocal pattern of residence makes perfect sense. In fact, by the turn of the century, there were numerous households in which both the senior male head of household and his son-in-law were absent, leaving mother and daughter to care for the family properties together. In the absence of men, the pooling of resources by means of an extended or multiple family was a very satisfactory economic arrangement. And if women were pooling economic resources in these extended or multiple domestic groups, so too were men as emigrants. Although absent, they were vital to the financial well-being of the household and in this sense, it is ultimately impossible to conceive of the Lanhesan household, and therefore of the Lanhesan family, as a localized entity.

Complex households, whether multiple or extended, were clearly common in Lanheses, hovering around one-quarter of all households in the parish between 1850 and 1927, with the important exception of the period between the 1860s and the mid-1880s. It is significant to note, however, that at only one point does the proportion of simple households drop below 50 percent, suggesting that at least half the population were successful in achieving the ideal of an independent household. The length of time it took to achieve this goal is clearly worth investigating, especially if it is reasoned that marriages in some part depended on the availability of housing. This can be done through the linkage of the rois data with marriage records.

Between 1840 and 1849, for example, fifty-five marriages were celebrated in Lanheses. In 1850, forty-five of these recently married couples could be linked to households included on the 1850 roll. Of the remaining ten, six involved couples who probably took up residence elsewhere (for the most part, the groom was from another parish and no further information on these couples exists in the Lanheses registers), and two involved marriages within the "aristocratic" class. Among the forty-five couples linked to households on the 1850 roll, a little more than a third were living in multiple households, twelve of them uxorilocally and five of them virilocally.[25] Almost half were living on their own in nuclear (3b) or potentially nuclear (3a) households. Five of them were on their own, but had an additional relative in the household with them: in one case a widowed parent (4a), in three cases a sibling of one of the spouses (4e), and in the final case an aunt (4d). Some of these latter households, although complex, might be more appropriately considered together with the nuclear households when independence from the senior generation is the issue. Although there is a strong indication that within ten years of marriage, almost two-thirds of the couples were able to set up their own household, the remaining third who were living with the parental generation and in a subordinate position within the household are not to be ignored.

There does not seem to be any significant difference according to whether the marriage was contracted at the beginning or the end of the decade. What we need to look at, however, is whether there was any difference in the ages at which these couples married—and indeed there is. The mean age for grooms who married during this decade and who were found in multiple households in 1850 was 26.8 and that of their brides was 26.5, both appreciably less than the mean for all marriages during that decade. The mean age for previously unmarried grooms who wed previously unmarried brides (that is, excluding the four marriages of a widow or widower) and who established an independent household was 30.1 and 26.8, respectively. Although there is little difference in these two groups between the brides, there is a significant difference between the two sets of grooms, suggesting that those who were able to establish separate households had waited longer to marry and had probably amassed some sort of income that permitted them to buy, build, or rent a separate house to shelter their new family. What we do not know for sure is whether the desire to be independent after marriage delayed the marriage of some couples, or whether the impossibility of living with the parents of either the young man or the young woman was the primary motivation to wait. In none of the cases of couples living in a multiple family situation was an earlier marriage prompted by premarital pregnancy, and there is no clear pattern according to birth order or marriage order. Five of the grooms were eldest sons, but three of these married uxorilocally. Five of the marriages involved three pairs of siblings, and in four instances the young couples were from well-to-do lavrador families who may have felt it necessary to ensure that at least one son or daughter married at home. That is, it is possible that multiple households were more characteristic of one segment of the population than of another. To this I will return shortly.

Of the fifty-four couples who were married between 1860 and 1869 who could be linked to the 1870 roll, almost two-thirds were living in independent households (3a or 3b) by 1870. In fact, to these we should probably add the households of three widows who married and subsequently lost their husbands within the same decade. Each of them was living alone with her children in 1870. Only two of the households on the 1870 roll that could be linked to marriages which took place in the parish in the preceding decade were multiple, both of them uxorilocal and occurring in 1869, just prior to the roll. In addition, there were four households extended laterally through the presence of a sibling/sibling-in-law (4e). It would appear that by 1870 newly married couples were establishing their own households with much more alacrity than twenty years earlier. The increase in the proportion of nuclear households shown on Table 3.13 is clearly a manifestation of this fact. Since the proportion of multiple households for this 1860–1869 marriage cohort is so small, it is futile to compare the mean ages at marriage of the two sets of couples (those living independently versus those living with parents) for this year.

This predominance of independent households among couples married within the decade preceding a roll continued into 1881. None of the couples married between 1870 and 1881 who could be linked to the 1881 roll were residing in a multiple household in 1881, and only three were extended laterally. Again, although we cannot be sure of what is cause and what is effect, delaying the age at marriage seems to have meant for couples marrying during the 1860s and 1870s that when they eventually did marry they had the possibility of establishing an independent household very quickly.

However, as one would predict given the distribution of household types on Table 3.13, this virtually exclusive trend toward the early formation of an independent household by newly married couples had reversed itself by 1887. Of the sixty-four couples who married between 1877 and 1887 and who could be linked to the 1887 roll, twenty-three were in nuclear family households (including two marriages in which one of the spouses had already died—3c and 3d) and eight more were single couples with no children (3a).[26] Together, these simple households comprised almost 50 percent of the marriages occurring between 1877 and 1887, and the mean age at marriage for this group of grooms and brides (excluding widows and widowers) was 32.3 and 31.3, respectively. If the households extended vertically or laterally (4a–4f) are added to these, then the couples who were able to establish their own household, or to assume the position of authority in a household, within ten years of their marriage make up 60 percent of all the couples who married during the late 1870s and early 1880s.

However, we cannot ignore the remaining 40 percent who were living in multiple family households, thirteen of them uxorilocally (including two where illegitimately born daughters brought their husbands to live with the unwed mothers) and twelve of them virilocally. The mean age at marriage for the grooms in these multiple households was 31.2 and for the brides 28.9. As in 1850, these means are lower than for the couples who were living as simple families, although this time appreciably lower for brides than for grooms. Does this suggest that there were extraneous circumstances that were delaying marriage for men, no matter what socioeconomic segment of the population they belonged to? One curious fact that this later roll allows us to see is that six of these couples who were living with either the bride's parents or the groom's parents in 1887 had been living in their own households (3b) six years earlier, in 1881. Four of these involved only children, in three cases the grooms were absent in 1887, and in all six cases the shift involved the consolidation of two separate households that were seemingly adjacent to one another in the same lugar and listed consecutively on the earlier roll.

It is possible that this tendency toward consolidation was pursued in order to avoid paying the extra taxes and tithes on an independent household. It is true that taxes imposed upon the rural peasantry were augmented significantly in 1882, by two, three, and even six times in the case of that associated with the transfer and registration of property (Sampaio 1979). This increasing tax burden continued into the 1890s, and was accompanied by a rise in interest rates, as well (Teles 1903). Yet, if the expansion of multiple households in the 1880s was a response to the new and onerous taxes, it is difficult to explain the fact that by 1899 the facility and proclivity with which newly married couples were able to establish independent households had again expanded. Consolidation may also have occurred to avoid having a woman live alone (in three cases a widow in the senior generation, in three cases wives with absent husbands and young children). In 1887 in general, the husbands of three young wives living virilocally and of five who were living uxorilocally were absent—that is, in a quarter of the multiple households of this decade.

Forty-seven percent of those marriages that occurred between 1889 and 1899 which could be linked to the 1899 roll were in nuclear family households, and 10 percent were composed of already widowed men or women; that is, virtually two-thirds of the couples who had married between 1889 and 1899 were in independent households by 1899. Only ten couples (17 percent) were living in multiple households, five of them virilocally and five of them uxorilocally (including one classified as 5h). Nine more were living in households that included members of the extended family. The mean age at marriage for grooms living in independent households in 1899 was 31.3, compared to a mean of 30.8 for the ten grooms in multiple households. The corresponding means for the brides was 29.0 and 27.1, respectively.

And yet the trend had shifted again by 1913. Among those couples who had married between 1903 and 1913, twenty-five of fifty-six were in nuclear family households, including three widowers who had remarried and two widows. Five more were living alone in their own household (including one widower who had remarried). Together these independent households comprised 53.6 percent of the marriages in this ten-year period during the early twentieth century. However, almost 36 percent of the couples married during this ten-year period prior to the 1913 roll were living in a multiple family situation in 1913, sixteen of them uxorilocally and four of them virilocally. Five more were extended through the presence of a niece (two), an aunt (one), a sister-in-law (one), or a combination of relatives (one). The mean age for grooms and brides living in independent households (3a and 3b) was 28.9 and 27.4, respectively; that for grooms and brides living in multiple households 26.9 and 27.1. As in 1850, the difference is negligible for brides, but quite dramatic for grooms. Eight of the grooms who married uxorilocally were from other parishes, and nine of these marriages involved jornaleiro couples.

In fact, when one analyzes by husband's profession the type of household in which young couples were living at their first appearance on the roll, it is evident that, especially during the early twentieth century, it was not only lavradores who were living in complex households, but jornaleiros and, to a lesser extent, artisans as well. In 1907, for example, 60 percent of the young lavrador grooms were in complex households, 55 percent of the jornaleiro grooms, and 44 percent of the artisan grooms. If the expansion in the number of jornaleiros during the first decade of the twentieth century is to be taken as a signal of the increasing proletarianization of the Lanhesan population, including those who moved in from other parishes, then the fact that almost as many of these young jornaleiro couples lived in complex households as did young lavrador couples is an indication that increasing proletarianization did not necessarily lead immediately to the proliferation of nuclear family households, although over the long term the proportion of multiple family households did indeed diminish significantly. It is important to note that in both 1907 and 1913, during a period when we know that emigration was common, slightly more than a third of the husbands of the younger couples living in multiple family households in each of those years were absent. In the majority of cases, these were uxorilocal households in which a young man left his wife and children with his wife's parents while he went abroad. The fact that in 1887 as many artisan households were multiple as were lavrador households is also related to male emigration. Certainly the proportion of married male *ausentes* had jumped from 14 percent of all males absent in 1881 to 39 percent in 1887.

To summarize, despite the short-term fluctuations, it seems that the pattern for differences in the mean age at marriage according to whether a couple established an independent household or moved into a multiple household was the same in 1913 as it had been a little more than sixty years before. Those who moved in with their parents married slightly earlier than those who established their own household soon after marriage. However, the proportions of these latter couples did fluctuate over time, and during their life cycles the composition of most households changed as individual family members moved in and out. It is certainly true that more than half of the households that can be traced through the late nineteenth century and into the early twentieth century passed through a multiple phase at some point in their cycle, and if one includes an extended family phase, we are dealing with the vast majority. Although the preference for nuclearity may have been a cultural norm in the past, it seems that each family accommodated itself to the realities of its personal situation, taking in a spinster sister, an illegitimate grandchild, or a widowed parent. Indeed, the preference for nuclearity has to be seen in the context of a culturally defined expectation that children will care for elderly parents, and family members for one another. Where this sentiment was not naturally felt, it was supported, as the late-eighteenth- and nineteenth-century testaments demonstrate, by promises of property bequests. When a multiple household headed by a widowed parent became an extended household headed by a son or son-in-law, generally the son or son-in-law continued to live in the house after the widowed parent had died. When a spinster sibling remained, the family may have been averting the problem of property division. Parents could, in fact, choose to leave the house to both children to ensure that an unmarried child would have a place to live throughout his or her life. In short, the system—if we can even call it a system—was flexible enough to allow individuals to adapt to certain opportunities or constraints that presented themselves at different points in time. Households expanded and contracted as economic conditions and family and individual migration patterns changed. Although the norm of nuclearity and independence was an ideal to be aspired to, and was clearly achieved by many couples, a range of phenomena could influence both the actuality and the timing for the attainment of this ideal.

Ethnographic data tend to support this interpretation of flexible and adaptive household arrangements. Villagers repeatedly use the word *conforme* (that is, depending on the situation at hand) to describe residence patterns of the past and present. That is, although they stress the ideal for each couple to live in their own household, and often view emigration as a means to achieve this end (as it certainly is today), *quem casa quer casa* is a preference rather than a rule. Factors such as the availability of housing (even houses that can be rented), the number of unmarried siblings left in a household, the availability of land on which to build a new house are all offered as important criteria influencing a residence decision. If it is necessary for two generations to live together, then better a daughter than a daughter-in-law, since daughters provide more care and affection (*carinho*). They also stress that it is best if at least one child remains to take over the paternal home, although which child is *conforme*. The tracing of various Lanhesan households through time clearly demonstrates that this, in fact, occurred over and over again. Some couples in their own neolocal and nuclear households lived long enough to welcome a married child into their home and to pass that home on to that child upon their death. Other households were taken over by groups of unmarried siblings. In short, what both ethnographic and historical data tend to suggest is that households in Lanheses were and remain processes rather than static facts. They respond to changing circumstances and conditions.

Yet, even when nuclearity is achieved, it does not imply total social, emotional, or economic independence from other members of the larger extended family. Family networks and kin obligations, as was noted earlier, transcend the local entity. Indeed, although some multiple households may have been an efficient adaptation to the constraints imposed by male emigration, not even they were necessarily self-contained labor units. Furthermore, in a rural economy characterized by extreme minifundia and a succession of tasks throughout the agricultural year, nuclear families that exchanged labor on the basis of bonds of kinship or even neighborship were equally effective. And in addition, these nuclear families could draw upon what was, by the late nineteenth century, a growing population of jornaleiros, particularly female jornaleiros, to meet some of the seasonal labor demands with which they might be faced. Such cooperation, particularly in the form of labor exchange between separate households, continues today and is a signal of the distinction that must be drawn between family and household.

## CONCLUSION

The discussion in this chapter has ranged widely. Associations between age at marriage, permanent celibacy, household structure, and emigration have been established, but these are not always the predictable and uniformly patterned associations delineated by a range of other scholars. This is primarily because emigration from northwestern Portugal has always been perceived as a temporary rather than a permanent departure, a necessary part of the local way of life and a constant for at least two-and-a-half centuries of recent history. Yet, if the Lanheses data are at all representative, it is equally true that in northwestern Portugal, as in some other parts of western Europe, emigration, age at marriage, and permanent spinsterhood all increased during times of economic, demographic, and even political crisis. When Antonio de Araujo Travessos wrote in 1792 that "the facility of living and abundance are the principle causes of marriages and the raising of children," he was stating what appears to be for most European populations, including the Portuguese, an evident truth.

Ansley Coale and a host of recent historical demographers have suggested that control of nuptiality is the most forthright response to changing economic conditions before and during the early stages of the demographic transition. One of the earliest demographers of Portugal, Balbi (1822), also perceived a connection.

> The young people of both sexes, instead of yielding to the penchants of nature by uniting themselves in the sacred union of marriage, pass their lives in libertinage; others, wait until they make a fortune before marrying; in waiting, the girls age and in each who waits until she is thirty-five to marry the state loses two-thirds of her fecundity.

Some have gone so far as to argue that delayed marriage is a conscious choice made to reduce the number of offspring born within a marriage, and that older brides are often preferred precisely because they have fewer childbearing years left. Drake (1969:146), for example, quotes from a Norwegian cottar who had married a woman several years his senior because "I thought that when I took such an old woman, the crowd of young ones would not be so great, for it is difficult for one in such small circumstances to feed so many." Although we cannot ignore Drake's cottar's remark, it is more likely, as Caldwell (1976) has observed, that the changes in ages at marriage have more to do with the economic and physical difficulties of establishing a new household than with a conscious decision to limit the size of the family. Yet the question does need further examination. Thus, it is to fertility that we turn in the next chapter.

# CHAPTER FOUR

# Having Children: Fertility in Lanheses

> Every human society is faced not with one population problem but with two: how to beget and rear enough children and how not to beget and rear too many. (Margaret Mead 1949:224)

## INTRODUCTION

Within the context of western Europe, the history of Portuguese fertility is at once familiar and unique. Although a downward turn has occurred, it came rather late—after 1920, and especially after 1930; that is, more than a century after historical demographers have pinpointed the decline in France, close to a half a century behind the decline in other parts of northern Europe (Germany, England), and a decade or two after Spain and Italy. In addition to the lateness of the so-called demographic transition, Portugal also demonstrates strong regional differences in the decline in fertility. Granted, such regional differences have also been found in other countries of western Europe and have led population economists like Ansley Coale and expert measurement demographers like Etienne Van de Walle to allow a cultural explanation into their models of the transition. "The cultural setting," claim Knodel and Van de Walle (1967) "influences the onset and spread of the fertility decline independent of socio-economic conditions."[1] Cultures are delimited by these scholars almost coterminously with language or communication frontiers. Thus, the French- and Flemish-speaking regions of Belgium differ (Lesthaeghe 1977), and the clusters of provinces in Spain with similar levels of fertility at specific periods approximate the diverse linguistic regions of that country (Leasure 1963).

In Portugal, however, the demarcation (even as of 1970) is along crude geographical lines; the northern region (including the districts of Bragança, Vila Real, Viana do Castelo, Braga, Porto, and Viseu) is characterized by comparatively high fertility; the central region (Aveiro, Guarda, Coimbra, Castelo Branco, and Leiria) by medium fertility; and the southern region (Portalegre, Santarém, Lisbon, Évora,

Setúbal, Beja, and Faro) by low fertility. In short, although all regions of Portugal, at an aggregate level, reduced their fertility levels appreciably between 1930 and 1970 (from rates that were more or less proximate at the beginning of the century), the southern districts (including the rural south) reduced their fertility on average by 41 percent while the northern districts (including what is considered the "industrialized" north) reduced theirs on average by only 21 percent (Livi Bacci 1971). What this suggests, particularly within the rural areas of north and south, is that there are important variations in regional sociocultural systems that have influenced and continue to influence fertility behavior. Indeed, even within the north, demographers such as Candido (1969) have described important local variations—for example, a lower level of fertility in those concelhos of the district of Viana do Castelo which border with Spain, and a higher level in those concelhos closer to the religious center at Braga.

Livi Bacci has examined some of these variations at an aggregate level, using both multiple and partial correlation analysis. He concludes that the contrasts between northern and southern Portugal cannot be satisfactorily explained by any of the "crude indices" (infant mortality, proportion of the population in the agricultural labor force, literacy, emigration) that he uses. He offers as an alternative explanation the "statistically unmeasurable variable" of religiosity which, as many scholars of Portugal have argued, is stronger in the north than in the south.[3] The impact of religiosity (especially Catholicism) on fertility is very controversial. Do the "measurable aspects" of this variable (church attendance or professed religious affiliation) have anything to do with beliefs and the way in which beliefs affect behavior (in this case fertility behavior)? Is it only a question of beliefs or of myriad other subtle facets of sociocultural life associated with religion, the Church, or small community living in general? Are we dealing not simply with a question of beliefs, but also with the regionally differentiated impact of the Catholic Church as an institution controlling, for example, the flow of birth control information, and, perhaps more importantly, the entire social and educational life of the rural community? With its seat in the northern provincial town of Braga and a close-knit network of priests in almost every village, the Catholic Church in northern Portugal has been and remains, even with recent political changes, much better organized than in the south.

Although the decline of overall fertility and in the crude birth rate occurred slowly in Portugal, and almost imperceptibly until the 1920s and 1930s, the birth rate and marital fertility in nineteenth-century

Portugal were themselves relatively low—a factor that has been reversed recently. (Portugal in 1960 had one of the highest rates of marital fertility in Europe). Emigration has been offered as one possible cause of this demographic feature. Indeed, as was demonstrated in Chapter Two, even pre-twentieth-century observers of Portuguese population trends perceived the possible connection between emigration and a lowered birth rate. Yet Livi Bacci has rejected, at the aggregate level, differences in rates of emigration (high in the north and low in the south) as a significant variable explaining the regional variations in fertility in Portugal. Rather, he concludes that "given the scarce elements at our disposal, a careful appraisal of the nature of Portuguese emigration becomes difficult and it is impossible to assess its role and impact on fertility" (Livi Bacci 1971:86). In a later section of this chapter, I will attempt to explore this impact further in the microlevel context of Lanheses, to the extent that the data permit. If sometimes more intuitively than statistically, I think we can present a rather strong picture of the association between emigration and marital fertility. If there is indeed a relationship, it will help to explain low overall fertility (marital and general), some of the individual differences in reproductive histories, and may eventually tell us more about migration patterns at local levels.

## MARRIAGE AND FERTILITY: DEMOGRAPHIC RELATIONSHIPS

In June of 1718, two young twenty-two-year-old third cousins, Domingos Alves and Maria Pereira, were married in Lanheses. Their life together lasted twenty-two years, terminating with Maria's death in 1741 at the age of forty-four. During those years, Domingos and Maria had six children. Although the first son was born only a little more than nine months after the marriage, the next five children were born at rather lengthy intervals, averaging approximately three years. Only the three youngest children married in the parish, one of them a daughter named Boaventura. Boaventura was twenty-eight when she wed Domingos da Costa in 1760. Their marriage lasted almost twice as long as that of her parents (forty-one years), yet they had only four children, the last born in 1772, when Boaventura was forty.

Boaventura and Domingos' eldest son Francisco da Costa Pereira married his third cousin Maria Josefa de Castro in 1796. Francisco, who had been in Spain prior to his marriage, was already thirty-two and his bride was thirty. Maria bore three children, the first almost nine months to the day after her marriage, the second four years after the first, and the third after an additional five years. All three were sons and all three married in the parish, the eldest, Manuel, in 1819 at age twenty-two, the middle son, José, in 1829 at age twenty-eight, and the youngest son, António, in 1826 at age twenty. António's wife, who was only sixteen at her marriage, died less than two years later, five days after giving birth to a son. António remarried in 1839, when he was thirty-three, a young woman of thirty-four, and sired three more offspring. Yet none of these children by his second wife married in the parish—two died as young adults and the third emigrated. Thus, only the son by his first wife carried on the family line, marrying in 1850, when he was twenty-two, a woman of twenty-five. They had seven children, four of whom married in the parish, three in their late twenties and one at age thirty-five. Among them, they produced only five children.

António's older brother Manuel married Domingas da Costa. She was also twenty-two and during thirty-years of marriage bore eleven children, roughly one every other year until she reached age forty-five. Only two of these children married in the parish, the second youngest son Manuel in October of 1870, when he was thirty-three, to his first cousin Maria da Costa Pereira. His bride was thirty and bore three children, the first fifteen months after the marriage, the second three years later, and the third approximately two-and-a-half years after the second in 1877. Although Manuel was marked as absent from the parish in 1881 and 1887, his obituary appears in the death register in 1914, three years after his wife had passed away. His eldest daughter Maria and his youngest son Manuel married in the parish, the former in 1900 when she was twenty-eight and the latter in 1915 when he was thirty-eight. After bearing one son in Lanheses, the daughter and her husband, a native of Vila Mou, moved to his parish. The son Manuel and his thirty-four-year-old wife had four children in ten years. Three of these children married natives of Vila Mou but only one, the eldest son, Manuel, who was twenty-six at his marriage, brought his wife to live in Lanheses. They had six children between 1944 and 1953, two of whom married in Lisbon, one of whom married in France, and one who died at four months.

This quick summary of some of the members of one Lanhesan family across several generations between the early eighteenth century and the mid-twentieth century demonstrates certain variations in fertility patterns in Lanheses over time, and tends to suggest that the fluctuations in the age at marriage that were discussed in the previous chapter are important to any understanding of the direction of those variations. As numerous historical demographers have pointed out, increases in the average age at which individuals in a population or community marry will reduce the number of years during which a woman can bear children—her so-called "period at risk"—and thus will affect the level of overall fertility. In this section, I will explore the impact of trends in age at marriage in Lanheses upon fertility. The underlying goal is to determine whether any birth control strategy, direct or indirect, is at the root of what are, in at least some of the above individual cases, moderated fertility histories.

Crude birth rates for the parish can be calculated for the late nineteenth century and the twentieth century. These rates were presented in Table 1.1 and indicate that Lanheses, like much of the rest of northwestern Portugal at the time, was not "suffering" from rampant fertility. In fact, these local rates were below that for the nation as a whole until 1930, and then rose above it. Furthermore, while the birth rate nationwide began a general decline after 1930, the birth rate in Lanheses increased temporarily. Only after 1960 was there a dramatic drop.

Although the national censuses only provide data beginning in the late nineteenth century, family reconstitution based on parish registers permits a deeper historical analysis of fertility. Based on this data, there are a number of measures of marital fertility that can be explored. Table 4.1 presents the age-specific marital fertility rates based on reconstituted and complete families for twenty-year marriage cohorts between the eighteenth and the mid-twentieth centuries. What the figures in this table indicate is that throughout these two centuries we are dealing with a "natural fertility" population. The key feature distinguishing the age pattern of natural fertility from some form of controlled fertility is the rate at which the marital fertility rates decline with age. The relatively constant rates shown in this data suggest natural fertility.

This constancy is more graphically apparent in Figure 4:1 which, in addition to illustrating the gradual slope of decline in these rates, also demonstrates that, with the exception of those women who married under age twenty, the age-specific marital fertility rates aggregated by half-century intervals were very similar throughout the period between 1700 and 1949. However, Table 4.1 does indicate that, as with the crude birth rate, there was an increase in both the age-specific rates and the total marital fertility rate after 1920. In fact, the fluctuations in the total marital fertility rate, although small, are nevertheless important to consider. In general, it appears that there was a decline in overall fertility toward the end of the eighteenth century, followed by an increase until the middle of the nineteenth

TABLE 4.1 AGE-SPECIFIC MARITAL FERTILITY RATES, 1700–1949

| Period | 15–19 | 20–24 | 25–29 | 30–34 | 35–39 | 40–44 | TMFR |
|---|---|---|---|---|---|---|---|
| 1700–19 | .214 | .512 | .394 | .274 | .269 | .165 | 8.07 |
| 1720–39 | .200 | .387 | .393 | .412 | .288 | .174 | 8.27 |
| 1740–59 | .207 | .483 | .379 | .355 | .269 | .164 | 8.25 |
| 1760–79 | .575 | .366 | .374 | .358 | .333 | .131 | 7.81 |
| 1780–99 | — | .370 | .331 | .334 | .277 | .138 | 7.25 |
| 1800–19 | .685 | .433 | .401 | .351 | .287 | .179 | 8.25 |
| 1820–39 | .537 | .391 | .408 | .354 | .305 | .162 | 8.10 |
| 1840–59 | .160 | .401 | .317 | .236 | .275 | .149 | 6.89 |
| 1860–79 | .500 | .310 | .396 | .321 | .279 | .133 | 7.19 |
| 1880–99 | .400 | .518 | .444 | .376 | .268 | .128 | 8.67 |
| 1900–19 | .364 | .367 | .361 | .331 | .266 | .149 | 7.37 |
| 1920–39 | .545 | .489 | .445 | .387 | .304 | .173 | 8.89 |
|  | (.500) | (.468) | (.444) | (.415) | (.322) | (.221) | (9.35) |
| 1940–49 | .461 | .468 | .348 | .363 | .211 | .139 | 7.64 |
|  | (.000) | (.466) | (.240) | (.466) | (.247) | (.400) | (9.09) |

NOTE: Since the figures for the 15–19 age group are often based on only a few cases, they are not reliable. The Total Marital Fertility Rate (TMFR) excludes this age category. In the final two periods, the second set of figures represents complete families for which the end of the union (indicated by the death of the husband or wife prior to 1970) is known. The first set includes all families who apparently remained in the parish, although neither of the parents had died by 1970.
SOURCE: Family Reconstitution Data, Lanheses.

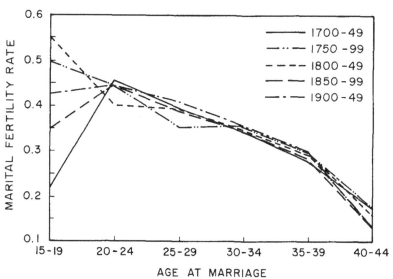

FIGURE 4.1 Age Specific Marital Fertility Rates by Fifty Year Intervals, 1700–1949

TABLE 4.2  MARITAL FERTILITY RATES BY PERIOD OF MARRIAGE
AND DURATION OF MARRIAGE, 1700–1949

| | Duration in Years | | | | |
|---|---|---|---|---|---|
| Period | 0–4.99 | 5–9.99 | 10–14.99 | 15–19.99 | 20–24.99 |
| 1700–19 | .366 | .300 | .195 | .128 | .067 |
| 1720–39 | .393 | .319 | .280 | .165 | .070 |
| 1740–59 | .359 | .322 | .235 | .154 | .061 |
| 1760–79 | .353 | .297 | .183 | .119 | .061 |
| 1780–99 | .338 | .268 | .160 | .108 | .048 |
| 1800–19 | .369 | .325 | .245 | .143 | .066 |
| 1820–39 | .406 | .311 | .212 | .100 | .021 |
| 1840–59 | .353 | .270 | .208 | .129 | .040 |
| 1860–79 | .319 | .221 | .152 | .098 | .043 |
| 1880–99 | .350 | .269 | .202 | .142 | .030 |
| 1900–19 | .374 | .282 | .192 | .138 | .049 |
| 1920–39 | .411 | .329 | .264 | .171 | .047 |
| 1940–49 | .447 | .286 | .197 | .109 | .023 |

NOTE: After 1920, all families are included that appear to have remained in the parish.
SOURCE: Family Reconstitution Data, Lanheses.

century which, in turn, was followed by another decline between roughly 1840 and 1880. The rate rose during the last two decades of the nineteenth century, but dropped again during the first two decades of the twentieth century. Clearly, there is some relationship between these fertility rates and the age at marriage for women. It is more than coincidence that female age at marriage reached one peak during the 1770s and a second peak during the 1860s and 1870s. Although I am not of the opinion that delaying marriage was necessarily a choice consciously made with the express purpose to reduce the number of children born within a marriage, it definitely had this result. The most curious aspect of these total marital fertility rates is the decline during the first two decades of the twentieth century at precisely the time when age at marriage itself dropped dramatically. Something other than a woman's age was probably affecting fertility rates at this time. To this point I will return in the next section.

Table 4.2 provides the marital fertility rates by period of marriage according to the duration of marriage by five-year intervals to age forty-four. Although this table does not differentiate women according to age at marriage, the periods when the overall mean age at marriage for women increased tend to coincide again with lower fertility rates, regardless of duration of marriage. Table 4.3 aggregates

TABLE 4.3 AGE-SPECIFIC MARITAL FERTILITY RATES BY PERIOD
OF MARRIAGE, AGE AT MARRIAGE, AND DURATION OF MARRIAGE,
1700–1949

| Age and Duration | Period of Marriage | | | | |
|---|---|---|---|---|---|
| | 1700–49 | 1750–99 | 1800–49 | 1850–99 | 1900–49 |
| Age 20–24 | | | | | |
| 0–4.99 | .430 | .389 | .387 | .423 | .450 |
| 5–9.99 | .367 | .353 | .340 | .337 | .345 |
| 10–14.99 | .310 | .313 | .275 | .326 | .302 |
| 15–19.99 | .219 | .206 | .185 | .154 | .201 |
| 20–24.99 | .076 | .128 | .092 | .078 | .061 |
| Age 25–29 | | | | | |
| 0–4.99 | .406 | .367 | .407 | .390 | .389 |
| 5–9.99 | .311 | .365 | .368 | .312 | .320 |
| 10–14.99 | .259 | .187 | .269 | .194 | .206 |
| 15–19.99 | .104 | .086 | .128 | .107 | .086 |
| Age 30–34 | | | | | |
| 0–4.99 | .340 | .330 | .402 | .334 | .375 |
| 5–9.99 | .278 | .185 | .250 | .213 | .219 |
| 10–14.99 | .066 | .080 | .119 | .081 | .122 |
| Age 35–39 | | | | | |
| 0–4.99 | .315 | .230 | .251 | .276 | .241 |
| 5–9.99 | .133 | .042 | .057 | .128 | .044 |
| Age 40–44 | | | | | |
| 0–4.99 | .102 | .048 | .090 | .030 | .000 |

SOURCE: Family Reconstitution Data, Lanheses.

these fertility rates according to duration of marriage and age at marriage by half centuries. Some of the variations for smaller time periods are probably lost in this table, and therefore make it hard to draw precise conclusions from it. There does appear to be a difference in the fertility rates of women married between twenty and twenty-four after fifteen to twenty years of marriage, and women married between thirty and thirty-four after five to nine years of marriage, the latter group showing higher fertility rates at the same biological age during all periods except the latter half of the eighteenth century. However, to suggest that this necessarily represents an attempt on the part of the younger marrying group to control their fertility is risky. It may be the result of less frequent sexual activity within marriage after fifteen years—which could or could not be seen as a form of deliberate family limitation—or with some other exogenous factor. The period effects of the late eighteenth and the late nineteenth century do show up on this table, as well.

Table 4.4 presents the average number of children per marriage by age at marriage for all women in complete families. Throughout the two-and-a-half centuries between 1700 and 1949, it appears that the younger a woman was at her marriage, the more likely she was to have more children. If any form of birth control was being practiced, it was apparently not effective in allowing women who had married at younger ages to curtail their fertility at a certain point when a desired number of children was reached. This is further substanti-ated, although not resoundingly, in Table 4.5, which presents the mean age at last birth for women marrying below and above age thirty by twenty-year marital cohorts. This table only includes women who reached at least age forty, and it is difficult to draw any conclu-sions from it. In general, those women marrying over thirty across the two centuries between 1700 and 1900 are slightly older at their last birth—which might indicate either family limitation or, again, reduced sexual activity among those couples who had married earlier and therefore lived together longer. The two periods when those marrying under thirty on average have children to a later point in life—the 1760s and the 1880s—are precisely those that emerge as unusual in other measures of fertility behavior. The period after 1920 is particularly interesting, since the difference increased dramatically to over three years. Is this an indication of the beginnings of some sort of attempt on the part of women married at younger ages to control or limit their family size?

One further measure, although a rough one, of the extent of family limitation is Coale and Trussell's index "little m," which compares

TABLE 4.4 AVERAGE NUMBER OF CHILDREN PER MARRIAGE BY AGE AT MARRIAGE, 1700–1949 (completed families only)

| Period | 15–19 | 20–24 | 25–29 | 30–34 | 35–39 | 40–44 |
|--------|-------|-------|-------|-------|-------|-------|
| 1700–49 | 7.1 | 6.1[a] | 4.9[a] | 3.5 | 2.4 | 0.4 |
| 1750–99 | 7.4 | 7.1 | 5.2 | 3.1 | 1.2 | 0.5 |
| 1800–49 | 7.7 | 6.2 | 5.9 | 4.0 | 1.5 | 0.6 |
| 1850–99 | 8.2 | 6.7 | 5.2 | 3.3 | 1.7 | 0.4 |
| 1900–49 | 8.1 | 6.9 | 5.3 | 4.1 | 1.9 | 0.8 |

[a] For each of these age groups, approximately 20 percent of the marriages were terminated by the death of one spouse well before the woman had reached age forty-four.
SOURCE: Family Reconstitution Data, Lanheses.

TABLE 4.5 AGE AT LAST BIRTH, 1700–1949

| Period | Women Marrying under 30 | | Women Marrying over 30 Who Reached Age 40 | |
|---|---|---|---|---|
| | No. | Mean Age | No. | Mean Age |
| 1700–19 | 32 | 39.9 | 11 | 41.6 |
| 1720–39 | 46 | 40.9 | 7 | 42.1 |
| 1740–59 | 32 | 40.5 | 10 | 39.7 |
| 1760–79 | 30 | 40.9 | 21 | 39.9 |
| 1780–99 | 20 | 40.3 | 15 | 40.5 |
| 1800–19 | 36 | 40.7 | 7 | 41.9 |
| 1820–39 | 48 | 39.4 | 16 | 40.8 |
| 1840–59 | 34 | 40.5 | 25 | 40.9 |
| 1860–79 | 27 | 38.7 | 33 | 40.2 |
| 1880–99 | 42 | 40.1 | 21 | 38.8 |
| 1900–19 | 46 | 39.1 | 17 | 40.6 |
| 1920–39 | 79 | 38.5 | 22 | 41.8 |
| 1940–49 | 47 | 36.8 | 10 | 39.9 |

NOTE: For women marrying in the 1940s for whom there is no record of death prior to 1970, an assumption is made that they reached age forty within the parish.

SOURCE: Family Reconstitution Data, Lanheses.

the age structure of an observed marital fertility schedule with the age structure of a "standard" natural fertility schedule (1974). The greater the value of "little m," the greater the level of fertility control. Conversely, negative values demonstrate that fertility is declining with age more slowly than in a standard schedule. The values of "little m" for the Lanheses data are included in Table 4.6. Negative values tend to predominate over positive values, and it is certainly not the case that a shift from a negative value, for example of −.110 in the 1720s and 1730s to a positive value of .046 in the 1740s and 1750s is necessarily an indication of more family limitation in the latter two decades than in the former. We have to remember that we are dealing with a relatively small population and, furthermore, Coale and Trussell themselves suggest that any value below 0.200 can be taken as evidence of little or no control. This makes the value of .274 during the latter two decades of the nineteenth century particularly puzzling. At the root of this figure are probably the unusually high age-specific rates for women who married between twenty and twenty-nine in comparison with both preceding and succeeding periods. Yet, this is precisely a period when women who married under thirty had

TABLE 4.6 VALUES FOR "LITTLE M" AND THE
MEAN SQUARE ERROR, 1700–1949

| Period | Little m | Mean Square Error |
|--------|----------|-------------------|
| 1700–1719 | .082 | .023 |
| 1720–1739 | −.110 | .004 |
| 1740–1759 | .046 | .006 |
| 1760–1779 | −.036 | .009 |
| 1780–1799 | −.047 | .001 |
| 1800–1819 | −.062 | .003 |
| 1820–1839 | −.070 | .001 |
| 1840–1859 | −.063 | .021 |
| 1860–1879 | −.066 | .009 |
| 1880–1899 | .274 | .000 |
| 1900–1919 | −.056 | .000 |
| 1920–1939 | .039 | .001 |
| (1920–1939) | −.139 | .005 |
| 1940–1949 | .165 | .015 |
| (1940–1949) | −.593 | .149 |
| 1700–1749 | −.011 | .005 |
| 1750–1799 | .070 | .004 |
| 1800–1849 | −.084 | .001 |
| 1850–1899 | .122 | .001 |
| 1900–1949 | .046 | .001 |
| (1900–1949) | −.094 | .002 |

NOTE: The more the observed rates deviate from the standard schedule, the higher the value of "little m" and the greater the likelihood of some form of fertility control. Any value of "little m" below 0.200 can be taken as evidence of little or no control, and values about 0.500 imply limitation of some form. Low values of the mean square error indicate that the observed rates conform well either to the standard natural fertility schedule or to an expected pattern of departure where fertility is controlled.

SOURCE: Family Reconstitution Data, Lanheses.

a mean age at last birth higher than women who married over thirty. This would seem to inhibit our ability to conclude that during these two decades, those women who married younger were attempting to limit their fertility in some way.

What conclusions can be drawn so far from this fertility data? I think we can reason that, based simply on these various statistical measures, family limitation was not extensive. Furthermore, as has

TABLE 4.7 RELATIONSHIP BETWEEN MOTHER'S
AGE AT MARRIAGE AND TOTAL NUMBER OF
CHILDREN, 1750–1949 (by twenty-year periods)

| Period | $r$ | $r^2$ | No. of Cases |
|--------|------|------|-------|
| 1750–1769 | −.79 | .59 | 36 |
| 1770–1789 | −.75 | .56 | 47 |
| 1790–1809 | −.66 | .43 | 35 |
| 1810–1829 | −.66 | .43 | 52 |
| 1830–1849 | −.58 | .38 | 70 |
| 1850–1869 | −.67 | .45 | 70 |
| 1870–1889 | −.66 | .43 | 79 |
| 1890–1909 | −.54 | .29 | 80 |
| 1910–1929 | −.60 | .36 | 51 |
|  | (−.41) | (.17) | (107) |
| 1930–1949 | −.66 | .43 | 160 |

NOTE: The calculations for 1750–1909 are based on complete
  families where it is known that the woman reached age 45;
  between 1910 and 1929, the first set of figures are for complete
  families and the second for families for which completeness is
  not established; the figures for 1930–1949 are calculated on
  the assumption that if there is no death before 45, the woman
  lived to that age in the parish.
SOURCE: Family Reconstitution Data, Lanheses.

been found in numerous other historical studies, the fertility levels of
Lanhesan women were affected by variations in the mean age at which
marriages were contracted. Women who married before age twenty-
four had roughly twice as many children as women who married in
their early thirties. And yet, age at marriage is certainly not the whole
story. Indeed, the correlation and regression coefficients for mother's
age at marriage and the total number of children born to a marriage
(Table 4.7) indicate that age provides only a partial explanation. Under "normal" circumstances, we would expect that as a mother's age
at marriage increases, the number of children she has decreases and,
in fact, all the correlation coefficients show this inverse relationship.
However, if we examine the $r^2$s—the proportion of the variance in
the number of children explained by mother's age at marriage—we
notice that beginning in 1790 they are consistently less than .50. Furthermore, a closer study of the more recent century (Table 4.8) reveals extremely low $r^2$s during certain decades (the 1870s and the
1900s). Thus, alternative factors need to be considered.

One of the variables frequently introduced is the level of infant

TABLE 4.8 RELATIONSHIP BETWEEN MOTHER'S
AGE AT MARRIAGE AND TOTAL NUMBER OF
CHILDREN, 1860–1949 (by decade)

| Period | r | $r^2$ | No. of Cases |
|--------|------|-------|--------------|
| 1860–69 | −.88 | .78 | 34 |
| 1870–79 | −.56 | .31 | 36 |
| 1880–89 | −.78 | .61 | 43 |
| 1890–99 | −.76 | .58 | 34 |
| 1900–09 | −.54 | .29 | 46 |
| 1910–19 | −.63 | .40 | 25 |
|  | (−.50) | (.25) | (43) |
| 1920–29 | −.73 | .53 | 26 |
|  | (−.42) | (.17) | (64) |
| 1930–39 | −.31 | .09 | 73 |
| 1940–49 | −.33 | .11 | 87 |

NOTE: The calculations for 1750–1909 are based on complete families where it is known that the woman reached
age 45; between 1910 and 1929, the first set of figures are
for complete families and the second for families for which
completeness is not established; figures for 1930–1949 are
calculated on the assumption that if there is no death before
45, the woman lived to that age in the parish.
SOURCE: Family Reconstitution Data, Lanheses.

mortality. As the argument goes, within peasant populations, there
was a strong motive to have many children in order to offset the
number of children who died in infancy or early childhood. Thus,
the larger the number of pregnancies, the larger the number of infant
deaths. Some historical studies (Knodel 1979) have in fact shown
quite the opposite relationship; that is, the average number of surviving children declines with increases in the age at marriage, and therefore with fewer pregnancies. One regional study of Portugal based
on an analysis of 1960 census data demonstrates only a weak correlation between fertility and infant mortality. Indeed, certain regions
of the south were characterized by low fertility and high infant mortality, whereas the district of Viana do Castelo was characterized by
relatively low infant mortality and moderate fertility (Candido 1969).

The data on infant and childhood mortality in Lanheses are unre-
liable until 1860. Until 1800 there were few children under fourteen
who could be matched to a baptismal record in order to determine
their age at death. Between 1800 and 1859, the deaths of children
under fourteen were recorded with more regularity, although whether

they were always reported is open to question. Again, only those
infants who could be positively linked to an entry in the baptismal
register can be considered. This population yields the following infant mortality rates (the number of infant deaths—under one year of
age—per 1,000 live births) for the first six decades of the nineteenth
century.

| | |
|---|---|
| 1800–1809 | 69 |
| 1810–1819 | 138 |
| 1820–1829 | 52 |
| 1830–1839 | 125 |
| 1840–1849 | 73 |
| 1850–1859 | 75 |

These rates are extremely low for a supposedly pretransition population and probably reflect problems with data on infant mortality.
Table 4.9 presents the more reliable post-1860 data. Although still
somewhat low, it should be noted that these rates for Lanheses are
within the range of what has been described for the district of Viana
do Castelo as a whole. Furthermore, when the deaths of illegitimate
children are omitted from the total number of children dying within
a year for each period, the infant mortality rates are even lower. Are
we to conclude on this basis that this region of Portugal had already
experienced the demographic shift, matching lowered fertility to a
lowered rate of mortality? The fertility data per se make such a conclusion problematic. It seems more reasonable to argue that the death
of an infant during the first year, in a society where women generally
breast-fed their children for at least a year, simply put a woman back
"at risk" earlier than if her child had survived. In fact, although the
average interval between the birth of a child who died within the
first year and the succeeding birth during the last four decades of the
nineteenth century was roughly one-and-a-half years, the average interval between births when the first child survived past a year is a
little more than two-and-a-quarter years. A comparison of the fertility histories of three couples married in the decade of the 1860s will
further illustrate the point. The first couple, Manuel da Silva and Ana
Gonçalves Rocha, were married in 1861. The groom, a poor potter,
was nineteen and his bride was twenty-five. During the next fourteen
years, they had ten children, only one of whom, the first-born daughter, survived to adulthood. This is the most extreme case of infant
mortality within a single family that exists among all the couples
married in the parish from 1860 on. Did this poor potter couple go
on having children because of some a priori notion about how many

TABLE 4.9 INFANT MORTALITY RATES, LANHESES, 1860–1959

| Period | No. of Baptisms | No. of Children Dying within 12 Months | Infant Mortality Rate | |
|---|---|---|---|---|
| | | | A | B |
| 1860–69 | 273 | 33 | 121 | 102 |
| 1870–79 | 239 | 44 | 184 | 155 |
| 1880–89 | 237 | 30 | 126 | 101 |
| 1890–99 | 281 | 22 | 78 | 60 |
| 1900–09 | 310 | 33 | 106 | 84 |
| 1910–19 | 263 | 23 | 87 | 80 |
| 1920–29 | 328 | 26 | 79 | 70 |
| 1930–39 | 435 | 23 | 53 | 46 |
| 1940–49 | 449 | 38 | 85 | 80 |
| 1950–59 | 473 | 17 | 23 | 34 |

NOTE: Column A includes all infant deaths; column B excludes the deaths of illegitimate children.

SOURCE: Parish registers, Lanheses.

children they wanted, or simply because nature was taking its course? The intervals between the births of their children follow and indicate a definite reduction in the amount of time between births when infants died soon after birth.

| | | *interval* | *status* |
|---|---|---|---|
| 1. | Maria Rosa | 2 mos. | lived |
| 2. | José | 35 mos. | died age 4 |
| 3. | Manuel | 31 mos. | died age 3 |
| 4. | Maria | 25 mos. | died same day |
| 5. | Maria | 13 mos. | died age 17 days |
| 6. | Maria | 11 mos. | died next day |
| 7. | Miguel | 13 mos. | died same day |
| 8. | Miguel | 10 mos. | died same day |
| 9. | Rosa | 11 mos. | died next day |
| 10. | José | 17 mos. | died same day |

There is no denying that seeing each baby die so soon was probably discouraging to Manuel and Ana, but in the end, she had just as many pregnancies as other women who saw more of their children survive to adulthood. For example, a comparable though slightly different fertility history is that of Rosa Rodrigues, who was twenty when she married António Rebouço in September of 1869. António was a lavrador, but a small-scale lavrador, and when he and Rosa married they moved into a house next door to Rosa's father and mother. During the next twenty years, Rosa had nine children, five of whom lived to adulthood. The intervals between the births of these children were as follows:

| | | | |
|---|---|---|---|
| 1. | Manuel | 10 mos. | died within the month |
| 2. | Maria | 18 mos. | lived |
| 3. | Joaquim | 41 mos. | died within two months |
| 4. | Rosa | 19 mos. | lived |
| 5. | António | 38 mos. | died within five months |
| 6. | Antónia | 19 mos. | lived |
| 7. | José | 31 mos. | lived |
| 8. | Luisa | 30 mos. | lived |
| 9. | Angelina | 42 mos. | died at 19 months |

Rosa was forty-one, two years older than Ana had been, when she terminated her childbearing. Her fertility history demonstrates even more dramatically the variations in birth intervals in association with whether an infant lives to a year or not. A third example is provided by the fertility history of José Alves and Luisa Gonçalves. José and Luisa married in 1868, when he was twenty-five and she twenty-six—thus, Luisa was roughly the same age as Ana. Like Manuel and Ana, they too were poor, though jornaleiros rather than potters. Like Rosa and António, they too had nine children, but only two died in infancy. Luisa also finished her childbearing when she was over forty, again later than Ana. The intervals between the births of Luisa's children were as follows:

| | | | |
|---|---|---|---|
| 1. | Sebastião | 2 mos. | lived |
| 2. | Maria | 27 mos. | lived |
| 3. | Rosa | 22 mos. | lived |
| 4. | António | 35 mos. | lived |
| 5. | Manuel | 27 mos. | died in two days |
| 6. | Maria Rosa | 21 mos. | lived |
| 7. | Manuel António | 26 mos. | lived |
| 8. | Maria Luisa | 24 mos. | died within month |
| 9. | Gracinda | 16 mos. | lived |

Although breast-feeding was common for at least a year, this does not necessarily mean that it was used forthrightly as a method of birth control. On the other hand, women were not necessarily unaware of the fact that their chances of getting pregnant again might be forestalled while they breast-fed, at least for a few months; it is obvious that the intervals between two healthy children seem to indicate that breast-feeding was somewhat effective in delaying the onset of ovulation. However, breast-feeding was practiced primarily because it was the best and cheapest source of nutrition, because a mother could easily feed her infant in the fields, and because when a child was weaned and fed *pappa*—a mixture of grain and cow's milk—the risks of death from gastroenteritis became greater. Such a concern was expressed, for example, by one elderly female villager who bore her children in Lanheses during the 1920s and early 1930s. Her first child was a daughter who died of enteritis when she was nine months old. Her mother blamed her death on the fact that she had little breast milk and was therefore forced to rely on a bottle almost immediately. Her second child, a son, was born a year after the first. She nurtured him and her succeeding children herself, and commented that perhaps for this reason they were all born approximately three years apart. Studies in other regions of Europe have substantiated the role of breast-feeding in the prevention of infant disease, and hence in the reduction of rates of infant mortality (Littell 1981, McLaren 1984).

Further consideration of the issue of family limitation and birth control will be developed in section four of this chapter, but it is apparent from what has been discussed so far that neither age at marriage nor infant mortality explains the whole picture of fertility in Lanheses. Furthermore, although they have not as yet been brought out sufficiently, there are individual differences in fertility histories that can be ascribed, I think, to more than individual differences in fecundity. It is to this question that I now turn.

### VIUVAS DOS VIVOS: EMIGRATION AND FERTILITY

> They leave (if they are married) their wives as widows, or single, unable to procreate, and if in ten years of absence they had remained and had had four children, these children would be the greatest richness for them and for the country. (Bezerra 1785:190)

Although Swedlund (1978:151) has argued that few of the many studies on migration and local mobility have been linked into the demographic transition model, the important relationship between migration and fertility is by no means novel. Davis (1963) included it in his discussion of a multiphasic demographic response, and Friedlander has explored it further, hypothesizing that "an adjustment in the reproductive behavior of a community in response to the rising of a 'strain' may differ depending upon the ease with which the community can relieve the 'strain' through outmigration" (1969:359).[4] In a later study (1983), Friedlander has demonstrated that the trade-off between emigration and marital fertility has been particularly characteristic of agricultural areas, although, except to suggest that it has something to do with man-land ratios, he does not give us a clear understanding of exactly why. Nor is there any precise differentiation in types of emigration—permanent or temporary. Indeed, it often seems that the underlying assumption is of a permanent departure. Yet differences in the pattern of emigration are, as has already been argued, crucial to an understanding of demographic behavior in Lanheses and northwestern Portugal generally, and a permanent departure was by no means a part of the initial migration plan for a number of Lanhesan emigrants in the past, as at present.

Doubters of certain elements of the multiphasic theory see a bias in the model. Knodel (1974), for example, suggests that socioeconomic conditions in backward areas, including high levels of illiteracy, themselves explain both outmigration and the slow spread of modern fertility levels. He concludes that there is "little evidence that migration from countryside to city retarded the adoption of family limitation." Although there may not be a direct link, especially in terms of a conscious choice between having fewer children or having more children emigrate once they have reached an appropriate age, it is impossible to dispose lightly of the indirect impact of migration on marital fertility in any consideration of demographic behavior in Portugal. The result of both population pressure and economic constraints, emigration from northwestern Portugal probably had the convenient effect not only of limiting nuptiality by eliminating a sizable proportion of men of marriageable age from the marriage pool (thereby increasing the population of spinster women), but also of limiting marital fertility through the occasional or even permanent absence of married men. Although perhaps not a conscious or deliberate method of family limitation or population control, at an aggregate level emigration had precisely this effect.

There are at least two ways in which emigration may have influenced marital fertility levels. On the one hand, the seasonal or temporary migrations to southern Portugal, Spain, and even to Brazil of married men reduced the so-called "period of risk" for their wives. The result was much more lengthy birth intervals between children than under normal conditions. On the other hand, those married men who departed and died abroad, or who simply never returned, truly left their wives as "widows of the living"—*viuvas dos vivos*. Their emigration had the result of prematurely aborting marriages at the height of their wives' fecund years, and therefore of permanently eliminating these women from the population of married women contributing to fertility levels within a community.

As indicated in an earlier chapter, the sex ratio of the married population in the parish since the late decades of the nineteenth century has been disproportionate in favor of women. It reached its lowest points in 1890 (78.1 males / 100 females) and in 1911 (72.5 males / 100 females). The evidence drawn from analyses of passport registers and the rois da desobriga tends to confirm that the number of married Lanhesan men who emigrated increased as the nineteenth century drew to its close and the twentieth century dawned. Although we have no systematic census data either on emigration or on sex ratios by marital status prior to 1864, the 1798 count made by Villas Boas yields a ratio of 87 males over 14 per 100 females over 14. Although these figures clearly include single men and women, other evidence, such as the death registers, suggests that both unmarried and married men were migrating and therefore were periodically absent during the late eighteenth century, as they were during the late nineteenth century. Indeed, it is very possible that for those marriages where no obituary notice for a husband could be found in the Lanheses registers, even though all other evidence—marriages and deaths of children, the death of the wife—indicate that the family lived their life in the parish, the husbands died abroad and their deaths went without verification and therefore without an official record in the Lanheses books.[6]

The impact of seasonal or temporary migrations on marital fertility has been the subject of a few recent studies in historical demography. Livi Bacci (1967), for example, isolates three areas of Spain where a deficiency of males has resulted from heavy emigration—the Canaries, the province of Asturias, and the province of Galicia. In comparison with other Spanish provinces, the latter two areas have been characterized by moderate fertility levels since at least 1860. Even more intriguing is Francine Van de Walle's study of the Italian-speaking canton of Ticino in the Swiss Alps (1975). Like the inhabitants of northwestern Portugal, the Ticinese demonstrate a strong attachment to their native land. In Ticino, as in northwestern Portugal, land was divided equally among children and therefore extremely fragmented. And finally, like the young man of Minho, the Ticinese "who worked abroad for several years in search of extra income had no intention of deserting the village where he would one day inherit a share of the patrimonial property" (1975:450). Thus the Ticinese, married or single, also migrated on a seasonal and temporary basis and, as a result, were also characterized by both late marriages and low marital fertility.

Menken (1979) has taken this discussion one step further by trying to estimate mathematically the impact of seasonal migration on fertility. She has devised a model for various ranges of fecundibility (the monthly probability of conception of a woman) and post-partum nonsusceptibility, and has found that consistently, as the number of months of physical absence increases, the birth probabilities decrease linearly. For example, in one of her hypothetical stages, when the fecundability is .15, the probability that the conception will lead to a live birth is .20, and the post-partum amenorrhea associated with a live birth is twelve months, then an absence of three months will reduce the birth probability by 11.2 percent. Clearly, if a seasonal pattern of migration of three or six months had this kind of effect, and then the migration were eliminated, the result could be a rise in fertility.[7]

Despite the limitations in migration data for Lanheses, especially prior to 1860, there are a number of ways to explore the possible impact of seasonal or temporary migrations from Lanheses on marital fertility. Table 4.10 shows the proportion of conceptions by season between 1700 and 1970. During the first half of the eighteenth century, only slightly more than half the infants born in Lanheses were conceived during the spring and summer months between April and September. For the next century and a half, however, almost two-thirds of the children born and baptised in the parish were conceived during the spring and summer. Only after 1900 does the early eighteenth-century pattern of more even seasonal distribution begin to emerge again. The pattern of seasonality prevalent in Lanheses during the latter half of the eighteenth century and throughout the nineteenth century is in sharp contrast to Bell's (1979) data on Italy. There he shows sharp dips in conceptions during the spring and summer months in comparison to the rest of the year, and relates it to a range of factors, including the demanding pace of work during the harvest season.

When the changes in the seasonality of conceptions in Lanheses are examined more closely, it is apparent that the twentieth-century shift did not really occur until 1920. At that point, whatever seasonal effects there had been which created marked differences in the timing of conceptions seem to have disappeared. Edward Shorter, in his book *The Making of the Modern Family* (1975), has suggested that the

TABLE 4.10 SEASONALITY OF CONCEPTIONS, 1700–
1970
(percent)

| Period | April–September | October–March |
|--------|-----------------|---------------|
| 1700–1749 | 52.1 | 47.9 |
| 1750–1799 | 64.7 | 35.3 |
| 1800–1849 | 64.5 | 35.5 |
| 1850–1899 | 60.8 | 39.2 |
| 1900–1949 | 55.3 | 44.7 |
| 1950–1970 | 45.6 | 54.4 |

NOTE: During 1960–70, there were over forty children born in France
but baptized in the village. They are excluded in the calculation.
SOURCE: Parish registers, Lanheses.

eventual evening out of seasonal conceptions is related to a general
process of modernization and to the "infusion of courtship and marriage by romance." In Lanheses, however, something else was probably occurring—the disruption in the mid 1920s, and especially after
1931 with the advent of political turmoil in Spain, of a pattern of
seasonal migration to Spain that had been part of the demographic
way of life of the parish for at least two centuries. As noted in the
previous chapter, this migration most likely occurred during the winter months, when the demands for labor in Lanheses were least. After
the grape harvest in late September or early October, men departed
for southern Spain, remained there until spring, and then returned in
time to aid their wives and families in the sowing and harvesting of
their fields.

Considering again the material presented in Chapter Three, there
seems to be a rough correlation (although not a dramatic one, with
the exception of the 1770s when spring and summer conceptions
rose to 74 percent of all conceptions) between an apparent increase
in the migration flow to Spain during the last three decades of the
eighteenth century and the first decade of the nineteenth century and
an increase in the number of conceptions occurring during the spring
and summer as opposed to the fall and winter. Conversely, during
periods when we think there may have been minimal seasonal emigration (the 1830s when spring and summer conceptions fell to 55.7
percent) or no emigration at all (the 1940s when spring and summer
conceptions represented 49.7 percent of all conceptions), a more equal
distribution is approached. Along a similar vein, it is also interesting
to reflect on the two decades between 1950 and 1970 in conjunction
with patterns of migration to France. Beginning in the later 1950s

and continuing through the 1960s, many married men emigrated to northern Europe alone, leaving their wives and families behind. While abroad, they worked primarily in construction. Although most returned for a month during the summer, it was also customary for these men to travel back to Portugal before Christmas, when construction work was at a halt, and to remain in the village for a couple of months before returning to France to resume their contract jobs. Simultaneously, and for the first time in 250 years, the number of conceptions that took place between October and March exceeded those that took place between April and September by more than 1 or 2 percent—in the 1960s by as much as 10 percent.

A second way to document the impact of seasonal or temporary migration is through an examination of individual fertility histories and birth intervals. In his important article on natural fertility, Louis Henry claims that in societies practicing little or no birth control, intervals between births vary from twenty-four months to somewhat less than thirty-six months. The primary factor causing variation is, in his view, the difference in the mean length of the "idle period"— that is, the length of time elapsing between parturition and the resumption of sexual relations or the reappearance of ovulation, whichever occurs later after confinement. We know that in many cultural contexts the former is affected by post-partum taboos and the latter by the culturally defined acceptable or "normal" number of months or years that a mother is expected to breast-feed her child.[8] Potter (1963) argues that intervals of up to thirty to thirty-three months can be readily accounted for, and anything over that should lead the analyst to suspect the presence of some form of family limitation or some other external nonbiological factor affecting fertility. If we are to conclude that widespread and deliberate family limitation was rare in Lanheses until well into the present century, then large intervals between births, when we find them, must have been the result of some other exogenous factor or factors. It is possible that we are seeing a series of unrecorded stillbirths; possible, but unlikely because it seems apparent that there were certain periods in Lanheses' history when lengthy birth intervals were more prevalent than at others. Thus at both an individual and an aggregate level there is something to explain.

Table 4.11 provides parity birth intervals for birth cohorts between 1700 and 1949 for children born in complete families, as well as the mean age of mothers at the births of these children. If we are to be suspicious of birth intervals greater than thirty-three months (2.75 years), then our attention is immediately drawn to the latter

TABLE 4.11 MEAN INTERVALS AND AGE OF MOTHER BY PARITY FOR
PERIOD–PARITY COHORTS, 1700–1949
(by year and decimal portions of year)

| Period | 0–1 | 1–2 | 2–3 | 3–4 | 4–5 | 5–6 |
|---|---|---|---|---|---|---|
| 1700–1749 | | | | | | |
| Interval | 1.36 | 2.37 | 2.54 | 2.50 | 2.68 | 2.79 |
| Mean Age | | | | | | |
| of Mother | 27.5 | 29.7 | 31.2 | 33.3 | 35.3 | 37.4 |
| 1750–1799 | | | | | | |
| Interval | 1.63 | 2.59 | 2.69 | 2.57 | 2.93 | 2.83 |
| Mean Age | | | | | | |
| of Mother | 29.7 | 31.0 | 32.4 | 33.4 | 34.4 | 37.5 |
| 1800–1849 | | | | | | |
| Interval | 1.49 | 2.42 | 2.55 | 2.74 | 2.76 | 2.77 |
| Mean Age | | | | | | |
| of Mother | 27.7 | 29.9 | 32.0 | 33.7 | 35.8 | 37.6 |
| 1850–1899 | | | | | | |
| Interval | 1.34 | 2.56 | 2.73 | 2.82 | 2.67 | 2.66 |
| Mean Age | | | | | | |
| of Mother | 29.4 | 31.2 | 32.9 | 33.9 | 35.5 | 36.2 |
| 1900–1949 | | | | | | |
| Interval | 1.29 | 2.39 | 2.64 | 2.65 | 2.54 | 2.48 |
| Mean Age | | | | | | |
| of Mother | 27.5 | 29.7 | 31.2 | 33.8 | 35.1 | 37.1 |

SOURCE: Family Reconstitution Data, Lanheses.

half of the eighteenth century (a mean interval of 2.93 between the
fourth and fifth births) and to the latter half of the nineteenth century
(a mean interval of 2.82 between the third and fourth births). Changes
in the mean age at marriage and therefore of the average ages of
mothers at the births of these later children do not appear to be
particularly important in explaining these differences. For example,
the mean age of mothers at the birth of their fourth child hovers
around 33.8 throughout the nineteenth and first half of the twentieth
century.

Information gleaned from a range of sources has suggested that
emigration to Spain probably increased during the late decades of the
eighteenth century and the first decade of the nineteenth century. If
we separate out the birth cohorts of the 1790s and 1800s, the longer
birth intervals following the third child are even more apparent.

|  | 0–1 | 1–2 | 2–3 | 3–4 | 4–5 | 5–6 |
|---|---|---|---|---|---|---|
| Interval | 1.57 | 2.55 | 2.70 | 3.03 | 3.02 | 2.90 |
| Mean Age of Mother | 28.1 | 30.2 | 32.7 | 33.9 | 36.8 | 39.7 |

Unfortunately, with the exception of a few death notices, we have no individual-level data for this period to help identify systematically those men who may have migrated after their marriage. However, an examination of the fertility histories of the wives of those men who had been absent in Spain prior to their marriage and who married during the decade of the 1790s reveals some particularly lengthy intervals. The assumption here, based simply on a broad ethnographic and historical knowledge of migration patterns, is that those men who had worked in Spain in their youth may have been quite likely to return there after a few children were born, to make money to support their growing families. There were forty-three marriages during this decade, and twenty-six of the grooms declared absences in Spain before marriage. Eighteen cases provide us with fertility histories. The remaining eight couples include four who appear to have left the parish, two who died childless, and two whose fate is uncertain. Interestingly, however, the bride of one of the latter two couples had an illegitimate child in 1798, six years after her marriage. On the baptismal record for this infant the "adulterous" woman's husband is recorded as being absent in Spain. For the eighteen couples with fertility histories, the mean intervals between the births of their children are as follows:

| 0–1 | 1–2 | 2–3 | 3–4 | 4–5 |
|---|---|---|---|---|
| 1.58 | 3.06 | 3.53 | 3.09 | 2.80 |

These indeed are unusually long intervals. Furthermore, two of the eighteen husbands died in 1804, one at age thirty-two and the other at age forty-four. Although it is only a guess, it is possible that these premature deaths were the result of illnesses contracted abroad—probably not an infrequent occurrence—and that these two men were fortunate enough to have made it back to the parish to die rather than to have died abroad and alone.

The data on emigration during the late nineteenth century is much more concrete and, in addition, both documentary sources and oral history provide us with information on specific individuals. Thus, it

TABLE 4.12 MEAN INTERVALS BY PARITY FOR
PERIOD–PARITY COHORTS, 1860–1949
(by year and decimal portion of year)

| | Intervals | | | | | |
|---|---|---|---|---|---|---|
| Period | 0–1 | 1–2 | 2–3 | 3–4 | 4–5 | 5–6 |
| 1860–69 | 1.1 | 2.2 | 2.3 | 1.8 | 1.0 | 1.2 |
| | 1.0 | 2.4 | 2.5 | 2.2 | — | — |
| 1870–79 | 1.5 | 2.6 | 2.9 | 3.2 | 2.1 | 1.7 |
| | 1.5 | 2.6 | 2.9 | 3.1 | 2.1 | 1.7 |
| 1880–89 | 1.5 | 2.4 | 2.7 | 2.4 | 3.1 | 2.6 |
| | 1.8 | 2.5 | 2.3 | 2.5 | 3.0 | 2.6 |
| 1890–99 | 1.2 | 2.2 | 2.9 | 2.8 | 2.5 | 2.3 |
| | 1.1 | 2.3 | 2.8 | 2.7 | 2.5 | 2.5 |
| 1900–09 | 1.1 | 2.6 | 3.1 | 2.5 | 2.3 | 2.4 |
| | 1.0 | 2.4 | 2.8 | 2.6 | 2.2 | 2.2 |
| 1910–19 | 1.5 | 2.4 | 3.1 | 3.1 | 2.8 | 3.0 |
| | 1.7 | 2.6 | 2.8 | 3.3 | 2.9 | 3.1 |
| | 1.5 | 2.5 | 3.1 | 3.2 | 2.9 | 3.0 |
| 1920–29 | 1.4 | 2.4 | 2.1 | 2.5 | 2.7 | 2.8 |
| | 1.5 | 2.3 | 2.1 | 2.6 | 2.6 | 2.5 |
| | 1.4 | 2.5 | 2.2 | 2.4 | 2.6 | 2.7 |
| 1930–39 | 1.5 | 2.3 | 2.5 | 2.5 | 2.5 | 2.3 |
| | 1.6 | 2.3 | 2.5 | 2.5 | 2.5 | 2.3 |
| 1940–49 | 1.2 | 2.4 | 2.5 | 2.7 | 2.4 | 2.4 |
| | 1.3 | 2.2 | 2.5 | 2.5 | 2.5 | 2.4 |

NOTE: The first row for each period includes all classes of families; the second
includes only complete families for which the end of the union is known and
the woman has reached the end of her fertile period; the third row (1910–
1929) includes both complete and incomplete families after 1920 where the
members of incomplete families are assumed to have lived to the end of
childbearing years.
SOURCE: Family Reconstitution Data, Lanheses.

is worth examining this period more closely. Table 4.12 provides the
mean intervals by parity for period-parity cohorts for each decade
between 1860 and 1949. It demonstrates that the intervals between
second- and third-born children and third- and fourth-born children
during the 1870s were especially long, as were the intervals between
second- and third-born children during the first decade of the twentieth century and between second- and third- as well as between third-
and fourth-born children during the second decade of the twentieth

century. The period after the turn of the century is particularly intriguing, since various sources indicate that the number of married Lanhesan men who emigrated to Brazil during that time increased dramatically.

Clearly, the aggregate figures indicate some sort of intervening variable affecting certain birth parities at particular points in time. Again, a more concrete understanding can be gained by looking at individual fertility histories in conjunction with data on absences documented in the rois da desobriga or through oral history (Table 4.13). Although somewhat prior to the dramatic increases in birth intervals, the first eight fertility histories on Table 4.13 (Group A) are selected from among the wives of twenty-nine married men who were marked absent in the 1850 rol da desobriga. The asterisked intervals are the ones that spanned the year 1850 and, for the most part, they are unusually long. Eight more women whose husbands were absent in 1850 and who had all their children prior to the mid-century mark (Table 4.13, Group B), also demonstrate some unusually long birth intervals. Although unverifiable, the suggestion here is that the absence of these men in 1850 is probably indicative of earlier absences. Indeed, three men marked absent in 1850 were still marked absent twenty years later, and by this time all were over fifty.

After 1870, and once the rois become more frequent, the evidence for repetitive emigration becomes more substantial. In instance after instance throughout the late nineteenth and early twentieth centuries, there appears to be a coincidence in the timing of a husband's absence from the parish and one or more lengthy birth intervals of his wife. Overall, for all marriages between 1850 and 1910 where a husband was marked absent on at least one of the rois da desobriga or where his emigration was established through passport registers, the mean interval between first and second child was 2.89 years (84 women) and between second and third child 3.98 years (67 women). Since the rois are our only continuous source of information on the migration of particular individuals, and the extant examples of these documents are sporadic until the turn of the twentieth century, this listing is a partial indication, at best, of seasonal and temporary male migrants. Certainly, the gap between 1870 and 1881 does not permit us to confirm an association between male migration during that decade and the lengthier birth intervals between second and third and between third and fourth children that emerge in the aggregate compilation included on Table 4.12.

As a whole, the wives of this subpopulation of identifiable migrants do stand out against the larger population. Indeed, when one

TABLE 4.13 FERTILITY HISTORIES OF SELECTED LANHESAN WOMEN, 1820–1960

| Date of Marriage | Mother's Age at Marriage | Birth Intervals | | | | | |
|---|---|---|---|---|---|---|---|
| | | 0–1 | 1–2 | 2–3 | 3–4 | 4–5 | 5–6 |
| Group A | | | | | | | |
| 28 / 11 / 1839 | — | 0.9 | 2.3 | 2.2 | 3.1 | 3.8* | |
| 17 / 04 / 1843 | 23 | 4.1 | 3.9* | 6.3 | 3.7 | | |
| 07 / 09 / 1843 | 31 | 0.8 | 2.8 | 5.0* | | | |
| 19 / 07 / 1845 | 31 | 3.9 | 2.7* | 2.2 | | | |
| 02 / 10 / 1845 | 25 | 1.5 | 2.2 | 3.0* | 2.7 | 4.3 | 1.7 |
| 21 / 08 / 1847 | 26 | 1.6 | 2.8* | 4.0 | | | |
| 19 / 08 / 1848 | 29 | 1.9 | 5.3* | | | | |
| 18 / 08 / 1849 | 29 | 2.6* | 3.1 | | | | |
| Group B | | | | | | | |
| 02 / 05 / 1829 | 27 | 0.9 | 1.8 | 2.5 | 5.8 | | |
| 23 / 06 / 1830 | 22 | 0.7 | 4.4 | 1.6 | 2.2 | 2.8 | 2.8 |
| 11 / 04 / 1831 | — | 1.2 | 4.1 | 2.8 | 3.1 | 2.9 | |
| 21 / 07 / 1831 | 22 | 2.2 | 3.2 | | | | |
| 25 / 04 / 1833 | 23 | 1.9 | 2.1 | 1.8 | 2.9 | 2.3 | 1.9 |
| 27 / 01 / 1837 | 29 | 0.3 | 3.1 | 2.9 | 5.0 | | |
| 06 / 09 / 1837 | 28 | 2.5 | 2.2 | 3.0 | | | |
| 08 / 07 / 1841 | 23 | 0.8 | 5.9 | | | | |
| Group C | | | | | | | |
| 04 / 02 / 51 | 24 | 0.7 | 1.5 | 5.6 | 4.3 | 1.3 | |
| 30 / 08 / 51 | 26 | 2.1 | 3.0 | 8.7 | | | |
| 23 / 02 / 52 | 23 | 0.3 | 4.2 | 9.2 | | | |
| 12 / 06 / 52 | 20 | 0.5 | 2.7 | 5.7 | 3.3 | 4.2 | |
| 26 / 09 / 53 | 21 | 1.0 | 2.7 | 9.7 | | | |

NOTE: Asterisked intervals are those spanning 1850 and are generally unusually long.
SOURCE: Family Reconstitution Data, Lanheses.

reverses the process by first selecting out from the marriage cohorts of the late nineteenth century and the first decade of the twentieth century those women with interrupted fertility histories (that is, with lengthy birth intervals), and then looking for migration information, in the majority of cases a male absence can be confirmed at about the time one would expect, given the fertility data. For the marriage cohort of the first decade of the twentieth century, the connection between lengthy intermediate birth intervals and emigration was also explored in the field through the collection of the migration histories of "suspect" men. Family members or fellow villagers were asked to recall the absences of particular men and repeatedly periods of absence recollected through oral history tended to coincide with a suspected absence suggested by a wife's fertility history. In short, all the evidence tends to support a conclusion that the seasonal or temporary absences of married men had an important impact on marital fertility levels in the parish through its impact on birth intervals. Men may have been marrying substantially earlier during the first decade of the twentieth century, but they were also migrating both more and farther.

That this pattern of behavior has continued well into the present century is suggested by a few examples drawn from the marriage cohort of the 1950s (Table 4.13, Group C). In the first case, we know that the husband migrated to Africa in 1953 after the birth of his second child and reemigrated in 1959 after the birth of his third child. In the second and third cases, the entire families are now residing in France, but both husbands were there alone between the births of their second and third children. In the fourth case, the husband first emigrated to France in 1956 after the birth of his second child. He continued to emigrate alone during the next decade, staying long enough on at least two visits home to leave his wife pregnant. The last case is similar to the second and the third. The husband emigrated to France in 1958 after the birth of his second child. In the late 1960s, his family joined him there. These five cases are by no means unique among the marriages contracted in Lanheses during the 1950s, and they suggest that just as seasonal or temporary migrations to Spain or Brazil affected the marriage cohorts of the eighteenth, nineteenth, and early twentieth centuries, so too has temporary migration to France affected the marriage cohorts of the mid-twentieth century.

Seasonal or temporary migrations of married men have clearly had an effect in lengthening birth intervals, but so too have more enduring forms of emigration; that is, emigration which, although initiated as a temporary departure, becomes permanent. Among the marriages contracted in Lanheses there were a number where the husband is known to have emigrated and where no death is recorded in the parish. As mentioned earlier, these men, in essence, left their wives as widows, but as widows who could not remarry (if they wanted to) because the fate of their husbands in far-off Brazil was not easily confirmed—hence "widows of the living" until death was a certainty. Some saw their husbands again after many years, but the insalubrious conditions of life in emigration had taken its toll—the men returned to die before their time. Many died abroad, and word was sent back to the parish. Under any of these conditions, the result was the premature termination of a marriage, sometimes well before a woman was through her childbearing years.

Although the data on emigration are scanty prior to the late nineteenth century, there are some indications that the early termination of marriages through the death of a spouse abroad was probably as much a part of the eighteenth-century demographic history of the parish as it was of the two more recent centuries. For example, Silvestre Castro married Maria Alves in 1721 when he was twenty and she was twenty-two. They had five children born at intervals of eleven months, seventeen months, thirty-one months, thirty-five months, and twenty-one months. Although there is no way to verify whether Silvestre was away from the parish for a time between the births of his third and fourth children (the thirty-five month interval), we do know that he died in Spain in 1734 at the age of thirty-four. Maria was thirty-six at the time and had her husband lived longer, she might have had at least two more children before completing her childbearing years.

A similar case is represented by António Afonso Novo and Francisca Luisa Pereira at mid-century. They married in 1746 when he was twenty-seven and she was twenty-one. They had four children at intervals of twenty months, twenty-four months, thirty-seven months, and thirty-one months. António died in Spain in 1757, leaving his wife a young widow of thirty-two. In 1764, Balthazar Pereira, a young man of twenty-two, married Maria Alves Franco, a woman six years older. In 1766, almost two years later, Maria gave birth to a son. In February of 1768, word was sent back to the parish notifying the priest of the death of Balthazar in Spain. His wife was thirty-three. Finally, from the latter part of the eighteenth century there is the marriage of Manuel António Sousa and Susana Pereira in 1781. He was thirty and she was twenty-four. They had two children, the first born ten months after the marriage and the second twenty-nine months after that. In August of 1785, Manuel died in Spain, leaving Susana a widow at age twenty-nine.

The three instances just cited all involved documented deaths, and there are several more throughout the eighteenth century. For the period between 1790 and 1809, when we think that emigration to Spain increased, there are nine marriages for which no death of a husband is recorded although by all other indications (the obituaries of the wives, the marriages and deaths of the children), the families of these men remained in the parish. Between 1780 and 1799, 16 percent of the grooms who married died before reaching age forty-five, compared to 13 percent between 1750 and 1769, and 2 percent between 1810 and 1829. Six of the forty-three grooms who married during the 1790s died within a decade of their marriage. Although these are not definite indications of actual emigration during the 1780s and 1790s, this is certainly a possibility.

From the mid-nineteenth century, we have, among others, the case of João Saraiva Araujo. He emigrated sometime around 1870 and never returned to the parish, leaving his wife a "living widow" at age thirty-six with four children to raise (three more died in infancy). This pattern of emigration seems to have passed on from father to sons. The eldest son, José, emigrated while still unmarried in 1892 at the age of thirty-six. The second son, Antão, was married in October of 1899 to Maria Costa Pereira. He was thirty-eight and she was twenty-eight. They had four children at intervals of nine months, thirty-three months, thirty-five months, and thirty-three months. The last child was born in January of 1909, when Maria was thirty-seven. At about that time, with Maria near but not quite at the end of her fecund years, Antão departed for Brazil. He may have had the intention of returning, but in 1913 his wife had a child by another man. "It was scandalous," recalled one of the now elderly villagers, "and he could not return for the shame of it. Of course, his absence was in part the reason for her misbehavior!"[9] Community attitudes aside, it is nevertheless clear that Maria was not at the end of her reproductive years, and had her husband remained, one or two more children might have been born legitimately to this marriage.

In fact, by the dawn of the twentieth century, the cases of wives abandoned by husbands who emigrated to Brazil increased dramatically, and few of them had the excuse for not returning that Antão Saraiva Araujo had. João Barbosa married Miquelina Oliveira Sousa on December 2, 1899. They were both twenty-one. They had four children at intervals of nine months (1900), twenty-nine months (1903), seventeen months (1904), and forty-two months. The last child was born in January of 1908 when Miquelina was twenty-nine. There is a record of Miquelina's death at age eighty in 1958 and records of the marriages of her three surviving children, but there is no further information on her husband. Data from the Rois da Desobriga and from oral history indicate that João was absent from the parish in 1905 and 1907—hence the long interval between the third and fourth children—and that he emigrated to Brazil for the last time in 1909 in the company of his brother, who also left behind a fairly young wife (of twenty-eight) and four children. Neither man returned. The explanation among descendents of why they never returned is that they were not able to make it rich in Brazil—as they expected—and were, therefore, "too ashamed to come back." But, again, the important result, in light of our discussion here, is that these two sisters-in-law, before either of them reached their thirtieth year, were through with their child-bearing despite the fact that they both could probably have borne at least four more children had their husbands been present.

The practice of leaving "living widows" continued into the 1910s and 1920s. Two sisters, Conceição Alves de Castro and Maria Alves de Castro were married within two years of one another, the former in 1913 at age twenty-three to a young man from the parish of Esturãos, and the latter in 1915 at age twenty-seven to a young man from Vila Mou. Both husbands were illegitimate sons. Maria had four children during the first nine years of her marriage. After the last child was born her husband left for Spain and never returned. Conceição had three children, the first born three months after her marriage, the second more than seven years later, and the last a little more than a year after the second. Shortly after her son, the first child, was born, Conceição's husband departed for Brazil, where he remained until after the First World War. He returned to the parish in 1920. Conceição became pregnant twice more. She lost her first daughter, born in 1921. Five months after her second daughter was born, in 1924, her husband left again, this time for France. He never returned. Conceição, to raise her son and daughter, worked for the Pimentas da Gama and in a range of other services such as cooking, washing clothes, and weaving. When her daughter was seventeen, they went to Lisbon for five years to work as domestic servants. They only returned to Lanheses after the Second World War was over.

A slightly later though similar example is provided by the case of "Tia Olivia," who died in 1981. Born in 1903, Olivia married in 1927. After seeing his wife give birth to a son nine months later, Olivia's husband departed for Brazil. Fifty years later, in January of 1979, he returned from abroad, and he came home to die. Throughout these years, Olivia worked hard to raise her only son, first as a jornaleira in the major lavrador houses, later fetching milk from households throughout the region and transporting it to the depository in Lanheses, and finally opening a small establishment on the feira where she sold bread and other food items. In addition, she was a skillful midwife who assisted at the births of numerous Lanhesans over the years.

There are examples during the postwar period of similar abandonments. The most interesting, although unusual in comparison with those discussed previously, is that of Maria dos Santos. Maria was the illegitimate daughter of Gracinda dos Santos. She was raised in her grandfather's home with her mother, spinster aunts, a married uncle and aunt, and several cousins. She grew up to be one of the prettiest young women in the parish, and as a result had many suitors who were "always after her baskets of flowers on festa days." In the summer of 1952, just as she was approaching her twenty-second birthday, she married Francisco da Silva, the son of a rather well-to-do lavrador family and a native of Fontão. She claims that she had never expected to marry so young, that she married "out of pride" because people were saying that she was "poor and could never become the wife of someone so well-off."

Maria and Francisco moved into a house in Corredoura that had been the home of Maria's great-grandparents. However, Francisco was already making plans to emigrate to Brazil, and a month after the marriage he left. Maria moved back into the big house in the Lugar de Seara and worked to pay off some of the debts her husband had incurred prior to his departure. Five years later she went to Brazil to join him, staying just long enough to conceive a child. Her husband, she claims, "did not treat her well," and she disliked Brazil. She returned to Lanheses to bear her child, a daughter Elisa who is now herself grown up and married. Elisa has seen photographs of her father but has never known him. Word about his whereabouts has filtered back to Maria over the years via other Lanhesans coming and going to Brazil. But he has never returned. Maria noted once, "I do not know if he is alive or dead, whether to pray for his health or for his soul!" Indeed, she lives with a kind of fear that he will appear on her doorstep one day and that she will have to assume her wifely duties toward a man she hardly knows and has not seen for almost thirty years. In the interim she has become an extremely independent women, essentially running a household full of aging and unmarried spinsters. Naturally, she has never been able to remarry. Nor was she able to emigrate to France, which she was keen to do in the 1960s to make some money. Until recently, a married woman had to have her husband's permission to secure a passport.

However, Maria dos Santos' case is almost unique. During the 1950s many women who married in Lanheses and whose husbands emigrated to Brazil eventually followed their spouses abroad. António Castro, for example, married Idalina Marques in 1954. He was twenty-four and she was twenty-two. They had two children in the next three years. In the winter of 1957, António emigrated to Brazil. Two years later, in 1959, Idalina traveled with her two sons to Brazil to join her husband, and there she has remained. Nelda Rios, whose own father spent three years in Brazil in the latter 1920s while his wife remained in the parish to raise their five children, did the same. Her husband left shortly after the birth of their first child in October of 1955. She joined him in 1958. All of her other children were born and baptized in Brazil, with the exception of the youngest, who was baptized in Portugal in 1968, when they were visiting over the Christmas holidays. Nelda and her husband have now returned to Lanheses in retirement, but all their children and two of her siblings and their families remain in Brazil.[10]

The real opportunities for female emigration have come with emigration to France. Numerous women married during the 1950s, whose husbands were among the first wave of Portuguese who departed for France in the late 1950s or early 1960s, have joined their spouses abroad. Those women who have married more recently, in the 1960s and early 1970s, have generally migrated with their husbands to France or joined them soon afterward. Among these younger brides, there has been a definite shift in attitude, in their definition of a Portuguese woman's role, and in their desires for the relationship they would like with their husbands. They no longer accept living apart as potential *viuvas dos vivos*. By the late 1960s, familial immigration eclipsed male wage-labor migration among the Portuguese entering France. These women have found employment abroad, and therefore supplement their husband's income not as rural agriculturalists but as salaried laborers, primarily in the domestic sector.[11] Their experiences abroad, and those of young women who emigrated while still single, have laid the basis for further changes in female life, including fertility, throughout northern Portugal.

To summarize, although detailed data on emigration from the parish of Lanheses is scanty prior to the latter part of the nineteenth century, the evidence available does suggest that for at least two centuries the Portuguese pattern of male-biased emigration has influenced fertility levels in the parish. The question remains, was emigration, together with a rising age at marriage and increases in the rates of permanent spinsterhood, an option taken because other mechanisms for reducing population—chiefly fertility control—were inconceivable? Perhaps. But more importantly, whether as a response to certain economic conditions, as an expression of certain ambitions, or as a result of a traditional division of labor that has deep historical roots, emigration certainly had the effect of reducing fertility and probably, therefore, contributed to the slower decline in fertility levels throughout Portugal in comparison with other regions of western Europe. It is therefore to the question of the demographic transition that we must turn in the final section of this chapter, for indeed it is by no means fully clear that the motivations for emigration among Lanhesans and among the northern Portuguese in general are the same as those that have prompted fertility control.

## THE SOCIAL AND CULTURAL CONTEXT OF THE DEMOGRAPHIC TRANSITION IN LANHESES

In most other regions of western Europe, where the demographic transition occurred more than a century ago, historians can only offer their best educated guesses about the reasons behind individual decisions to restrict family size or the possible causes of specific demographic characteristics associated with limited fertility. The lateness of the decline in Portugal, however, permits the use of sociological and anthropological research techniques to pursue the changes in attitudes and social behavior that precipitated a decline or, conversely, the attitudes or social systems that maintained the pre-decline patterns of fertility and other demographic behavior.[12]

Although high ages at marriage and emigration have both been discussed as factors that have indirectly influenced the lateness of the decline in fertility in Lanheses in particular, and probably in northwestern Portugal more generally, there are a range of alternative nondemographic factors that need to be considered. It is within the context of a rather abundant theoretical literature dealing with these alternatives that I would now like to discuss fertility behavior in the parish of Lanheses.

One approach forwarded to explain the demographic transition is rooted in the opposition between motivations and techniques. This dichotomy was first raised by the Swedish demographer Gosta Carlsson (1966), who argued that the fertility transition is best viewed as a situation wherein already well-established mechanisms of family limitation are employed by couples to adjust fertility to a new set of structural or motivational forces rather than as innovative behavior resulting from the knowledge of and access to new methods of birth control. That is, he suggested that the techniques were already there, or at least some were, and that it was a change in motivations that led to the more extensive use of these techniques or a search for new and more effective techniques.

More recently, John Knodel (1977) has proposed that it is not a question of either adjustment or innovation but of both, and that the transition should be viewed as the product of their coincidence as they work sometimes alone and sometimes in conjunction. What Knodel argues, with direct reference to Carlsson, is that in order to support the thesis of adjustment, the claim has to be made that fertility control was already present within a population. Low marital fertility may be one indication of its presence, but it is not, Knodel says, necessarily so. As section three of this chapter has demonstrated, other phenomena can produce a similar result in the absence of fertility control.

Etienne Van de Walle (1980), in an essay that among other things evaluates the types of evidence we have at our disposal to determine the extent and nature of fertility control, tends to concur with Knodel's conclusion. "Motivations," he claims, "are not necessarily strong enough in all societies to allow fertility to decline—although there are always some strongly motivated individuals." Furthermore, birth-control technology is not always readily available despite the fact that some reasonably effective methods are described in the historical literature. Both elements must be present for fertility to decline successfully. Conversely, the lack of information about or access to birth control technology and/or the absence of any incentives to limit family size will help to maintain fertility at high levels.

In fact, neither Knodel nor Van de Walle is particularly innovative in their compromise position. More than a decade ago, Ansley Coale (1971) suggested that the problem of structural change versus technological change be viewed in terms of a series of prerequisites that have to be present before a major fall in fertility can occur:

1. Fertility must be considered to be a result of conscious choice—that is, couples must be aware that control of family size is both possible and acceptable;
2. reduced fertility must be advantageous within a perceived socio-economic context;
3. effective techniques of fertility reduction must be available.

Despite some disagreement over where the emphasis should be placed, clearly there are a number of broader questions that underlie all these arguments; to what extent is the fertility decline (or even a decline in the age at marriage) an indication of significant structural and cultural changes in local social systems, and what are these changes; to what extent is fertility decline associated with a process of modernization, and what are the components of that modernization such that fertility comes to be viewed as a result of calculated choice and its control to be advantageous; has access to better forms of birth control been the decisive factor, and at what point did these better methods replace older methods, if they did?

Underlying these three broader questions is another opposition—that between modernization and culture. In what might almost be called the traditional view, the shift from high to low fertility has been associated with a number of social and economic changes commonly attributed to a process of modernization—urbanization, expanding education, changes in women's roles, an increasing emphasis on the nuclear family, and even secularization. Yet, as was pointed out in the introduction to this chapter, demographers such as Coale have recently begun to question the general applicability of the modernization theory of demographic transition, pointing out that levels of modernity are by no means consistent among countries that have supposedly passed through the transition. Certainly, France stands out as an excellent example of the negative case—a country that underwent the transition as early as the eighteenth century but that was still at the time very much an agrarian society.

Livi Bacci (1971), as we have seen, comes to the same conclusion with regard to regional differences in Portuguese fertility, falling back on religion as the single most predictive variable to explain persistent high fertility levels in the north in comparison with the south. He is certainly not alone in this conclusion about the impact of religiosity (Lockridge 1984, Van de Walle 1980). To some, religion is a variable to be subsumed within modernization. To others, it is more closely associated with attitudes and beliefs, and therefore with culture. The problem demographers have is that culture, or "habits of the mind," as Van de Walle calls it, cannot easily be measured. Thus, culture often becomes a residual category that will explain that which cannot be explained by socioeconomic differences. To many anthropologists, for whom the socioeconomic differences are as much a part of culture as are the "habits of the mind" to which they are related, the entire approach is limiting.

A second body of theories about fertility and the demographic transition relates to issues of economic rationality. All of them essentially argue that fertility is a decision based on an evaluation of the number of children desired (some notion of the "ideal" family size) in the context of income, prices, the costs of raising children, and the benefits accrued. With precise and skillful premeditation, couples supposedly decide upon the number of children they both need and can afford. There is an implicit assumption that the methods for birth control are available and that it is a changing perception of the value of children in terms of the contributions they can make to the household which is decisive in bringing about a transition. The rationality thesis has been applied repeatedly to the study of peasant societies, the argument being that both the labor and the love of children (especially succor in later life) are obstacles to the desirability of family limitation.[13] Where familial production has prevailed, large families are preferred.

Caldwell (1982) has recently reinterpreted the rationality thesis. He views the demographic transition as the result of social rather than economic changes. The social changes have primarily to do with a shift in the direction of "intrafamilial flows of wealth" as they are influenced by family obligations—primarily as a concomitant of education—as we shall see shortly.

These theories about the causes and nature of the demographic transition delineate a number of questions that can and have been addressed to the Lanhesan population, primarily in the course of unstructured interviews with both men and women. In general, villagers of both sexes emphasized the fact that effective methods of control are a very recent phenomenon. They repeatedly described their country as "poor and backward." Coitus interruptus and certain folk methods of douching were mentioned, and some individuals may have practiced them, but they were not considered either widespread or foolproof. Male informants observed that the former "took the pleasure out of marriage." Female informants commented that they had heard about the latter but never talked to anyone about help for themselves. Indeed, the women tended to stress their general naiveté where pregnancy was concerned. "We did not know anything in those days. Girls were innocent when they married. Today a girl of twelve knows what I did not know even after I was married."

Ignorance of birth control was viewed by some informants as a way for men to dominate women (a female response) and for the rich to dominate the poor (an attitude of both men and women). For  example, one woman commented, "They [the men] needed to have ignorant wives. Then the children came. They are like that—they want to fill an empty stomach."

Domination was equally imputed as the motive behind the anti-birth-control doctrines of the Roman Catholic Church. By encouraging the poor to have large families, poverty was perpetuated and the status quo could be maintained. Older women in particular admitted to believing that avoiding children was a sin. The fear that this engendered in the course of religious confession, when some women were asked why they had so few children, was brought back to the marital bed. One woman, for example, who had only two children, admitted to telling the priest that her husband wanted no more—"I do not go to confession to lie." She was severely chided. From the male perspective, it was through their wives that the Church controlled their lives. It must be remembered, of course, that these responses are emerging today during a period when the influence of the village priest is changing. Yet it speaks to the power that the Church and its officers had over the basically illiterate populations in the not too distant past, and to one aspect of the way in which religion influences fertility behavior.[14]

The role of the Church and religion in relation to the absence of any real ability to control family size has to be considered in another light. Questions about ideal family size raised with older informants, particularly female informants, appeared to make little sense. A similar response has been recorded by Schneider and Schneider (1984) among Sicilians. In general, the number of children one had was viewed as a matter that was neither predictable nor controllable. It was "up to God" or "what God decided to give me." This element of fatalism permeates the spoken Portuguese of the rural populations. Something will only happen, *se deus quiser*—if God is willing. Whether it is rational or not is beside the point! Caldwell's (1982) general thesis that these references to God and religion may be "closer to the truth" than numerical explanations for fertility decisions is indeed applicable to the Lanhesan population until fairly recently.

If there were means available, albeit the oldest and simplest of them, it is not apparent that Lanhesans of the past were necessarily motivated to use those means nor that they were particularly motivated to have large families, either. One woman, for example, who was married in the early 1950s, drew a distinction between living in the countryside and living in the city. Soon after her marriage, she and her husband, who was in the Republican Guard, went to Lisbon. They lived in a small room, and after the birth of her first child she sought advice about how to avoid having more children because there was simply "not enough space where we lived to have more children." In the countryside, she pointed out, "there is more space and the children can go out at will. They are safe and there are lots of people around to watch out for them." The implication of her statement was that there were fewer motivations in the countryside to limit family size, although admittedly some individuals were, for their own reasons, strongly motivated. If Lanhesans attribute the new knowledge of birth control to the emigrants returning from France, it is evident that not only are new techniques available abroad, but also new motivations are engendered, including that prompted by the limited space and alienation of urban life in cities like Paris, Lyon, and Marseilles.

If there were not until quite recently strong and prevailing motivations to limit family size, what of the reverse? Were the peasants, artisans, and day laborers of Lanheses motivated to have large families? Such a question is difficult to address because again, older villagers do not necessarily see it as something over which they had any control (we "accept what God gives us"), and younger villagers are already influenced by the preference for small families. Several villagers mentioned the approval bestowed by the State in the form of prizes for women with numerous children during the Salazar era. Yet this is a fairly recent phenomenon. The historical data certainly underscore the perception of children as a source of additional labor or income in middle age and as a source of security in old age. Yet were these incentives strong enough to influence fertility behavior? It is impossible to answer this question without reconsidering the character of the social and economic system in northwestern Portugal.

Indeed, it is difficult to see the benefits of a large family in a region that has been overpopulated since the twelfth century, and where the land has been parcelized for almost as long. Plots averaging less than a hectare in size could easily be farmed by a married couple and one child.[15] Furthermore, if children were of economic value to the familial mode of production, why were they sent abroad at such a young age? Granted, as emigrants or as day laborers they contributed to the family income by turning over wages or sending remittances. This cash in some instances led to the purchase and/or rental of new plots of land or new farm animals. Yet probably for as many who faithfully stimulated the flow of wealth back to the parental generation there were equal numbers lost to their parents forever. Furthermore, at a certain point at least some offspring demanded compensation from their parents for their labor. This is evident in the wills that speak of wages owed to children. Finally, those children who were farmed out as domestic and/or agricultural servants (*criados*) earned little else than their keep. Wealth flowed back into the family of origin only in the sense that the burdens of supporting that particular child were relieved. In short, while northwestern Portugal and Lanheses were characterized by a familial mode of production (in contrast to the capitalist mode in the south of Portugal), in general it was of small enough scale to make a motivational connection between this mode of production and a desire for large families tenuous. However, Caldwell's thesis of intergenerational wealth flows cannot be dismissed totally, for it is true that the value of children as social insurance in old age has been strong in northwestern Portugal.

Bringing into question the motivational relationship between peasant farming and large families does not undermine the need to explore further the impact of specific regional socioeconomic differences on fertility. At an aggregate level, it is impossible to understand fully some of the more subtle differences between the rural proletarian system of agriculture of southern Portugal and the peasant system of the north, and particularly the way in which the latter has survived precisely because of emigration. Until very recently, emigration from the south has been rare, and that which exists today is primarily in the form of a permanent departure to Lisbon. This issue is subject to further exploration, and certainly awaits more intensive examination of communities in southern Portugal similar to the present study of a community in the northwest. In the southern proletarian system, there is a much greater disjunction between reproduction and production, between those with the economic power, who gain the most from production, and the worker families who only have control over their own reproduction. Families are more nucleated, and the flow of wealth is between landlord or his intermediary and the day laborer. Work is seasonal, owing to a large extent to the cultivation of export crops such as cork and olives, and unemployment is high. In short, there is no obvious advantage to larger families when the returns of labor are beyond the control of the family. Despite the progressive proletarianization of the north during the latter part of the nineteenth century, a greater proportion of the population of the south had no matters of inheritance to solve, no restrictions on early marriage, no ideology calling for the ownership of some land prior to marriage (procured in the north through emigration or rental). Thus, a solution in the form of family limitation probably had to come earlier, and was not impeded as in the north by the strength of religious institutions. It is in this sense that culture is not simply a matter of beliefs and values (including religious beliefs), but the entire social and economic system.

It has been established by several demographers that although the final downward trend in fertility began in Portugal in the 1930s, in the north of Portugal, and in Lanheses, it is of later date. With regard to new motivations, villagers ascribe the change in attitude primarily to education. Education is important in two respects. For the adults themselves, it is the foundation for a greater sense of control over their lives. It erodes the sense of fatalism embodied in a religious view of the world. In short, education combats ignorance. Whereas the phrase *educar os filhos* used to mean to teach children manners and respect (to raise them well), it now has the modern meaning of schooling. Thus, Lanhesan parents today are eager to provide their children with schooling and a brighter future. A definite and quite conscious connection is made between fewer children and the ability to achieve this end. Yet it is a connection made in the context of the greater accessibility of the educational system, greater prosperity, and less reliance on the agricultural way of life that "yields nothing." Said one male informant, "the greater sin today is not having enough to feed all the children." In a sense, there is indeed a shift in obligations that can perhaps be phrased as a shift in the direction of wealth flows associated with changes in the roles of children (Caldwell 1982). In the past, if the agricultural season demanded, children simply did not go to school, but helped their parents in the fields. Today this is no longer the case, not only because of new state legislation that makes schooling obligatory but also because of the new value attached to education. Clearly, education is a different form of investment from that in a child who as a migrant, day laborer, or extra hand could mean the potential purchase or rent of an additional plot of land. Education has other ramifications, the chief one being upward social mobility. If schooling takes their children out of unskilled manual labor and out of agricultural work, it has achieved its ends for this new generation of parents.

Lanhesans are quick to point out that couples today only have the children they want (*só tem o que quer*). An ideal family size is definitely embodied in this statement. They attribute the change in attitude to *o modernismo*, and in this phrase they encompass the latest methods of birth control. Yet, they are also quick to point to the fact that the Catholic Church has also changed its tune. To avoid children is no longer a sin. Only abortion is a sin. Thus, together with the changing values that stress the education of fewer children, the growing distaste for an agricultural way of life, and the lucrative alternatives offered particularly by emigration to France was a reformulation of Church doctrine itself.

The impact of this shift on the demographic transition in Lanheses is not to be underestimated. It has made family limitation thinkable. Villagers can still be religious (in the sense of feeling that they are not sinning) and yet actively control the number of children they have. That they have increasingly chosen to do it with methods that are unapproved by the Catholic Church is a sign of a much more far-reaching change in the nature of religious belief. Much like American Catholics, Portuguese Catholics in rural villages like Lanheses are today picking and choosing among those doctrines they will follow and those they will ignore. Many believe vociferously that the Church has no place in the private lives of families, as it had in the past. Yet they will continue to be married in the church, to baptize their children in the church, and to give money to the various confrarias so that they can be given a decent burial.

In general, the Lanhesan field data lend support to Coale's tripartite model for the demographic transition. With changes in Catholic doctrine, family limitation became acceptable. With new goals set for the social and economic advancement of one's children, family limitation became advantageous. With new techniques available, particularly after the collapse of the Salazar regime, family limitation has become possible.

## CONCLUSION

A few recent studies of demographic regimes in western Europe have hinted at the significance of emigration as a factor contributing to a slower fertility decline (Livi Bacci 1977, Knodel 1974). In this chapter, the dynamics of this impact have been illustrated, primarily at an individual level. At an aggregate level, the result of these individual behaviors was something that looks like a self-equilibrating demographic system of low or minimum growth that can easily be interpreted as a conscious attempt at population control. However, for married men in particular, migration was not and is not a deliberate and conscious attempt to limit family size but a response to the economic pressures placed upon young families, and is made in the context of a traditional division of labor whereby men migrated and women stayed at home to take care of the fields and raise the children. Nevertheless, in view of the impact of these individual decisions to migrate on the fertility of the population as a whole, it is legitimate to ask what disrupted the system and led to the period of population growth after 1920 and the fact that, in 1960, Portugal, and especially northern Portugal, had one of the highest marital fertility rates in western Europe?

David Heer's (1966) attempts to reconcile Malthusian and economic interpretations of the effects of prosperity on fertility are extremely useful to suggest a possible framework for analysis. Heer argues that in an initial phase of economic development and modernization, fertility is more likely to increase (in the short term), and then, once all the other social changes associated with economic development begin to occur, the long-term result is a decline in fertility.

By several indications, and despite the Depression and the Second World War, the economic situation of Lanhesans did begin to ameliorate at this time. New schools were built, roads linking the village to the local provincial town and the marketplace were improved, and during the Second World War a great deal of money, by village standards, was made by some in local tin mines.

To Heer's hypothesis can be added MacFarlane's (1980b) formulation of three different models for pretransition populations. The first model he dubs "classic"—a society in which high mortality balances high fertility. As mortality declines, so too must fertility in order to reach a new point of equilibrium. The second he calls a "crisis" model—a society wherein births exceed deaths and population surpluses are periodically eliminated through war, famine, or disease. These crisis events restore a tolerable equilibrium. When they are eliminated, a new solution has to be found, and one such solution is fertility control. The third model is a homeostatic model—"a society wherein fertility and mortality are below their possible ceilings." In these latter societies, a rise in fertility, resulting possibly from a decline in age at marriage, would be the stimulus for an eventual transition. The latter model, MacFarlane suggests, is most characteristic of societies in which the "individual prevailed over the group." He also argues that which model predominates depends upon the regional demographic cultures of the pretransition populations, and that these cultures vary, depending on such factors as the way land is owned, the way families are defined, and the way property is transmitted. Clearly, it is this latter homeostatic model that prevailed in Lanheses. The element of individualism is present in the freedom of choice connected with inheritance and in the prevalence of emigration as an individual or at most nuclear-family solution to economic pressure.

Thus, a possible answer to the rise in birth and fertility rates after 1920 is threefold: that social and economic changes were occurring which facilitated earlier marriages; that seasonal and longer distance migrations were reduced if not essentially halted during the 1930s and 1940s; and that there was, as yet, no conscious adoption of any form of family limitation because other "unconsciously rational" factors (age at marriage, emigration, permanent celibacy) had served in the stead of family limitation to offset population growth. In addition, and influencing the fact that effective birth control remained largely unpracticed, was the creation of Salazar's Estado Novo (New State) in 1932. The Estado Novo restored the Catholic Church to a powerful position in the social life of the country. Essentially, the Church remained in that position until the revolution of 1974.

The consequences of the rising birth rates after 1920 are quite apparent: the rampant outmigration of the 1950s and 1960s, as the birth cohorts of the post-World War I period grew to maturity. Indeed, new policies for settlement in the African "overseas territories" were formulated at this time, partly as a politically advised population solution. In addition, fortunately for Portugal, the countries of northwestern Europe were experiencing postwar economic growth and were desperately in need of manpower. In the years between 1960 and 1974, France alone accepted close to a million Portuguese immigrants. The decline in population in Lanheses by almost 4.5 percent between 1960 and 1970 clearly shows that emigration to northern Europe was a solution for this parish, as well. Thus the cycle was repeating itself such that, by the mid-twentieth century, the areas of Portugal with highest emigration were also the areas with highest  fertility.

However, in the 1980 world of tightening labor markets, migration can no longer serve Portugal, nor Lanheses, as a panacea for population pressure. In addition, young couples no longer accept the traditional division of labor that kept so many husbands and wives geographically apart for innumerable years of their married lives between 1700 and the present. As a result, individual, deliberate, and conscious efforts at birth control have necessarily begun to have their place in modern rural Portugal, facilitated by the collapse of Salazarism in 1974. The explanation in the village for the new generation of married couples is that "they learned it in France." The knowledge brought back from that country has placed pressures upon the Portuguese government to take an active role—rather than the historically passive role embodied in emigration—in population control and, in the late 1970s, a planned parenthood program was finally introduced.

# CHAPTER FIVE

# Children Out of Wedlock: Illegitimacy in Lanheses

> Sexual behavior has never anywhere been con-
> fined to procreative behavior, procreative be-
> havior confined to marriage, and marriage con-
> fined to the official celebrations established by
> society. (Laslett 1980c:xiii)

## INTRODUCTION

In his book *The Making of the Modern Family* (1975), the historian
Edward Shorter speaks of two sexual revolutions. One comprises, of
course, the post-World War Two changes in sexual mores that have
given us, among other things, significant rates of out-of-wedlock births.
The other is a sexual revolution that occurred between the mid-eighteenth and the mid-nineteenth centuries, and that was also marked
by a dramatic increase in the rate of illegitimacy in western Europe
from rates that had been between 1 and 4 percent in previous centuries. The interim period between these two revolutions (roughly
1880 to 1940) was characterized by plummeting illegitimacy in a
number of European nations that were at different stages of social
and economic development.

Various theories have been forwarded to explain both the rise in
European illegitimacy after 1750 and its subsequent decline in the
latter part of the nineteenth century, theories that range from correlations of strictly demographic variables to those which associate it
with the increasing secularization of society. Some explanations are
quite specific to a particular case at a particular time, as, for example, John Knodel's (1967) discussion of the influence of prohibitive
nineteenth-century German marriage laws upon German nonmarital
fertility.[1] Others are more all-encompassing. Shorter, Knodel, and Van
de Walle (1971) suggest that the decline in nonmarital fertility in
western Europe after 1850 was part of the demographic transition
itself, and that both are explained by the increasing knowledge about
and use of improved methods of birth control.

One of the major arenas of debate among those offering more
comprehensive theories is that which exists between David Levine of

the "marriage frustrated" school of thought and Edward Shorter of the "promiscuity rampant" school. Levine argues, in his book *Family Formation in an Age of Nascent Capitalism* (1977) that in situations where uncertainty intervenes between courtship and marriage because of adverse social or economic conditions, illegitimacy is likely to be high because couples' expectations to marry are dashed—their marriage is frustrated, or at least postponed. The major demographic relationship that he calls upon to support his thesis is the one between age at marriage and illegitimacy—when one is high, the other is also likely to be high. Essentially, Levine argues that over time sexual behavior outside marriage has been fairly constant, but that other conditions (material constraints) had the effect of making what might have been legitimate births into illegitimate ones.

Edward Shorter (1971, 1973, 1975), on the other hand, maintains that the surge in illegitimacy in Europe between 1750 and 1850 was due to a change in courtship practices, to the expanding freedom of women resulting from new patterns of employment, and to a greater emphasis on the individual, which made women into "pleasure-seekers"—in short, that for all these reasons the rate of sexual activity among young people outside marriage increased. Tilly, Scott, and Cohen have challenged Shorter's discussion of the changing nature of women's work as it may have increased their independence and therefore influenced their sexuality. "Rising rates of illegitimacy," they argue, "did not signify a sexual revolution. They followed instead from the structural and compositional changes associated with urbanization and industrialization" (Tilly, Scott, and Cohen 1976:470). Yet, if this serves to explain rising rates of nonmarital fertility in the burgeoning cities of western Europe, how do we explain rising rates of illegitimacy in rural areas? Can we speak of the same weakening of kin control in the countryside? Knodel and Hochstadt (1980), in a study comparing rural and urban rates of illegitimacy in Imperial Germany find that in regions where nonmarital fertility is generally low, rates in the cities are higher than those in the countryside; conversely, in regions where illegitimacy is generally high, levels in the cities are below those in rural areas. They conclude that regional differences and therefore local customs are more significant than the rural/urban contrast per se in explaining variations in nonmarital fertility. What they mean precisely by "local customs" is unclear in this particular discussion, but other historians (Laslett 1980, Levine and Wrightson 1980) have suggested that in rural areas dominated by single-family farms, where there is greater parental control and more concern for the legitimacy of an heir, rates of illegitimacy are lower than in rural areas characterized by a landless proletarian agricultural labor force.

A somewhat different direction for discussion focuses on the relationship between illegitimacy and social class. On the one hand, critics of Shorter's view, like Fairchilds (1978), note that the attitudes of lower classes are frequently interpreted, in the past and at present, through the eyes of the middle classes.[2] Based on her own study of a fascinating collection of pregnancy declarations in Aix-en-Provence (1727–1789), Fairchilds distinguishes among several types of relationships that have resulted in out-of-wedlock pregnancies: those in which the socioeconomic status of the male is higher; those in which the participants share the same status; and those based on short-term encounters (rape, prostitution). She documents a shift over time, with relationships based on inequality becoming less frequent after 1750, as relationships of equality become more frequent.[3] De Pauw (1972), using similar sources in Nantes, arrives at similar conclusions.

Finally, there is the work of Laslett (1980a) and Laslett and Oosterveen (1973) on the so-called "bastardy-prone subsociety." They have drawn our attention to the fact that among the population of women having illegitimate children throughout European history was a subgroup of women who had more than one child out of wedlock and who were frequently connected to one another by ties of kinship or marriage. These repeaters contributed significantly to levels of nonmarital fertility. When the illegitimacy ratio has risen, the proportion of repeaters has tended to rise as well, and at a faster pace.

Whether any of these hypotheses about historical illegitimacy helps to explain the character of illegitimacy in Lanheses is the subject for discussion in this chapter. However, the broader underlying problem is to try to explain why Portugal as a whole stands out within the context of both Mediterranean Europe and Catholic Europe in having unusually high illegitimacy rates well into the present century (Hartley 1975:38–39). Although a change has occurred since the nineteenth century such that a phenomenon essentially most characteristic of certain districts in the north, as well as the city of Lisbon, has now become more prevalent in certain southern districts and the city of Lisbon (Livi Bacci 1971:74), this regional shift has nevertheless happened within a cultural and socioeconomic framework that makes Portugal distinct from her cultural and/or geographical neighbors. Furthermore, the northern half of the country is supposedly the most Catholic part. Why were earlier rates higher?[4]

Ethnologists have come to know Catholic, but especially Latin Catholic or Mediterranean Europe as an area where "virgins are vigilated" (Schneider 1971) and crimes of honor are committed, where chastity is next to godliness and reputation is everything. If these are ideals, and illegitimacy is used as a measure of the effectiveness of these ideals, then Spain, Italy, and Greece are masters at putting their ideals into practice. Portugal, on the other hand, is quite another matter. Are we then to abandon these codes of social evaluation where Portugal is concerned, to claim that they have little or no meaning there? Are we to argue that there is something in the culture and history of Portugal which differentiates it from its Mediterranean neighbors? Or are we to insist that Portugal is not really part of the "Mediterranean culture area" at all, at least as that culture area is defined by the so-called honor-shame complex (Peristiany 1965, Davis 1977). Indeed, its inclusion is problematic to several analysts of the anthropology of the Mediterranean (Boissevain et al. 1979), as well as to the great Portuguese geographer Orlando Ribeiro, who described his country as belonging culturally to both the Mediterranean and the Atlantic. In Ribeiro's schema (1945), northern Portugal was clearly an Atlantic region, a classification that is in agreement with Kenny's (1963) formulation of the "Atlantic fringe" European culture area. Yet, even within this culture area one runs into problems as far as illegitimacy is concerned, especially if one draws upon another "Atlantic fringe" country, Ireland, as a point of comparison. Sundbarg, in his *Aperçus Statistiques Internationaux*, published in 1908, noted that as early as the 1870s the differences in levels of illegitimacy between Portugal and Ireland were quite apparent, despite the fact that in both countries age at marriage was late and the proportion of lifelong celibates was high.[5]

A more basic issue that these variations in illegitimacy and their relationship to codes of conduct raises is outlined quite perceptively by Barrett (1980) in an article on bastardy in Taiwan. He notes that there are various levels at which the phenomenon of illegitimacy can be analyzed: its statistical prevalence, its socioeconomic context; its meaning for the parents or for the bastards; and finally, its prevalence as perceived by the local people, and what their understanding of it is. Anthropologists of China, he claims, have tended to focus on the latter two questions and therefore to misrepresent the extent of illegitimacy in Taiwan. "There is," he adds, "no necessary relation between the perception [of illegitimacy] and actual prevalence." His point has implications for studies of illegitimacy elsewhere in the world (including Portugal), if not for anthropological and historical research in general.[6] It provides a second underlying problem to be addressed in this chapter and takes us right back to a question that

Kingsley Davis (1939) posed several decades ago—why does illegitimacy occur despite the norms and sentiments against it? Illegitimacy in Lanheses will be explored at each of Barrett's levels of analysis in an attempt to integrate prevalence with meanings, variations with socioeconomic context, and to reconcile norms with behavior.

## THE PREVALENCE OF ILLEGITIMACY IN LANHESES: OVERALL TRENDS AND DEMOGRAPHIC RELATIONSHIPS

In his volume of *Lusitanian Sketches*, William Kingston describes an encounter with a woman of the countryside who, over her arm, carried a basket with four infants inside. When asked if they were all hers, the woman replied, "Oh no, senhor . . . they are children without fathers found this morning in our village and I am taking them to the *roda* (foundling wheel)" (1845:302). Kingston remarked that "it was a sight at first glance to frighten Malthus, though one at which both he and his disciples might ultimately rejoice, as the inmates of these establishments are very short-lived." This passing observation made by an Englishman is one of the few examples to be found in travel literature which hints at the problem of illegitimacy in rural Portugal during the first half of the nineteenth century. To gain a more complete understanding of the extent of this phenomenon prior to 1864, it is necessary to explore the parish registers.

Throughout the eighteenth, nineteenth, and early twentieth centuries, out-of-wedlock births have been recorded in the baptismal books of Lanheses. Although the fathers of these children were occasionally mentioned during the first several decades of the eighteenth century, by the middle of that century this practice was abandoned, and both the father and paternal grandparents were registered as "unknown" (*incógnito*), despite the fact that within a small village an illegitimate child's paternal heritage was probably very much known! In only one instance did a mother remain unidentified, a stranger who appeared at the home of a lavrador couple in December of 1823, refused to give her name, but asked for help because she was about to give birth. In short, *pai incógnito* (father unknown), in addition to consistent use of either the phrase *filho ilegítimo* (illegitimate child) or *filho natural*, (natural child) are definite markers of an out-of-wedlock birth. These baptisms were registered matter-of-factly by the parish priest in much the same format as the record of a baptism for a legitimate child. Only once did one of Lanheses' priests make what might be considered a moral comment. In 1817, a certain Dona Joaquina (Dona implies a well-to-do status) had her illegitimate child baptised. She gave her name, but refused to declare where she was from—perhaps, as the priest speculated, "in order to hide her sin."

In addition to these filhos ilegítimos or filhos naturais, there are approximately thirty cases throughout the two-and-a-half centuries between 1700 and 1950 of foundlings (*expostos*) like those carried by the woman Kingston encountered in the 1840s being baptised in Lanheses. However, it is not always clear whether these were the children of women living in Lanheses, of women from other villages who deposited their unwanted infant at the doorstep of a Lanhesan, or infants brought from another village or one of the nearby provincial towns to be raised by a Lanhesan couple, childless or not. A little more will be said about expostos later in the chapter, but for the moment they are excluded from consideration in the discussion of illegitimacy.

Table 5.1 presents the total number of illegitimate baptisms by ten- and twenty-year intervals between 1700 and 1969, as well as the illegitimacy ratio—the percentage of total baptisms that were illegitimate. There are significant problems associated with this ratio (Laslett and Oosterveen 1973, Knodel and Hochstadt 1980), chief among which are the fact that a sharp increase in either the proportion of unmarried women at risk in the population, or in the level of marital fertility itself, will significantly alter it. Nevertheless, it is the only possible measure of nonmarital fertility for a microlevel study where no data on the distribution of the local population by sex, age, and marital status are available. With these shortcomings in mind, it is, I think, safe to argue that the illegitimacy ratio does provide a fairly accurate indication of long-term trends. Furthermore, it is possible to suggest, as I will shortly, that the impact of a rise in the proportion of celibate women in the local population is in fact crucial to a full understanding of the patterns of nonmarital fertility in Lanheses in particular and northern Portugal more generally.

What Table 5.1 demonstrates first is that prior to 1750, the point at which other historians have discovered a take-off in illegitimacy in western Europe in general, nonmarital fertility was by no means insignificant in Lanheses, although it did indeed increase thereafter (with the exception of the period between 1840 and 1859, when it dropped temporarily back to early eighteenth-century levels). However, it was during the final decades of the nineteenth century and the first two decades of the twentieth century that the number of illegitimate births in Lanheses seems to have reached outstanding proportions. Even as late as 1939, it remained high (and here the

TABLE 5.1 ILLEGITIMACY RATIOS IN LANHESES, 1700–1969

| Period | No. of Illegitimate Baptisms A | No. of Expostos[a] B | Total Baptisms C | Illegitimate Ratio A/C |
|---|---|---|---|---|
| 1700–09 | 16 | 2 | 239 | 6.7 |
| 1710–19 | 25 | 4 | 227 | 11.0 |
| 1700–19 | | | | 8.8 |
| 1720–29 | 21 | 3 | 214 | 9.8 |
| 1730–39 | 14 | 2 | 239 | 5.8 |
| 1720–39 | | | | 7.7 |
| 1740–49 | 16 | 1 | 243 | 6.6 |
| 1750–59 | 23 | 2 | 227 | 10.1 |
| 1740–59 | | | | 8.3 |
| 1760–69 | 23 | 3 | 199 | 11.5 |
| 1770–79 | 12 | 2 | 186 | 6.4 |
| 1760–79 | | | | 9.1 |
| 1780–89 | 22 | 3 | 181 | 12.1 |
| 1790–99 | 15 | 4 | 169 | 8.9 |
| 1780–99 | | | | 10.6 |
| 1800–09 | 21 | 3 | 188 | 11.2 |
| 1810–19 | 15[b] | 0 | 202 | 7.4 |
| 1800–19 | | | | 9.2 |
| 1820–29 | 28 | 0 | 267 | 10.9 |
| 1830–39 | 27 | 0 | 255 | 10.6 |
| 1820–39 | | | | 10.7 |
| 1840–49 | 17 | 0 | 261 | 6.5 |
| 1850–59 | 21 | 0 | 241 | 8.7 |
| 1840–59 | | | | 7.6 |
| 1860–69 | 31 | 0 | 273 | 11.3 |
| 1870–79 | 36 | 0 | 239 | 15.1 |
| 1860–79 | | | | 13.1 |
| 1880–89 | 24 | 0 | 237 | 10.1 |
| 1890–99 | 39 | 2 | 281 | 13.9 |
| 1880–99 | | | | 12.2 |
| 1900–09 | 43 | 0 | 310 | 13.0 |
| 1910–19 | 34 | 0 | 263 | 12.9 |
| 1900–19 | | | | 13.4 |

TABLE 5.1 ILLEGITIMACY RATIOS IN LANHESES, 1700–1969 (*cont.*)

| Period | No. of Illegitimate Baptisms A | No. of Expostos[a] B | Total Baptisms C | Illegitimate Ratio A/C |
|---|---|---|---|---|
| 1920–29 | 31 | 0 | 328 | 9.4 |
| 1930–39 | 34 | 0 | 435 | 7.8 |
| 1920–39 | | | | 8.5 |
| 1940–49 | 16 | 0 | 449 | 3.6 |
| 1950–59 | 14 | 0 | 473 | 2.9 |
| 1940–59 | | | | 3.2 |
| 1960–69 | 6 | 0 | 386 | 1.5 |

[a] Expostos are abandoned children who may or may not be illegitimate.

[b] This total excludes a woman who was passing through Lanheses and who remained anonymous in the baptismal record.

NOTE: During the first six decades several of the illegitimate children baptized in Lanheses were the offspring of black slaves. If these children are omitted from the calculations, the ratios for these decades are as follows:

| | |
|---|---|
| 1700–1709 | 5.1 |
| 1710–1719 | 9.4 |
| 1720–1729 | 9.8 |
| 1730–1739 | 5.8 |
| 1740–1749 | 5.8 |
| 1750–1759 | 8.5 |

In the period 1960–1969, children born in France of Lanhesan parents but baptized in Lanheses are excluded from the total number of baptisms.

SOURCE: Parish registers, Lanheses.

dramatic fall in the ratio might indeed be accounted for by a sharp rise in marital fertility associated with the steadily declining age at marriage). After 1940, however, nonmarital fertility declined rapidly until it became almost negligible in the decade of the 1960s.

Figure 5.1 plots the trends in illegitimacy together with trends in the mean age at marriage and in premarital pregnancy. With the exception of the period between 1820 and 1860 and again between 1900 and 1920, there appears to be a direct relationship between fluctuations in the mean age at marriage and fluctuations in the proportion of illegitimate births. It is precisely such a relationship that Levine (1977) has documented for the English parishes he has studied, and certainly the data from Lanheses after 1850 seem to indicate that as marriage was postponed to an unprecedented age, as it was increasingly "frustrated," the number of illegitimate births rose to unprecedented levels. Clearly, there is some connection between

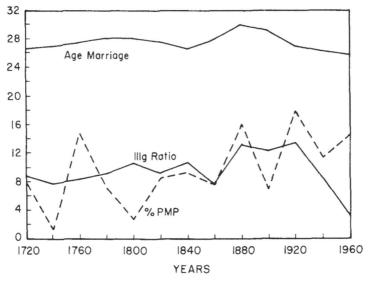

FIGURE 5.1 Trends in the Female Mean Age at Marriage,
Illegitimacy Ratio, and Proportion Premaritally Pregnant, 1700–1970

changes in the average age at which Lanhesan women tended to marry
for the first time and levels of nonmarital fertility. However, the nature of that connection, particularly given the contrary trends in these
two phenomena during the first two decades of the twentieth century, is neither straightforward nor assuredly predictable.

In order to examine this connection further, it seems useful to explore other characteristics of the population of illegitimate children
and their mothers, especially in contrast to the population of women
having children within wedlock. Table 5.2 compares the mean ages
at first birth for mothers of legitimate children with those for mothers of first-born illegitimate children. With the exception of the period between 1800 and 1819 (the difference here is small) and that
between 1920 and 1939, mothers of illegitimate children were consistently younger than mothers of first-born legitimate children, and
in general by an average of 2.3 years until 1920. That the two exceptions are both periods at the heart of a decline in the mean age at
marriage could be important. The trend roughly parallels that which
Levine (1977) and Levine and Wrightson (1980) have described for
the parishes of Colyton and Shepshed throughout the eighteenth century, although the differences in the two mean ages are generally
greater in Lanheses. Furthermore, the Lanheses data also indicate that
for a rather lengthy period of time, and even as the illegitimacy ratio

TABLE 5.2 MEAN AGES, MOTHERS OF LEGITIMATE AND
ILLEGITIMATE CHILDREN

| Period | Mean Age at Marriage A | Mother's Mean Age at First Birth | | B − C | A − C |
| | | Legitimate Children B | Illegitimate Children C | | |
| --- | --- | --- | --- | --- | --- |
| 1740–59 | 27.4 | 28.4 | 27.8 | 0.6 | −0.4 |
| 1760–79 | 28.2 | 29.9 | 26.6 | 3.3 | 1.6 |
| 1780–99 | 28.2 | 30.2 | 26.5 | 3.7 | 1.5 |
| 1800–19 | 27.6 | 27.9 | 28.3 | −0.4 | −0.7 |
| 1820–39 | 26.6 | 27.9 | 26.0 | 1.9 | 0.6 |
| 1840–59 | 27.9 | 28.9 | 26.1 | 2.8 | 1.8 |
| 1860–79 | 30.1 | 30.8 | 26.1 | 4.7 | 4.0 |
| 1880–99 | 29.2 | 28.5 | 26.1 | 2.4 | 3.1 |
| 1900–19 | 26.9 | 27.1 | 24.7 | 2.4 | 2.2 |
| 1920–39 | 26.2 | 27.3 | 28.6 | −1.3 | −2.4 |
| 1940–59 | 25.7 | 26.3 | 26.0 | 0.3 | −0.6 |

NOTE: The mean ages for legitimate children are grouped according to the marriage
cohort of the mother; for illegitimate children the mean is figured according to the
period when the first illegitimate child was born. During several decades, the mean
age at the birth of the first child for mothers of legitimate children is lower or closely
proximates the mean age at marriage. These were periods when many women were
marrying at higher ages and not having any children at all and thus not appearing
in the calculations of the mean age of mothers of legitimate first-borns; or periods,
such as the last, when premarital pregnancies were high.
SOURCE: Family Reconstitution Data, Lanheses.

rose to outstanding proportions, the average age for the mothers of
first-born illegitimate children remained fairly constant, hovering at
around twenty-six. The single exception is the period between 1800
and 1819, a period characterized by political turmoil in Portugal.
Finally, precisely when the mean age at marriage dropped suddenly
during the first decade of the twentieth century, so too did the mean
age for mothers of illegitimate children. The unusual figure in the
present century is the dramatic jump in the age of these women during the period between the two world wars.

The mean ages calculated in Table 5.2 are for unmarried women
marrying for the first time. Although single women made up the bulk
of mothers of illegitimate children throughout the two-and-a-half
centuries between 1700 and 1950, it is worth noting that there were
a few instances of married women, widows, and slaves giving birth
to children out of wedlock or as the result of adultery. The slaves,

five of whom gave birth between 1700 and 1719 and four of whom gave birth between 1740 and 1759, were the "property" of members of the Abreu-Pereira-Cirne-Brito family (ancestors to the Almada lineage), and of Padre Francisco Franco of the Casa da Barrosa and his heirs. All of them are identified as being black, and were probably brought from Brazil, where many of their owners had lived and/or had business or governmental dealings. We can only speculate as to who sired their offspring. Four widows gave birth to illegitimate children during the eighteenth century, eight during the nineteenth century, and three between 1900 and 1949. Some of these widows had more than one child out of wedlock. In only one instance was one of these widows successful in marrying the father of her child. Fewer were the married women who had children who were identified as illegitimate—as filho adulterino. Two cases occurred during the first half of the eighteenth century; one during the latter half of the same century; and four between 1900 and 1949. It is important to note that five of these women were living without their spouses at the time of the illegitimate birth; that is, their husbands were identified in the register as being abroad, in Brazil or Spain, as emigrants. Obviously, it is only in such cases that a married woman's child could truly be called the issue of adultery. A more problematic case with a reverse outcome (such a child recognized as legitimate) is discussed later in the chapter.

Before drawing any conclusions about these illegitimate children and, more importantly, their mothers, let us examine a few more demographic variables, one being the extent of premarital pregnancy. Shorter (1971) has used fluctuations in the rate of conceptions prior to marriage to support his argument of increased sexual promiscuity. Where illegitimacy and premarital pregnancy are plotted together, he notes, they tend to rise together. When they diverge it must indicate, he continues, that either more or less emphasis was being placed upon saving a girl's honor or the honor of her family through marriage, although why this should vary in the short run if there is, as he is arguing, a definite shift in social mores, is a question he does not adequately address.

In Lanheses (Figure 5.1), the relationship between premarital pregnancies (the percent of first births occurring within seven months after marriage) and illegitimate births does not appear to be clear-cut, although in general the former peaks at precisely the same periods as the latter—that is, between 1860 and 1879 and between 1900 and 1919, a pattern which would tend to support Shorter's argument and suggest that by the latter part of the nineteenth century

TABLE 5.3 RATIO OF PREMARITAL PREGNANCIES TO ALL
PREGNANCIES OUTSIDE OF MARRIAGE AND MEAN AGE OF MOTHERS
AT BIRTH WITHIN SEVEN MONTHS OF MARRIAGE,
1700–1959

| Period of Birth | No. Illegit. Births A | Births within 8½ Months of Marriage | | | Births within 7 Months of Marriage | | | Mean Age of Mother at First Birth |
|---|---|---|---|---|---|---|---|---|
| | | No. B | Total A + B | Ratio B/A + B | No. C | Total A + C | Ratio C/A + C | |
| 1700–19 | 41 | 12 | 53 | 22.6 | 6 | 47 | 12.8 | 31.4 |
| 1720–39 | 35 | 3 | 38 | 7.9 | 1 | 36 | 2.8 | 20.3 |
| 1740–59 | 39 | 11 | 50 | 22.0 | 10 | 49 | 20.4 | 26.9 |
| 1760–79 | 35 | 11 | 46 | 23.9 | 5 | 40 | 12.5 | 31.4* |
| 1780–99 | 37 | 3 | 40 | 7.5 | 2 | 39 | 5.1 | 26.5 |
| 1800–19 | 36 | 10 | 46 | 21.7 | 6 | 42 | 14.3 | 27.0 |
| 1820–39 | 55 | 12 | 67 | 17.9 | 8 | 63 | 12.7 | 23.2 |
| 1840–59 | 38 | 7 | 45 | 15.5 | 7 | 45 | 15.5 | 25.9 |
| 1860–79 | 67 | 17 | 84 | 20.2 | 14 | 81 | 17.3 | 27.6 |
| 1880–99 | 63 | 10 | 73 | 13.7 | 7 | 70 | 10.0 | 29.5 |
| 1900–19 | 77 | 25 | 102 | 24.5 | 18 | 95 | 18.9 | 26.6 |
| 1920–39 | 65 | 18 | 83 | 21.6 | 14 | 79 | 17.7 | 29.1 |
| 1940–59 | 30 | 34 | 64 | 53.1 | 23 | 53 | 43.4 | 23.3 |

* If three widows in their forties are omitted, two of whom married widowers, the mean
is 28.4.
SOURCE: Family Reconstitution Data, Lanheses.

sexual activity outside of marriage in Lanheses was on the increase.
Certainly, premarital pregnancy fluctuates much more dramatically
than illegitimacy, and there is one great period of divergence in the
latter part of the eighteenth century when illegitimacy rises above 10
percent while premarital pregnancies fall to 3 percent. The other important point of departure is in recent times, when premarital pregnancies account for more than half of all nonmarital conceptions
(Table 5.3). The diverging paths of these two measures of nonmarital
conceptions after 1920 must be linked in some way with the declining age at marriage in the context of improving socioeconomic conditions which made it more possible for a young man to marry the
girl he had "got in trouble" and save her honor. Could it also be
that there was some sort of renewed emphasis on such an obligation?
This is a question I will return to later.

It should be stressed that the plot of premarital pregnancies on
Figure 5.1 only includes births occurring within seven months of a

TABLE 5.4 PERCENTAGE OF WOMEN IN A MARRIAGE COHORT
WHO WERE PREGNANT AT THE TIME OF MARRIAGE, 1700–1959

| Period | No. Marriages | % of Women in Cohort at Least 2 Weeks Pregnant | % of Women in Cohort at Least 2 Months Pregnant |
|---|---|---|---|
| 1700–1719 | 102 | 17.6 | 5.9 |
| 1720–1739 | 97 | 4.1 | 1.0 |
| 1740–1759 | 82 | 25.6 | 12.2 |
| 1760–1779 | 88 | 18.2 | 5.7 |
| 1780–1799 | 88 | 5.7 | 2.3 |
| 1800–1819 | 94 | 17.0 | 6.4 |
| 1820–1839 | 106 | 18.9 | 7.5 |
| 1840–1859 | 128 | 5.5 | 5.5 |
| 1860–1879 | 124 | 25.0 | 11.3 |
| 1880–1899 | 134 | 12.7 | 5.2 |
| 1900–1919 | 130 | 33.1 | 13.8 |
| 1920–1939 | 156 | 20.5 | 8.9 |
| 1940–1959 | 203 | 28.1 | 11.3 |
| 1700–1749 | 246 | 11.8 | 5.3 |
| 1750–1799 | 211 | 11.8 | 5.2 |
| 1800–1849 | 256 | 15.6 | 7.0 |
| 1850–1899 | 330 | 15.4 | 7.2 |
| 1900–1949 | 387 | 23.2 | 11.1 |

SOURCE: Family Reconstitution Data, Lanheses.

woman's marriage. That is, the woman must have known that she was pregnant at the time of her marriage. Tables 5.3 and 5.4 (the latter simply defines premarital pregnancy with reference to women in a marital cohort rather than with reference to first births to a marital cohort) include what might be considered all possible premarital pregnancies (children born within eight-and-a half months after marriage). The distinction here is between marriages where sex before marriage was likely, and marriages that may in fact have been prompted by a pregnancy.[7]

Table 5.5 presents the mean intervals between marriage and the birth of the first child for these two subpopulations of premaritally pregnant women, as well as the mean ages at marriage for those who were single at the time of their marriage. Although the number of cases is small for some periods, it does seem that throughout the nineteenth century many women who had conceived a child out of wedlock married the father of the child just as the pregnancy began

TABLE 5.5 MEAN INTERVALS BETWEEN MARRIAGE AND FIRST BIRTH, AND MEAN AGES AT MARRIAGE FOR SINGLE WOMEN WHO WERE PREGNANT AT MARRIAGE, 1700–1959

| Period | Those Giving Birth within 7 Months | | | Those Giving Birth from 7 to 8½ Months | | | Overall Mean Age at Marriage | Mean Age at Marriage, Total Pop. |
|---|---|---|---|---|---|---|---|---|
| | No. | Inter-val | Age | No. | Inter-val | Age | | |
| 1700–19 | 6 | .46 | 29.7 | 6 | .66 | 25.1 | 28.0 | 26.5 |
| 1720–39 | 1 | .31 | 19.9 | 2 | .64 | 27.0 | 24.7 | 26.9 |
| 1740–59 | 10 | .29 | 26.6 | 1 | .60 | NA | 26.6 | 27.4 |
| 1760–79 | 5 | .11 | 28.2 | 6 | .66 | 26.5 | 27.4 | 28.2 |
| 1780–99 | 2 | .14 | 26.3 | 1 | .67 | 23.6 | 25.4 | 28.2 |
| 1800–19 | 6 | .36 | 26.6 | 4 | .66 | 25.2 | 26.1 | 27.6 |
| 1820–39 | 8 | .29 | 26.1 | 4 | .67 | 29.5 | 27.4 | 26.6 |
| 1840–59 | 7 | .34 | 25.5 | 0 | — | — | 25.5 | 27.9 |
| 1860–79 | 12 | .34 | 26.8 | 5 | .64 | 30.7 | 27.9 | 30.1 |
| 1880–99 | 7 | .42 | 29.0 | 3 | .65 | 26.5 | 28.3 | 29.2 |
| 1900–19 | 18 | .41 | 25.1 | 7 | .66 | 25.8 | 25.3 | 26.9 |
| 1920–39 | 14 | .32 | 25.9 | 4 | .66 | 24.7 | 25.6 | 26.2 |
| 1940–59 | 23 | .29 | 23.0 | 11 | .66 | 26.1 | 24.5 | 25.7 |
| 1700–49 | 13 | .33 | 27.2 (25.8) | 7 | .67 | 25.9 (26.3) | 26.7 | 26.7 |
| 1750–99 | 11 | .23 | 27.3 (25.6) | 7 | .66 | 25.9 (26.0) | 26.7 | 28.2 |
| 1800–49 | 18 | .33 | 26.4 (26.3) | 8 | .66 | 27.4 (27.0) | 26.7 | 27.3 |
| 1850–99 | 22 | .36 | 27.1 (26.3) | 8 | .64 | 29.1 (30.2) | 27.6 | 29.3 |
| 1900–49 | 41 | .33 | 24.9 (23.1) | 17 | .65 | 25.0 (24.1) | 24.9 | 26.6 |

NOTE: Numbers in parentheses are the medians. Scales for intervals are as follows: 3 months = .25; 4 months = .33; 5 months = .41; 6 months = .50; 7 months = .58; 8 months = .67.

SOURCE: Family Reconstitution Data, Lanheses.

to be apparent (between four and five months). What we do not know precisely is the nature of the pressures that led a couple to marry rather than to let a child be born illegitimately. Although the mean ages at marriage for women who had their first child within seven months would seem to indicate that they were younger at the time of marriage than the population as a whole, the median ages calculated for fifty-year intervals indicate great diversity during the

eighteenth century and some diversity, though less, during the nineteenth century. Although not included in the calculation of mean ages
on Table 5.5, it should be noted that three of the women who were
premaritally pregnant between 1700 and 1719 were widows (of a
total of thirteen widows who remarried during this period). Only
one, however, had her child within seven months. In the 1760s, all
three widows who remarried were pregnant, but again only one was
expecting a child imminently. I mention this because it would perhaps suggest that pregnancy, or at least the granting of sexual favors,
may have been used as a marital strategy, especially by widows left
with young children. Certainly these widows were more fortunate
than those who ended up giving birth to a new child out of wedlock.
At the very least, and coupled with the data on illegitimate births, it
suggests that it was certainly not unusual for widows to engage in
sexual activity after the death of their husbands.

The majority of women who had their first child within eight-and-
a-half months of their marriage were definitely pregnant (mean intervals under .67, or 8 months) although they may not have known it
at the time that they were wed. For some, engagement was clearly a
license for premarital sex, a factor at least suggested for the early
eighteenth century by the fact that five mothers of illegitimate children were registered as being "engaged" (*esposada*) to a certain young
man. Each of these women married her fiancé shortly after the birth
of the child. Curiously, during the eighteenth century the women who
had their first child within eight-and-a-half months of marriage were
younger than the overall population at the time of their marriage;
but during the nineteenth century, they seem to have been roughly
equivalent in age.

Clearly, a comparison between the data on premarital pregnancy
and that on illegitimacy leaves us with several questions, chief among
which is one already raised. What pressures led some young men to
marry the girl they had "got into trouble" while others did not? Are
there perhaps some differences in the population of women who were
premaritally pregnant and those who ended up giving birth to an
illegitimate child? Although specific references to engaged couples
disappear in the registers by the mid-eighteenth century, it is possible
to arrive at an estimate of how many of these mothers of illegitimate
children married, at least within the parish, and to derive some understanding of whom they married. During the eighteenth and nineteenth centuries, there was little change in the proportion of women
who successfully married after having a child out of wedlock—roughly
one-fifth (21.7 percent). In the present century, this proportion de-

clined to 16 percent. Examining the data more closely, we see that the latter two decades of the eighteenth century particularly stand out. The number of illegitimate births was high (10.6 percent), the number of women at least two months pregnant at marriage low (2.3 percent), and the number of mothers of illegitimate children who subsequently married very few (4.2 percent). It may be no accident that this coincides with a period when the emigration of young men to Spain was, by all indications, high. Was emigration an escape from the responsibilities of a wife and child, or did the young man leave, promising his girlfriend that he would marry her once he had made his fortune abroad?

Of course, we cannot readily assume that the mothers of "natural" children were marrying the fathers of their children or that these children were in all cases the offspring of young courting couples. Indeed, if one examines the individual cases, enormous variations appear. Of the twelve women who had illegitimate children during the first half of the eighteenth century and who subsequently married in the parish, six were wed within six months to the fathers of their children; another had three illegitimate children within four years by the same man (to whom she was esposada), and married him eight months after the last child was born; two more married the fathers of their children fourteen and twenty-eight months later (one of these married a mulatto slave); two married widowers six and seven years later (one of them had had three illegitimate children); and the last married a man seven months later (whether he was the father is unclear).

Of the fourteen women who married during the latter part of the eighteenth century, only three were married within six months to the fathers of their children; another two married the fathers more than six months later—one two years later; three married widowers, one eight years after the birth of her third illegitimate child, another fourteen years later at age forty-four and after two illegitimate children, and a third when her illegitimate child was ten years old; one married eleven months later, pregnant again, but not necessarily to the father of the first child; the rest married anywhere from two to eight years later, probably to other men.

The patterns of marriage for the mothers of illegitimate children during the eighteenth century seem to have continued during the nineteenth century, although by the end of the century we begin to see in some cases a much longer interval between the birth of an illegitimate child and marriage to the father of that child. Of the sixteen women who married between 1800 and 1850, five married the father of their child within six months, and another four married the father within two years (one of these had two children illegitimately); the rest married anywhere from eleven months to fourteen years later, and of these one was already pregnant again, another had had two children six years apart out of wedlock, and a third had seen her illegitimate child die. During the latter half of the nineteenth century, two women married the fathers of their children within six months and another four within a year (of these latter four, one had had three illegitimate children and another was pregnant again); three more married the father of their child more than a year later, one of these six years later, another two years after the birth of a second child and when she was pregnant with a third; four married widowers, two after having had four children illegitimately (one after three) and generally between five and eight years after the birth of the last child; one married the father of her child in 1897 after twenty years had passed and only three days before his death—clearly a case of last-minute legitimization, about which more will be said later; the rest were married anywhere from ten months to seven years later to men whose relationship to the illegitimate children is uncertain. One of these was pregnant at the time of her marriage, whereas the illegitimate children of two more had already died.

During the first half of the present century, a practice that clearly started in the late nineteenth century seems to have emerged even more forcefully. Of the fourteen women who married after having had an illegitimate child, four married the fathers of their children from three to fourteen years later, and three of these were pregnant again at the time of their marriage; two married the fathers of their children within six months; the rest married anywhere from sixteen months to seven years later, and two of them were pregnant at the time of their marriage. Of the five women who had illegitimate children in the 1950s and who subsequently married, one married the father of her child ten years later, and three more married seven, seven, and ten years later outside the village—two as immigrants living in the Lisbon area, and the third as an immigrant in France.

Summing up the two-and-a-half centuries between 1700 and 1949, it seems that of the seventy-eight single women who had at least one illegitimate child and who subsequently married, 54 percent married without question the fathers of their illegitimate children, although the interval between the birth of their child and their marriage varied enormously, especially by the end of the nineteenth century and the early decades of the twentieth century.

There are some important observations to make about the marriage of these mothers of illegitimate children, but I would like to reserve them for later in the chapter and at this point turn to one final aspect of the demographic data that should be addressed—so-called "repetitive bastard-bearing" in Lanheses. No matter how one looks at it, it is quite apparent that repeaters, women who had more than one illegitimate child, contributed significantly to the extent and nature of illegitimacy in Lanheses between 1700 and the mid-twentieth century. Approximately 50 percent of all the children born illegitimately in Lanheses during two-and-a-half centuries were born to these women—during the nineteenth century; the proportion was over 50 percent. In addition, more than one-quarter of all the women who had illegitimate children in Lanheses were women who had more than one illegitimate child. These proportions are well above those cited by Levine (1977) for even his protoindustrial towns of Shepshed and Colyton after 1750! Indeed, in the agricultural villages he studied, Levine found that repetitive bastard-bearing was relatively infrequent, and therefore explains his data with reference to the ability of women with several illegitimate children in towns like Colyton and Shepshed to find work and support themselves independently.

The Portuguese village data also indicate that at precisely the time when illegitimacy (and premarital pregnancy) reach their highest levels—between 1860 and 1879 and between 1900 and 1919—so too do the percentage of illegitimate children who were born to repeaters and the percentage of women having illegitimate children who were repeaters (Table 5.6). These trends lend support to the conclusions of both Levine and Laslett that at times of increasing illegitimacy, repetitive bastard-bearing is disproportionately influential. It should also be noted that during the last two decades of the eighteenth century (when illegitimacy rose and premarital pregnancy declined), the proportion of illegitimate children born to repeaters rose to above 50 percent, and the number of women having more than one child out of wedlock to more than a third of the total. What, we might ask, do the late eighteenth and late nineteenth centuries have in common?

Repeater mothers were generally younger than the overall population of mothers of illegitimate children at the time of their first illegitimate birth. The differences are greatest (over three years) between 1760 and 1819 and between 1860 and 1879. In addition, a greater proportion of repeaters were native-born (that is, Lanhesans) than were mothers of a single illegitimate child. Levine (1977) found that in Colyton 60 percent of the repeaters were natives of the town. In Lanheses, for most of the period under consideration in this study, the proportion is well above this, reaching almost 90 percent during the latter part of the eighteenth century and the first half of the twentieth century. The comparative figures for mothers of one illegitimate

TABLE 5.6 ILLEGITIMATE CHILDREN BORN TO REPEATERS,
1700–1959

| Period | No. of Women with at Least One Illegitimate Child | % of These Who Had More Than One Illegitimate Child | % of All Illegitimate Children Born to Repeaters |
|---|---|---|---|
| 1700–19 | 32 | 18.7 | 38.1 |
| 1720–39 | 30 | 16.6 | 32.4 |
| 1740–59 | 32 | 15.6 | 37.5 |
| 1760–79 | 26 | 15.3 | 31.2 |
| 1780–99 | 25 | 36.0 | 37.1 |
| 1800–19 | 28 | 21.4 | 42.1 |
| 1820–39 | 36 | 27.8 | 51.8 |
| 1840–59 | 25 | 28.0 | 48.6 |
| 1860–79 | 45 | 42.2 | 64.4 |
| 1880–99 | 43 | 32.5 | 58.2 |
| 1900–19 | 43 | 32.5 | 60.8 |
| 1920–39 | 45 | 22.2 | 45.3 |
| 1940–59 | 20 | 25.0 | 44.4 |

SOURCE: Parish registers, Lanheses.

child are 77.8 percent native-born between 1750 and 1799, and 76.0 percent between 1900 and 1949. The lowest proportions are during the first half of the eighteenth century, when 54.8 percent of the mothers of one illegitimate child were natives of Lanheses, as were 58.3 percent of the repeaters. In general, these figures tend to suggest that illegitimacy in Lanheses was very much a Lanheses phenomenon; that is, it was not a behavior pattern that can be attributed in large part to outsiders who moved in to Lanheses for whatever reason, although, as we will see, women born in Lanheses of non-native parents (especially caseiros) contributed disproportionately to the repeater population during the latter decades of the nineteenth century and the early decades of the twentieth century.

Clearly, the discussion so far has indicated that despite any modern-day denials of the importance of illegitimacy in the demographic history of Lanheses, it was a rather prevalent phenomenon with some distinctive characteristics. Even if some current residents admit that it existed in the past, and that it has occasionally happened in more recent times (in fact, some stress that it is more rampant now because of increasing sexual freedom and declining morality), they tend to draw distinctions within the population of women who had children out of wedlock. Indeed, statistics on the extent of repetitive bastard-bearing suggest such distinctions. It is to some of these differences that I would now like to turn, reserving a final explanation of the statistical trends, and particularly of period effects, to the conclusion of the chapter, after all the evidence is in.

## THE SOCIOECONOMIC CONTEXT OF ILLEGITIMACY

A number of historians working with nonmarital fertility data in different regions of western Europe have described variations in the character of illegitimate births according to the socioecomic background of the mothers of illegitimate children. Chaunu (1966:196–197), for example, differentiates between two groups of mothers of illegitimate children, each associated with a distinct agricultural system in rural France: in the open field areas, he argues, out-of-wedlock births originated in the prenuptial privileges between boys and girls of the same class and age, while in the *bocage* or closed field regions, illegitimacy was the result of the rights that masters exercised over their servants. Bouvet (1968:53), in his study of the parish of Trouarn, wonders whether some of the mothers of illegitimate children were not, in fact, prostitutes—"Marie Ancelle, day laborer, had at least six children without one finding any mention of a father."Lawrence Stone, in his monumental study of family and domestic life in England between 1500 and 1800 (1977), describes three types of sexual encounters: the seduction of one servant by a fellow servant (status equals); the seduction of servants by those of higher social status; and straight promiscuous illegitimacy. Shorter (1971) places a time dimension on roughly similar categories and speaks about a significant shift from manipulative sex to expressive sex, the former yielding to the latter by the nineteenth century. The work of Fairchilds (1978) and De Pauw (1972) with pregnancy declarations in different regions of France lends further support to the "types" delineated by Shorter and Stone. Although no such pregnancy declarations exist for Portugal, various factors, including oral history, seem to indicate that the circumstances which led to a nonmarital pregnancy were as diverse as those elsewhere in western Europe. Although each situation could be considered unique, there are some general patterns that emerge which permit a delineation of a similar set of types for the northwestern Portuguese parish.

### The Infelicitous Servant

That women have been and remain the mainstay of the agricultural way of life in northern rural Portugal is a fact which has been emphasized repeatedly in this volume. Indeed, the word servant, *criado,* applies most appropriately in the countryside to an individual who does agricultural work, or, in the case of the female *criada*, both agricultural and domestic work. Young girls, often from large families, were customarily sent out to work as servants for well-to-do lavradors or for the local landed aristocracy. In some instances, these young women simply worked for a wealthier peasant family in their own village, moving in to become part of another household. In others, they were sent to neighboring villages or to a nearby provincial town. Many of these girls left their families as young teenagers, and, outside the supervision of their parents, some of them were inevitably taken advantage of, whether by their employers or by young male servants living and working in the same household.

Although the evidence is slim for the eighteenth century, there are a few indications of the existence of these "infelicitous servants" in the records of Lanheses. As early as December 1707, a young woman from a village in the concelho of Valença (further north) gave birth to an illegitimate child in Lanheses and declared the father to be Braz Dantas da Gama of S. Paio Aguiar, the son of a well-to-do aristocratic family, most likely a family for whom she had worked before coming to Lanheses. Another young woman, again not a native of the parish, gave birth to an illegitimate daughter six months later and named Gabriel de Freixo Malheiro of the town of Viana do Castelo as the father, again an individual from a family of means. We do not know precisely why these two women were in Lanheses at the time that they gave birth. Had they come or been sent to serve in a new household? Certainly, the high number of non-natives who gave birth to illegitimate children in Lanheses, especially during the first half of the eighteenth century, suggests that such young women were an important part of the local population. Unfortunately, the rare occasions on which the fathers were actually named in the baptismal records makes it virtually impossible to identify their socioeconomic status with any certainty. They could, in fact, just as well have been status equals of these non-native criadas as their employers. In 1714, for example, Ana Gonçalves of Sopo (concelho of Caminha) gave birth to a son. Only when this young man marries in 1742 do we learn that his father was a certain João Rodrigues, a native of Areosa (concelho of Ponte de Lima) but a resident of Lanheses. Both mother and father were most likely servants in Lanheses at the time that their son was conceived. They had never married, however. Although hardly statistically overwhelming, cases such as those just cited suggest the possibility of sexual encounters between servants or between servant and employer, both of which resulted on occasion in an illegitimate birth. Furthermore, not only were young women moving into Lanheses and giving birth to children conceived elsewhere, but equally there were young women of Lanheses who went to serve in other villages or towns, conceived a child while away, and then returned to give birth to the child in their native village.

Although the majority of household absences recorded in the late nineteenth-century rois da desobriga are those of male heads of household or young single men, there are several instances in which young women in their teens and twenties are also absent. In some cases, these absences are concentrated within particular families— poor and landless families with several mouths to feed. Sending two or three daughters out to serve was a strategy used to reduce the number of dependents and, even if they were paid little or nothing at all, they were at least sustained in their employer's household. In 1899, for example, twenty-one daughters of Lanhesan households were absent, women whose mean age was a little more than fifteen; in 1907, twenty-two were absent, with a mean age of eighteen and a half. Among both the 1899 and the 1907 absent women were four groups of sisters, although entirely different groups. Both sisters in one of the 1899 groups subsequently had an illegitimate child baptized in Lanheses. Similarly, in 1907 two sisters who were both absent in that year eventually had out-of-wedlock children who were baptized in Lanheses. What we do not know, of course, is how many may have conceived and given birth to children in the parish or town where they were employed. Furthermore, in none of the cases where we know of an illegitimate birth is the paternity of the child certain. Yet, among one of the groups of four sisters who were absent in 1907 was an eighteen-year-old, Delia Lima Pereira, and her experience in service is known to us through oral history.

Delia was baptized in 1888, the fourth of twelve children born to Manuel Pereira and Catarina Lima. Manuel and Catarina were second cousins, descended on his paternal side and her maternal side from António Pereira and Ana Lima. Catarina's parents were potters who had arrived in Lanheses from a village near the city of Braga in the middle of the nineteenth century to work for a potters' household from the same village, which was already well established in the parish. Catarina was one of eleven children born after the couple had settled in Lanheses. Her husband, Manuel, was also a potter, having learned the trade as a young man. Although his own father was born in the neighboring village of Fontão, the family on his paternal side has a long history in Lanheses. His maternal grandparents, however, came to Lanheses from villages elsewhere in the region sometime after their marriage.

As essentially landless artisans, Delia's parents were poor and, consequently, all the daughters were sent out to serve. Delia first left home at the age of seven. When she began in service, she earned three *vintens* (0$060) a year. By the time she was twenty, she was earning five *tostões* (5$000) a month; and by the age of forty (in the late 1920s), her salary had risen to 150$000 per month. Everything she earned she gave to her parents, and, in addition, some of her more kindly employers frequently sent her home at Christmas with baskets full of potatoes, sugar, and codfish. During her career in service, she worked in the region (including serving as a maid for the Almada family) and in Lisbon. Although she never talked about it, the baptismal records indicate that in 1916, when she was twenty-eight, Delia gave birth to a daughter. The child died. She then went to work in the northern coastal town of Afife for a well-to-do couple. Early in 1917, the mistress of the household passed away, and her employer soon began to turn his attentions to her. She became pregnant and gave birth to another daughter in 1918.

When her employer's family discovered what had happened they were dismayed. "They thought of me," she said, "as lowly (*muito baixeira*) and they discouraged my employer from marrying me. I was only a servant!" She also admitted that her father was angry with her, "ashamed at what she had done," and did not want to see her at home. She took her daughter and went to Lisbon, accepting employment only in households where they were both welcome. She remained in Lisbon for five years, working primarily as a cook. However, in 1923, as her father was dying, he called her back to the village, "perhaps with some remorse." After his death, she remained with her mother (who died in 1943) and eventually inherited the major portion of her parents property (the têrço). She bought out the shares of her siblings in the paternal home and continued to live there with her daughter (who never married) until her own death in 1982. Her daughter still lives in the house (which she has renovated) with a young niece.

Delia was the only one of the spinster daughters of Manuel Pereira and Catarina Lima (three of eight who survived to adulthood never married) to give birth to children out of wedlock. However, the family itself was one that was gossiped about because several of the daughters "did not behave themselves" (*não se comportar bem*). In fact, one of Delia's older sisters, Rosa, caused what was perhaps an even greater scandal. Rosa was extremely pretty and at eighteen married a man who was almost twice her age. They had no children, and while her husband was away in Spain she became the mistress of the local colonel. Later, he "passed her on to the village chaplain." "Perhaps," one old-timer speculated, "she thought that she was quite safe because she had not conceived with either her husband or the colonel." But soon she was pregnant with the chaplain's child. When her husband returned from Spain, he accepted the child as his own and the infant was registered as a legitimate son. "But, the people of the village knew better because the boy was the spitting image of his real father." After the birth of her son, Rosa "became very religious," and eventually the incident was forgotten. However, her behavior, together with that of her sister Delia, made it difficult for some of the other sisters to marry locally. Three eventually left, and two of these wed in Lisbon. Another had a fiancé, but when other young men began to laugh at him and imply that his fiancée, like her sisters, may have already been "used," he abandoned her. "As time passed, she aged beyond the point of being able to successfully find a husband." However, she worked for many years for the Almadas and eventually amassed enough money to buy a house on the feira which, upon her death, she bequeathed to her goddaughter.

Clearly, Rosa's story suggests that relationships between young women of poor families and men of wealth or of higher-status families could take place in Lanheses itself. Although Rosa was not a criada at the time, the Rois da Desobriga of the latter half of the nineteenth century indicate that servants in Lanhesan households, although not abundant, did exist. For example, in the 1850 roll, twenty-three of 210 households had at least one servant (11 percent), some (the Almadas and the Tinocos) as many as seven or eight. The total number of servants was forty-three, and of these seventeen were men and twenty-six were women. Three decades later, in 1881, slightly fewer than 10 percent of the households had a servant, and the population was made up of twenty-nine women and seven men. Many of these servants were quite young:

|          | 1881 | 1899 |
|----------|------|------|
| Under 15 | 3    | 1    |
| 15–19    | 7    | 0    |
| 20–24    | 6    | 5    |
| 25–29    | 1    | 1    |
| 30–39    | 6    | 5    |
| Over 40  | 6    | 8    |

By the end of the century, only 7 percent of the households had live-in servants and again there were four times as many criadas as criados. However, fewer of them were very young. Indeed, the servants over forty were generally women who had remained with one household for a lengthy period of time. What is more difficult to discern, since these criadas are most often listed on the rois with a first name only, is whether any of them gave birth to illegitimate children. Furthermore, even if this connection could be made, it has already been noted that the father of the child was not identified after the mid-eighteenth century. Yet again, oral history provides us with a few cases in which criadas in Lanhesan households found themselves in the unfortunate condition of carrying their employer's child.

One such woman was Amelia da Rocha, who was born in 1863 and who lost both her mother and father when she was very young. She went to live with one of her mother's sisters, a spinster who owned a small house in the Lugar de Seara and who made her living as a weaver (*tecedeira*). When she was in her mid-twenties, Amelia went to work as a servant for João da Quinta, a wealthy lavrador and entrepreneur in the village who had a large house on the feira. João da Quinta and his wife had no children of their own. In 1892, João da Quinta's wife died and Amelia's aunt, perhaps feeling that it was inappropriate for a young woman to live alone with a widower who was only nine years her senior, asked her niece to return to live with her. However, João da Quinta insisted that he "thought of Amelia as a daughter" and that he wished for her to remain in his household. Amelia's aunt agreed. In 1898, Amelia became pregnant with João da Quinta's child. Although João da Quinta continued to urge her to remain in his household (without any promise of marriage), Amelia decided at that point to return to live with her aunt, "feeling disgust, ashamed by what had happened to her." "From that time on, for the rest of her life," her illegitimate daughter recounted, "my mother went around with her head bowed down." Meanwhile, João da Quinta went on to father several other children with women who worked for him as servants or as day laborers. Amelia's daughter was raised knowing who her father was and when he passed by she addressed him as *pai*. However, he paid little attention to her and her mother never spoke to him again and never married.

## The Abandoned Namorada

Although some mothers of illegitimate children were from poor families who, by necessity, were forced to send their daughters out to work as servants or as day laborers in conditions that might not always have been best for the protection of their purity, there were also daughters of what might be considered more respectable or well-to-do lavrador households who "made a mistake." Villagers claim, when discussing these young women, that the blame lies with parents who did not watch over their daughters closely enough—as one informant commented, citing, as the Portuguese often do, a popular adage: *quem fez o ladrão é a ocasião* (what makes a robber is the occasion). Often, these were girls whose children were fathered by their current boyfriends, and frequently the conception occurred during the summer months when young people were out in the fields working together or enjoying the activities of one of the numerous summer festas (Table 5.7). Indeed, festas were the occasions for courtship and perhaps promises of marriage.

Once the child was conceived, the young man could choose to marry the girl or not to marry her. Until quite recently, Portuguese law gave no protection to the mother of an illegitimate child unless she was a minor, and there was, therefore, no legal recourse that would either require the girl to reveal the identity of her child's father or require the boy to assume any responsibility whatsoever for the child he had sired. Nothing except social pressure could force him to marry the girl, and often social pressure, especially peer group pressure, worked in quite the opposite direction. However, as one villager noted—and this is significant in light of explanations for changes in patterns of historical illegitimacy set forth by some scholars—after 1930 courtship behavior altered in such a way as to result in more marriages than there had been previously. The demographic data reflect this shift: premarital pregnancy rates continue to rise while illegitimacy experiences a rapid decline.

> In the past a young man might have had several girls whom he was courting and whom he visited on a Sunday afternoon, none of them very serious. Young men today stay with one girl, a girl they may have been "conversing with" for many years.[8] If this girl gets pregnant, everyone knows who the father is because they know that she was only seeing one boy. In the past, if a girl gave herself to a young man and he was not that serious about her anyway he would think "if she allowed me to take advantage of her, how many more will she allow?" The young men were scrupulous about whom they chose to be their wife.

Another villager indicated that some of these abandoned namoradas became part of the group of women who had more than one child out of wedlock—*o pão já era incerto* (The bread was already

TABLE 5.7 SEASONALITY OF ILLEGITIMATE BIRTHS, 1700–1959

| Birth Cohorts | Total No. | Percent of Total | | | |
|---|---|---|---|---|---|
| | | B. Jan–Mar C. Apr–Jun | B. Apr–Jun C. July–Sept | B. July–Sept C. Oct–Dec | B. Oct–Dec C. Jan–Mar |
| 1700–1719 | 41 | 26.8 | 39.0 | 19.5 | 14.6 |
| 1720–1739 | 35 | 25.7 | 34.3 | 22.8 | 17.1 |
| 1740–1759 | 39 | 20.5 | 41.0 | 20.5 | 17.9 |
| 1760–1779 | 35 | 22.9 | 57.1 | 8.6 | 11.4 |
| 1780–1799 | 37 | 29.7 | 32.4 | 29.7 | 8.1 |
| 1800–1819 | 36 | 25.0 | 41.6 | 16.7 | 16.7 |
| 1820–1839 | 55 | 23.6 | 29.1 | 23.6 | 23.6 |
| 1840–1859 | 38 | 23.7 | 34.2 | 15.8 | 26.3 |
| 1860–1879 | 67 | 29.8 | 29.8 | 19.4 | 20.9 |
| 1880–1899 | 63 | 30.1 | 31.7 | 20.6 | 17.5 |
| 1900–1919 | 77 | 29.9 | 33.7 | 16.9 | 19.5 |
| 1920–1939 | 65 | 23.1 | 33.8 | 24.6 | 18.5 |
| 1940–1959 | 30 | 26.7 | 30.0 | 13.3 | 30.0 |
| 1700–1749 | 92 | 26.1 | 38.0 | 19.5 | 16.3 |
| 1750–1799 | 95 | 24.2 | 43.1 | 21.0 | 11.6 |
| 1800–1849 | 108 | 25.0 | 36.1 | 19.4 | 19.4 |
| 1850–1899 | 151 | 28.5 | 29.8 | 19.8 | 21.8 |
| 1900–1949 | 158 | 25.3 | 33.5 | 20.9 | 20.2 |

NOTE: B = period of birth; C = period of conception.
SOURCE: Parish registers, Lanheses.

doubtful). On the other hand, even if a young man did not marry his namorada right away after learning that she was pregnant, he might marry her several years later, "seeing that she remained *seria* (serious/sincere) and well-behaved." In earlier discussion of the subsequent marriage of mothers of illegitimate children, such cases clearly existed, especially during the late nineteenth and early twentieth centuries. Again, oral history provides us with recent, but I think typical, examples of the experiences of these "abandoned namoradas."

Virginia was born in 1931 to a respectable lavrador family in Lanheses who owned and rented several plots of land. When she was eighteen she went to Lisbon to work as a servant for the Almada family. Her father did not want to let her go because it was not economically necessary, but when she pleaded with him, he finally consented. She remained in Lisbon for three years. Then one of the other maids in the household became pregnant and the Condessa Almada decided to send all her Lanhesan girls back to the village. It was during the summer when she returned home that Virginia "arranged" her own child. The father was a young man from the neighboring village of Vila Mou whom she had met at a festa. He watched for her when she was out on errands, taking meals to her brothers or milk to the depository. At first she tried to avoid him when he attempted to speak to her alone, but eventually she began to meet him secretly. He promised her marriage and finally she gave in to him.

When she told her namorado that she was pregnant, he urged her to get rid of the child in town, but she refused. Her father was very angry with her, but he did not throw her out. Her baby was born the following April, and three months after his birth her namorado left for Lisbon to find work. When he returned for Christmas he began to arrange the papers for their marriage. But then he received a letter from an uncle in South America who urged him to emigrate. He changed his mind about marrying Virginia and left. Although he sent money from time to time, he never returned, and Virginia raised her son on her own, working first in the village at a range of jobs and later once more in Lisbon as a domestic servant.[9]

A second and somewhat variant example is provided by the case of Margarida Sousa, the fourth child of Manuel de Sousa and Maria Franco. Manuel de Sousa was a lavrador descended from a family of long lineage in Lanheses. Maria Franco was abandoned on the foundling wheel in Viana do Castelo. We do not know when and why she came to Lanheses, but in 1886 she was married to Manuel, a man almost twenty years her senior. Margarida was born in 1893. Her two elder brothers (born in 1888 and 1891) emigrated with their father to Brazil in 1903 and remained there. Her father returned in 1913 to discover his daughter, just twenty years old, pregnant with her namorado's child. However, instead of marrying her, her namorado left the parish. "If she had not been abandoned," speculated one villager, "she might not have arranged the others." In 1921, a son was born out of wedlock and in 1935 another daughter. It seems that Margarida continued to live in her parents' household until her death in 1956. Like her sister Maria, who had an illegitimate child in 1917, she never married.

### Women with No Shame

Although Margarida de Sousa is technically a repeater, Lanhesans who remember her describe her in different terms from those they use for yet another group of women who contributed significantly to illegitimacy in the parish. These latter women simply "had no shame" when it came to arranging children out of wedlock. They "had the vice." Some of them were "prostitutes without a license" whom young men of the village visited; others were widows or married women whose husbands were absent and who "could not live without a man"; others have been described as vulgar (*muito popular*), rough (*bruto*), and wild (*brava*), as women who got around, working as jornaleiras for various households. Some of them were from poor families, "not brought up with the proper education"; others were women who came from neighboring villages to work in Lanheses.

One such woman was Antónia Gonçalves, one of many children of a poor caseiro family who came to Lanheses sometime between 1892 and 1895 from the village of Santa Marta to work the lands of the wealthy Pimenta da Gama family. Antónia, like her brothers and sisters, was sent out to work as a day laborer at a young age. "She had the freedom which agricultural work involves," observed one villager. "It is easy to get lost among the cornstalks down by the river's edge and she was a devil for arranging children." Antónia had seven illegitimate offspring, the first in 1904 when she was twenty, the last in 1921, and each, apparently, by a different father. She continued to support herself in agricultural work and as a carteira transporting wood from the mountains. She lived with her parents and raised her children "with no shame at all." "Nothing stopped her from continuing to do what she had been doing and she had too little education to avoid having more." One of her daughters had two illegitimate children of her own, the first when she was twenty. Another daughter was pregnant prior to her marriage and a second child, born many years after the first, is reputedly not her husband's child, although legally registered as such. In addition, although none of Antónia's other sisters had illegitimate children baptised in Lanheses, her sister Teresa married a boatsman, the illegitimate son of Rosa Araujo, when she was twenty-two and already one month pregnant; and her brother Francisco married at nineteen a girl of seventeen who bore her first child five months later.

## The "Bastardy-Prone Subsociety"

If Antónia is any indication, certain families seem to have been particularly susceptible to the most extreme forms of sexual nonconformity. Servants, jornaleiras, and the daughters of caseiros, individuals from families at the bottom of the socioeconomic scale, contributed significantly to illegitimate or potentially illegitimate births throughout Lanheses' history.[10] During the last four decades of the nineteenth century, women from these socioeconomic groups comprised more than 50 percent of all the women in Lanheses who had at least one illegitimate child. In addition, virtually half of the jornaleiras in particular had more than one child out of wedlock. During the first half of the present century, the trends have been little different, although the number of repeaters has declined, especially after 1940.[11] Even if one examines the socioeconomic background of the women who were premaritally pregnant at the time of their marriage, one finds almost one-fifth (19.2 percent) between 1860 and 1900 and more than a quarter (26.3 percent) between 1900 and 1959 were jornaleiras or daughters of jornaleiros. The comparable figures for lavradeiras or the daughters of lavradores were 57.7 percent and 64.5 percent. Yet, of greater interest are not those who managed to marry and "save face," something which was clearly more customary for women from lavrador families, but those who bore the child they were carrying illegitimately, those for whom "saving face" was either irrelevant or impossible. Furthermore, it is important to examine particular families as a whole rather than individual women who mothered illegitimate children or individual couples who had clearly engaged in premarital sex.

It is precisely through an examination of families rather than individuals that one comes closest to what has been labeled by some historians as the "bastardy-prone subsociety." Laslett (1980a:217) has defined this subsociety as consisting of "a series of bastard-producing women, living in the same locality, whose activities persisted over several generations, and who tended to be related by kinship or marriage." Furthermore, among the women who were part of this subsociety were many who had more than one illegitimate child. The data from Lanheses tends to support the existence of some sort of subsociety or at least subpopulation, even when one considers only the most immediate family relationship, sisterhood. Between 1740 and 1959, approximately one-fifth of all the women who had at least one illegitimate child were related as sisters; the proportion is closer to a third if the focus is on the nineteenth century. Furthermore, these related groups of women had more than a quarter (27.3 percent) of all the illegitimate children baptized in the parish after 1740. Between 1860 and 1939 there were five sets of three sisters who had among them twenty-eight illegitimate children.

One more indication of the kinship basis of at least some illegitimacy in Lanheses is the extent to which women who had illegitimate children were themselves born out of wedlock. Between 1740 and

1959, 13 percent of the mothers of illegitimate children fell into this category, and if women who were labeled as exposta are added, the proportion rises to 15.7 percent.

One example of a poor and "bastardy-prone" family was that of José Alves and Ana Ferreira, a couple who were married in 1868. Ana was a jornaleira, born to jornaleiros in 1841. Her parents, who were married in the parish in 1834, were both natives of other villages in the district of Viana do Castelo, her mother from Neivas, her father from Vila Chá. Her mother, who was born around 1800, had an illegitimate child in 1828 who died four years later. At the time of her marriage she was one month pregnant with a second child. The couple resided in the Lugar de Corredoura. Although there is no record of his death, Ana's father was no longer a member of the household in the rol da desobriga of 1870, and her two brothers were both marked absent in 1870 and 1881. In the 1871 arrolamento dos bens, Rosa Gonçalves is listed as a lavradeira with a property evaluation of 0$960. It seems that over the years she and her husband, by whatever means, had been able to improve their economic condition somewhat, although what little there was hardly enhanced the social and economic status of her daughter, son-in-law, and their offspring. In the 1850, 1870, and 1881 rois, a woman named Henriqueta, a foundling, is included as a member of the household. Why she was there is not clear, but she too had two children out of wedlock, one born in 1862 and the other born in 1865. Only the second was listed in the 1881 roll.

José Alves was a jornaleiro who had come to Lanheses to work for the Tinocos some time prior to his marriage in 1834. He was born in Esturãos, a village to the east of Lanheses in the concelho of Ponte de Lima. He died in 1904 at the age of sixty-one. José and Ana had nine children, two of whom died in very early infancy. Of those who survived to adulthood (three sons and four daughters), four married—three of the daughters remained spinsters. In addition, three of the daughters had illegitimate children baptised in Lanheses between 1893 and 1932. The fourth, a "very beautiful girl" according to one old-timer, went to Lisbon and had children out of wedlock there. In fact, all of the daughters of José Alves and Ana Ferreira were described by several villagers who remembered them as poor "prostitutes" (this is a loosely used epithet) from a poor and disreputable family.

Each of the daughters who gave birth to out-of-wedlock children in Lanheses had more than one: Maria had four (although only one lived past childhood); Rosa had three, all of whom survived; and

Gracia, the youngest daughter who, in adult life, was the servant of Padre Fraga, had three, two of whom survived. Only Rosa married, and when she did it was to a widower who was almost thirty years older (he was sixty-nine and she was forty) and the father of her last illegitimate child, born three years prior to the marriage. The eldest of Rosa's illegitimate children, a daughter born in 1901, herself had a son out of wedlock in 1937.

Although the behavior of the daughters of José Alves and Ana Ferreira in large part accounts for the description of this family by those who remember them as "disreputable," the sons drew equal criticism. The eldest son who was lame, married a *jornaleira* almost ten years older in 1895. When he died in 1902, his death record described him as a "beggar" (*mendigo*). The middle son, born in 1875 was infamous, a "pilferer" (*gatuno*) who stole what he could—chickens, hams, rabbits—from fellow villagers. His wife, a poor jornaleira with one leg shorter than the other, had been in love with a young carpenter. But when her father insisted that she marry José Alves' son, her boyfriend left for Brazil and never returned.

This couple had five daughters, the eldest of whom had three illegitimate children of her own between 1931 and 1941. Only one married in the village, to another poor jornaleiro. The youngest son, Manuel, married a woman who had already borne three illegitimate children, and two years after his death in 1921, she had another. This woman, Rosalia, was a jornaleira who was originally from the village of S. Julião Moreira de Lima. She was related to Manuel in the third degree of consanguinity, presumably through Manuel's father, who had lived in S. Julião prior to his arrival in Lanheses. Manuel and Rosalia had two sons and a daughter. The daughter had an illegitimate child herself in 1941. Furthermore, Rosalia's own illegitimate daughter, born in 1909, two months prior to her mother's marriage, had six illegitimate children herself, the first two by the same father and subsequent children by different fathers. "Her mother," said one villager, "was a prostitute, and she was too!"

## THE MEANING OF ILLEGITIMACY

Almost fifty years ago, the social historian Paul Descamps, noting that many Minhotan women never marry, commented that it was not exceptional to find them with children born out of wedlock. "If the parish priest," he added, "admonishes the poor sinner, she excuses herself by saying that she does not know how it happened. Public opinion finds nothing to add to it all" (Descamps 1935:72).

A little less then a century earlier, William Kingston had come to the same conclusion.

> The female peasantry who depart from the paths of strict morality are not treated by their parents and acquaintances with the same rigor as in the more righteous England. They are compassionated for their misfortune more than punished for their fault and it is only when they obstinately persist in an evil course of life that they are turned away from their paternal homes. (Kingston 1845:304)

Were Lanhesans as accepting of these unwed mothers and their illegitimate offspring as Descamps and Kingston suggest? Clearly, what has been discussed so far indicates that public opinion was probably not uniform. Indeed, there are several different levels at which to explore the attitudes toward, and therefore the meaning of illegitimacy. First, it is important to consider the attitudes and motivations of the mothers themselves: was it something they were ashamed of or something they engaged in with any deliberation? The different circumstances that may have led to out-of-wedlock births described in the previous section would suggest some variation. Second, it is necessary to explore, to the extent that it is possible, the attitudes of the parents of girls who gave birth to illegitimate children: did they disdain their daughters, banish them from sight, or were they accepting, even forgiving and, if so, why? Third, the attitudes of the larger community toward what was obviously a prevalent form of behavior should be evaluated: to what extent were overriding norms challenged? To answer these questions for the parish of Lanheses is not easy, since the data available is neither systematic nor rich. What follows is therefore a suggestive and wide-ranging argument based on diverse evidence; both historical and ethnographic. Much of it relates more, although not exclusively, to the "abandoned namoradas" or "one-time errers" than to the repeater population or the "bastardy-prone" subpopulation. To the latter I will return in the conclusion of the chapter.

One test of the status of unwed mothers and illegitimate children, and therefore of the attitudes toward them, is the extent to which they were included in any division of property. As noted earlier in this chapter, until very recently a father was neither obligated to recognize a child as his nor to contribute any support. Yet there are numerous cases, as has been shown, of illegitimate children being legitimated through marriage and therefore sharing equally with any siblings born subsequently. Furthermore, there are two marriages that took place in the 1890s which were, it would seem, expressly for the purpose of facilitating the rights of an illegitimate child in the absence of any other legal offspring and heir. One of these cases was discussed in Chapter One. In November of 1891, José Tinoco de Sá Furtado Mendonça, the proprietor of the Casa and Quinta da Barrosa, married (with a dispensation for a relationship of "first degree illicit affinity"—most likely a reference to a common-law relationship) Francisca Rosa da Silva, a jornaleira by whom he had had two illegitimate children in the 1870s. He was seventy-five and she was fifty-five, and seventeen months later he died. His legitimated son Miguel became the new heir to a massive (by northern Portuguese standards) and important piece of property.

On a slightly less grand scale, and six years later, João Gonçalves Abrigueiro, the eldest and bachelor son of a well-to-do lavrador family with property in the lugar of Roupeiras de Cima married Maria Luisa Pereira, the mother of his illegitimate son José, who had been born twenty years earlier, in August of 1877. (Maria Luisa had given birth to another illegitimate child, presumably not João Abrigueiro's child, in 1862. The fate of this child is unknown—he was present in the 1870 roll but not in that of 1881.) João Abrigueiro was eighty-one at the time of his marriage and his bride was sixty-one. Three days after the marriage, the groom passed away. There is no extant will, but given the timing of the marriage and the legitimization that accompanied it in the marriage register, we can only conclude that the recognition of an heir was its express purpose. Maria Luisa, herself one of three illegitimate children born to her mother and namesake Maria Luisa, had lived with her son in a house in Roupeiras de Baixo and, subsequent to her marriage, she appears to have moved into her husband's house in Roupeiras de Cima. By 1907, her son José is no longer included on the roll and she is living with a nephew, Domingos, instead.

Although these are both cases of men who eventually married the mothers of their illegitimate children in order to establish a legal heir, there is a case in the books of testaments of the parish where a father recognized his illegitimate son as his universal heir although he had never married the mother of his son. António Pereira de Castro was the eldest of six children born to Maximo Pereira Castro and Luisa Maria Puga, a couple married in July of 1764 and presumably a rather well-to-do peasant family. (The families of both had been in the village since the beginning of the eighteenth century.) Of their six children, four married, one died as a teenager, and the youngest probably left the village. Of the four who married, António was the last, postponing his wedding until 1816 when he was fifty, and well after both his parents had died and his two younger brothers had married (in 1795 and 1801, respectively; a sister married in 1811 at age thirty-six). António wed his second cousin, Margarida Alves Fiusa, a woman who was only a year younger than him and therefore unable to give him any legitimate heirs.

In April of 1837, shortly before his death, António made a will and designated his illegitimate son Albino as his sole heir. Albino was born in 1809 to a certain Maria Josefa, daughter of Manuel Teixeira and Francisca Rosa, all natives of Figueirão, but residents of the lugar of Roupeiras. Maria Josefa had a second son (Guilherme) born illegitimately in 1814 and married in 1842 to the daughter of lavradores Pascoal Franco and Mariana Farrulla. Although there are records of the deaths of Albino's and Guilherme's maternal grandparents, Francisca Rosa in 1811 and Manuel Teixeira in 1817 (the latter listed as *pobre*—poor—on his obituary), there is no record of the death of their mother Maria Josefa. Was Albino raised by his father? All we know is that in 1837 when the will was made he was living in his natural father's household. By this time he too was married, also to a second cousin on his paternal side. In his will, António Pereira de Castro asks his wife (to whom he gives usufruct rights to half of his property) to remain in his natural son's company until the end of her life to "direct and teach him"; and he asks his son "always to respect and remain in the company of his wife." However, when Margarida passed away three years later, she was living with her sister and brother-in-law and not with her husband's illegitimate son and legal heir. She left her own property to her sister's children (especially to a single niece and godchild).

Albino also inherited, though not exclusively, some land from a childless aunt who died only thirteen days after his father. Furthermore, in December of 1826, António Pereira de Castro and his wife named Albino as heir to a prazo they farmed which was leased from the Convent of Santa Ana in Viana do Castelo. Their motive, as always, was "for the love they had for him and for the obedience and respect with which he had treated them . . . as do all good children." The stature gained by Albino as a result of these inheritances is apparent in the 1855 electoral roll—he is among the more wealthy lavradores listed. Indeed, the house of the "Maximos," the nickname given to this lineage by present-day villagers, still stands as an example of one of the more substantial lavrador households of the past. Clearly, Albino's case indicates that if a man had no legitimate offspring, an unlegitimated child was perfectly acceptable as an heir not only by his natural father, but also by his natural father's family.[12]

That the acceptance of illegitimate offspring permeated all levels of Lanhesan society is evident in the joint will, dated November 1816, of Pedro Marinho Brandão de Castro and his wife Dona Luisa Rego Mesquita, proprietors of the Casa da Torre. This family, of aristocratic background and with property and kinship connections in the town of Viana, had been present in the village since at least the seventeenth century. There are indications of illegitimate children fathered by the male members of the family dating back to this time. For example, a natural son was born to a spinster named Maria de Castro in 1694 and baptized Jacinto. At Jacinto Marinho's marriage in 1712 we learn that his father was Dom Pedro Marinho Brandão, most likely the grandfather of the Pedro Marinho Brandão who died in 1816. The younger Pedro Brandão had three legitimate children baptized in Lanheses in 1774, 1776, and 1778. In the joint will, he and his wife recognize their son Francisco and daughter Rosa (the third child Pedro must have died) as their heirs. However they also mention a certain Dona Josefa Luisa, "daughter of the testador" (Pedro Brandão) and ask their legal heirs "not to scorn her." "As such," they continue, "Dona Josefa has been raised by us, always in our company, serving us in our illnesses, and for these benefits, we have recorded in a notarized agreement a donation for her marriage and money for her support, and in this will we confirm all that we have bestowed upon her." The will goes on to say that if for some reason Dona Josefa does not want to remain in the company of the two legal children Francisco and Rosa, she is to be given the house and land in the Lugar de Arco for her own use. At no point is there any indication of Dona Josefa's natural mother. All we do know is that both Pedro Brandão and his legal wife accepted this out-of-wedlock child, raising her in their own home and looking after her needs at their death.

Although the examples cited indicate that some illegitimate children did inherit from their natural fathers, it was more customary for a child born out of wedlock to be recognized by and inherit from the maternal side, if at all. In his brief observations on illegitimacy in northern Portugal, Descamps (1935:72) noted this fact: "In Minho, an illegitimate child belongs to the mother, or better still to her family who do not deny her legal right to inherit because of her sin." Indeed, succession through the female line, in addition to the frequent transmission of names, including nicknames, through the mother were two factors that Descamps cited to underscore the "matriarchal' (I prefer "matricentric") character of northwestern Portuguese rural society.[13]

There are numerous cases in the books of testaments of illegitimate children being designated as their mothers' heirs, or of these unwed mothers themselves inheriting from their own parents. In 1809, for example, João Alves Franco died and named his spinster daughter Maria and her daughter (his granddaughter) Joana as the recipients of his têrço ("they can choose whatever appears best to them in my lugar and household"). In addition, he leaves them his *cabana* and the *eira* in Barreiro, which was most likely used for the production of clay roof tiles. Maria, as the heir to the têrço, was of course expected to assume responsibility for a third of all her father's debts, as well. The remaining property and debts were to be divided equally among the rest of his children. In a will of 1826, Catarina da Rocha mentions that her daughter Custodia, who married in 1811 and went to reside in Fontão, received half of a prazo as a dowry upon her marriage. Custodia had had an illegitimate child in 1806. Is it possible that the dowry was a condition for marriage made by the future-son-in-law who had perhaps even fathered the illegitimate child?

In a will of 1807 made jointly by two spinster sisters, Francisca and Gracia Granja, all the property is left to their son and nephew (respectively), Manuel, and his wife Quiteria. If Francisca died first, Gracia was to have usufruct rights, and vice versa. Francisca and Gracia were two of three children born to António Gonçalves and Maria Granja. The illegitimate child Manuel was born one year before his widowed grandfather died in 1772. Finally, Catarina de Azevedo, who died in 1842, left her property to her two (of three) illegitimate children Maria and Francisco, born in 1785 and 1792, respectively, and designated her spinster daughter as the recipient of the têrço. She acknowledged in this will that none of her children had inherited from their fathers.

There is one other piece of evidence that also tends to suggest that, although they may have been ashamed of what their daughters had done, not all parents ostracized them or banished them from their households. An appreciable number of these young women who had had a child out of wedlock continued to live with their parents. This is apparent if we simply look at the number of households in the rois da desobriga that were made up of a single woman and her children and the number of households that were extended downward by the addition of one or more grandchildren of the head of household (Table 5.8). It should be noted again that the 1850 and 1870 rolls did

TABLE 5.8 PATTERNS OF RESIDENCE OF UNWED
MOTHERS, 1850–1920

| Year | Number of Households With | | |
| | Unwed Mothers Living Alone | Extended by an Illegitimate Grandchild | Others |
| --- | --- | --- | --- |
| 1850 | 10 | 3 | |
| 1870 | 10 | 6 | |
| 1881 | 6 | 13 | 1 |
| 1887 | 8 | 12 | 3 |
| 1892 | 9 | 10 | 1 |
| 1899 | 12 | 12 | |
| 1907 | 10 | 15 | 2 |
| 1913 | 8 | 12 | 1 |
| 1920 | 12 | 7 | 1 |

NOTE: The "other" category includes households that are extended
by another relative in addition to the illegitimate grandchild and,
in 1892, one household in which a mother of an illegitimate child
is living with a sister in addition to her own offspring.
SOURCE: Rois da Desobriga, Lanheses.

not include children under seven, and therefore probably underrepresent the extent of both types of households we are focusing on—that is, for both of these years some of the single women living alone may have been single women living with their illegitimate offspring, and some of the nuclear households may in fact have been extended households that included grandchildren born out of wedlock. These by no means account for all the women who had illegitimate children in Lanheses between 1850 and 1920. Clearly, some subsequently married and therefore formed nuclear households of their own, others may have left the parish, and still others were part of households classified as multiple by the presence of a married sibling and his or her spouse and offspring. Certainly, however, there were a number of parents who accepted the illegitimate grandchild or, in some cases, grandchildren.

What conclusions can be drawn based on patterns of residence and inheritance practices that clearly did not discriminate against unwed mothers and their offspring? It is possible to argue that at least some members of the older generation, the parents of the daughter who had gone astray, may have viewed the birth of a child out of wedlock as a way of binding the mother, their daughter, to them, perhaps

even more firmly than a virgin spinster daughter. Marriage meant a
change in allegiances from the family of orientation to the family of
procreation. It meant, at least ideally, the formation of a new household, laboring primarily for one's husband and children rather than
for one's parents. If the chances of marriage for a woman who had
had an illegitimate child were reduced (and they were for many
"abandoned namoradas"), she would be more likely remain with her
own parents. Indeed, some of them probably chose not to marry
once abandoned, feeling that no man but the natural father would
treat their child properly. In short, an unwed mother would continue
to labor on her parents' land and to succor them in their old age
long after her other siblings had married and directed their loyalties
elsewhere. Such help provided by an offspring was clearly necessary
to aging parents, and it was therefore logical, where the occasion
arose, to reinforce the bond by designating these daughters as heirs,
including, perhaps, heirs to the paternal home. Making them heirs
was on the one hand a gesture of gratitude and on the other hand an
extra inducement for the maintenance of allegiance, care, and devotion.

This is, perhaps, one explanation for the tolerant attitude of at
least some parents. Furthermore, it must be understood within the
context of a system of property devolution wherein an illegitimate
grandchild was in no way a threat to the corporate kin group. Unlike
other areas of the Mediterranean, which were characterized by patrilineal partible inheritance and joint family structure (Hammel 1968,
Kunkel 1966), or nineteenth-century Ireland where a stem family system and patrilineal impartible inheritance predominated (Arensberg
1937), in most of northwestern Portugal, and certainly in Lanheses,
no such corporate kin group based on shared tenancy existed. But if
this possibly accounts for the motivations of the parents of wayward
daughters, what of the daughters themselves? Certainly, some did
marry eventually, but others did not, and why they did not has in
part been explained with reference to the demographics of emigration. Just as parents may have viewed a daughter's "mistake" as a
reinforced guarantee of their old-age security, the young woman herself may have had a similar outlook. Before discussing this outlook
more fully, however, let us explore more precisely the relationship
between emigration, the sex ratio of the unmarried population, and
illegitimacy.

In one of the rare discussions of the connection between sex ratios
and illegitimacy, Knodel and Hochstadt (1980) point out that opinions about determining factors have been diametrically opposed. Some

have argued that it is an excess of women which leads to high illegitimacy, while others have asserted that it is an excess of men which is most crucial. In their attempt to systematically test the relationship between these variables with data from Imperial Germany, Knodel and Hochstadt conclude that it is by no means predictable, and that the source of the sex ratio imbalance itself must be carefully considered. In the rural northwestern Portuguese case, as was already noted in Chapter Three, the imbalance is clearly the result of a particular pattern of outmigration which created an excess of single women in the countryside. What precisely is the relationship between heavy male outmigration, high levels of permanent spinsterhood, and extensive illegitimacy?

In Chapter Three, northwestern Portugal was compared with rural Ireland, one country with high levels of female celibacy and the other with high levels of male celibacy. As was mentioned at the outset of the present chapter, these countries also differ in their levels of non-marital fertility, and thus a comparison is again useful. In the simplest demographic terms, the disproportionate number of women in the rural Portuguese countryside, especially toward the end of the nineteenth century, would logically account for high levels of illegitimacy, in contrast to rural Ireland where women tended to leave the countryside in massive numbers. However, the situation is more complex than simple demographics would indicate. It is important to direct attention, as Dixon (1978) emphasizes, both to the opportunities and motivations to either reproduce or not reproduce.

Let us first consider the status and roles of women as they relate to the question of opportunity. It has been noted repeatedly that the division of labor in Portugal has been such that women perform a large share of the major agricultural tasks. Although there appears to be some disagreement in the ethnographic literature, it is safe to argue, I think, that in Ireland, the women's sphere has been much more in the strictly domestic sphere. Indeed, the English agricultural observer Arthur Young wrote in his eighteenth-century travelogue that women in Ireland "do not even make hay" (a literal comment which, in the present context, has a figural meaning!). Travelers to northern Portugal at the same period and throughout the nineteenth century, as was pointed out in Chapter Two, recorded completely opposite observations. Thus, while rural Ireland has been characterized by sex segregation in public life (Sklar 1977), in northwestern rural Portugal the interaction of the sexes in the world beyond the domestic sphere has been and remains extensive, despite the ideology embodied in numerous popular adages which defines the household as a woman's "proper place." Descamps (1935:84) drew the appropriate conclusion about where this "agricultural order" might lead: "Married men and single women enjoy great license. This is the result of the enormous numerical disequilibrium among the sexes and of their mingling in the life of the fields, and this from a very tender age." The role of women in the rural economy of northern Portugal has provided ready occasions for illicit sexual activity. That young Portuguese women were themselves aware of the pitfalls of work in the fields is evident in the following popular verse:

Minha mãe mandou me a herva
Eu a herva não sei ir
Que o lameiro tem buracos
Tenho medo de cair

My mother sent me to the pasture
To the pasture, I do not know the way
Because the swamps have holes
I am afraid of falling

If agricultural work provided the opportunity to engage in sexual activity outside of marriage, what about the question of motivation? Although we can only speculate about the "sexuality" of young peasant girls in Lanheses' historical past, or about the ability of peasant men to lead them skillfully into an activity which they may not have known much about, there is a more concrete conclusion we can make, I think, about motivations in relation to the demographic structure of the parish and the region in general. The unbalanced sex ratio of the unmarried population clearly made marriage impossible for a significant proportion of young women. Yet, no marriage meant no children (at least legally), and therefore the possibility of no one to take care of you in your old age.

It can be argued, therefore, that, faced with the prospect of lifelong spinsterhood, and in the context of a society where the nuclear family was the ideal and where married siblings were not necessarily obligated to take care of their unwed sisters (though many did), some young women may have conceived of a child out of wedlock as a strategy for social security, as a way to insure protection and support in the future when they themselves were old and frail. Even if originally used as a strategy of entrapment, as it may well have been by some in the context of a marriage market that was more unfavorable for women than for men, abandonment once the deed was done, although shameful initially, may have had its long-range benefits. One villager, talking about some of the unwed mothers of more recent times, commented: "Look at them today, they are like fish in water with their children and grandchildren about them." Indeed, given the wary attitude toward marriage discussed in Chapter Three, some women may have seen this as the preferable course of action.

Although the disproportionate sex ratio resulting from a sex-biased pattern of emigration is convincing to explain differences in patterns of illegitimacy between Portugal and Ireland, we are still left to wonder whether emigration is important simply because it created a society of spinsters in Portugal. Can a consideration of emigration also lend further understanding to the fact that premarital pregnancies swelled to their apex at precisely the same time as the illegitimacy ratio, and, for that matter, repetitive illegitimate births, as well? It is possible to suggest that emigration equally had an effect in weakening the Portuguese family as a result of the frequent and often long-term (if not permanent) absence of male heads of household. Although young single men seem to have dominated the stream of emigrants from Portugal to Brazil in the first half of the nineteenth century, by the last quarter of the century, as economic conditions worsened and population grew, married men became increasingly important among those who left their country in search of new riches, or simply of a source of additional support for their burgeoning families. If we accept for the moment the argument that it is men (fathers and brothers) who protect the honor of their women, then in many families there were no men around to perform this role—to keep young women out of trouble or to insist upon a subsequent marriage before a child was born. Despite the fact that northern Portugal can perhaps be characterized as matricentric, mothers, acting as heads of households in the absence of a spouse, simply could not perform the same role, for they were viewed as sources of succor and support, not of authority and castigation.

Although individual-level data on emigration are limited, there are, nevertheless, a few cases in which absence at a particular point in time can be documented and shown to coincide roughly with an out-of-wedlock birth. For example, Manuel Pereira is marked absent in the rois of 1907 and 1913, and by 1920 his wife is a widow. Several of his daughters had children out of wedlock, one in 1906, another in 1910, another in 1915, and the youngest in 1923. António Ferreira is marked as absent in 1907. His daughter Luisa had an illegitimate child in 1904 and a second in 1907. Her parents died soon afterwards and Luisa, living alone, went on to have several more children out of wedlock. Francisco Fernandes was not present in

Lanheses at the time that both the 1910 and 1913 rois were compiled. His unwed daughter Maria had a child in 1911. Francisco Rodrigues was clearly a long-term emigrant, absent in 1907, 1913, 1920, and 1927. In 1930, his youngest daughter Lucinda (born in 1905) gave birth to an illegitimate child. Her father may still have been absent; all we know is that he was buried in the parish in 1940. For none of these cases am I arguing that it is the absence of the male head of household that exclusively explains the wayward daughter or daughters. Rather, I am simply suggesting that it be considered together with factors such as low socioeconomic status (which is indeed characteristic of all the examples cited above), and therefore the necessity for many of the young women from these households to go out to serve or work as day laborers—both situations, as has been shown, in which illegitimate conceptions were a likely outcome.

The suggestion that the absence of parental or masculine authority and control has some significance for a complete understanding of trends in Lanhesan illegitimacy can be further substantiated by pointing to the cases of married women, who, especially during the early part of the present century, committed adultery after their husbands had departed. In two of these cases, as noted in Chapter Four, the husbands never returned to Lanheses because when they found out what their wives had done they were "too ashamed to come back." In another case, not only did the mother have two children by someone other than her husband, but a daughter of hers (born legitimately) in turn had six.

A violation of marital chastity was, in fact, a more serious "crime" than was the loss of virginity by an unmarried woman, especially if that unmarried woman came from a poor family and therefore had little chance of marrying anyway. This lends support to theses proposed by some anthropologists of the Mediterranean (Goldschmidt and Kunkel 1971, Schneider 1971) who draw a connection between varying forms of family structure and inheritance and different attitudes toward pre- and post-marital continence. The patriarchal family characteristic of rural Ireland, and of other regions of the Mediterranean where illegitimacy rates are low, has been associated with an emphasis on keeping the family patrimony intact and preserving the honor and name of the patriline. That is clearly not of central importance in northwestern Portugal.

There is one further point to make about the relationship between emigration and illegitimacy in northwestern Portugal. The availability of wage employment has been emphasized by several historians in their explanations of high rates of illegitimacy. In general, these discussions have focused on regions of protoindustrialization. The Lima Valley was certainly not such a region during the period under consideration in this study, although there were some opportunities for small-scale domestic industry. More importantly, the roles of women in agriculture, to a large extent the result of heavy male emigration, as well as the local opportunities for domestic service, were what made it possible for them to be self-supporting. Such work not only set the context for illicit sexual activity, but provided sustenance for the fruits of such activity. If a girl found herself pregnant, she could work to raise her child, and the pressures, therefore, to conform to the laws of morality did not exist in Portugal as they did in rural Ireland, where an unmarried (and perhaps unmarriageable if she had an illegitimate child) woman remained dependent upon her father or brother. That many of the jobs in domestic service in more recent times have shifted to Porto and Lisbon may provide a partial explanation for the regional shift in illegitimacy after the first half of the present century.

One explanation for the low illegitimacy rates of rural Ireland is that single men far outnumbered single women—that the women left. A potential rebuttal is that rural Irish girls may have had illegitimate children, but they had them elsewhere. Those unfortunate enough to become pregnant out of wedlock and without hope of marrying the father left or were sent off by their parents to give birth in the cities or abroad (Sklar 1977). To point to illegitimacy, therefore, as an indication of the more faithful adherence of Irish women to Catholic mores could be misleading (McKenna 1974). Yet, some studies have demonstrated that even among Irish immigrants abroad, illegitimacy rates are relatively insignificant, and Sklar (1977) has argued quite convincingly that even when the out-of-wedlock births among these immigrant populations are considered, Ireland still ends up with comparatively low levels of nonmarital fertility. In his study of illegitimacy in Scotland, Smout (1980) finds the Irish to be an extremely moral group, and concludes:

> It is difficult not to associate this with the nature of 19th century Catholicism in Ireland, with the great strength of the priests and the emphasis on the worship of Mary and the holiness of the virgin state. It would probably also be naive not to imagine that there is a relationship with the scarcity of land in Ireland. After the famine with late marriage for males and few holdings to go round, the teaching of the priests was reinforced by a quite separate economic sanction. For immigrant industrial workers in Scotland the eco-

nomic situation was obviously of another kind, but the cultural and moral habit formed in Ireland would not immediately collapse. (Smout 1980:209)

What Smout's discussion raises is the question of the relationship between religion, or, conversely, secularization, and nonmarital fertility. Although one would like this relationship to be straightforward, data are strongly to the contrary. For example, De Pauw (1972) argues for France that negligible illegitimacy and a high degree of religious observance coincide in Brittany and along the eastern slope of the Massif Central, while weak religiosity and high illegitimacy coincide in the southwest. Yet, in regions such as the Département de Nord, the Pas-de-Calais, and Alsace, all characterized by "strong religious observance;" nonmarital fertility is high. In short, the relationship between these two variables, religiosity and illegitimacy, is by no means clear-cut. As Hartley (1975) notes in her broad analysis of illegitimacy, it is not just being Catholic that is important, but the nature of that Catholicism. Furthermore, she adds, what is central are not the religious beliefs per se, but the sanctions imposed for any transgression of those beliefs. By entering into a discussion, however brief, of religion—and the comparison with Ireland will be carried further—one is necessarily entering into the realm of community attitudes toward out-of-wedlock births.

Much has been written about the Irish Catholic Church, and I do not intend discuss it in depth. However, there are a few general points that will bring differences in the nature of Catholicism and their impact on illicit sexual activity into sharper focus. Most of those who have commented on the Church in Ireland conclude that it was and remains an extremely powerful institution within the rural countryside, and that its influence over the moral life of its parishioners has been great indeed. One observer stated, "in no other country in the world probably is religion so dominant an element in the daily life of the people, not even in Spain where devotion to the Church and earnest piety are so deeply rooted in the hearts of the people" (Plunkett 1905; quoted in Connell 1968:151). Another called Ireland a "Catholic culture as it existed in the Middle Ages" (Devane, quoted in Blanshard 1962:3). Scheper-Hughes (1983) points to the heavily Jansenist character of Irish Catholicism, which literally suppressed sexual activity.[14]

The Irish Catholic Church was also a truly national church, and, by the middle of the nineteenth century, had come to be identified as the protector of a population fighting English Protestants for its freedom (Sklar 1977, Davis 1963). Larkin (1976:649) has argued that, faced with the threat of a loss of identity, the Roman Catholic Church gave the Irish a "substitute symbolic language and a new cultural heritage"; and Kennedy (1973:35) has noted, "to the degree that religious and political institutions of Ireland reinforced one another, the ideology of Roman Catholicism would have a more pervasive influence, a potent factor especially in the area of policy concerning sex and family." Blanshard (1962:139–140) is most precise about this infiltration into private sexual matters:

> Courtship is the business of the Irish priest, and petting is the business of the Irish priest and even the etiquette of the marriage bed— as well as birth control, abortion, mixed marriages, illegitimacy, sodomy, masturbation, divorce, sex education. . . . The Irish accept such supervision of personal conduct with far more docility than their fellow Catholics in Latin American countries . . . where the Catholic sexual code is more honored in the breach than in the observance.

He concludes that Irish priests have become somewhat embarrassed by the triumph of their sexual standards, "exalting virginity to the point that it has become a national catastrophe and condemning the sins of the flesh to such an extent that a guilt complex permeates rural Ireland." [15]

Portugal is quite another case, despite the fact that today we think of it as one of the most Catholic countries of western Europe. As was pointed out in Chapter One, Church and State were often at loggerheads and, at certain points in the country's history, anticlericalism was rampant. Although it played a major role in Portuguese overseas expansion, the Portuguese Catholic church was never the champion of nationalist causes to the extent that the Catholic Church was in Ireland. Furthermore, although Irish priests are known to have practiced what they preached in relation to morality and celibacy, this does not seem to have been the case where the Portuguese priesthood is concerned. Diatribes on the immorality of Portuguese clerics were cited in Chapter One. Parish registers have left indications that these priests were responsible for at least some of the out-of-wedlock conceptions in northern Portugal.

Today, throughout the north of Portugal one hears the comment that priests "are men like other men"; that is, they are expected to have sexual desires and in order to realize these desires they have no choice but to engage in illicit sex. Many mothers were and remain wary of having their daughters spend any time alone in the company

of priests, a problem that disturbs some of the young and more sin-
cere members of the "new" priesthood. In short, there is a certain
skepticism where priests are concerned, and therefore about the morality which they preach. Furthermore, there are some indications
that the rigorous sanctions against young women who "found themselves in trouble" in Ireland were not imposed in Portugal. In fact,
some villagers in Lanheses talked about the friendly and joking relationships which some of their local clerics had with some of the more
infamous unwed jornaleira mothers. There certainly appears to have
been no attempt to deny the sacraments of baptism or marriage either
to these children or to their mothers.

If a certain skepticism for the morality supposedly preached from
the pulpit by the Catholic clergy has existed in northern Portugal,
this does not mean that the northern Portuguese peasantry are any
less Catholic. Furthermore, in more recent times, particularly during
the reign of Salazar or Salazarism between 1926 and 1974, the Catholic Church regained or improved its hold over the countryside. Indeed, this new-found power, supported by the State, may contribute
to an explanation of trends in nonmarital as well as marital fertility.
In Lanheses, after 1930, premarital pregnancy continued to rise, while
illegitimacy began its downward and, so far, irreversible decline. According to villagers, the priest who officiated in the parish at this
time exercised a great deal of control over the morality of his parishioners. He was responsible, for example, for the practice of men and
women standing separately during the mass. (Even today, all the men
stand at the front in a group and the mass of women stand behind
them.) This priest may have been influential in discouraging out-of-
wedlock conceptions, and if they did occur, encouraging marriages
prior to the birth of the child.

Finally, there is one more factor beyond religious beliefs and insti-
tutionally embodied morality that provides some indication of community attitudes toward illegitimate offspring: the marriage prospects of the population of unwed mothers. As indicated earlier in the
chapter, between 1700 and 1900 approximately 20 percent of unwed
mothers subsequently married. During the first half of the twentieth
century, the proportion was 15 percent. Fifteen to 20 percent is by
no means negligible, especially if we realize that this only includes
women who married in the parish. Even some of the women with
more than one illegitimate child were able to contract a marriage
later in life, often, admittedly, to widowers who may have been the
fathers of their youngest child. There is, for example, the case of
Dores da Rocha, who married in 1901 at the age of thirty after hav-

ing given birth to four illegitimate children (only two survived) during the 1890s. When she married it was to a widower who was more than twenty years older, a poor beggar from San Pedro de Arcos. He lived for two years more and the couple had no children. A year after his death Dores remarried, again to a widower twenty years her senior. Her second husband was from Mujães and worked in the mines. They had two sons, the first born within seven months of their marriage. Both sons went off to Spain as young men, married there, and have never returned to the parish. Dores' second husband died in 1916, and in 1928 Dores herself died, drowning in a well into which she fell after drinking too much.

Although there are several indications that illegitimacy was not an object of extreme opprobrium in Lanheses itself, within the district as a whole, at precisely the period that one might suspect on the basis of Lanheses data, there does appear to have been somewhat of a public outcry. In the 1860s, on the editorial pages of one of the more important regional newspapers of the latter part of the nineteenth century, O Vianense, public attention was directed toward the increasing numbers of infants who were being abandoned on the local rodas in the towns of Viana do Castelo and Ponte de Lima.[16] In an article of July 17, 1862, the foundling institutions were called "incentives for licentiousness and prostitution rather than institutions of charity."

> Today, it seems that these establishments are destined for the children of all single women, even for those who, neither ashamed to be mothers, nor to abandon their children, continue in the same manner of living, or become mercenary wet nurses raising the children of others.

The writer called upon parish priests to assume more responsibility for what was going on and to point out to mothers their "natural, moral, and religious obligations to succor their own children." In another article three months later, it was noted that in Portugal there were, at the time, six expostos for each thousand infants born, whereas in England the rate was only four per hundred thousand. In 1863, a commission was established to study the problem of expostos, and in 1864 it was concluded that "public demoralization and scandalous prostitution are at the root of the shocking increase in the number of foundlings" (O Vianense 24-9-1864).

This rather vociferous outcry might lead one to conclude, as Shorter has for regions elsewhere in western Europe at a somewhat earlier period in time, that promiscuity was on the rise, if not already out of hand. Yet an examination of exposto records clearly indicates that not all the children who were abandoned on the foundling wheels were infants born out of wedlock, and therefore the result of "a corruption of customs." Many were the offspring of legally married parents who, finding themselves in dire economic straits, left their newborn child temporarily until they could better care for him. Frequently, notes were attached to the infant indicating such reasons (including claims by some mothers that they had insufficient breast milk) and informing the institution of the child's name so that he could easily be identified when they came to reclaim him. Needless to say, many of these parents never saw their child again, since the mortality rates in these foundling institutions was quite high.[17]

That the dire economic straits to which these unfortunate parents referred were a reality has been pointed out already in earlier discussions of rising prices and increasing land fragmentation during the late nineteenth century. Furthermore, although more research needs to be carried out on the problem of abandoned children in Portugal, the evidence suggests that it was by no means a new phenomenon. Expostos appear in the baptismal, marriage, and death registers of Lanheses throughout the period under study in this book, and cursory examination of the registers of neighboring villages indicates that it was equally prevalent, if not more so, elsewhere in the region. Furthermore, the rodas themselves were old—one in the Rua dos Caldeireiros in Porto having been established in 1688. Indeed, in an examination of the number of exposto children in Porto during the latter part of the eighteenth century, Costa (1789) cites a total of 14,435 infants abandoned between 1770 and 1785.

If any preliminary conclusion can be drawn based on the problem of expostos in the nineteenth century, it should be that, like the general rise in illegitimacy, in the mean age at marriage, in emigration, and in permanent female spinsterhood, it was a manifestation of the grave economic difficulties experienced by the rural populations of northwestern Portugal as the nineteenth century drew to its close.

## CONCLUSION

The discussion of the socioeconomic context of illegitimacy in Lanheses suggests that it cannot be treated uniformly. Even in a small village, there were important variations in who had out-of-wedlock children and in the circumstances behind their conception. Furthermore, the extent to which the actions of these unwed mothers were considered shameful or the degree to which they or their families felt shame after the fact also varied. It appears that censorship through shame applies not to the loss of virginity or to the fact of illicit pregnancy, but to the subsequent behavior of the unwed mother. Only those who flaunted their sexuality and who demonstrated little concern about the opinions of others (that is, those for whom the informal mechanisms of social control simply did not work) were considered truly "shameless." There is an extremely important difference between the phrase *ter vergonha* (to feel or have shame) and the phrase *sem vergonha* (to be without shame).

What this suggests is that the codes of honor and shame, as they are applied to the behavior of women in the Mediterranean region, are different depending upon the position of those women within a socioeconomic hierarchy, and upon the roles associated with that position. The status of the one "Dona" registered in the Lanheses baptismal book who had a child out of wedlock called for her to be "too ashamed to give her name and therefore to openly admit her sin." On the other hand, the illegitimate offspring of young women who, as jornaleiras or criadas, worked by necessity outside the home and beyond the watchful eye of their fathers, were much more numerous on the baptismal rolls. The connection between their activities in the public domain and a weaker feeling of shame or sin associated with an illegitimate birth (*ter vergonha* becomes the state of being *sem vergonha*) is no coincidence.

Although the early ethnographic literature of the Mediterranean left us with a notion that women in this part of the world do not work outside the boundaries of home, Gilmore (1982) has drawn our attention to numerous studies which indicate that in fact this is by no means a universal Mediterranean phenomenon. Variations in women's roles, in the strength and character of the code of honor and shame, and in the nature of illegitimacy depend, I would suggest, on the prevailing system of land tenure, on the dominant form of family organization, and on the complexities of the system of social stratification. In northern Portugal, where properties were and remain small, where the nuclear family was and is the basic unit of ownership despite life cycle phases of extended or multiple family households, and where the agricultural population included both landed and landless, women played an important part in the nondomestic labor force. Their behavior could not be and was not totally controlled, as was and is the behavior of women in other regions of both the Christian and Muslim Mediterranean, where the system of economic production and the division of labor based upon it have essentially confined women to the domestic sphere, very often in large extended households based on joint tenureship.

Furthermore, the fact that Portuguese women inherited equally with men and were often the favored recipients of the têrço reinforced their economic independence and their role in the extradomestic village world. Even in comparison with that of her counterparts in Catholic Ireland, the status of the Portuguese spinster was much less precarious. As a spinster, she normally remained in her parents' household until their death. Whether as primary heir or joint heir, she generally had a right to remain there even after they passed away. To my mind, parents would be much more accepting of an illegitimate grandchild than would a brother be of an illegitimate niece or nephew. Thus, Irish women, who were essentially disenfranchised within the rural environment if they did not marry, would be more likely either to avoid an illegitimate child, if they chose to remain in the countryside and in a brother's household, or to emigrate.

Although I have suggested that the more or less equal division of property in northwestern Portugal may provide one context within which to understand the character of illegitimacy in this region of northwestern Portugal, the relationship between forms of inheritance and illegitimacy is by no means straightforward. Khera (1981), for example, in her work on the Austrian peasantry, finds exactly the reverse. High illegitimacy is associated with regions where impartible inheritance, late marriage, and low nuptiality prevail, and low illegitimacy with regions characterized by partibility, early marriage, and high nuptiality. In northwestern Portugal, high illegitimacy, partibility, late marriage, and low nuptiality coincide.

Clearly, the sex-biased pattern of emigration that undermined the marriage prospects for numerous young women is an intervening variable. Emigration provided an escape valve for the young man who did not want the responsibility of a wife and children. From the woman's point of view, having assessed the dismal hopes for marriage in light of unbalanced sex ratios and difficult economic conditions, giving oneself to a fiancé and thereby running the risk of out-of-wedlock pregnancy may have been a last-ditch effort to win a spouse. For some it worked; for others it backfired. On the other hand, with no hope of marriage, an illegitimate child was the only way to fulfill one aspect of womanhood denied within legal bounds. While it is probably impossible to claim that this was a conscious strategy aimed at guaranteeing social security in old age, it did have this result. Certainly, many of these illegitimate offspring, especially first-born offspring, were probably conceived in a context of naiveté (in the case of namorados), if not female exploitation (in the case of criadas and some jornaleiras).

The other fact which has to be remembered in connection with the northwestern Portuguese countryside is that landless day laborers and tenant farmers comprised an important proportion of the population. Both Laslett (1980b) and Khera (1982) suggest that among the landless, matters of inheritance and land tenure were not vital issues for consideration, and thus parental control to avoid illegitimate births was less severe. There certainly does seem to be a strong association between an increase in the proportion of landless agricultural laborers, sharecroppers, and tenant farmers toward the end of the nineteenth century and during the early twentieth century, and a rise in illegitimacy. Again, however, it is important to consider what this change in the socioeconomic composition of the population meant for women's roles and the increasing number of occasions for premarital/illicit sexual activity that it generated.

That nonmarital fertility was so high and remained high well into the present century further substantiates the fact that deliberate fertility control was not part of a demographic plan of action in Lanheses or in northwestern Portugal. To meet this goal, nonmarital fertility would have to be controlled as well, and clearly it was not. The decline in illegitimacy during the present century can be attributed to a number of factors. Foremost, of course, is the general downward trend in the age at marriage, coupled with a rise in the rate of nuptiality such that more births that might have been illegitimate became premarital pregnancies. The rise in the mean age of mothers of first-born illegitimate children above the mean age of mothers of first-born legitimate children is not accidental. These unwed mothers may have seen several marriage opportunities pass them, and at age thirty viewed giving in to a man as their only option in order to secure a husband. Of course, for many this strategy was unsuccessful and some subsequently had several more illegitimate offspring, forced as they were to work as jornaleiras to feed their first infant. Equally important to an explanation of the diverging paths of illegitimacy and premarital pregnancy after 1930 was the fact that emigration dropped off dramatically during the 1930s and 1940s. Young men who remained at home were exposed to greater community pressure, if not to priestly and male family pressure, to marry the young women they had impregnated.

Recently, Goody (1983:212) has suggested that where women married early, their virginity was more important than where women married in their mid- to late twenties.

> Where women marry young, the code of honor can be more easily sustained, the breaches being both less frequent and more serious. Moreover the courtship of adolescents is restricted, possibly pre-empted by parental choice. On the other hand, later marriage for women makes pre-marital chastity more difficult to maintain; choices are freer, courtships are longer and delays in marriage lead if not always to illegitimacy at least to bridal pregnancies and to the acceptance of mantle children.

Underlying this difference are probably varying attitudes toward women, which are associated fundamentally with definitions of their status and roles. In the first case, a woman as a young bride is a treasured object who will be brought into the paternal household and whose major duty will be to add heirs, preferably male heirs, to the patriline. She must be untainted so that paternity can be certain. In the second case, characteristic of northwestern Portugal, men are looking for something different or at least something in addition—women who can work and therefore contribute to the economic success of the new household, sharing equally in the labor.

# CONCLUSION

We constantly walk in life between two visions:
one proceeds us, splendid and brilliant, like the
luminous light which guided the march of the
Hebrew people in the desert; the other follows
us, pale and beautiful, like the ideal virgins in
Scottish folksongs. They are hope and nostalgia.
(Julio Dinis 1947:24–25)

CULTURAL anthropology is a discipline that focuses on the minutiae
of daily life and on the way in which people layer their experiences
with meaning. In one sense, emigration, and especially "emigration
to return" can be viewed in the Portuguese context as an ideology
that defines or gives meaning to experience. Although emigration to
return is not unknown in other areas of southern Europe, it is particularly strong in Portugal, where it is expressed through the deeply
cultural sentiment of *saudade*. Saudade roughly translates as nostalgia or yearning—nostalgia or yearning for the homeland, and particularly for the village where one was born and the family one has left
behind. Saudade embodies a Januslike approach to life—a simultaneous looking to both the past and the future. It is distinctly different
from the ethos of *la miseria* which has been described to characterize
the world view of the southern Italian peasantry (Friedmann 1953,
Bell 1979). Saudade is melancholic, but it is also hopeful.

Yet emigration to return embodies more than a cultural sentiment
or world view. It is also a socially determined strategy, pursued by
groups of individuals within a particular social and cultural context.
The nature of emigration varies from one part of Portugal to another. Emigration to return is most characteristic of the northwest,
where it has been a means by which the population of the region has
preserved small inheritances and avoided total penury. Emigration
has made survival in the face of both limited resources and constant
population pressure possible. In this sense it has indeed served to
perpetuate a way of life. But emigration has also been, for the few
who were particularly fortunate, an avenue for social and economic
mobility, and in this second sense it equally embodied and embodies
ambition. That is, it has accommodated the more fluid and graduated
socioeconomic structure which has distinguished this region of northern
Portugal for several centuries.

This book has attempted to demonstrate the impact of emigration as both cultural ethos and social strategy on a range of other demographic phenomena, and thus its impact on the roles of women in northwestern Portuguese society. Saudade and social strategy contribute equally to an explanation of the thirty-five- or forty-year-old spinster who waits patiently for her namorado to come back to her; or of the "widow of the living" who copes as best she can with the farm and the children until her husband returns. If the data from Lanheses are at all representative, emigration from northwestern Portugal is closely related (though not always causally) to high ages at marriage, high female celibacy, lowered fertility, and high illegitimacy. From the strictly demographic point of view so well delineated by Guttentag and Secord (1983), it is the unfavorable sex ratio (an oversupply of women) resulting from male-biased emigration which has influenced both sexual behavior and sexual mores. Yet this sex ratio must, as they admit, be viewed within a cultural context which takes into account such factors as the distribution of political and economic power, the degree of openness or fluidity in a society, and the balance between the sacred and the secular. All of these factors will affect the relationships between men and women—for example, the degree to which the virginity of women is highly prized, or the freedom and autonomy that women can expect. Guttentag and Secord (1983) have proposed a theoretical framework that transcends localities to look at the commonalities generated by similar demographic and structural conditions.

Anthropology is by nature a comparative discipline. Although this book has focused on the demographic behavior of the population of a single parish in northwestern Portugal, this behavior has been projected consistently against that of numerous other European populations. Thus, the goals of the volume have been more than monographic. It is primarily through this process of comparison that the structural and cultural similarities and differences which underlie population processes (including the emergence of an unbalanced sex ratio) can be discerned. It is only within a comparative framework that one can address the question of whether regions that share similar geo-cultural and structural conditions also share similar patterns of demographic behavior despite perhaps quite distinct political histories. It is only with such an approach that we will begin to solve some of the puzzles of demographic association. Why, for example, do some regions characterized by late marriage, low nuptiality, and impartible inheritance have high illegitimacy, while others have low illegitimacy? Or why in some populations where partible inheritance is the custom do people marry early and more frequently, and consequently have few children out of wedlock, while in others partible inheritance leads to late marriage, low nuptiality, and high rates of illegitimacy? We know today that these relationships are not as clear-cut as when originally proposed by Habakkuk (1955).

Although the above questions are posed hypothetically at this point, and with no intention or ability to answer them fully, in this book it has been suggested that migration streams, the socioeconomic composition of the population, the roles of women that have emerged on the basis of the first two factors, and even the nature of religiosity may act as intervening variables, and are certainly worthy of consideration. Indeed, it may be profitable to frame a comparison among regions in western Europe that might comfortably be labelled *matricentric*. In such regions women have a certain degree of autonomy because they are property owners in their own right and because they generally establish an independent household after marriage rather than become members of a corporate kin group. They are essentially partners with the male household head, and their labor is valued by both the family of orientation (hence delayed marriages) and the family of procreation (hence proven productivity may be more esteemed than virginity).

If we adopt such an approach, northwestern Portugal and the coastal regions of the province of Galicia in Spain should be considered together as a single demographic region. Not only are they alike geographically, but they also share similar socioeconomic conditions and migration traditions. The roles of women in these two regions are also somewhat similar. But such comparisons can extend further. Boissevain (1979:92), for example, refers to the strong female orientation of Maltese society, and suggests a promisingly testable hypothesis that "where attachment to landed property for economic purposes is minimal and where there is a village outward economic orientation, the mother-daughter tie is allowed freer play and matrifocal-uxorilocality results."

Still further afield, the demographic system described for Lanheses shares many features with that described by Lee (1977), who uses the term "matrifocal" to characterize certain demographic patterns in Bavaria. We need to know more than Lee tells us about patterns of migration, although other sources, particularly some of the work of John Knodel, have indicated an unbalanced sex ratio in southern Germany which is similar to that in northwestern Portugal. We also need to know more about the economic, social, and cultural roles of Bavarian women, and about their relationship to land and inheritance, before a more systematic comparison can be made. To what extent, for example, are children and husbands in Bavaria referred to, as they are in northwestern Portugal, with reference to their mothers and wives? (For example, in Lanheses all the descendents of a certain Clara de Sousa who was married at the turn of the century are known as "as Claras.") Naming practices, whether formal or informal, are not incidental. The face that there was a tendency in northwestern Portugal to give daughters the family names of their mothers and sons those of their fathers (see "Note on Names" in Appendix One) not only underscores the importance of mother-daughter ties in this region, but also indicates a flexible inheritance system wherein the notion of preservation of patrimony is weak.

The variable of religiosity might also be more adequately addressed through such "extra-national" regional comparative analyses. At several points in this volume, northwestern Portugal was contrasted to Ireland to ferret out differences that might explain variations in demographic trends. One of these differences (though by no means the only one) between countries that were characterized by both extensive emigration and high ages at marriage during the latter part of the nineteenth century, lies in the nature of Catholicism. The weakened influence of the Catholic Church is also a variable explored briefly by Lee in the Bavarian context, although he does not conclude that it alone can explain the high levels of illegitimacy which characterize southern Germany. Brittany, where rates of female celibacy are high and rates of illegitimacy low, might also serve as an appropriate region to consider in the same light, although there is no systematic study containing the kind of data on a range of demographic, socioeconomic, and cultural features such as those included in this book which would make such a comparison possible at this point.[1]

In a sense, I am proposing a cultural-ecological approach to the understanding of demographic regimes in Europe that goes beyond a consideration of single factors to a consideration of the total social and cultural environment. McQuillan (1984) has paved the way with his recent consideration of modes of production and demographic patterns in nineteenth-century France. Even within the regions mentioned so far, there are subtle differences that cannot be ignored. Lison-Tolosana (1976) has described three different patterns of inheritance and corresponding family systems within the single Spanish province of Galicia. These differences seem to follow variations in a landscape which moves from coastal fishing in the west to more mountainous agro-pastoralism in the east. Although Bauer's (1983) population of agro-pastoralists in the Sierra del Caurel in eastern Galicia share some features with the lavradores of Lanheses, they practice a form of preferential inheritance which is quite distinct from trends in Lanheses. In the Sierra del Caurel, emigration, it seems, is an alternative rather than a complement, and women are chosen as heirs only when there is no adequate male candidate. Yet a distinction between mountain-valley and coastal cultures per se does not encompass all the differences. It is remarkable how strikingly similar are the patterns of demographic behavior in Lanheses and in the Swiss mountain valley of Ticino (Van de Walle 1975). Finally, Lanhesans themselves hint at differences between the way they do things and the way things are done in closely neighboring parishes such as Fontão and Perre. Although at this point such differences can be neither verified nor explained, they present us with challenging puzzles for future research.

It is evident that such a broad comparative approach will sacrifice the detail of intensive local analysis, although it is only on the basis of the latter that the former can proceed. I have produced in this volume an analysis of a local population, but frequently within a comparative framework so that processes, patterns, and associations can emerge. Although the population trends in Lanheses over the last two-and-a-half centuries demonstrate numerous short-term changes, until quite recently they also demonstrate a strong thread of continuity that links living Lanhesans to their historical past. This element of continuity revolves around the repeated choice of emigration as a strategy for survival for those who have left and for those who have been left behind. Seasonal, temporary, and international migration are all part of a logically connected social system which is deeply embedded within Portuguese culture. What, then, of the future for Lanheses and Portugal in a world of tightening labor markets and increasingly reduced possibilities for emigration? Although the ideology to return is as strong among Portuguese immigrants in France as it was among their fathers, grandfathers, and great-grandfathers who went to Brazil and Spain, for the first time in almost eighty years Lanheses experienced a significant decline in population during the decade of the 1960s. In addition, the birth rate fell below twenty— the result not only of increasing attempts at fertility control, but also of the fact that the age and sex structure of the population has changed. More young women are emigrating and having their children elsewhere.

As mentioned in an earlier chapter, in the late 1970s family planning became a state-supported option. This is, in fact, the first attempt at the government level to take an active role in population control. Yet this does not mean that the problem of population pressure is solved and that the smaller birth cohort of the 1960s will not be confronted with the necessity to emigrate in the late 1980s and 1990s, if emigration is possible. This is a much more educated cohort who no longer want to work on the land. Today their problem is outright unemployment rather than underemployment. Furthermore, emigration to France has brought a kind of consumer modernism that far outdistances local development, whether industrial or agricultural. The gaps among needs and aspirations and opportunities are widening.

One has to wonder, therefore, if a scene I witnessed during the summer of 1978 was very different from a scene that might have occurred more than a century ago in the household of some other Lanhesan family. Young Zézinho (a diminutive nickname for José) was going off to Venezuela to work in his uncle's restaurant. He was fourteen, one of two children of Rosa da Silva and Joaquim Fernandes. He had dropped out of school and could find no work in Lanheses. To assuage his mother's tears, he told her that he was going to make a lot of money and then return to build a new house on the plot of land adjacent to his parents' house. She asked him to write to her, knowing that he would not write frequently and that when the letters came she would have to have her daughter or her husband read them to her, for she could not read herself. He was her only son and despite his intention to return, she wondered if he ever would. As the car which took him and two other Lanhesan youths to Porto to catch the plane pulled away from the house, Rosa, her daughter, and other members of the family spoke little. But the tears on their cheeks spoke much of the anguish of emigration, a phenomenon in which the Portuguese have invested for so long both their hope and their nostalgia.

## Sources: The Parish Registers and Other Documents

AFTER 1563, during the second-to-last meeting of the Council of Trent, all Portuguese parishes were required to have two registers, one for baptisms and one for marriages.[1] The registers of Lanheses, housed for the most part in the District Archives in the town of Braga, date from the final decade of the sixteenth century (1593), although only those dating from the mid-seventeenth century on were examined for purposes of the present study. Luckily, there are no gaps in the Lanheses records; the same cannot be said for some of the neighboring parishes in the region. It was only in the middle of the nineteenth century, however, that the regulations set forth by the Council of Trent were scrupulously adhered to by all Portuguese parish priests, and the Lanheses documents themselves reflect this more rigorous application. The information included in post-1860 records is much more complete than that from any previous period. This is the result of a series of public decrees dated between 1859 and 1863 which specified precisely what information was to be included in each type of entry. Only in 1911 did the Portuguese state begin civil registration, and from that time on there are duplicate records, one set in the local parishes, and the other in the justice offices of each district.

Reflecting the progressive move toward greater systematization, the registers for Lanheses change format over the two-and-a-half centuries between 1700 and the present. During the early eighteenth century, the baptismal records provide the name of the child (given names only), date of birth, date of baptism, sex and legitimacy, the names of parents, their place of birth (if one or the other was a native of another parish), and their place of residence (the lugar where they lived), and the names, marital status, and lugar of residence of the godparents. In 1747, the names, place of birth, and place of residence of both paternal and maternal grandparents were added, and with this new information, the format of baptismal records remained unchanged until 1860, when further information was included. The following is an example of how such entries read throughout the later part of the eighteenth and much of the nineteenth centuries:

Isabel, legitimate daughter of Manuel Alves and his wife Isabel Alves, natives and residents of this parish in the lugar of Seara, granddaughter on the paternal side of Pedro Alves, native of the parish of Fontão and resident of this parish and his first wife Ana Gonçalves, native of the parish of Santa Leocadia Geraz de Lima and on the maternal side of Domingos Martins and his wife Caterina Alves, natives and residents of this parish and the lugar of Seara; born on the 28th of January, 1747 and I Father and Curate Francisco da Rocha baptized her in the baptismal font of this church on February 2, 1747. The godparents were Pascoal Franco of the lugar of Seara and Isabel, spinster, daughter of Miguel Gonçalves and his wife Isabel Alves of Taboneira, and I Father and Curate made this record in the presence of Domingos Martins and José de Sousa, all of this parish.

In 1860, the place where the parents were married was added to the baptismal record. In addition, although not completely systematically until 1911, the profession of the parents is given, as well as the age and profession of godparents. In some instances, the priest recorded the date of marriage of the child in the margin, but this seems to have been a discretionary rather than an obligatory practice.

In general, the interval between birth and baptism throughout the eighteenth and nineteenth centuries rarely exceeded five days, and most frequently occurred within four days. On several occasions, children were baptised *em perigo da vida* (in danger of their life) very soon after birth either by the priest or by the midwife, and this fact was duly recorded on the register. These were often cases where the word *morto* or *obiit* appeared in the margin next to the baptismal entry. That is, the infant did indeed die although clearly every effort was made to have him baptised first. In only four instances (two of them in the 1930s) in over two hundred and fifty years did an individual whose birth record could not be found turn up in some other document. In short, it appears that the baptismal records for Lanheses are virtually complete. Verifying the extent of completeness was necessary, given the low birth rates during the last decades of the nineteenth century. Once it could be established, at least for the latter part of the nineteenth century and the twentieth century, that the registration of births was systematic and the birth rate was generally accurately represented, something did indeed need explanation; that is some extraneous factor or factors must have been responsible for low birth rates.

The marriage registers start out in 1700 as simply as the baptismal registers. Until 1747, the only information provided are the date, the name, and the marital status of the groom, his parents, his place of birth, the name and marital status of the bride, her parents and her place of birth, whether the marriage was contracted with or without any "impediment" (i.e. a dispensation for consanguinity), and the names of the witnesses. Beginning in 1725 the question of whether or not the groom had to justify his absences from the parish appears, although we do not know if this has to do with a sudden increase in emigration or a change in the regulations or custom of recording.

In 1747 the names and places of birth and residence of both sets of grandparents were also added. The following is an example of a marriage record dating from the latter part of the eighteenth century, a format that again remained unchanged until 1860.

> Francisco João Castinheira, legitimate son of Francisco João and his wife Josefa Rodrigues, grandson on the paternal side of João Gonçalves Castinheira and his wife Ana Gonçalves of the parish of San Pedro de Arcos, and on the maternal side of José Domingues and his wife Maria Rodrigues of this parish; was received in my presence on the third of August, 1789 in the company of Caterina Rodrigues, legitimate daughter of António Alves and his wife Maria Rodrigues; granddaughter on the paternal side of Bento Alves and his wife Andresa da Costa, the latter of the parish of Fontão and the former of the parish of Santa Marta, vicinity of Viana; and on the maternal side, granddaughter of Francisco Rodrigues Caleiro and his wife Felicia Rodrigues of this parish; the banns having been published, and there being no impediment, with the exception of the groom having been absent in parts of Spain for which reason he showed me a matrimonial license, to receive them. Assisting at this marriage were the witnesses . . . (names follow).

Beginning in 1860, the ages of both the bride and groom were included on the marriage register and appear to have been extremely accurate. (Of course, a complete verification of individuals born in other parishes but married in Lanheses was not made, although spot checks tended to support the accurate recording of ages on the marriage registers.) The place of residence (the lugar) of both the bride and groom and their professions were also added in 1860.

As is customary among historical demographers, only so-called "complete families" whose continued presence in the parish could be established were used for most of the analyses of various aspects of fertility. Completeness is generally determined by a marriage record followed (if the woman is in her fertile years) by the births of children and terminated by the deaths of both husband and wife registered in the book of obituaries. For more recent families in which only one spouse had passed away as of 1970, oral history or an obituary where the individual's marital status was recorded as *casado* (married) rather than *viuvo* (widowed) helped to establish continued presence in the village. Those couples who married in the parish and then moved elsewhere were for the most part easy to separate out. Generally, the groom was from another parish, and a safe assumption is that the couple moved to the groom's parish after their union. Although the proportion of usable families fluctuated over the entire period, the average is approximately 75 percent. There were also several cases, especially during the latter part of the nineteenth century, of couples in which the wife died a widow but there was no record of the husband's death. In many instances, other documents or oral history confirmed that these men had died abroad as emigrants. Despite the fact that these families, in a strict historical demographic sense, would be considered incomplete, they have been considered in some of the discussion, especially that dealing with the effect of emigration on fertility.

The death records contain the least information prior to 1860, and it is highly likely that at least throughout the eighteenth century there was an underreporting of infant, and perhaps even some early childhood, deaths. This is confirmed, for example, by the birth of a subsequent child who is given the same name as one who presumably died, but for whom no obituary can be found. It is also confirmed by the fact that parents, in their wills, frequently listed all their children, and occasionally some children who were born to them and recorded in the baptismal register go without mention. Yet we have no record of their death in the parish. Emigration and exogamous marriage are, of course, possibilities, but parents often mentioned such facts in their wills, as well. Where alternative sources have clearly indicated a death at some point, it was included on the record for a particular family, and in general it has been necessary to work within the constraints set by the limitations of the mortality records.

For the purposes of the historical demographer, there are also limitations to the death records for adults, limitations that generally relate to the difficulties of record linkage. More precisely, there are variations in the format of the death entries depending on the age and marital status of an individual. It seems that minors (after 1800 the word *menor* is frequently included on the death notice of a child under seven), teenagers, and very young unmarried adults were identified as the son or daughter of a certain man and his wife (or a certain woman in the case of a child born illegitimately). However, older unmarried adults were buried with an entry which simply gave their name and status and no other identification. Since the baptismal record only indicates the given name of an infant at birth, and since there was no consistent formula about what family names a child would be given (see the note on naming below), the fact that the names of the parents of unwed adults was not included on the death records has made the problems of calculating permanent celibacy prior to 1860 very difficult. Record linkages were made with extreme caution, which has probably hampered the possibility of any sound estimate of permanent celibacy prior to 1860, although clearly it did exist. The following is an example of a death record for a single adult female, and is representative of the format that such entries took throughout most of the eighteenth and nineteenth centuries.

> On the 5th of September, 1747, Luisa Gonçalves, spinster, of the lugar of Devesa with all the sacraments was buried in sepulchre number 46, leaving her clothing to pay for the passing of her soul.

On this entry, the word *pobre* (poor) was included, a designation clearly supported by the fact that she was forced to leave her clothing as compensation for the masses which were to be said on her behalf. Whether Luisa was a spinster of thirty who may still have married had she lived or a spinster of fifty or more who had passed the marriage age we do not know for sure.

In the case of married individuals who died, the name of their living spouse is generally included on the entry and thus matching is facilitated. This is also generally true for widows (such as *viuva de João Rodrigues*), though less true for widowers, who are simply identified as *viuvo*. Although neither systematic nor precise, the death records do on occasion provide other information: for example, socioeconomic status (such as the use of *pobre* or *mendigo*, (beggar), whether the individual died with or without a testament (in a few cases an oral will was made and recorded as part of the obituary) and, more rarely and vaguely, what the person died of (generally a reference to a *moléstia*, (disease). Throughout much of the latter part of the eighteenth century, and on occasion during the nineteenth century, the parish priest of Lanheses also recorded death notices of parishioners who were abroad, a piece of evidence useful in an assessement of emigration.

In 1860, the quality of the death records in terms of completeness improved enormously. In fact, they became quite detailed. The following is a good example:

> On the 25th of March, 1862, at five in the afternoon in the house of António da Rocha of the lugar of Rocha of this parish of Lanheses, concelho and district of Viana do Castelo, Diocese of Braga, Maria Luisa Pereira, peasant woman, age of fifty-two and six months, wife of António da Rocha, parishioner of this parish, legitimate daughter of José Pereira and Francisca Luisa Pereira, granddaughter on the paternal side of Francisco Gonçalves and Ana Pereira and on the maternal side of Simão Luis and Domingas Gonçalves da Granja, died. She received all the sacraments and made no will. She left behind her a son and a daughter and was buried in the parish church in sepulchre sixty.

The practice of indicating whether or not and how many children were left ceased after 1911.

Although the parish registers form the core of the documentary sources used in this study, there are a few other materials that have been useful. Among the village "archives," somewhat in disarray, in the home of the parish priest are three books of testaments covering the period between 1742 and 1859. There are no books dated any earlier or any later; either they never existed or they have been lost. These wills are discussed in detail in Chapter One, and there is little need to say more about them here except that not everyone made a will and that some wills not included in the livros dos testamentos may be available in the rich notarial records for the district of Viana do Castelo. These latter records are discussed below.

The other major source included in these parish "archives" are the so-called rois da desobriga. These are lists of households kept by the parish priest to keep track of who had confessed and taken communion in any one year and who had paid the annual tithe. Households are ordered by lugar, and numbered. The name of the head of household is given, followed by other members of the household and their relationship to the head, including servants (criados). Those who were absent from the village and therefore had not confessed are so indicated with a letter *A*. This record of *ausentes* has also been very useful evidence in an evaluation of the extent of emigration. Beginning in 1881, the ages of each member of the household is also provided on the rois, although on cross-checking with parish register data these ages are not always accurate. Furthermore, in the few extant rois prior to 1881 children who have not taken their first communion (that is, children under seven or eight) are not included. However, by linking these households with reconstituted families it is possible to correct some of this inaccuracy. Rois for the following years have survived in the parish archives: 1850, 1851, 1852, 1870, 1881, 1887, 1892–1899, 1901–1927. For purposes of this study only selected years between 1892 and 1927 were systematically analyzed. Whether any other rois for Lanheses exist we do not know. There are none among the records for the parish kept in the District Archives in Braga.

The only other useful material about Lanheses among these District Archives are notarial records dating to the 1820s and early 1830s, when Lanheses was still a vila. In fact, the notarial records for the entire Concelho of Viana do Castelo are housed in Braga. However, a search primarily for documents pertaining to the residents of one village would have been an enormously time-consuming task, since these records are classified by the name of the notary rather than by the native parish of a particular client. It would have taken me far astray from the central focus of the book, and I therefore limited myself to the three more easily accessible volumes relating to the vila of Lanheses. It seems apparent from examining these three books that the peasants of the region were deeply involved in various legal procedures having to do with the sale of land, the mortgaging of land, the payment of debts, the bequeathing of property (indeed, notarial records probably supplement and expand on the books of testaments), and the general settling of differences. A more systematic study of these notarial records awaits future research or a future researcher.

Among other sources mentioned in the book is a series of electoral rolls dating between 1835 and 1870 that are housed in the Municipal Museum in Viana do Castelo and procured for me with the help of Rui Feijó. These electoral rolls at first simply list the names of men who were eligible to vote by virtue of having paid a proportionate tax on their property. Later on, their profession and age is also included. In the same archive there is an arrolamento dos bens dated 1871 that lists every head of household, his or her profession, a figure evaluating the extent of the taxable property, the number of oxen teams in his or her possession (generally none or one, occasionally two), and the number of adult males (over 21) living in the household. Finally, there are a few documents pertaining to local elections in the parish during the time when Lanheses was a vila. They provide information on who the various presidents and judges ( juizes) of the village junta were.

Among other documents kept by the local priest are the records of the various parish brotherhoods (*confrarias*). These are discussed in Chapter One. They are primarily useful for the information they contain on loans taken by parishioners. Finally, the research included a systematic reading of local newspapers published in Viana do Castelo during the latter half of the nineteenth century and an analysis of passport registers housed in the Civil Government Offices of the Concelho of Viana do Castelo. These latter documents are discussed in the test.

## NOTE ON NAMES

Any individual generally had two family names. However, there was no universal pattern to which of the four family names a child would be given. Nor was there necessarily any fixed order to the names. Thus, the offspring of José da Silva Rodrigues and Ana Castro Fernandes could have had any one of a dozen or more last names, including simply Rodrigues or Fernandes. Indeed, there seems to have been some tendency for daughters in the family to receive their mother's names and sons to receive their father's names. Thus, siblings could have different last names. But the fact that none of this is predictable makes record linkage difficult when there is no other clue to identification (as in the death registers before 1860). Furthermore, individuals were frequently identified by nicknames, particularly nicknames that had to do with geographical sites in the parish, such as João Rodrigues dos Possos or Ana Victoria de São João. Often this was necessary because there were several adult men or women with virtually identical names. Women were very frequently identified by nothing more than their given names, such as Maria de Jesus of Outeiro.

## Recognition Which the Inhabitants of This Village Made of Their Practices and Customs 10 November, 1779

THEY recognize that they have an obligation to pay the Reverend Priest (*abbade*) each year a tenth of the corn, olives, and wine that they harvest on their land and also that which they bring has to be among the best of what they harvest. They also recognize that they must pay the priest a tenth of all the wheat, rye, and linen which they harvest. Of each ovenful of tiles which are baked, they are accustomed to pay one *moio* to the priest. For sheep, the custom is to pay one for every ten; a half for every five; and those with fewer than five, 0$025 reis per head. For each calf the customary payment is 0$005 reis. For every ten beehives, the payment is one; for every five, one; and those with fewer than five pay nothing. For honey, it is the custom to pay one liter for every ten. For ten suckling pigs, the fee is one; for five, it is half, and for less than five the fee is 0$025 reis per head. For each litter of chicks, the fee is one hen; no tithe is due on fruit, vegetables, beans, and wood.

For the *premicia*, married couples pay five *quartos* per household, alternating one of corn with one of rye. Widowers pay half of the above and single people a quarter; and even if in one household two or more married couples live together, the premicia is paid only once on St. Michael's Day. Each couple also pays one egg on St. Michael's Day and again at Easter.

The mordomos of the Confraria of Jesus, on the day of the festa, give an offering to the reverend priest, and in addition to the offering for the mass, three *tostões* in money and a chicken. For each wedding, the reverend priest receives 0$240 reis money; for each certificate required by a parishioner, the fee is 0$200 reis and for those from other parishes, if it is a certificate of banns, 0$240, and for any other 0$120 reis. For each baptism, the fee is one chicken, and for the *desobriga* (release from obligation) one tostão per household. For attendance to a funeral each sacerdote should be given a small offering of 0$020 reis. For each church service with mass the reverend priest is to be paid 0$240 in money, a portion of bread and two glasses of wine, and if it is a mass in the presence of the body he is due 0$900 and each other sacerdote present should be paid 0$240 and 0$010 reis worth of white bread and a glass of wine.

The heirs of those who have died have the custom of celebrating three offices of ten priests each: the first in the presence of the body; the second at the end of the month; the third at the end of the year. For the first, the reverend priest is to be paid the offering described above, as are the priests who assist in the mass. For the second and third offices, the priest is to be paid 0$240. For the annual prayers, the reverend priest is paid 1$440, and he in turn has the obligation to issue candles to be carried during the prayers. For the sons of families it is customary to carry out a mass with five priests and one in which the parish priest is involved. For this service he is to be paid 0$240 if the child is over seven and for those who die under this age a mass is given for the sum of 0$100.

Each year, the inhabitants of the parish should pay 0$640 to the person who serves as the mordomo of the cross. They also declare that the candles used in the *Missa de Dia* (Mass of the Day) each Sunday and on Holy Days should be paid by the mordomo of the cross and that he is obliged to give the reverend priest, at Easter, one goat and two hens and that the same mordomo will pay each of the priests who assists in the rites in honor of the patroness of the church 0$100. They also say that the reverend priest is obliged to say Mass each Monday and for this service married couples will pay a half *alqueire* of corn on St. Michael's Day each year, even if several couples live in one household; and that widows and widowers, bachelors and spinsters will pay a quarter, and that the priest is obliged to provide the candles for this mass. Further they say that the mordomos of the brotherhoods of the church are accustomed to light the daily mass and that he who forgets it will be fined 0$050.

Lastly, the residents of this parish say that they understand the habits and customs and obligations recognized above and that they all promise to fulfill them well as their ancestors have done and that in recognition of this fact they make this act and all sign below, with the exception of the women because they do not know how to sign.

[Signatures and marks (x's) are affixed at this point and these in turn are followed by this addendum:]

And the residents of the parish declared that the obligation that couples have to pay a half alqueire of corn each year to the reverend abbade for the Monday masses is only applied to those houses that constitute one household, given that many couples live together in one household, all of them are only obliged to pay half an alqueire and that this also applies to widows/ers and bachelors and spinsters.

# NOTES

## INTRODUCTION

1. Holism is an extremely common-sense anthropological notion that encourages the researcher to attend to all the parts of a system and the way in which they are integrated to form a whole. It also underscores an appreciation of both the long- and short-term consequences of a change in the system.
2. Indeed, Cohn (1982:252) points out that "many anthropologists . . . have turned to history as a means of escaping the assumptions of an unchanging, timeless, native culture."
3. This is precisly the underlying implication of Laslett's significant, if controversial, book *The World We Have Lost*, or of William Goode's coining of the phrase "the family of western nostalgia."
4. Although I agree with Freeman (1981) that the present cannot necessarily be taken as a faithful guide to the past (indeed this would be to commit all the errors of structural functionalism all over again), this approach can nevertheless guide us into areas of questioning that we might not otherwise consider.
5. See the appendix for a brief discussion of the historical records used in this study.
6. Dyke and Morrill (1980) express this compatibility in terms of a combination of approaches, one they call ethnographic, which relies on informants' accounts, and the other documentary, which relies on the written record. They point to the fact that orally recollected genealogies are frequently inaccurate, telescoping time or distorting, purposefully or unconsciously, biological reality. Documentary information can, in their view, provide a check upon the ethnographic genealogy. Thus, they have looked to the documentary record in search of more accurate demographic information. What they have missed in their approach is precisely what the historians are looking for in their application of what they consider to be an anthropological ethos; that is, that these records can provide cultural information in addition to demographic information.
7. Kennedy (1973), for example, has addressed the relationship between women's status and differential mortality in Ireland. More recently, Guttentag and Secord (1983) have explored the impact of different sex ratios (high or low) on sexual behavior, sexual mores, patterns of nuptiality and divorce, family stability, and so on. They argue, for example, that a high sex ratio is linked with an emphasis on the sexual purity of women who are, in this context, prized objects. Conversely, a low sex ratio can be linked with high illegitimacy, remarriage only for men, and so on. Although there are clearly cultural factors that create exceptions to the rule (Ireland is one case), the study is provocative.

8. Eugen Weber (1976) has also explored the issue of migration in his study of the peasant populations of France in the late nineteenth and early twentieth centuries. In his work, he calls migration "an industry of the poor," implying that it was *the* alternative in the absence of other local industrial opportunities. See Kertzer (1984b) for further comments.

9. For an excellent discussion of this issue see Watson (1975).

10. In the guise of structural-functionalism, it has equally been a part of the theoretical underpinnings of the disciplines of sociology and anthropology. For one of the best explications, see Gluckman's (1968) discussion of the so-called "equilibrium model."

11. Friedlander has in fact continued to explore the issue of change and multiple response, and in a recent article in *Demography* (1983) has concluded that "emigration and marital fertility decline are substitute responses," especially among rural, agricultural populations. His more recent work will be discussed further in Chapter Four.

12. The sociologist Robert K. Merton, in his classic essay on manifest and latent functions, makes a similar point: "It need not be assumed that the *reasons* advanced by people for their behavior ('we act for personal reasons') are one and the same as the observed consequences of these patterns of behavior. The subjective disposition may coincide with the objective consequence, but again, it may not" (Merton 1967:78).

13. I am alluding here to the sentiment of sociocentrism discussed by ethnographers of both Spain (Caro-Baroja 1957, Freeman 1979, Pitt-Rivers 1954) and Italy (Bell 1979, Silverman 1975). In Italian, the word used to express this concept is *campanilismo*, which refers literally to a common bond among those who live within hearing distance of their village church bell, and figuratively to village chauvinism. Although Kenny and Kertzer (1983) conclude that *campanilismo* is primarily an "urban concept" manifested among migrant populations, it does have its counterpart in the village environment as well, emerging, for example, during annual religious festivals. This is precisely the context in which Riegelhaupt (1973) discusses sociocentrism in Portugal.

CHAPTER ONE. THE PARISH OF LANHESES

1. Leal (1873, 4:93) quotes from the Roman Tito Livia: the consul Decio Junius Brutus wanted to cross the river (the Lima) to make war on the Gallicians about 135 A.D. Seeing that his soldiers feared to cross it, he took the flag of the eagles from the hand of the standard bearer. He crossed and from the other side called to each of his soldiers by name to prove that he had not lost his memory. This served as a stimulus to the Roman legions. See similar discussions in Padre Jeronymo Cortador de Argote (1732) and Denis (1846).

2. The bridge over the Lima River at the town of Ponte de Lima was part of an important military road linking the city of Braga with the Galician

city of Tuy. Indeed, traces of Roman settlements have been found throughout the region.

3. See a fuller discussion of this period in Portugal's history in Marques (1972).

4. Marques (1972:28) notes that even at this time the system of land tenure in Tras os Montes was different from that in Minho. "The *aforamentos* were given to a people who divided among themselves the chores as among Romans in the curia municipal, or among Russians in the mir."

5. Marques points out that forty-three of the seventy-four *vilas novas* and *aldeias novas* are located in the north, in the district of Porto.

6. See Balbi (1822) for one of the earliest analyses of Portugal's population prior to the nineteenth century.

7. A couto was a piece of property marked by the authority of the king with specific boundaries, in which the lay brothers (*donatorios*) administered justice, collected rents, foros, and other revenues—even taxes. The tenant-farmers (*colonos*) made payments in agricultural products, in pensions, or in services to the seigneur. Balbi (1822) referred to these coutos as "comprising several hamlets and small populations which still enjoy in some areas the right to have a special jurisdiction for civil causes of little importance." He described them as belonging to bishops and friars, in contrast to *honras*, which were seigneuries given to laics by the king. See the discussion in Denis (1846). Coutos were officially abolished in 1790 (Leal 1873).

8. In 1560, the monastery and farmlands were united with the monastery of S. Domingos, and Dominican monks remained in possession until 1834, when the convent of S. Salvador was, like many others throughout Portugal, confiscated. The farmlands and monastery buildings were publically auctioned and purchased by Senhor Valadares of Valadares do Minho, a patriot who had returned from Brazil. The Portuguese word *freguesia* (parish) is sometimes derived from the Latin *filtu gregis*—son of the church—indicating the religious connection as far back as Roman times. See Oliveira (1950) for further discussion.

9. The number of households in each of the five provinces was counted as follows: Minho, 55,066; Tras os Montes, 35,616; Beira, 66,804; Estremadura, 65,178; Alentejo, 48,804; Total, 271,468. Balbi estimated the number of households in the Algarve (which was omitted at the time) to have been approximately 18,532.

10. This position was shared with the Rochas of the neighboring village of Meixedo.

11. Costa (1868) lists Dr. Gonçalo Mendes de Brito, a judge of the court and superintendent of tobacco in Lisbon, and his brother Francisco de Abreu Pereira, sergeant-major of the *comarca* (judicial district) of Barcellos as senhores of Lanheses, sharing this patronage with the Rochas of Meixedo.

12. In the 1930s, there was a fire in the city hall in Viana do Castelo, and many documents were destroyed.

13. Vila Mou had 79 households, Meixedo 87, and Fontão 122.

14. This cadastre was given to a monk in the monastery at Alcobaça seventeen years after the tragic death of Villas Boas during the Napoleonic invasion.

15. 100 *reis* = 10 *centavos* = 1 *tostão*. The notation for 100 *reis* is 0$100. For 10 *mil reis*, 10$000.

16. In the judicial district (*comarca*) as a whole there were 39,964 men, 49,249 women (sex ratio of 81 men per 100 women), 17,461 boys and 17,523 girls, 1,177 clerics, 14 monasteries with 315 monks, 5 nunneries with 189 nuns, and 257 markets. Meixedo and Fontão were also listed as belonging to the couto of Lanheses, with 86 and 92 households, respectively, and total populations of 388 and 402, respectively. The difference of almost 10,000 people between adult males (presumably over 14) and adult females is worth noting—even at this time, prior to the massive exodus to Brazil, emigration had its impact upon the male population of the district. The other twelve coutos in the comarca of Viana were Bertiandos, S. Fins, Queijada e Bahosa, Aboím de Nobrega, Sahariz, Gomide, Baldreu, Sibões, Rendufe, Boure, Paredes Seccas, and Souto.

17. Costa (1789:v) in fact claims that Viana began its decline in importance in the mid-eighteenth century as the city of Porto increasingly absorbed much of its commerce.

18. See Francisco Cyrne de Castro's article on cholera in the district of Viana do Castelo (1952).

19. See Dias (1949) for an excellent discussion of the geography of Minho.

20. See, for example, Freeman (1970). Sampaio (1923:480) describes the people of Minho as being quite skillful at finding subterranean currents of water and capitalizing on them, whether in underground or above-ground aquaducts. Even today, during the dry months of summer, there are disputes over the use of canalized water for irrigation.

21. The ownership of plots of land in other villages is the result of village exogamy and inheritance practices.

22. Silbert (1968:53) cites a petition requesting the retention of common lands (*baldios*) submitted in the early 1820s by the village of Ancora in the concelho of Viana. The villagers claimed that without their common lands there would be no underbrush, without underbrush, no manure, and without manure, no agriculture. "We ask," said the petition, "that the common lands be left alone, without partitions or fences." Discussion of the baldio question went on, sometimes heatedly, throughout the nineteenth century (see Cabral 1974). In 1904, the baldios of Lanheses were finally divided, and each household was allocated two plots—one in the foothills and the other higher up in the mountains. According to one village informant, most Lanhesans by this time approved of the division. Those who were opposed were the few men who had flocks of sheep or who worked in activities related to the harvesting of pine trees.

23. Recently, as a result of the building boom caused by emigrants to France, two new lugares have been created through the conversion of land that was once agricultural into residential areas.

24. Many of these shops and cafés are of recent origin, the result of the new prosperity. However, dry goods stores, bakeries, and taverns were a part of the mercantile past on the village square. The Casa do Povo is primarily a rural credit institution that was first established during the early years of Salazar's Estado Novo. Its responsibilities have been expanded during the post-Salazar era.

25. The Conde de Aurora, who was a property owner in the Lima Valley, has written a book entitled *Roteiro da Ribeira Lima* (1929), which describes many of the solares of the local nobility. The word *fidalgo* derives from the words *filho* and *de algo*—son of someone.

26. For a discussion of the emphyteusis system in Portugal see Carvalho (1814).

27. A fire in the Camara Municipal of Viana do Castelo in the 1930s destroyed all previous property records. New ones were made in 1940 for land ownership at that time, and they are periodically updated.

28. The Furtado Mendonças were a family who came to the region from Angola in the early nineteenth century. In a will dated October 1812, Padre António da Rocha Franco, Maria Micaella's brother, declared that the property of his patrimony was part of the vinculo of his uncle Francisco Alves Franco, and he bequeathed the major part of it to his nephew Miguel Tinoco, "heir of the Casa da Barrosa."

29. A *prazo* is a termed lease agreement for the rental of property. An *alquiere* is a dry or liquid measure of varying capacity throughout the country. In upper Minho it was equivalent to about 17.8 liters.

30. To attempt to reconstruct the history of this particular prazo is fascinating. It was apparently inherited by José Martins' grandmother Mariana Goncalves in 1742 on the death of her husband João Alves, a widower whom she had married in 1729 and who was a resident of Casal Maior (and presumably the tenant on the prazo). In 1742, her rights to the prazo were apparently challenged by a man from the concelho of Geraz de Lima, but the case was settled in her favor. Presumably, when Mariana died in 1762, she passed the prazo on to her only surviving daughter Ana, who in 1773 married Bento Martins. Ana died in 1783, and presumably passed title in the prazo on to her eldest son José. When José died (he married in 1803 at age 29) he left his property to his brother João—he had no children of his own. His brother João had married a young women from another parish but was residing in Lanheses.

31. The testators had no children of their own and, two years after Isabel Gonçalves died, João Franco de Castro remarried. He died in 1854 and no new will seems to have been recorded. The heir, Isabel, born in 1825 (her relationship to the testators is unclear) as one of several daughters of José Correia and Luisa da Costa, married in 1851 a young man from a village across the Lima River. She appears to have left Lanheses.

32. Francisca married six months after Manuel Morais' death at the age of twenty-five. It is not clear if she stayed with Luisa Gonçalves or not. She did remain in the village, however.

33. Deaths in Spain were not uncommon and were frequently recorded in

the parish obituary register, presumably on the basis of information sent to the parish priest. In the Livros dos Testamentos there are two wills that appear to have been made by young men who died in Spain, one dated 1753 and the other 1762. The first testator, José, age twenty-three, son of Silvestre of Lobatos, stated that he was "in the city of Cordoba in the kingdom of Spain, sick in bed, and in the company and care of friends." He gave his share of his parents' house to his brother João. Further discussion is in Chapter Three.

34. In February of 1835, ten months before her daughter Luisa's marriage to José António Rodrigues (José Alexandre) of Meixedo, Isabel Francisca de Castro recorded with the notary Francisco José Mesquito Rego of Lanheses the bestowing of a dowry upon her daughter. Presumably, she wanted some way to legitimize her daughter's right to her property. The text of this note is revealing and is translated here in part: "It was said that she (Isabel Francisca de Castro), living in the third state (widowhood), had this said daughter (Luisa Francisca de Castro), whom she raised under her jurisdiction, whom she sent out to serve as a maid in different houses, until, at the age of sixteen, she was placed in the service of José Caridade of Vila Franca, where she spent four years, and then the grantor, needing her daughter in her own company to serve her, was obliged to take the case before the justice of Barcellos in order to have her daughter released from the service of José Caridade. The mother won the case and her daughter was entrusted to her on the condition that she pay the wages (0$500) owed the daughter as well as for the cost of a suit of clothing (0$300); and which wages were never paid to this day with the exception of some necessary clothing; and because said daughter is now contracted to marry and the mother is pleased about it, she (the mother) is now obliged to pay said wages. In addition, the mother recognizes the daughter's right to her legitimate inheritance, comprising the residence in Sobral and the fields in Trogal (mortgaged to Santo António of Meixedo and Santo António of Lanheses for 23$000) and Ponte de Linhares on the condition that the daughter cares for her until she dies, for which care she will be paid wages. The mother states that she is the senhora and administrator of what is hers until death. The mother recognizes that all that her daughter and husband acquire or purchase on their own is theirs because they are not entering into an association; but rather the daughter and her husband are like servants."

35. See Weinberg (1972) for a discussion of the way land is divided according to its nature and value in Swiss mountain villages.

36. This couple had three other surviving children: a son Bento born in 1783 and married in 1811; a daughter Rosa born in 1785 and married in 1811; and a son José born in 1804, whose fate is unknown. The heir Ana died a spinster in 1860 at the age of sixty-one.

37. For this study, only those notarial records which pertained to Lanheses when it was a vila (between 1790 and 1835) were consulted. See Appendix One for further discussion.

38. Lison-Tolosana (1976) describes a similar system of inheritance in the interior of Spanish Galicia. In fact, within this single province of Spain, he notes three quite distinct patterns of inheritance which correspond to three family types. See also O'Neill (1983, 1984) for a discussion of inheritance in northeastern Portugal.

39. Ezequiel de Campos (1943) has described the accumulation of enormous amounts of property in the hands of religious corporations as one of the major obstacles to the development of the agricultural sector in Portuguese history.

40. Several popular adages embody these regional differences between northern and southern Portugal: "The Minhotan is submissive to his priests; the Alentejan is proud and independent"; "The Minhotan is religious by tradition; the Alentejan is religious by conviction." See Sanchis (1976) for others.

41. Riegelhaupt (1981) has recently done extensive research on the Maria da Fonte movement. See also Pinto (1979).

42. See Franca (1980) for a contemporary statistical study of regional variations in religious behavior in Portugal.

43. In Candido Furtado Coelho's statistical study of 1861, four major convents are listed for the District of Viana do Castelo. In addition, he estimates one cleric for every 178 of the civil population.

44. The English traveler William Young made a similar remark: "But I must be permitted to state my perfect conviction that no guarantees whatever can exist as to female honor or female purity in a state society where, under the mask of religious duties, females of every class are subjected to the contamination of such men as the great majority of the Portuguese clergy" (Young 1828:4). See also Pardoe (1832:ii:327).

45. Almeida (1921) cites a similar circular of almost a century earlier issued by Bishop Morato.

46. Analysts of the Church in Portugal have frequently attempted to classify priests into a series of types. Ortigão (1887), for example, distinguished between *padres das missões* (mission priests), *padres d'aldeia* (village priests), and *padres da sala* (salon priests). The mission priests he further subdivided into adventurers who travel to Africa or Brazil for the love of the life of the emigrant, in search of mercantile rewards or to involve themselves in the intrigues of colonial politics; and mystics, a rarer type who view themselves as martyrs. He described the village priest as "ordinarily the best of men": "On ordinary days, he mutters the mass of souls at daybreak in an abbreviated Latin and then goes to prune the vines, weed the onions, graft the lemon trees, or hunt partridges, trudging through the mountains, leaping over ditches, and returning home at the ringing of the ave marias with the quail hunters leading him, his rifle over his shoulder, extending good evenings to his right and left throughout the village, slapping the shoulders of the men, pinching the cheeks of the girls with the good carnal joviality of his old colleague of Meudon, the Reverend Rabelais" (Ortigão 1885:24). The third type, on the other hand, was part of

the *mise en scène* of the aristocratic salon of the Portuguese city, "a servant of neuter sex" who involved himself in the lives and activities of the upper classes.

More recently, Cabral (1981) has differentiated between the "modern priest," the "antiquated priest," and the "curer priest," acknowledging that at present the majority of priests belong to the first category. These are clerics who no longer wear ecclesiastical garb on a daily basis and who generally teach in a secondary school (*liceu*) in addition to officiating over a parish. They are, for the most part, opposed to traditional festas and to superstitious beliefs. They live in modernized houses and drive automobiles.

47. Fortunato de Almeida, in his monumental history of the Portuguese Church (1921), also refers to scandals connected with the fact that priests were living with their children.

48. I participated in this celebration of the patroness saint in December of 1975. At that time, the new village choir that my husband and I had organized sang a hymn about the Virgin Mary from the church balcony as the procession got underway. It was a very beautiful hymn that we had recently taught the choir and that the villagers had not yet heard. The word *mãe* (mother) was repeated over and over again, as she was called upon to help the faithful in all their troubles. Many of the parishioners were brought to tears in what was one of the most moving religious ceremonies I have ever witnessed. Virgin Mary, motherhood, and the mother saint of the parish were all brought together in a way which was clearly emotionally meaningful to many of those attending the mass that afternoon. To speak of a lack of religious faith and belief after observing the reactions to this hymn is impossible.

49. For a more complete discussion of the festa of Senhor do Cruzeiro in Lanheses, see Brettell (1983).

50. As noted at the end of the previous section of this chapter, although testaments clearly indicate that at death's door saving one's soul was of momentous importance to testators (thus the requests for various masses at various prices), in only one instance was property transmitted to the Church through this particular vehicle. However, it is evident that the Church already owned vast properties (confiscated and restored at various points in history), which were tilled by peasants who paid an annual rent. And in numerous other ways it extracted wealth from its congregations.

CHAPTER TWO. EMIGRATION IN
PORTUGUESE HISTORY

1. Faria is equally concerned about the *falta de gente* among the noble classes, but here cites as major causes two different factors: the primogeniture (*morgado*) system of inheritance, and the lavish doweries bestowed upon elder daughters at the expense of younger offspring, who remain unmar-

ried. Clearly, for both social classes (rich and poor) his major concern was why so few children married.

2. This migration to Spain was probably in some way a result of the Spanish occupation of Portugal between 1580 and 1640. Once the pattern was established, it most likely continued. In the Greenlee Collection of the Newberry Library, Chicago, there is a letter written by Felipe II dealing with recommendations to halt this migration flow from Portugal to Spain (Manuscript 1623).

3. It should be noted that the point of view which bemoaned a severe loss of population was not based on entirely accurate facts. The population of Portugal remained stationary at approximately 1,200,000 between 1540 and 1640, and then increased after the mid-seventeenth century to reach a figure of 2,500,000 by the mid-eighteenth century (Boxer 1961).

4. A discussion of the brasileiro follows shortly.

5. The bibliography includes several studies of nineteenth-century emigration to Brazil.

6. Pereira (1981) mentions negotiations directed to replacing black slaves with immigrants. See also Serrão (1974).

7. Teles (1903) distinquishes between emigration rates in more central districts, such as Aveiro and Coimbra, which fluctuated largely in response to crises affecting the export of monocultural agricultural products cultivated in these areas, from emigration in the northwest where polycultural and subsistence agriculture prevailed.

8. For further discussion of property laws, see Brandão and Rowland (1980).

9. While only a small piece of local evidence, the *Aurora de Lima* in July of 1889 reported the auction of seven properties in Lanheses in order that back taxes and debts could be paid.

10. For the rural classes, Teles (1903) tells us, military service "only spoiled and demoralized a young man, giving him vices, exposing him to illness, and putting him finally on a road without profession and without means." See also Descamps (1935) and Pereira (1981).

11. Foreigners as well as natives discussed the brasileiros. For example, the following observation was made by Juliette Adams in her travel book, *La Patrie Portugaise*, published in 1896: "The Portuguese returned from Brazil always choose the town, the village, the hamlet where they were born. They generally build a home on a small property and remain complacent in the realized dream" (Adams 1896:324).

12. References to the Galicians in Portugal are numerous. For example, the following observation was made by James Murphy during a trip to Portugal in 1788: "The laborers chiefly employed here are natives of Galicia, a province of Spain: hence, they are called galegos. Their number is computed at eight thousand in Oporto alone and the whole kingdom is thought to contain not less than fifty thousand of these industrious adventurers. If this statement is correct (and I do not give it on light authority), and that each man lays up, on an average, eighteen pence per week, then the most

profitable trade of Portugal is carried on by the Galicians; for their savings, according to this calculation, amount to one hundred and ninety five thousand pounds per annum which they carry to their own country. Those who have witnessed their manner of living, will admit that the sum is stated rather below than above the truth; for they are the most economic people in the world. They are fed gratuitously at the gates of convents, lodged in cellars, stables, or cloisters, and clothed in rags in which they usually repose. Yet, many of them possess lands and houses in their own country, whither they return at stated periods to divide their hard earned pittance with their families and finally retire, as soon as they have made sufficient to live independent of labors, to spend the evening of life in the simple enjoyment of domestic felicity" (Murphy 1795:16). Similar references are made in Link (1801:206–207) and Descamps (1935:64).

13. See Cesar (1969) and Brettell (1978) for further discussion.

14. The First Parliamentary Inquiry on Emigration refers to these "small-scale" returned emigrants, as well: "those who come back not with massive fortunes, but at least with sufficient funds to live in comfort, and for them emigration has not been disadvantageous because they return with capital which they use in the country and with which they develop the public wealth" (p. 177). The inquiry report goes on to contrast these brasileiros who return to their native villages with those of larger fortune who settle in Porto or in "more important regions in Minho where they become involved in commerce or live off the income from property they have in Brazil." A characterization of these Porto brasileiros can be found in Julio Dinis' novel *Uma Familia Inglesa*.

15. Another observer of the province of Minho had this to say about the engajadores: "Before leaving, the engajadores read them the *good word* to prove to them that happiness awaits them: they point to the palaces, quintas, and belongings of their neighbors whose fathers and grandfathers, like them, had nothing; they show them the sun that brilliantly breaks through the clouds, but hide from them the storm, whose destruction, from far away, they cannot see, nor even suspect" (Costa 1874:274).

16. A *conto* = 1000 escudos or 1000$000.

17. See Pereira (1981) for a discussion of the politics of emigration in relation to remittances.

18. For example, Silva (1868:326) writes: "From households where often families support twenty-five people, vigorous day laborers leave for all parts of the kingdom to dig the vines, to harvest the corn fields, to help in all services of agricultural work."

Thirty years earlier an Englishman noted: "The population of Alentejo is supposed to have diminished during the last century, while the Entre-Douro-e-Minho has become unable to support its increasing numbers, many of whom annually emigrate from their happy valleys and offer their services to the inhabitants of other provinces. Influenced, however, by similar habits and by the recollection of a common theme, these poor people keep together, ranging from place to place" (Carnarvon 1836:II:109).

And a German traveler similarly observed at the dawn of the nineteenth century: "Yet the increase of this industrious and cheerful people is too great for their unfruitful soil, and a great number annually emigrate, some with an intention of settling elsewhere, and others to acquire property and return. These men help the farmers of other provinces in their harvests and other branches of husbandry, traveling about in considerable numbers under the command of a captain and living in huts" (Link 1801:333).

19. In 1858, for example, 155 ships from Portugal docked in Rio de Janeiro—60 originating in Lisbon, 44 in Porto, 2 in Viana do Castelo, 1 in Setúbal, 1 from Faial, 3 from Madeira, 39 from Cabo Verde, 3 from Launda, and 1 from Macão.

20. These passport registers are incomplete because they only count legal emigration. Toward the end of the nineteenth century, numerous individuals left for Brazil illegally or with a simple paper issued by a notary rather than with an official passport.

21. The differences in the national censuses between the *de jure* and the *de facto* population demonstrate the fact of emigration. The figures are somewhat at variance with those drawn from the rois, but given the seasonality of migration, possible incompleteness in the rois, and perhaps different definitions of what constituted an absence, the disparities are not serious. These figures, drawn from a range of sources, are simply meant to demonstrate that the Lanhesan population, like the population of the region as a whole, was definately a migrating population.

|      | De jure | De facto | DJ-DF (difference) |
|------|---------|----------|--------------------|
| 1864 | 1191    | 1207     | + 16               |
| 1878 | 1140    | 1034     | −106               |
| 1890 | 1073    | 1000     | − 73               |
| 1900 | 1028    | 1029     | + 1                |
| 1911 | 1200    | 1087     | −113               |
| 1920 | 1161    | 1083     | − 78               |
| 1930 | 1218    | 1265     | + 47               |

22. It is important to note that the mobility of this female population is itself an indication of the difficult economic conditions of the later nineteenth century.

23. Stanislawski (1959) has suggested that the division of labor which places farming in the hands of women has much deeper historical roots dating back to the Celts.

24. For further discussion see Brettell (1979, 1982).

CHAPTER THREE. FAMILY AND HOUSEHOLD

1. The fact that for a number of decades the mean age at marriage for women is higher than that for men is explained in part by a problem with the

data. Since marriages generally occurred in the bride's village, and since an appreciable number of grooms came from other villages, we simply have more confirmed ages for brides than for grooms. Only after 1860 were the ages of both brides and grooms provided on the marriage registers themselves, and some spot-checking with the registers of the native villages of in-marrying grooms has shown these ages to be recorded reasonably accurately. However, this problem with the data should not detract from the fact that there were indeed cases throughout the demographic history of Lanheses where wives were older than their husbands.

2. See the discussion of European Culture Areas in volume 36 of the *Anthropological Quarterly*. The issue of culture areas in relation to demographic patterns is raised again in Chapter Five below, in connection with the discussion of illegitimacy, and in the Conclusion. See Rowland (1983) for further exploratory discussion of the marriage pattern "typology" and its relevance for Portugal. Kertzer (personal communication) has raised the question of whether Wrigley's model applies any better to other regions of the Mediterranean.

3. Several volumes published as part of the Princeton Fertility Project give these variations in age at marriage on a regional basis for a number of European nations. See for example Lesthaeghe (1977); Knodel (1974); Coale, Anderson, and Harm (1979).

4. For an excellent ethnographic description of the problems of a joint family household in the throes of dissolution, see Wolf (1968).

5. Douglass (1971) has demonstrated the importance of the timing of the selection of an heir and its relationship to rural out-migration through a comparison of two Basque villages, one where the heir is identified while still a child and socialized into the role, and the other where offspring compete to gain the favor of their parents.

6. Livi Bacci (1971) has also drawn attention to the differences in forms of land tenure and economic exploitation between northern and southern Portugal in order to explain the broad regional variations in patterns of nuptiality. For the northern region, he points, somewhat confusingly, both to the practice of *morgado* (entailed, impartible primogeniture) and to that of partibility, without carefully distinguishing among different socioeconomic levels.

7. Vinovskis does not discuss the inheritance of land in his study of demographic trends in New York State in the mid-nineteenth century (1978), but he does demonstrate a relationship between the number of unimproved acres of land per person in agriculture and the average ages at which people married.

In cross-cultural anthropological literature in general, marriage has for a long time been viewed as a contract rooted in economic considerations and very often closely associated with the question of succession—succession not only to wealth and property, but also to the power and authority that accompany these.

8. In fact, it is also possible to argue that the early death of a father may

have resulted in the delayed marriages of offspring, especially older off-spring whose continued labor input became even more necessary to the survival of the household. Daughters may have gone out to serve or work as day laborers; sons may have emigrated. Elliott (1976) has argued that the early deaths of fathers in seventeenth-century London, Essex, and Hertfordshire forced daughters to migrate as servants and therefore to de-lay their marriages.

9. Professor Allan Williams of Exeter University brought to my attention a particularly apt comment in this regard made about the Portuguese by António Vieira in the seventeenth century. Vieira stated, "God gave the Portuguese a small country as a cradle and the whole world as their grave."

10. See Rowland (1981).

11. Although the more accepted argument is that there is a direct relation-ship between grain crop prices and the economic well-being of the peas-antry, an alternative interpretation is probably worth considering. High grain prices may reflect low crop yields which, for the small-scale subsist-ance peasant farmer, means that there is little surplus produce to sell. As a result, he has less cash available and his debts for taxes and other nec-essary goods will increase. The result could be a greater tendency to delay marriage and/or to opt for emigration as a means to procure the necessary cash. Low grain prices as a measure of good crop yields would mean that there is more cash on hand, making emigration less necessary and mar-riage more feasible.

12. Bell (1979) notes the minimal number of marriages contracted during the month of March in southern Italy, and links it to the Lenten season. March appears to be an unpopular month for marriages in Lanheses as well, but I did not pursue questions in the field related to seasonality and therefore cannot confirm the association with Lent. If there is some con-nection, however, it would tend to reinforce arguments linking certain forms of demographic behavior (beyond fertility) to religiosity, and perhaps stand as another measure of the degree of religiosity. Bell also finds May to be a popular month for marriage in southern Italy. May does not emerge as the month of most marriages in Lanheses at any time between 1700 and 1970.

13. Mitterauer and Sieder (1982:66) have suggested that a younger groom married to an older bride, and particularly a bride who had been wid-owed, may not only have affected authority relationships, but also influ-enced sexuality within marriage.

14. In this group was one man who bought and sold gold and who married a well-to-do spinster almost twenty years older than himself who had in-herited the bulk of her wealthy uncle's estate. He was called an opportun-ist by those who remembered him. Also included were two brothers who emigrated to Brazil and returned to open small businesses in the parish. One had no children—he married at thirty a well-to-do woman of the same age. The other married young and had eight children, of whom sev-eral died. Another man in this group had married, as a widower, a wealthy

heiress from Fontão. Yet another was described by villagers as poor, but all of his sons were enterprising and successful and may have bought land in the parish for their father. Another was an only son who married the daughter of caseiros. They had nine children and his wealth has therefore dissipated. Several more men listed as *proprietários* in 1945 were natives of other parishes.

15. Since the phrase "permanent celibacy" is used by demographers and historical demographers to encompass conveniently both spinsterhood and bachelorhood, I will use it here. The word is totally appropriate, since in its original sense (Oxford English Dictionary) celibacy refers to the "state of living unmarried" and a celibate is a "confirmed bachelor or spinster." To some, the word implies asexuality or at least an absence of sexual activity. Although this meaning is not attached to the definition in the Oxford English Dictionary, this more modern connotation is in no way implied in my use of the word here. In short, it simply refers to the unmarried state with or without sexual involvement.

16. Prior to 1860, when a new set of regulations was issued by the Church regarding the format for parish registers, the names of parents were not consistently given in the obituary notices of individuals who had reached adulthood. In fact, such identification was infrequent. Because of the peculiarities of Portuguese naming practices and because only Christian names were provided on baptismal records, the task of matching the deaths of various individuals to their births or to their families of orientation is extremely difficult. In this study, it was only done when there was no doubt about an individual's identity, and doubts increase as one moves back in time in the records. For example (and hypothetically), a certain Maria Luisa de Castro who died in 1790 could have been the daughter of any number of couples bearing offspring during the first six or seven decades of the eighteenth century who had a daughter christened Maria, Luisa, or Maria Luisa and who had the name Castro as one of the family names of either the father or mother. Although there seems to have been some tendency through most of the eighteenth and nineteenth centuries for daughters to take the family names of their mother and sons to take the family names of their father, there are enough exceptions to make guesses hazardous at best. The result is that prior to 1860, it was also difficult to establish age at death for a number of unmarried individuals. Furthermore, there were so many problems and exceptions with the pre-1750 data (including the presence of slaves, illegibility, and the omission of marital status for a number of men), that the tabular data begins only in 1750.

17. Some of these were quoted to me by Lanhesans, others by native Portuguese outside the village; still more can be found in Lima (1938:214–215).

18. The famous Portuguese *fadista*, Amalia Rodrigues, has enshrined this desire in her song "Uma Casa Portuguesa."

19. The confusion arises in part because no clear distinction has been made between the concepts of family and household. For clarification, see Wall (1983).

20. A more complete description of these rois can be found in the appendix.
21. First, a 2c category has been added to account for coresident singles of unknown relationship. Second, a 3e category designates single women living with their illegitimate offspring, and a corresponding multiple household category (5h) designates single women as heads of households living with one of their married illegitimate offspring and his or her family. Third, the extended family categories (Laslett's 4a through 4d) have been broken down further for some analyses to mark more precisely the vertical or lateral relative or relatives present in the household. An otherwise nuclear household extended through the presence of a grandchild, very often an illegitimately born grandchild, is an important phenomenon to consider and keep apart from a household extended vertically downward through the presence of a nephew or niece. Similarly, a vertical extension upward made by the presence of a widowed mother/father or mother-in-law/father-in-law very often represents a shift in authority from what was originally a multiple household (5b–5e), and should therefore be distinguished from vertical extension through an aunt or uncle. Included among these extended family households are households headed by a widow or widower rather than by a married couple. Between one time period and another, one or the other spouse may have died but the composition of the household (that is, the presence of extended family members) remains unchanged. Fourth, the multiple household categories have been "multiplied" for some analyses in order to explore the general issue of matricentrality in northwestern Portuguese rural society. Matrilocal or uxorilocal household, where the husband moves in with the wife's kin after marriage, are distinguished from patrilocal or virilocal households, where the wife moves in with the husband's kin after marriage. Furthermore, households where the couples in both generations are complete and those where the senior generation is composed of a widow or widower are differentiated. Again, it seems logical to retain these households headed by a widow or widower in the multiple category until there is a death (whereupon they would become simple nuclear households) or until a son or son-in-law is listed as the head of household (whereupon it becomes a household extended vertically upward [4a]). Fifth, for some of the discussion a separate category of types (7a through 7e) has been created. These types take into account the impact of emigration on household structure. Figure 3.3 provides a key to all these categories.
22. The total number of households counted on each of these rolls are close enough to the total number of households enumerated in the national censuses to suggest reasonably accurate recording, although an increase in the number of households by forty-seven in the six years between 1864 and 1870 seems out of proportion and is somewhat disturbing, particularly given the fact that during the decade of the 1860s the marriage rate was only 5.4 per annum. The data for 1870 are definately accurate, since individuals who married after 1870 but before 1881 are still marked as single. The 1870 figure, however is so close to the 1878 figure on the national census that at least the trend to growth is accurate, although the

years during which it occurred are in doubt. Indeed, as the discussion points out, some of the increase in the sheer number of households between 1850 and 1870 is accounted for by an expansion in the number of solitaries, particularly single solitaries. On occasion couples married in the parish, who by all indications from the parish records should have been present in the village, could not be linked to the rois. This could indicate a temporary absence, an oversight on the part of the priest, or the caution with which record links were made.

23. Again, both these figures are underestimated, since the households exclude children under seven during these two years. The amended figures show 26.1 percent of the households in 1850 and 17.5 percent of the households in 1870 made up of seven or more people. All these proportions represent a de jure population—that is individuals marked *ausente* are included.

24. This possibility was made most evident to me in the late 1970s when I was in the field. My husband left to return to the United States for six weeks, and several villagers offered to take me into their homes for that time. They could not understand my preference to live in a house by myself. Since then, whenever I have returned alone to the village, I have always boarded with a family.

25. This includes two households classified as 6a. One is a case of a widowed son-in-law living with his father-in-law and the other a case of an illegitimate daughter and her husband living with the bride's unmarried father.

26. Six of these simple families involved a widow or widower who remarried.

## CHAPTER FOUR. HAVING CHILDREN

1. See Knodel's further development of this line of thinking in his 1977 article.

2. Candido (1969) comes to a similar conclusion.

3. A number of other historical demographers have recently made similar statements in their work in other areas of western Europe. Van de Walle (1980:172), for example, suggests that the long resistance to adoption of birth control by populations that would otherwise be motivated in favor of it may have been associated with certain "philosophical and religious outlooks" that made it simply unthinkable. Kenneth Lockridge (1984) and his colleagues in Sweden have explored regional differences in the process of secularization and their relationship to fertility patterns. Regions of high fertility tend to coincide with regions of low secularization, and vice versa. See also Lesthaeghe (1977).

4. Even Friedlander recognizes that this is not a new idea, noting that it harks back to the view of emigration as a "safety valve" for population pressure.

5. Individual cases where the husband's death abroad or his permanent de-

parture could not be substantiated through oral history or some other document were excluded from the calculation of age-specific rates based on family reconstitution (they would be classified as "incomplete" families). Yet such cases would clearly have an effect on any sort of aggregate calculation of fertility.

6. This is simply a suggestion on my part. In fact, when I raised the possibility with the current parish priest that a man born in another parish yet married to a Lanhesan woman might nevertheless have been buried in his native parish, he rejected the idea as totally contrary to custom. A man, he insisted, prefers to be buried where he spends his adult life, alongside his wife, and together with his children. Conversely, when a Lanhesan woman moved to live with her husband in his parish, she was buried there.

7. Massey and Mullan's (1984) study of sex-selective seasonal migration from the town of Gaudelupe, Mexico came to my attention after completion of this manuscript. It lends support to Menken's simulated hypothesis. It also demonstrates an interesting difference between the fertility levels of women whose husbands are legal migrants and those whose husbands are illegal migrants. The former group, with husbands away for longer periods, have lower fertility.

8. The literature on these cultural factors is rich. See, for example, Nag 1976.

9. Although this informant meant by this remark that Maria had no man present to "control" her behavior, there is a further observation to be made. Given the regularity of births approximately every two to two-and-a-half years for a woman whose husband was present, there would have been little opportunity between pregnancy and breastfeeding for a married woman to involve herself in extramarital affairs and risk a child. Furthermore, if her husband were present, the child would have been considered his unless he raised strong protest.

10. Nelda's father António returned to Brazil in 1958, when his youngest unmarried daughter decided to join her sister there. He went to accompany her, but remained for four years, working with his son-in-law, who owned a commercial establishment. Today he travels to Brazil to visit his children and grandchildren—*nem sempre lá, nem sempre cá* (neither always there nor always here). Another son-in-law, who spent some time in France, has returned to Lanheses to set up a carpentry workshop. António works a little with him. The Rios family has always emigrated. António's father spent time in Spain, in Brazil, and in France during and after the First World War. Neither his mother nor his wife, however, ever went abroad.

11. For further discussion of the role of women in Portuguese migration to France, see Brettell 1978, 1982.

12. Sune Akerman and his colleagues at Uppsala University in Sweden have adopted such an approach. Parts of northern Sweden also experienced the demographic transition late enough in the present century for it to be pos-

sible to carry out interviews in conjunction with family reconstitution. They are trying to discover at what point it became acceptable and fashionable to limit family size and why. See also Schneider and Schneider (1984).

13. See Mamdani (1972) and Mueller (1976) for alternative views on this issue. Mamdani argues in what is essentially a discussion of the failure of family planning in India, that what is rational is rational in a cultural context.

14. Although McLaren's (1984) arguments in favor of the presence of conscious and deliberate methods of family limitation in the historical past are convincing, he ignores the potential impact of a large institution like the Catholic Church.

15. Lehning (1984) makes a similar argument in his study of the Loire region of France, where farms were also small. See also Schneider and Schneider (1984).

CHAPTER FIVE. CHILDREN OUT OF WEDLOCK

1. Livi Bacci (1977) calls upon similar phenomena to explain nonmarital fertility in Italy. See also Lee (1977).

2. MacFarlane (1980a) also emphasizes the fact that whereas one stratum of a society may see out-of-wedlock births as an offense, another may not.

3. In fact, Shorter himself differentiates between types of encounters that may have led to illegitimate births, arguing that all types were present throughout history, but that at certain points in time one type may have been more prevalent than the others. He refers to the "bundling" of engaged couples, relationships based on master-servant exploitation, the "hit-and-run" contacts associated with temporary cohabitation, and, finally, "true romantic love." Stone (1977) distinguishes between betrothed couples, seduction, and promiscuity. Goode (1964) formulates as many as fourteen categories.

4. Even on Shorter, Knodel, and Van de Walle's map of nonmarital fertility in nineteenth-century Europe, northern Portugal stands out as one of the "blackest" areas. Indeed, Laslett (1980:33) suggests that in both Portugal and Scotland, space (that is, regional variations) seems to have been more important than time. Within northern Portugal, the district of Viana do Castelo, where Lanheses is located, has never demonstrated the highest rate of illegitimacy, nor has illegitimacy been negligible. Clearly, what is needed is more detailed research in order to ferret out local causes and variations. Brian O'Neill (1981) suggests, based on data gathered in a small village in Bragança (the region of highest illegitimacy in the nineteenth century), that the important factor is patterns of inheritance. Yet if property disenfranchisement leads to illegitimacy, what about rural Ireland? Certainly, there is a difference between pre- and post-mortem transfers, which is important to consider.

5. Leffingwell (1892), in an early and often cited study of illegitimacy, also mentions Portugal and Ireland in one breath as a way of puzzling over the

impact of religion. How, he asks himself, can countries that are supposedly equally Catholic and where Catholic morals are supposedly equally upheld, have such different patterns of illegitimacy? He concludes by rejecting religion as the most significant variable and focuses his attention instead upon a multiplicity of causes, including courtship practices and familial variations.

6. MacFarlane (1980a) also raises this question, noting that the lack of an historical perspective among anthropologists who have considered the problem of illegitimacy has led us to an often erroneous conclusion that the differences between actual behavior and norms are an indication of the "breakdown of society." Prior to my own exploration of the historical material in Lanheses, I was confronted with normative statements about illegitimacy—it is rare and always has been, it has always been a moral sin—and this despite the fact that the woman who was responsible for my starting work in Lanheses in the first place (a migrant worker in France) had herself had an illegitimate child in 1954. Only after I began working with the parish records did I begin to realize how extensive nonmarital fertility was in the not-too-distant past.

7. An elderly informant recounted to me a comment that had been made to him by a female villager who was pregnant prior to her marriage. "The first child," she said, "comes in a short amount of time. After that, it takes longer and is more regular."

8. The expression, *conversados*, is also used to refer to couples who are "going together." It is a less serious relationship than that between *namorados*, and is probably the more appropriate term to refer to the succession of young men with whom a girl might be "conversing" on a Sunday afternoon.

9. Virginia's life history is more fully developed in my book *We Have Already Cried Many Tears* (1982).

10. As indicated in an earlier chapter, professions are included in the parish registers after 1860, although the priests were occasionally negligent. Although it was noted that one has to interpret the use of the term *lavrador* rather broadly to describe landholding peasants of varying degrees of wealth (including lavradores-rendeiros), the distinction between a lavrador and a jornaleiro was probably accurate. After 1930, there is a tendency to describe the profession of many women as simply *domestica* (domestic) despite the fact that the majority of them most likely did some agricultural work. This reflects a trend in national census figures to ignore the labor of peasant women in agriculture. They are treated as "unemployed."

11. O'Neill (1981) finds a similar predominance of jornaleiras giving birth to illegitimate children in a Tras os Montes village during the late nineteenth century.

12. A French woman who recorded her observations of Portugal in a travel account arrived at similar conclusions: "A curious particularity of the customs in Portugal, one which apparently contradicts the tendency to jealously protect the family, is that they hardly scorn bastards. The wife often

accepts them, if they are born before her marriage, and even afterwards, as her proper children, and like her own children, they take part in inheritance" (Adams 1896:325).

13. The third factor Descamps mentions is the significant role of women in the rural agricultural economy.

14. Larkin (1972) argues that the highly pious and moral character of Irish Catholicism is in fact the result of a post-Famine devotional revolution.

15. This "guilt complex" is thoroughly and skillfully analyzed by Scheper-Hughes in her study of mental illness in rural Ireland (1979c).

16. Douglass (1984) describes a similar phenomenon for southern Italy at approximately the same period.

17. For example, a quick perusal of the exposto records for the concelho of Viana do Castelo in 1846 and 1847 showed that of 274 children who were abandoned during those two years, 114 died. In the 1860s the names of two Lanhesan women appear as wet nurses. Simoa Luisa, a married woman, took a child Lourenço, born on September 4, 1862. The child died on September 18. In July of 1864, Ana Marinho of Lanheses took a baby girl of three months with a six-month subsidy.

### CONCLUSION

1. This lacuna should be corrected by the recent publication of Martine Segalen's book *Quinze Générations de Bas Bretons (1720–1980)* (Paris: Presses Universitaires de France, 1985).

### APPENDIX ONE. SOURCES

1. For a more complete discussion of the history of parochial registers in Portugal as a whole see the article by M. Felix (1958).

## BIBLIOGRAPHY

Abelson, Andrew
    1978   "Inheritance and Population Control in a Basque Village before 1900." *Peasant Studies* 7:11–27.
Adams, Juliette
    1896   *La Patrie Portugaise: Souvenirs Personnels.* Paris: G. Havard Fils.
Almeida, Fortunato de
    1921   *História da Igreja em Portugal.* Coimbra: Imprensa Acadêmica.
Amzalak, M. B.
    1923   *As Memórias Econômicas de António de Araujo Travessos.* Lisbon.
    1947   *As Doutrinas da População em Portugal nos Séculos XVII e XVIII.* Lisbon.
Anderson, Michael
    1971   *Family Structure in Nineteenth-Century Lancashire.* Cambridge: Cambridge University Press.
    1976   "Marriage Patterns in Victorian Britain: An Analysis Based on Registration District Data for England and Wales, 1861." *Journal of Family History* 1:55–79.
Andorka, Rudolf
    1978   *The Determinants of Fertility in Advanced Societies.* London: Methuen.
Anonymous
    1623   *Nota a Pedro de Contreras para que la Junta Grande se Ocupe de la Prohibición de lo que Viene de Portugal.* Madrid, May 21.
    1873   *First Parliamentary Inquiry on Portuguese Emigration.* Lisbon.
A.P.D.G.
    1826   *Sketches of Portuguese Life, Manners, Costumes, and Character.* London.
Aranha, Wenceslau de Brito
    1900   *Bibliographie des Ouvrages Portugais pour Servir à l'Étude des Villes.* Lisbon.
Araujo, José Rosa de
    1957   "A Serra de Arga," *Arquivo do Alto Minho* 7:89–110.
Arensberg, Conrad
    1937   *The Irish Countryman.* New York: Macmillan.
Arensberg, Conrad, and Solon T. Kimball
    1940   *Family and Community in Ireland.* Cambridge: Harvard University Press.
Argote, Padre Jeronymo Contador de
    1732   *Memórias para a História Eclesiástica do Arcebispado de Braga.* Lisbon.

Augé, Marc
1982 *The Anthropological Circle*. Cambridge: Cambridge University Press.
Aurora, Conde de
1929 *Roteiro da Ribeira Lima*. Porto: Livraria Simões Lopes.
Balbi, A.
1822 *Essai Statistique sur le Royaume de Portugal et d'Algarve*. Paris.
Barrett, Richard
1980 "Short-term Trends in Bastardy in Taiwan." *Journal of Family History* 5:293–312.
Barros, Henrique de
1972 *A Estrutura Agrária Portuguesa*. Lisbon: Editôra República.
Barros, Dr. João de
1910 *Geografia d'Entre Douro e Minho e Tras os Montes*. Porto: Biblioteca Pública, Colecção de Manuscritos Inéditos (originally 1789).
Barros, José Joaquim Soares de
1789 *Memória Sobre as Causas da Diferente População de Portugal em Diversos Tempos da Monarquia*. Lisbon.
Bauer, Rainer
1981 "Property, Marriage, and Population Change in the Sierra Caurel during the 19th Century." Paper presented at the Society for Spanish and Portuguese Historical Studies, Toronto.
1983 *Family and Property in a Spanish Galician Community*. Ph.D. dissertation, Stanford University.
Bell, Rudolph
1979 *Fate and Honor, Family and Village: Demographic and Cultural Change in Rural Italy since 1800*. Chicago: University of Chicago Press.
Berkner, Lutz K.
1972 "The Stem Family and the Developmental Cycle of the Peasant Household: An Eighteenth-Century Austrian Example." *American Historical Review* 77:398–418.
1976 "Peasant Household Organization and Demographic Change in Lower Saxony, 1689–1766." In Ronald Lee (ed.), *Population Patterns in the Past*. New York: Academic Press.
Berkner, Lutz K., and Franklin Mendels
1978 "Inheritance Systems, Family Structure, and Demographic Patterns in Western Europe, 1700–1900." In Charles Tilly (ed.), *Historical Studies of Changing Fertility*. Princeton: Princeton University Press.
Berkner, Lutz K., and John W. Shaffer
1978 "The Joint Family in the Nivernais," *Journal of Family History* 3:150–162.
Bettencourt, José de Sousa
1961 *O Fenômeno da Emigração Português*. Luanda: Instituto de Investigação Científica de Angola.
Bezerra, Manuel Gomes de Lima
1785 *Os Estrangeiros no Lima*. Coimbra.

Birot, Pierre
n.d.    *Portugal.* Lisbon: Colecção Horizonte No. 31.

Blanshard, Paul
1962    *Freedom and Catholic Power in Spain and Portugal.* Boston: Beacon Press.

Boissevain, Jeremy, et al.
1979    "Towards a Social Anthropology of the Mediterranean." *Current Anthropology* 20:81–93.

Boisvert, Colette Callier
1968    "Remarques sur le Système de Parenté et sur la Famille au Portugal." *L'Homme* 8:87–103.

Bourdelais, Patrice
1981    "Le Poids Démographique des Femmes Seules en France (2ème Moitié du XIX Siècle)." *Annales de Démographie Historique* 5:215–227.

Bourdieu, Pierre
1962    "Célibat et Condition Sociale." *Études Rurales* 5/6:32–135.

Bouvet, Michel
1968    "Trouarn: Étude de Démographie Historique." *Cahiers des Annales de Normande* 6:17–204.

Boxer, Charles
1961    *Four Centuries of Portuguese Expansion, 1415–1825.* Johannesburg: Witwatersrand University Press.

Branco, Camillo Castello
1966    *O Senhor do Paço de Ninães.* Lisbon: Parceria A. M. Pereira.

Brandes, Stanley
1976    "La Solteria, or Why People Remain Single in Rural Spain." *Journal of Anthropological Research* 32:205–233.

Brandão, Fatima, and Robert Rowland
1980    "História da Propriedade e Comunidade Rural: Questões de Método." *Análise Social* 16:173–207.

Braun, Rudolf
1978    "Early Industrialization and Demographic Change in the Canton of Zurich." In Charles Tilly (ed.), *Historical Studies of Changing Fertility.* Princeton: Princeton University Press.

Brettell, Caroline B.
1978    *Hope and Nostalgia: Portuguese Migrant Women in Paris.* Ph.D. dissertation, Brown University.
1979    "Emigrar Para Voltar. A Portuguese Ideology of Return Migration." *Papers in Anthropology* 20:1–20.
1982    *We Have Already Cried Many Tears: The Stories of Three Portuguese Migrant Women.* Cambridge, Mass: Schenkman Publishing Company.
1983    "Emigração, a Igreja, e a Festa Religiosa no Norte de Portugal: Estudo de um Caso." *Estudos Contemporâneos* 5:175–204.
1984    "Emigration and Underdevelopment. The Causes and Conse-

quences of Portuguese Emigration to France in Historical and Cross-Cultural Perspective." In Thomas Bruneau et al. (eds.), *Portugal in Development: Emigration, Industrialization, and the EEC*. Ottawa: University of Ottawa Press.

Burguière, André
1979 "Endogamie et Communauté Villageoises: Pratique Matrimoniale à Romaine Villes au XVIIIème Siècle." *Annales de Démographie Historique* 3:313–336.

Cabral, João Pina
1981 "O Paroco Rural e o Conflito entre Visões do Mundo no Minho." *Estudos Contemporâneos* 2/3:75–110.

Cabral, Manuel Villaverde
1974 *Materiais para a História da Questão Agrária em Portugal, Séculos XIX e XX*. Porto: Editorial Inova.
1977 *O Desenvolvimento do Capitalismo em Portugal no Século XIX*. Lisbon: Regra do Jogo.
1979 *Portugal no Alvorada do Século XX*. Lisbon: Regra do Jogo.

Caldas, Eugenio Castro, and Manuel dos Santos Laureiro
1963 *Niveis de Desenvolvimento Agrícola no Continente Português*. Lisbon: Gulbenkian Foundation, Centro de Estudos Agrários.
1966 *Regiões Homogêneas no Continente Português*. Lisbon: Gulbenkian Foundation, Centro de Estudos Agrários.

Caldwell, John
1976 "Towards a Restatement of Demographic Transition Theory." *Population and Development Review* 2:321–366.
1982 *Theory of Fertility Decline*. New York: Academic Press.

Campomanes, D. Pedro
1762 *Noticía Geográfica del Reyno Y Caminos de Portugal*. Madrid.

Campos, Ezequiel de
1943 *O Enquadramento Geo-Econômico da População Português Através dos Séculos*. Lisbon: Edição da Revista Occidente.

Candido, L. Morgado
1969 *Aspectos Regionais da Demografia Portuguesa*. Lisbon: Instituto Gulbenkian de Ciências, Centro de Economia e Finanças.

Cardoso, Padre Luis
1767 *Catálogo Alfabético de Todas as Frequesias dos Reinos de Portugal*. Lisbon.

Carlsson, Gosta
1966 "The Decline in Fertility: Innovation or Adjustment Process." *Population Studies* 20:149–174.

Carnarvon, Henry John
1836 *Portugal and Galicia*. 2 vols. London: John Murray.

Caro-Baroja, Julio
1957 "El sociocentrismo de los pueblos españoles." In *Razas, Pueblos, y Linajes*. Madrid: Revista de Occidente.

Carqueja, Bento
1916 *O Povo Português*. Porto: Livraría Chardron.

Carvalho, Vicente António Esteves de
1814  *Memória Sobre a Origem e Progressos da Emphyteuse e sua Influência Sobre a Agricultura em Portugal.* Lisbon.

Castro, Armando de
nd  *A Revolução Industrial em Portugal no Século XIX e XX.* Lisbon: Col. Lumiar.

Castro, Francisco Cyrne de
1952  "A Colera Morbus no Distrito de Viana do Castelo." *Arquivo do Alto Minho* 4:106–119.

Cesar, Guilhermino
1969  *O Brasileiro na Ficção Portuguesa.* Lisbon: Parceria A. M. Pereira.

Chaunu, Pierre
1966  *La Civilization de l'Europe Classique.* Paris: Arthaud.

Chojnacka, Helena
1976  "Nuptiality Patterns in an Agrarian Society." *Population Studies* 30:203–226.

Cisternas, J. Pinto et al.
1975  "Consanguinity in Spain, 1911–1943: General Methodology, Behavior of Demographic Variables, and Regional Differences." *Social Biology* 26:55–71.

Coale, Ansley
1971  "Age Patterns of Marriage." *Population Studies* 25:193–214.
1973  "The Demographic Transition Reconsidered." *Proceedings.* International Population Conference. Liège, 1:53–72.

Coale, Ansley, Barbara Anderson, and Erna Harm
1979  *Human Fertility in Russia since the Nineteenth Century.* Princeton: Princeton University Press.

Coale, Ansley, and James Trussell
1974  "Model Fertility Schedules: Variation in the Age Structure of Childbearing in Human Populations." *Population Index* 40:185–258.

Coelho, Eusebio Candido Furtado
1861  *Estatística do Distrito de Viana do Castelo.* Lisbon: Imprensa Nacional.

Cohn, Bernard
1982  "Anthropology and History in the 1980s: Toward a Rapproachement." In Theodore Rabb and Robert Rotberg (eds.) *The New History.* Princeton: Princeton University Press.

Connell, K. H.
1968  *Catholicism and Marriage in the Century after the Famine. Irish Peasant Society: Four Historical Essays.* Oxford: Clarendon.

Cortesão, Jaime
1942  *O Que o Povo Canta em Portugal.* Rio de Janeiro: Livros de Portugal Lda.

Costa, Afonso
1911  *Estudos de Economia Nacional: O Problema da Emigração.* Volume I. Lisbon.

Costa, Agostinho Rebelo da
  1789  *Descrição Topográfica e Histórica da Cidade do Porto*. A. Alvarez Ribeiro.
Costa, Alexandre de Carvalho
  1959  *Lendas Históricas e Etimológicas Respeitantes as Cidades, Vilas e Lugares de Portugal*. Porto.
Costa, António da
  1874  *No Minho*. Lisbon: Imprensa Nacional.
Costa, Padre António Carvalho da
  1868  *Corografia Portuguesa e Descripçam Topográfica*. Braga: D. Gouveia (2nd ed.; 1st ed. 1706–1712).
Costa, Francisco
  1928  *A Divisão da Propriedade no Minho e a sua Influência na Emigração e no Urbanismo*. Braga.
Costigan, Arthur William
  1787  *Sketches of Society and Manners in Portugal*. London: T. Vernon.
Cruz, António
  1970  *Georgrafia e Economia da Província do Minho nos Fins do Século XVII*. Porto: Centro de Estudos Humanísticos, Universidade de Porto.
Dalrymple, Major William
  1777  *Travels Through Spain and Portugal in 1774*. London: J. Almon.
Davis, John
  1977  *The People of the Mediterranean: An Essay in Comparative Social Anthropology*. London: Routledge and Kegan Paul.
Davis, Kingsley
  1939  "Illegitimacy and Social Structure." *American Journal of Sociology* 45:215–233.
  1963  "The Theory of Change and Response in Modern Demographic History." *Population Index* 29:345–366.
Denis, Fernando
  1846  *Portugal Pittoresco ou Descripção Histórico deste Reino*. Lisbon: Typ. de L. C. da Cunha.
De Pauw, Jacques
  1972  "Illicit Sexual Activity and Society in Eighteenth-Century Nantes." *Annales E.S.C.* 27:1155–1182.
Descamps, Paul
  1935  *Portugal: La Vie Sociale Actuelle*. Paris: Firmin-Didot.
  1959  *Histoire Sociale du Portugal*. Paris: Firmin-Didot.
Dias, Jorge
  1949  *Minho, Tras os Montes, Haut Douro*. Lisbon: Congrés International de Geographie.
Dias, José Sebastião da Silva
  1960  *Correntes de Sentimento Religioso em Portugal*. Coimbra: Universidade de Coimbra.
Dinis, Julio
  1947  *Serões da Província*. Volume I. Porto: Livraria Civilização.

1964　*A Morgadinha dos Canaviais.* Porto: Livraria Civilização.

Dion-Saletot, Michelle
1971　"Endogamie et Système Economique dans un Village Français." *Sociologia Ruralis* 11:1–18.

Dixon, Ruth
1971　"Explaining Cross-Cultural Variation in Age at Marriage and Proportions Never Marrying." *Population Studies* 25:215–233.
1976　"The Roles of Rural Women: Female Seclusion, Economic Production and Reproductive Choice." In Ronald Ridkin (ed.), *Population and Development: The Search for Selective Intervention.* Baltimore: Johns Hopkins University Press.
1978　"Late Marriage and Non-Marriage as Demographic Responses: Are They Similar?" *Population Studies* 32:449–466.

Douglass, William A.
1971　"Rural Exodus in Two Spanish Basque Villages: A Cultural Explanation." *American Anthropologist* 73:1100–1114.
1974　*Echalar and Murelaga: Opportunity and Rural Exodus in Two Spanish Basque Villages.* New York: St. Martin's Press.
1984　*Emigration in a South Italian Town: An Anthropological History.* New Brunswick, N.J.: Rutgers University Press.

Drake, Michael
1969　*Population and Scoiety in Norway, 1735–1865.* Cambridge: Cambridge University Press.

Dyke, Bennett, and Warren T. Morrill
1980　*Genealogical Demography.* New York: Academic Press.

Elliott, Vivien Brodsky
1976　"An Analysis of Age at First Marriage in 17th-Century London, Essex, and Hertfordshire." *Newberry Papers in Family and Community History*, No. 4.

Eversley, D.E.C.
1965　"Population, Economy, and Society." In D. V. Glass (ed.), *Population in History.* London: Edward Arnold.

Fairchilds, Cissie
1978　"Female Sexual Attitudes and the Rise of Illegitimacy." *Journal of Interdisciplinary History* 8:627–667.

Faria, Armindo de
1960　*Minho: Dossel de Portugal.* Lisbon.

Faria, M.
1951　"O Uso dos Apelidos em Portugal." *Brotéria* 52:164–184.

Faria. Manuel Severim de
1974　"Dos Remedios para a Falta da Gente." In Antonio Sergio (ed.), *Antologia dos Economistas Portuguesas (Século XVII).* Lisbon: Biblioteca Nacional (originally 1655).

Fel, Edit, and Andres Hofer
1969　*Proper Peasants.* Chicago: Aldine Publishing Co.

Felgueiras, Guilherme
1932　*Espadeladas e Esfolhadas.* Porto: Ed. Pátria Gáia Portuguesa.

Felix, M.
1958  "Les Registres Paroissiaux et l'État Civil au Portugal." *Archivum* 8:89–94.

Flandrin, J. L.
1979  *Families in Former Times*. Cambridge: Cambridge University Press.
1980  "Repression amd Change in the Sexual Life of Young People in Medieval and Early Modern Times." In Robert Wheaton and Tamara Hareven (eds.), *Family and Sexuality in French History*. Philadelphia: University of Pennsylvania Press.

Franca, Luis de
1980  *Comportamento Religioso da População Portuguesa*. Lisbon: Morães Editores.

Freeman, Susan Tax
1970  *Neighbors: The Social Contract in a Castilian Hamlet*. Chicago: University of Chicago Press.
1979  "The 'Municipios' of Northern Spain: A View from the Fountain." In R. Hinshaw (ed.), *Currents in Anthropology: Essays in Honor of Sol Tax*. The Hague: Mouton.
1981  "From Present to Past: The Genealogical Approach to Local History." Paper presented to the Society for Spanish and Portuguese Historical Studies, Toronto.

Freire, A. Braamcamp
1905  "Povoação de Entre Douro e Minho no Século XVI." *Arquivo Histórico Português* 3:241–273.

Friedl, Ernestine (ed.)
1967  "Appearance and Reality: Status and Roles of Women in Mediterranean Societies." *Anthropological Quarterly* 40 (special issue).

Friedlander, Dov
1969  "Demographic Responses and Population Change." *Demography* 6:359–381.
1983  "Demographic Response and Socioeconomic Structure: Population Processes in England and Wales in the 19th Century." *Demography* 20:249–272.

Friedmann, F. G.
1953  "The World of 'La Miseria.' " *Partisan Review* 20:218–231.

Gaskin, Katharine
1978  "Age at First Marriage in Europe before 1850: A Summary of Family Reconstitution Data." *Journal of Family History* 3:23–33.

Gilmore, David
1982  "Anthropology of the Mediterranean Area." *Annual Review of Anthropology* 11:175–205.

Girão, Aristides
1960  *Geografia de Portugal*. Porto: Portugalense Editôres (3rd ed.; 1st ed. 1940).

Girão, Aristides, and Fernanda Velho
1944  *Demografia e Ocupação do Solo Continental*. Coimbra: Centro de Estudos Geográficos.

Gluckman, Max
1968 "The Utility of the Equilibrium Model in the Study of Social Change." *American Anthropologist* 70:219–237.

Godinho, Vitorino Magalhães
1955 *Prix et Monnaies au Portugal.* Paris: Armand Colin.
1971 *Estrutura da Antiga Sociedade Portuguesa.* Lisbon: Coleção Temas Portuguesas.

Goldschmidt, Walter, and Evalyn Kunkel
1971 "The Structure of the Peasant Family." *American Anthropologist* 73:1058–1076.

Golini, Antonio
1968 "The Influence of Migration on Fertility." *Genus* 24:93–108.

Goode, William J.
1964 *The Family.* Englewood Cliffs: Prentice-Hall.

Goody, John
1973 "Bridewealth and Dowry in Africa and Eurasia." In J. R. Goody and S. J. Tambiah (eds.), *Bridewealth and Dowry.* Cambridge: Cambridge University Press.
1976 *Production and Reproduction: A Comparative Study of the Domestic Domain.* Cambridge: Cambridge University Press.
1983 *The Development of the Family and Marriage in Europe.* Cambridge: Cambridge University Press.

Greven, Philip Jr.
1970 *Four Generations: Population, Land and Family in Colonial Andover, Massachusetts.* Ithaca: Cornell University Press.

Guichard, François
1978 *Atlas Démographique du Portugal.* Bordeaux: Publications Maisons de Sciences de l'Homme.

Guimarães, Avelino da Silva
1890 *A Crise Agrícola Portuguesa.* Porto: Typografía A. J. da Silva Teixeira.

Gusmão, Alexandre de
n.d. *Cálculo Sobre a Perda do Dinheiro do Reino.* Lisbon.

Guttentag, Marcia, and Paul Secord
1983 *Too Many Women: The Sex Ratio Question.* Beverly Hills: Sage Publications.

Habakkuk, H. G.
1955 "Family Structure and Economic Change in Nineteenth-Century Europe." *Journal of Economic History* 15:1–12.

Haines, Michael
1979 *Fertility and Occupation: Population Patterns in Industrialism.* New York: Academic Press.

Hair, P.E.H.
1967 "Bridal Pregnancy in Rural England in Earlier Centuries." *Population Studies* 20:233–243.
1970 "Bridal Pregnancy in Earlier Rural England Further Examined." *Population Studies* 23:59–70.

Hajnal, J.
    1965  "European Marriage Patterns in Perspective." In D. V. Glass and D.E.C. Eversley (eds.), *Population in History*. London: Edward Arnold.
Hammel, Eugene
    1968  *Alternative Social Structure and Ritual Relations in the Balkans*. Englewood Cliffs: Prentice-Hall.
Harrison, W. H.
    1839  *The Tourist in Portugal*. London: Robert Jennings.
Hartley, Shirley
    1975  *Illegitimacy*. Berkeley and Los Angeles: University of California Press.
Heer, David M.
    1966  "Economic Development and Fertility." *Demography* 3:423–444.
Henry, Louis
    1961  "Some Data on Natural Fertility." *Eugenics Quarterly* 8:81–91.
Henry, Louis, and Jacques Houdaille
    1978  "Célibat et Age au Mariage aux XVIII et XIX Siècles en France." *Population* 33:43–61.
Herculano, Alexandre
    1873  "A Emigraçâo." *Opúsculos*. Lisbon: Livraria Bertrand (4th ed.), pp. 105–282.
Hufton, Olwen
    1974  *The Poor of Eighteenth-Century France*. Oxford: Clarendon Press.
Iszaevich, Abraham
    1974  "Emigrants, Spinsters, and Priests: The Dynamics of Demography in Spanish Peasant Societies." *Journal of Peasant Studies* 2:292–312.
Iturra, Raul
    1980  "Strategies in the Domestic Organization of Production in Rural Galicia." *Cambridge Anthropology* 6:88–128.
Jegouzo, G.
    1977  "Le Célibat Paysan en 1975." *Population* 34:27–42.
Jegouzo, G., and J. L. Brangeon
    1974  "Célibat Paysan et Pauvreté." *Économie et Statistique* 58:3–13.
Kennedy, Robert E., Jr.
    1973  *The Irish: Emigration, Marriage and Fertility*. Berkeley and Los Angeles: University of California Press.
Kenny, Michael
    1963  "Europe: The Atlantic Fringe." *Anthropological Quarterly* 36:100–119.
Kenny, Michael, and David Kertzer (eds.)
    1983  *Urban Life in Mediterranean Europe: Anthropological Perspectives*. Urbana: University of Illinois Press.
Kertzer, David
    1984a  "Anthropology and Family History." *Journal of Family History* 9:201–228.

1984b    *Family Life in Central Italy, 1880–1910.* New Brunswick, N.J.: Rutgers University Press.

Khera, Sigrid
1981    "Illegitimacy and Mode of Land Inheritance among Austrian Peasants." *Ethnology* 20:307–322.

Kingston, William
1845    *Lusitanian Sketches of the Pen and Pencil.* London.

Knodel, John
1967    "Law, Marriage, and Illegitimacy in Nineteenth-Century Germany." *Population Studies* 20:279–294.
1970    "Two and a Half Centuries of Demographic History in a Bavarian Village," *Population Studies* 24:353–376.
1974    *The Decline of Fertility in Germany, 1871–1939.* Princeton: Princeton University Press.
1977    "Family Limitation and the Fertility Transition: Evidence from the Age Patterns of Fertility in Europe and Asia," *Population Studies* 31:219–249.
1979    "From Natural Fertility to Fertility Limitation: The Onset of the Fertility Transition in a Sample of German Villages." *Demography* 16:493–521.

Knodel, John, and Steven Hochstadt
1980    "Urban and Rural Illegitimacy in Imperial Germany." In Peter Laslett et al. (eds.), *Bastardy and Its Comparative History.* Cambridge: Harvard University Press.

Knodel, John, and Mary Jo Maynes
1976    "Urban and Rural Marriage Patterns in Imperial Germany." *Journal of Family History* 1:129–168.

Knodel, John, and Etienne Van de Walle
1967    "Demographic Transition and Fertility Decline: The European Case." In *Proceedings of the International Population Conference.* Sydney: International Union for the Scientific Study of Population.

Kochanowicz, Jacek
1983    "The Peasant Family as an Economic Unit in the Polish Feudal Economy of the Eighteenth-Century." In Richard Wall (ed.), *Family Forms in Historic Europe.* Cambridge: Cambridge University Press.

Koebel, William
1909    *Portugal:-Its Land and People.* London: A. Constable and Co.

Kunkel, Evalyn
1966    *The Structure of the Family in Peasant Society: A Comparative Analysis.* Ph.D. Dissertation, University of Michigan.

Larkin, Emmet
1972    "The Devotional Revolution in Ireland 1850–1875." *American Historical Review* 77:625–652.
1976    *The Historical Dimensions of Irish Catholicism.* New York: Arno Press.

Laslett, Peter
  1965  *The World We Have Lost.* New York: Scribner's.
  1977  *Family Life and Illicit Love in Earlier Generations.* Cambridge: Cambridge University Press.
  1980a  "The Bastardy-Prone Sub-Society." In Peter Laslett et al. (eds.), *Bastardy and Its Comparative History.* Cambridge: Harvard University Press.
  1980b  "Introduction: Comparing Illegitimacy over Time and between Cultures." In Peter Laslett et al. (eds.), *Bastardy and Its Comparative History.* Cambridge: Harvard University Press.
  1980c  "Preface." In Peter Laslett et al. (eds.), *Bastardy and Its Comparative History.* Cambridge: Harvard University Press.
  1983  "Family and Household as Work Group and Kin Group: Areas of Traditional Europe Compared." In Richard Wall (ed.), *Family Forms in Historic Europe.* Cambridge: Cambridge University Press.
Laslett, Peter, and Karla Oosterveen
  1973  "Long-Term Trends in Bastardy in England, 1561–1960." *Population Studies* 27:255–286.
Laslett, Peter, and Richard Wall (eds.)
  1972  *Household and Family in Past Time.* Cambridge: Cambridge University Press.
Leal, Augusto Soares Barbosa de Pinho
  1873  *Portugal Antigo e Moderno.* Lisbon: Livraria Editôra de Mattos.
Leasure, William
  1963  "Factors Involved in the Decline of Fertility in Spain, 1900–1956." *Population Studies* 17:271–285.
Lee, Ronald
  1977  "Introduction." In Ronald Lee (ed.), *Population Patterns in the Past.* New York: Academic Press.
Lee, W. R.
  1977  "Bastardy and the Socioeconomic Structure of Southern Germany." *Journal of Interdisciplinary History* 7:403–425.
Leffingwell, Albert
  1892  *Illegitimacy and the Influence of the Seasons upon Conduct.* London: Swan.
Lehning, James
  1984  "The Decline of Marital Fertility: Evidence from a French Department, La Loire (1851–1891)." *Annales de Démographie Historique* 8:201–217.
Lerner, Daniel
  1958  *The Passing of Traditional Society: Modernizing the Middle East.* New York: Free Press.
Lesthaeghe, Ronald J.
  1977  *The Decline of Belgian Fertility, 1800–1970.* Princeton: Princeton University Press.
Levine, David

1977    *Family Formation in an Age of Nascent Capitalism.* New York: Academic Press.

Levine, David, and Keith Wrightson
1980    "The Social Context of Illegitimacy in Early Modern England." In Peter Laslett et al. (eds.), *Bastardy and Its Comparative History.* Cambridge: Harvard University Press.

Lima, Fernando Pires de
1942    *Cantares do Minho.* Porto: Portucalense Editôra.

Lima, Joaquim Pires de, and Fernando Pires de Lima
1938    *Tradições Populares de Entre Douro e Minho.* Barcelos: Companhia Editora do Minho.

Link, Henry
1801    *Travels in Portugal.* London: T. N. Longman.

Lison-Tolosana, Carmelo
1971    *Antropología Cultural de Galicia.* Madrid: Siglo XXI de España Editores.
1983    *Belmonte de Los Caballeros.* Princeton: Princeton University Press.
1976    "The Ethics of Inheritance." In J. G. Peristiany (ed.), *Mediterranean Family Structures.* Cambridge: Cambridge University Press.

Littell, Ulla-Britt
1981    "Breast Feeding Habits and Their Relations to Infant Mortality and Marital Fertility." *Journal of Family History* 6:182–194.

Livi Bacci, Massimo
1967    "Fertility and Nuptiality Changes in Spain from the Late 18th to the Early 20th Century." *Population Studies* 22:211–237.
1971    *A Century of Portuguese Fertility.* Princeton: Princeton University Press.
1977    *A History of Italian Fertility during the Last Two Centuries.* Princeton: Princeton University Press.

Lockridge, Kenneth
1984    *The Fertility Transition in Sweden: A Preliminary Look at Smaller Geographic Units, 1855–1890.* Report 3, Demographic Database, Umea University. Umea, Sweden.

Lopreato, Joseph
1961    "Social Stratification and Mobility in a Southern Italian Town." *American Sociological Review* 26:585–596.

Loring, George B.
1891    *A Year in Portugal.* London: G. P. Putnam.

Macedo, Duarte Ribeiro de
1675    *Discurso Sobre a Introdução das Artes no Reino.*

Macedo, Jorge de
1951    *A Situação Econômica no Tempo de Pombal.* Porto: Livraria Portugalia.

MacFarlane, Alan
1977    *Restructuring Historical Communities.* London: Cambridge University Press.

1980a "Illegitimacy in English History." In Peter Laslett et al. (eds.), *Bastardy and Its Comparative History*. Cambridge: Harvard University Press.

1980b "Demographic Structures and Cultural Regions in Europe." *Cambridge Anthropology* 6:1–17.

Machado, J. T. Montalvão

n.d. *Como Nascem e Morrem os Portugueses*. Lisbon.

McKenna, Edward E.

1974 "Marriage and Fertility in Post-Famine Ireland: A Multivariate Analysis." *American Journal of Sociology* 80:688–705.

McLaren, Angus

1984 *Reproductive Rituals*. London: Methuen.

McQuillan, Kevin

1984 "Modes of Production and Demographic Patterns in Nineteenth-Century France." *American Journal of Sociology* 89:324–346.

Mamdami, Mahmood

1972 *The Myth of Population Control: Family and Caste in an Indian Village*. New York: Monthly Review Press.

Manique, Luiz de Pina

1970 *A População de Portugal em 1798. O Censo de Pina Manique*. Paris: Fundação Calouste Gulbenkian.

Marques, A. H. de Oliveira

1972 *History of Portugal*. New York: Columbia University Press.

Marreca, António d'Oliveira

1903 *Parecer e Memória sobre um Projecto de Estadística História e Memórias de Academia Real das Ciências de Lisboa*. Lisbon.

Martins, J. P. de Oliveira

1885 *Política e Economía Nacional de Portugal*. Lisbon: Magalhães e Moniz.

1956 *Fomento Rural e Emigração*. Lisbon: Guimarães & Ca Editores (originally 1887–1892).

Massey, Douglas S., and Brendan P. Mullan

1984 "A Demonstration of the Effect of Seasonal Migration on Fertility." *Demography* 21:501–517.

Mead, Margaret

1949 *Male and Female*. New York: William Morrow and Company.

Mendels, Franklin

1969 *Industrialization and Population Pressure in Eighteenth-Century Flanders*. Ph.D. Dissertation, University of Wisconsin.

Menken, Jane

1979 "Seasonal Migration and Seasonal Variations in Fecundability: Effects on Birth Rates and Birth Intervals." *Demography* 16:103–109.

Merton, Robert K.

1967 *On Theoretical Sociology: Five Essays, Old and New*. New York: Free Press.

Miguez, Alberto
1967  *Galicia: Exodo y Desarrollo.* Madrid: Editorial Cuadernos para el
      Dialogo.
Mitterauer, Michael, and Reinhard Seider
1979  "The Developmental Cycle of Domestic Groups: Problems of Re-
      construction and Possibilities of Interpretation." *Journal of Family
      History* 4:257–284.
1982  *The European Family.* Chicago: University of Chicago Press.
Morgado, Nuno Alves
1979  "Portugal." In W. R. Lee (ed.), *European Demography and Eco-
      nomic Growth.* Amsterdam: Groomheim.
Morris, R. J.
1970  *Cholera 1832: The Social Response to an Epidemic.* New York:
      Holmes and Meier.
Mosher, William D.
1980  "Demographic Responses and Demographic Transitions: A Case
      Study of Sweden." *Demography* 17:395–412.
Mueller, Eva
1976  "The Economic Value of Children in Peasant Agriculture." In Ron-
      ald Ridkin (ed.), *Population and Development: The Search for Se-
      lective Interventions.* Baltimore: Johns Hopkins University Press.
Murphy, James
1795  *Travels in Portugal.* London: A. Stratton.
Nag, Moni
1976  *Factors Affecting Human Fertility in Non-Industrial Societies: A
      Cross-Cultural Study.* New Haven: Human Relations Area Files.
Nazareth, J. Manuel
1977  "Familia e Emigração em Portugal: Estudo Exploratório." *Eco-
      nomia e Sociologia* 23:31–50.
Netting, Robert McC., et al. (eds.)
1984  *Households: Comparative and Historical Studies of the Domestic
      Group.* Berkeley and Los Angeles: University of California
      Press.
Neves, L. Quintas
1963  "A Partilha das Aguas da Rega nas Tradições Rurais do Norte do
      Portugal." *Actas* do Congresso Internacional de Ethografia (Santo
      Tirso). Volume 3, pp. 361–384.
Oliveira, Padre Miguel de
1950  *As Paróquias Rurais Portuguesas: Sua origem e formação.* Lisbon.
O'Neill, Brian J.
1981  "Proprietários, Jornaleiros, e Criados numa Aldeia Transmontana
      desde 1886," *Estudos Contemporâneos* 2/3:31–74.
1983  "Dying and Inheriting in Rural Tras-os-Montes." *Journal of the
      Anthropological Society of Oxford* 14:44–74.
1984  *Proprietários, Lavradores e Jornaleiros.* Lisbon: Publicações Dom
      Quixote.

Ortigão, José Duarte Ramalho
1885    *As Farpas.* Volume I. Lisbon: David Corrazzi.
Paço, Afonso de
1932    "Sogras e Cunhados na Cancioneiro Popular e no Adagário." *Actos de Congresso Internacional de Etnologia,* 3:10–31.
Pardoe, Julia
1832    *Traits and Traditions of Portugal.* 2 vols. London: Saunders and Otley.
Percheiro, D. A. Gomes
1878    *Portugal e Brazil: Emigração e Colonisação.* Lisbon.
Pereira, Miriam Halpern
1971    "Demografia e Desenvolvimento em Portugal na Segunda Metade do Século XIX." *Análise Social* 25/26:85–117.
1981    *A Política Portuguesa de Emigração, 1850–1930.* Lisbon.
Peristiany, John (ed.)
1965    *Honor and Shame: The Values of Mediterranean Society.* London: Weidenfeld and Nicolson.
Pery, Gerardo
1875    *Mouvement de la Population en Portugal.* Paris: Guillaumin et Cie.
Picão, José Silva
1947    *Através dos Campos: Usos e Costumes Agrícolas Alentejanas.* Lisbon: Neogravura Limitada.
Pinto, Manuel
1979    "A Igreja e a Insurreição Popular do Minho de 1846." *Estudos Contemporâneos* 0:83–134.
Pitt-Rivers, Julian
1954    *The People of the Sierra.* London: Weidenfeld and Nicolson.
Potter, R. G.
1963    "Birth Intervals: Structure and Change." *Population Studies* 17:155–160.
Ravenstein, E. G.
1885    "The Laws of Migration." *Journal of the Royal Statistical Society* 48:167–277.
Reis, Jaime
1981    "Aspectos Econômicos de Viana do Castelo em 1840: Um Inquérito Esquecido." *Estudos Contemporâneos* 2/3:143–198.
Reis, Matos
1980    "História Econômica—Os Preços dos Cereais em Ponte de Lima." *Almanaque de Ponte do Lima.*
Ribeiro, Orlando
1945    *Portugal, O Mediterrâneo e o Atlántico.* Coimbra: Coimbra Editora.
1970    *Ensaios de Geografia Humana e Regional.* Lisbon: Editôra Sá da Costa.
Richards, Toni
1977    "Fertility Decline in Germany: An Econometric Appraisal." *Population Studies* 31:537–553.

Riegelhaupt, Joyce
 1973   "Festas e Padres: The Organization of Religious Action in a Por-
        tuguese Parish." *American Anthropologist* 75:835–851.
 1981   "Camponeses e Estado Liberal: A Revolta de Maria da Fonte."
        *Estudos Contemporâneos* 2/3:129–142.
Ross, Ellen, and Rayna Rapp
 1981   "Sex and Society: A Research Note from Social History and An-
        thropology." *Comparative Studies in Society and History* 20:51–
        72.
Rowland, Robert
 1981   "Ancora e Montaría, 1827: Duas Frequesias do Noroeste Segundo
        os Livros de Registro Das Companhias de Ordenação." *Estudos
        Contemporâneos* 2/3:199–242.
 1983   "Family and Marriage in Portugal (16th–20th Centuries): A Com-
        parative Sketch." Paper presented to the 8th Annual Meeting of
        the Social Science History Association.
Sampaio, A
 1923   *Estudos Históricos e Econômicos*. Porto: Livraria Chardron.
Sampaio, Francisco
 1978   "Viana na Segunda Metade do Século XIX: O Jornal o Vianense."
        *Cadernos Vianenses* 1:68–73.
 1979   "Análise Qualitativa das Estatísticas Demográficas do Districto de
        Viana na Segunda Metade do Século XIX." *Cadernos Vianenses*
        2:189–204.
Sanchis, Pierre
 1976   *Arraial. La Fête d'un Peuple: Les Pélérinages Populaires au Por-
        tugal*. Paris: Écoles des Hautes Études en Sciences Sociales, Thèse
        IIIe cycle.
Santos, Fernando Piteira
 1962   *Geografia e Economia da Revolução de 1820*. Lisbon: Europa
        America.
Scheper-Hughes, Nancy
 1979a  "Inheritance of the Meek: Land, Labor and Love in Western Ire-
        land." *Marxist Perspectives* 2:46–77.
 1979b  "Breeding Breaks Out in the Eye of the Cat: Sex Roles, Birth
        Order, and the Irish Double Bind." *Journal of Comparative Fam-
        ily Studies* 10:207–226.
 1979c  *Saints, Scholars, and Schizophrenics: Mental Illness in Rural Ire-
        land*. Berkeley and Los Angeles: University of California Press.
 1983   "From Anxiety to Analysis: Rethinking Irish Sexuality and Sex
        Roles." *Women's Studies* 10:147–160.
Schneider, Jane
 1971   "Of Vigilance of Virgins: Honor, Shame and Access to Resources
        in Mediterranean Societies." *Ethnology* 10:1–24.
Schneider, Jane, and Peter Schneider
 1984   "Demographic Transition in a Sicilian Rural Town." *Journal of
        Family History* 9:245–272.

Segalen, Martine
1980  "The Family Cycle and Household Structure: Five Generations in a French Village." In Robert Wheaton (ed.), *Family and Sexuality in French History*. Philadelphia: University of Pennsylvania Press.

Serrão, Joel
1974  *A Emigração Portuguesa*. Lisbon: Colecção Horizonte.

Shorter, Edward
1971  "Illegitimacy, Sexual Revolution, and Social Change." *Journal of Interdisciplinary History* 2:237–272.
1973  "Female Emancipation, Birth Control and Fertility in European History." American Historical Review 78:605–640.
1975  *The Making of the Modern Family*. New York: Basic Books.

Shorter, Edward, John Knodel, and Etienne Van de Walle
1971  "The Decline of Non-Marital Fertility in Europe, 1880–1940." *Population Studies* 25:375–393.

Sieder, Reinhard, and Michael Mitterauer
1983  "The Reconstruction of the Family Life Course: Theoretical Problems and Empirical Results." In Richard Wall (ed.), *Family Forms in Historic Europe*. Cambridge: Cambridge University Press.

Silbert, Albert
1968  *Le Problème Agraire Portugais au Temps des Premières Cortes Liberales (1821–1823)*. Paris: Presses Universitaires de France.
1978  "Economia e Sociedade de Portugal Meridional em Principios do Século XIX." *Economia e Sociologia* 24:13–23.

Silva, José Verissimo Alvares da
1872  *Memória Histórica Sobre a Agricultura Portuguesa Considerada Desde o Tempo dos Romanos até ao Presente*. Lisbon.

Silva, L. A. Rebello da
1868  *Memória Sobre a População e a Agricultura de Portugal*. Lisbon.

Silveira, António Henriques da
n.d.  *Racional Discurso Sobre a Agricultura*. Lisbon.

Silverman, Sydel
1968  "Agricultural Organization, Social Structure, and Values in Italy: Amoral Familism." *American Anthropologist* 70:1–20.
1975  *Three Bells of Civilization*. New York: Columbia University Press.
1976  "On the Uses of History in Anthropology: The Palio of Siena." *American Ethnologist* 6:413–436.

Simões, Nuno
1934  *O Brasil e a Emigração Portuguesa*. Coimbra: Imprensa Universitária.

Sklar, June
1974  "The Role of Marriage Behavior in the Demographic Transition: The Case of Eastern Europe Around 1900." *Population Studies* 28:231–241.
1977  "Marriage and Non-Marital Fertility: A Comparison of Ireland and Sweden." *Population and Development Review* 3:359–375.

Smith, Daniel Scott
  1977   "A Homeostatic Demographic Regime: Patterns in West European Family Reconstitution Studies." In Ronald Lee (ed.), *Population Patterns in the Past*. New York: Academic Press.
  1978   "Parental Power and Marriage Patterns: An Analysis of Historical Trends in Hingham, Massachusetts." In Michael Gordon (ed.), *The American Family in Socio-Historical Perspective*. New York: St. Martin's.
Smout, Christopher
  1980   "Aspects of Sexual Behavior in Nineteenth-Century Scotland." In Peter Laslett, et al. (eds.), *Bastardy and Its Comparative History*. Cambridge: Harvard University Press.
Stanislawski, Dan
  1959   *The Individuality of Portugal*. Austin: University of Texas Press.
Stone, Lawrence
  1977   *The Family, Sex, and Marriage in England 1500–1800*. New York: Harper and Row.
  1982   "Family History in the 1980s: Past Achievements and Future Trends." In Theodore Rabb and Robert Rotberg (eds.), *The New History*. Princeton: Princeton University Press.
Stys, W.
  1957   "The Influence of Economic Conditions on the Fertility of Peasant Women." *Population Studies* 11:136–147.
Sundbarg, G.
  1908   *Aperçus Statistiques Internationaux*. Stockholm.
Swedlund, Alan C.
  1978   "Historical Demography and Population Ecology." *Annual Review of Anthropology* 7:137–173.
Taylor, James
  1958   *A Portuguese-English Dictionary*. Stanford: Stanford University Press.
Teles, Basilio
  1903   *A Carestia da Vida nos Campos*. Porto: Livraria Chardron.
Thomas, Keith
  1963   "History and Anthropology." *Past and Present* 24:3–24.
Thomson, E. P.
  1972   "Anthropology and the Discipline of Historical Context." *Midland History* 1:41–55.
Tilly, Charles (ed.)
  1978   *Historical Studies of Changing Fertility*. Princeton: Princeton University Press.
Tilly, Louise, Joan Scott, and Miriam Cohen
  1976   "Women's Work and European Fertility Patterns." *Journal of Interdisciplinary History* 3:447–476.
Ulrich, Ruy Ennes
  1905   *Estudo Sobre a Condição Legal das Ordens e Congregações Religiosas em Portugal de 1834 até 1901*. Coimbra: Imprensa Universitária.

Vandelli, Domingos
  n.d.  *A Memória Sobre a Preferência que em Portugal se Deve Dar a Agricultura Sobre as Indústrias.* Lisbon.
Van de Walle, Etienne
  1968  "Marriage and Marital Fertility." *Daedalus* 97:486–501.
  1980  "Motivations and Technology in the Decline of French Fertility." In Robert Wheaton and Tamara Harevan (eds.), *Family and Sexuality in French History.* Philadelphia: University of Pennsylvania Press.
Van de Walle, Francine
  1975  "Migration and Fertility in Ticino." *Population Studies* 29:447–462.
Vasconcellos, Joaquim Leite de
  1958  *Etnografia Portuguesa: Tentame de Sistematização.* Volume 4. Lisbon.
Verdon, Michel
  1980  "Shaking Off the Domestic Yoke, or the Sociological Significance of Residence." *Comparative Studies in Society and History* 22:109–131.
Villas Boas, José Gomes de
  n.d.  *Descrição Geográfica e Econômica da Provincia do Minho.* Lisbon.
Vinovskis, Maris A.
  1971  "American Historical Demography: A Review Essay." *Historical Methods Newsletter* 4:141–148.
  1974  "The Field of Early American History: A Methodological Critique." *The Family in Historical Perspective* 7:2–8.
  1978  "Marriage Patterns in Mid-Nineteenth-Century New York." *Journal of Family History* 3:51–61.
Wall, Richard (ed.)
  1983  *Family Forms in Historic Europe.* Cambridge: Cambridge University Press.
Wallerstein, Immanuel
  1974  *The Modern World System: Capitalist Agriculture and the Origins of the European World Economy in the Sixteenth Century.* New York: Academic Press.
Watson, James L.
  1975  *Emigration and the Chinese Lineage.* Berkeley and Los Angeles: University of California Press.
Weber, Eugen
  1976  *Peasants into Frenchmen: The Modernization of Rural France 1870–1914.* Stanford: Stanford University Press.
Weinberg, Daniela
  1972  "Cutting the Pie in the Swiss Alps." *Anthropological Quarterly* 45:125–131.
Willems, Emilio
  1962  "On Portuguese Family Structure." *International Journal of Comparative Sociology* 3:65–79.

Wolf, Eric
    1962    "Cultural Dissonance in the Italian Alps." *Comparative Studies in Society and History* 5:1–14.
Wolf, Margery
    1968    *The House of Lim.* Englewood Cliffs: Prentice-Hall.
Wrigley, E. Anthony
    1969    *Population and History.* New York: McGraw-Hill.
    1978    "Fertility Strategy for the Individual and the Group." In Charles Tilly (ed.), *Historical Studies of Changing Fertility.* Princeton: Princeton University Press.
    1982    "The Prospects for Population History." In Theodore Rabb and Robert Rotberg (eds.), *The New History.* Princeton: Princeton University Press.
Yanagisako, Sylvia Junko
    1979    "Family and Household: The Analysis of Domestic Groups." *Annual Review of Anthropology* 8:161–205.
Young, William
    1828    *Portugal in 1828.* London: Henry Colburn.

LIBRARY OF CONGRESS CATALOGING-IN-PUBLICATION DATA
Brettell, Caroline.
Men who migrate, women who wait.

Bibliography: p.
Includes index.
1. Lanhezes (Portugal)—Population—History
2. Portugal—Emigration and immigration—History—Case
studies. 3. Fertility, Human—Portugal—Lanhezes—
History. 4. Marriage—Portugal—Lanhezes—History
I. Title.
HB2082.L36B74 1986      304.6'09469'12      86-11270
ISBN 0-691-09424-1

CPSIA information can be obtained at www.ICGtesting.com
Printed in the USA
BVOW09s0502160714

359298BV00020B/1045/P